Nature's Burdens

UTAH STATE UNIVERSITY PRESS
Logan

Nature's Burdens

*Conservation and American Politics,
the Reagan Era to the Present*

Daniel Nelson

© 2017 by the University Press of Colorado

Published by Utah State University Press
An imprint of University Press of Colorado
5589 Arapahoe Avenue, Suite 206C
Boulder, Colorado 80303

The University Press of Colorado is a proud member of
Association of American University Presses.

The University Press of Colorado is a cooperative publishing enterprise supported, in part, by Adams State University, Colorado State University, Fort Lewis College, Metropolitan State University of Denver, Regis University, University of Colorado, University of Northern Colorado, Utah State University, and Western State Colorado University.

ISBN: 978-1-60732-569-7 (paperback)
ISBN: 978-1-60732-570-3 (ebook)

Library of Congress Cataloging-in-Publication Data

Names: Nelson, Daniel, 1941– author.
Title: Nature's burdens : conservation and American politics, the Reagan era to the present / Daniel Nelson.
Description: Logan : Utah State University Press, [2017] | Includes bibliographical references.
Identifiers: LCCN 2016044403 | ISBN 9781607325697 (pbk.) | ISBN 9781607325703 (ebook)
Subjects: LCSH: Conservation of natural resources—Government policy—United States—History—20th century. | Conservation of natural resources—Government policy—United States—History—21st century. | Environmental policy—United States—History—20th century. | Environmental policy—United States—History—21st century.
Classification: LCC S930 .N45 2017 | DDC 333.720973—dc23
LC record available at https://lccn.loc.gov/2016044403

Cover illustration © handini_atmodiwiryo/Shutterstock

Contents

Preface

This book began as an attempt to trace the development of American environmentalism in the period after the buoyant and triumphant 1960s and 1970s, when the issues had seemed both obvious and compelling and so much was being accomplished. The more recent period has been markedly different, with a variety of observers pointing to reaction, decline, complacency, and organizational senescence at the same time news reports often list positive developments and even political victories. My first decision was to narrow the scope of the study to what has traditionally been known as conservation, "the care and preservation of natural resources," leaving aside a host of topics related to air and water pollution, toxics, and energy. This approach made sense for a variety of reasons, not least the growing importance of land and water protection, wildlife, and biodiversity as well as the ongoing effort to define the requirements of long-term ecological health. Indeed, the recognition of conservation as a distinctive and vital activity, related to but not subordinate to parallel efforts to grapple with other environmental challenges posed by modern society, has itself been one of the of the major developments of this period.

The changes of the post-1980 years have been notable and include a more comprehensive and science-based approach to conservation; profound changes in the environmental "infrastructure," the organizations that actively promote environmental protection and the practice of conservation management; the flowering of the land trust movement; increased emphasis on the preservation of native forests, including "old-growth" forests; more attention to wildlife, especially threatened or endangered wildlife and controversial "keystone" species; and, in the very recent past, growing recognition of the importance of climate change in conservation planning. At the same time there have been intense and determined campaigns to prevent opponents from turning back the clock on public land regulations and management. A common theme to all these activities has been the difficult and often perplexing task of trying to define long-range goals at a time when nature is under assault from many quarters and a return to the conditions of an earlier day is impossible. In this setting, "restoration," a commonly used term, now has a narrow and often technical meaning, involving the implementation of principles based on prior experiences rather than efforts to mimic those settings and experiences.

Conservation has often proven to be a difficult, uphill climb. Most recent campaigns have encountered strong, often heated resistance, which helps to explain the limitations of many conservation victories, especially in the political arena. The other major element that has tempered any tendency toward complacency is a growing realization, based mostly on the work of activist scientists, of how much remains to be done. Among other things, the successes of the last quarter-century have provided a sobering view of the larger challenges that lie ahead.

I am indebted to Mansel Blackford, Jerome Mushkat, Vicky Hoover, and Peg Bobel, all experts in their respective spheres, for reading the manuscript in its entirety; to Jay Turner, who read chapters 3 and 4; and to Bill Brown, who read the section on the Adirondacks. They offered many helpful suggestions for improvements, but I alone am responsible for the ultimate result.

Once again, I am indebted to Lori for her assistance and support.

Abbreviations

ACE	Army Corps of Engineers
ANSCA	Alaska Native Claims Settlement Act
AMC	Appalachian Mountain Club
ANILCA	Alaska National Interest Lands Conservation Act
BLM	Bureau of Land Management
CBD	Center for Biological Diversity
CERP	Comprehensive Everglades Restoration Plan
DEIS	Draft Environmental Impact Statement
EIS	Environmental Impact Statement
EPA	Environmental Protection Agency
EPIC	Environmental Protection Information Center
FERMAT	Forest Ecosystem Management Assessment Team
FLPMA	Federal Land Policy and Management Act
FOE	Friends of the Earth
FEIS	Final Environmental Impact Statement
FWS	Fish and Wildlife Service

FSEEE	Forest Service Employees for Environmental Ethics
HCP	Habitat Conservation Plan
HRV	Historical Range of Variability
ICCAT	International Commission for the Conservation of Atlantic Tunas
ISC	Interagency Scientific Committee
IUCN	International Union for the Conservation of Nature
LAC	Limits of Acceptable Change
LTA	Land Trust Alliance
MPA	Marine Protected Area
MMS	Minerals Management Service
MSLDF	Mountain State Legal Defense Foundation
NEPA	National Environmental Policy Act
NFMA	National Forest Management Act
NMFS	National Marine Fisheries Service
NPS	National Park Service
RARE	Roadless Area Review and Evaluation
SCLDF	Sierra Club Legal Defense Fund
SEACC	Southeast Alaska Conservation Council
SLOSS	Single Large or Several Small
TNC	The Nature Conservancy
TPL	Trust for Public Land
TWS	The Wilderness Society
WRLC	Western Reserve Land Conservancy
Y2Y	Yellowstone to Yukon

Nature's Burdens

Introduction

My home is approximately two miles from northeast Ohio's Cuyahoga Valley
National Park, one of the new national parks of the 1970s that reflected the
vigor and militancy of environmentalism activism during those years. The
park resulted from a decade-long campaign to preserve the picturesque valley from urban sprawl, with preservation understood to include the area's
historical and cultural heritage as much as its ecological character. At 33,000
acres, Cuyahoga Valley is relatively small for a national park and constrained
by urban development on every side. Yet the park is augmented by a corridor that follows the route of a nineteenth-century canal for more than 100
miles, and by local park systems; in my county, for example, the local parks
total more than 13,000 acres. A few date from the pre–World War II period,
but most have been added since the 1960s, and that is true for the adjacent
counties as well. Park management has evolved as the parks have multiplied,
with greater attention to environmental education and wildlife. In addition,
a regional land trust holds easements on more than 45,000 acres, nearly all
added since the 1990s. The easements protect farms, estates, and other prop-

DOI: 10.7330/9781607325703.c000

erties, many with wooded and riparian areas and an impressive variety of wildlife. In recent years a natural history museum has embarked on an ambitious campaign to preserve rare and sensitive ecosystems, and it now owns more than 5,000 acres.

There is more good news. Bald eagles, great blue herons, and wild turkeys are now relatively common, as are beavers and coyotes; black bears are occasionally sighted. The Cuyahoga River, which was severely polluted in the 1960s and the subject of one of the riveting anecdotes of that era—"the river that burned"—is greatly improved, thanks to restrictions on discharges, restoration efforts, removal of several upstream dams (with additional removals planned for the near future), and a painfully slow updating of local sewage treatment facilities. Like parks and wildlands everywhere, Cuyahoga Valley and the other parks provide "ecosystem services" as well as recreational opportunities and wildlife habitat. They improve air and water quality, moderate temperature changes, protect against flooding, and increase property values.

These successes reflect shifts in public attitudes toward nature over the last half century—increasing concern about urban sprawl, loss of green space, and air and water pollution as well as desires to preserve and encourage wildlife, protect native plants, and enlist nature in creating a more attractive and appealing community. But the actual changes had more specific origins: they resulted from the growth of environmental activism, most explicitly expressed in the appearance of a variety of voluntary organizations, and the arrival of park administrators and other public officials steeped in environmental science and receptive to environmental concerns. Those administrators have made passive recreation (such as hiking, bird-watching, and nature photography), ecological restoration, and environmental education the hallmarks of park management, blurring distinctions between services to humans and preservation of natural settings.

Yet there are also limits and perplexing problems. The region's parks, individually and collectively, are still too small and fragmented to constitute meaningful "cores," large areas relatively undisturbed by humans, or to provide habitat for most threatened or endangered species or, indeed, for many others that once were common. Several major dams still compromise water flow and inhibit aquatic life; and the rivers are still sufficiently polluted to preclude many fish species. Most of the parks, together with the region's rivers and lakes, are under attack from invasive plants and animals. Some native species—white-tailed deer and other "edge" dwellers, raccoons, opossums, skunks, and foxes—have become overabundant, emphasizing the imbalances that appear as "nature" gradually reclaims an area. Finally, there are major issues of resiliency as the climate warms and plants and animals are forced to adapt.

With slight variations this account could be repeated for hundreds of other places, capturing the state of conservation in the United States today. Land conservation has accelerated over the last quarter century; new ideas about the preservation of nature have been debated and translated into policy; environmental organizations have grown larger, more numerous, and more varied; restoration projects abound; and far more is known about what is or will be needed to avoid the most dire consequences of resource exploitation. Wetlands have fared less well; rivers, lakes, and oceans are in worse shape, and most species of wildlife face a perilous future. The resulting picture is thus one of dramatic insights and positive changes coupled with a spectrum of obstacles ranging from bureaucratic inertia to the narrow particularism of many environmental groups and the popularity of libertarian and reactionary political ideologies in some quarters. Conservation campaigns have always generated concerted opposition and have typically required years, even decades, to achieve even modest results. In recent decades, however, the opposition has became more vociferous and determined, just as the need for concerted, systematic, and timely action has become more compelling. Government—with significant but sporadic exceptions—has often been unable or unwilling to act, raising the specter of an accelerating loss of biodiversity and wholesale extinctions, perhaps comparable to the events of 65 million years ago that killed off most living things, including the dinosaurs.

∽

The idea of conservation, meaning, as the dictionary tells us, the "care and preservation of natural resources," emerged at the end of the nineteenth century and focused almost exclusively on public lands and wildlife. The overriding goal was to segregate a few notable areas and a few representative species that were judged to have great public value. The intent was not to lock them away, as in an attic trunk or safe deposit box ("lock up" has been a favorite calumny of anticonservationists) but to regulate human use in order to preserve the resource and, in the case of wildlife, to ensure sustainable populations. But what constituted acceptable use? The answers were provided by agents of the government bureaus that administered the nascent federal conservation system, notably the US Forest Service (1905), the National Park Service (1916), the Bureau of Biological Survey, ultimately the Fish and Wildlife Service (1940), and, in some cases, the state agencies that provided parallel services together with individuals working in diverse fields, usually involving private lands and resources. The government officials were increasingly skilled professionals who had to balance the conflicting pressures of conservationists, who argued for more emphasis on preservation, with those of user or commodity groups that sought greater use and exploitation. As a result, public policy oscillated, reflecting the varying influence of the managers and pressure groups they dealt with. In the post–World War II years, as the economy revived after years of depression and wartime controls, the pendulum swung decisively toward greater economic activity and less restraint. More than at any previous time, the Forest Service became an ally of the timber industry, the Park Service emphasized tourism and recreation, the Fish and Wildlife Service accommodated hunters and commodity producers, and Congress became infatuated with large and intrusive public works, dams and interstate highways in particular. Thus, in 1949, the distinguished naturalist Joseph Wood Krutch could write that "what is commonly called 'conservation' . . . is not really conservation at all . . . only a more knowledgeable variation of the old idea of a world for man's use only."[1]

The backlash against the excesses of the postwar era, together with rising concerns about the safety of novel technologies such as nuclear energy largely determined the timing and substance of the new era of environmental sensitivity that followed. The environmentalism of the 1950s, 1960s, and 1970s had two distinct but overlapping dimensions. One was a wide-ranging campaign to reduce environmental abuses (primarily air and water pollution), protect society against dangers such as nuclear fallout and hazardous wastes, and clean up polluted areas; the other, which is the starting point of this study, was a renewed effort to conserve natural resources shorn of the compromises and accommodations that had marked the postwar era. Preserving nature, however it was perceived, became the dominant theme of contemporary conservation. Organized in an ever expanding group of voluntary associations, activists found a receptive audience in Congress and many state legislatures and soon came to devote as much attention to them as they did to the conservation agencies. The result was a remarkable series of laws that extended the reach of existing agencies, forced them to deemphasize or abandon alliances with commercial interests and become more accountable to the public, and introduced policy innovations on subjects as diverse as wildlife preservation and fire management.

This process accelerated through the 1960s and 1970s and was most acutely reflected in the Wilderness Act(1964), the Endangered Species Act (1973), and the Alaska National Interest Lands Conservation Act (ANILCA, 1980), which demanded new approaches to land and wildlife conservation over vastly larger areas. The Wilderness Act and the Endangered Species Act had enormous potential but little immediate impact; ANILCA, on the other hand, instantly designated over 100 million acres, largely for noncommercial purposes. The implications were impossible to disregard. ANILCA galvanized opponents as no other act of that decade. In 1980 they helped elect Ronald Reagan, the first chief executive since the 1920s who did not at least give lip service to the cause of conservation.

Reagan and his appointees had a substantial impact on public policy, national politics, and ultimately the practice of conservation. They were hostile to most conservation measures and to the environmental organizations, and sought in many cases to turn back the clock. But they also faced intense congressional opposition and aggressive lobbying by environmental groups, and soon found that their supposed mandate had largely evaporated. Unable to make fundamental changes, they contented themselves with imposing budgetary reductions, undermining or simply disregarding the policy revisions of the preceding decade, and increasing national forest timber harvests, which had bipartisan support in Congress and in many western states. In retrospect, however, their most significant change, and critical legacy, was to recast conservation as a partisan cause, another example of the more general polarization that increasingly characterized Washington politics. In later years the Clinton and Obama administrations brought different perspectives, greater sympathy, and far more energy to conservation issues but had little success in persuading Congress to adopt new laws. They and their allies depended on executive actions and administrative procedures to advance their conservation agendas. An increasing partisan setting thus ensured that the years after 1980 would be a time of heightened conflict, frequent paralysis, and what prominent political scientists have characterized as "green drift," in marked contrast to the pattern of the 1970s.[2]

In this climate, so different from that of the 1960sand 1970s, what options remained? Three developments stand out and largely define the role of conservation in contemporary society. First, environmental organizations successfully defended the legal status quo. They worked energetically to see that no major laws were repealed or substantially revised; indeed, aggressive lobbying and litigation actually extended the scope of many of them, a tendency most vividly illustrated in the conflicts over wilderness designations in the early 1980s and wildlife policy in the Pacific Northwest in the late 1980s and in Washington in the mid-1990s. The legacy of the 1960s and 1970s proved to be as resilient as the heartiest of threatened species.

Second, private land conservation became increasingly important and by the early twenty-first century had resulted in a land conservation system that in some respects paralleled the public lands. The private system was national in scope but fragmented, difficult to characterize and evaluate, and, in contrast to the federal and state land systems, was managed by private groups and was largely invisible to the public. Its long-term impact will depend on the continued activism of people and organizations that have, to date, been both ingenious and successful.

The third development was the emergence of a potent scientific voice, which provided a compelling rationale for a variety of conservation causes, promoted the protection of animals and plants, and injected a new sense of urgency into the larger cause. In the 1980s a growing number of scientists, biologists and ecologists in particular, began to argue that the problem with contemporary conservation was not too much attention to the preservation of natural resources but too little. Population growth, urbanization, and industrial development had led to an accelerating loss of biological diversity and an alarming rise in plant and animal extinctions; projecting these trends into the future suggested a bleak and perhaps unlivable future for all the Earth's inhabitants. By implication, Reagan and his allies were profoundly short-sighted. But many environmentalists were also oblivious to the larger threat. They were satisfied with national parks and wilderness areas that were too small to be meaningful except as tourist destinations and with campaigns to save whales, eagles, and other iconic species when their overriding concern should have been the habitats that sustained whales, eagles, and thousands of other known and unknown species. Too often they based their strategies on what seemed politically achievable rather than what was necessary and essential.

The scientists' answer to these limitations, often expressed in a shorthand formula, "cores, corridors, and carnivores," introduced a new way of thinking about plants and animals and indirectly about conservation in general. Its central message was the inadequacy of the status quo, despite the achievements of the preceding quarter century and mounting political pressures to do less. By the last years of the twentieth century this message was inescapable and broadly influential.

The following account charts the course of American conservation in these critical decades. It is a story of persistent activism, conflict, and frustration, but also of striking achievements, including many that would not have even been contemplated in earlier years. It is also an account of how new or revised ideas and policies about human relationships to plants, animals, and their surroundings have become a vital feature of modern environmentalism. Above all, it records the first steps in a race against time, with the hope of disproving biologist Les Kaufman's conclusion that "life on the planet advances irreversibly, like a ratchet, toward greater impoverishment."[3]

NOTES

1. Joseph Wood Krutch, *The Voice of the Desert: A Naturalist's Interpretation* (New York: William Morrow, 1955), 199.

2. Christopher McGrory Klyza and Davis Sousa, *American Environmental Policy, 1990–2006: Beyond Gridlock* (Cambridge, MA: MIT Press, 2008), 296.

3. Les Kaufman, "Why the Ark Is Sinking," in *The Last Extinction*, 2nd ed., ed. Les Kaufman and Kenneth Mallory (Cambridge, MA: MIT Press, 1993), 1.

1

An Auspicious Legacy

The achievements of the conservation community prior to 1980 included a national park system second to none, a pioneering National Wilderness Preservation System, a variety of other protected lands, a complex body of rules governing their management, and general recognition that government was necessary to protect vulnerable plants and animals. Yet there were also significant omissions and what in retrospect appeared to be badly misguided policies. This mixed legacy was the result of decisions and activities that largely date from two periods of conservation activism, the years to the 1950s and a "golden age" of congressional initiatives, the 1960s and 1970s.

ORIGINS

American conservation originated at the end of the nineteenth century as a reaction to the increasingly visible degradation of the continent's resources. The vast forests of Appalachia and the Great Lakes states had largely vanished between the 1870s and 1900, as had the bison herds of the Great Plains,

DOI: 10.7330/9781607325703.c001

many species of freshwater fish, most wolves, bears, and other large carnivores, migratory birds, white-tailed deer, and wild turkeys. Nature was under
siege and seemed about to succumb. What could be done? A commonsense
answer was to preserve the best of what remained and to restrain, via laws
and regulations, the uses of the public domain. Thus, many states began to
regulate hunting and fishing and restrict the uses of rivers and lakes. More
ambitious initiatives occurred in the West, where the federal government
still owned most of the land. The first national park (Yellowstone) dated
from 1872, and the great Sierra Nevada parks (Sequoia, Yosemite, and Kings
Canyon) were added in 1890. The official rationale came later, in the National
Park Act of 1916, the outgrowth of an extended battle over a proposed dam at
Hetch Hetchy Valley in Yosemite, which the park defenders lost. Perceiving
the parks' vulnerability under existing law, they strongly promoted the 1916
act, which defined the national parks' mission as conserving "scenery," "natural and historical objects," and "wildlife" and managing them so they would
be "unimpaired for the enjoyment of future generations."[1] The legislation
also created an administrative agency, the National Park Service, to uphold
that charge.[2]

In the meantime Congress had given the president the power to designate
"forest reserves," and by the turn of the century there were "reserves" totaling more than 30 million acres, mostly in rugged mountainous country and
entirely in the West. The reserves were not exactly parks or nature preserves.
At first their purpose, apart from conserving public water supplies and holding rapacious loggers at bay, was uncertain. Gradually, however, a kind of
hybrid approach, combining public ownership and management with a variety of human uses, emerged. It became known, although not officially until
1960, as multiple use.

The most dramatic break with the past came with the presidency of
Theodore Roosevelt, who almost single-handedly made conservation a feature of progressive government. Roosevelt had a lifelong fascination with
birds and was a respected ornithologist; he was well informed on wildlife
issues generally and was a personal acquaintance of the leading naturalists
of his time, including his uncle Richard Roosevelt, who was an expert on
fish and water resources. He cultivated important political allies, including
Representative John F. Lacey (R-IA) and Gifford Pinchot. The soft-spoken
Lacey, a leader in the effort to preserve archaeological sites and wildlife,

immediately recognized Roosevelt's potential as a reformer and worked closely with him. In 1906 Lacey persuaded his colleagues to pass the Antiquities Act, which gave the president the power to unilaterally create national monuments, a power that Roosevelt instantly seized and used to the utmost.[3]

Pinchot had long been one of the president's closest friends and advisors. Scion of a wealthy Pennsylvania family, he had studied forestry in France and became the first professional forester in the United States. He made his family lands a model of scientific forestry, set up a forestry program at George Vanderbilt's vast estate near Ashville, North Carolina, and joined the federal government. A Roosevelt intimate by the mid-1890s, he became the head of the Interior Department's Division of Forestry in 1898 and, with Roosevelt's support, engineered its transfer from the hidebound Interior Department to the Agriculture Department, renamed as the US Forest Service. There Pinchot aggressively implemented his view of conservation based on national planning, sustainable forestry, watershed protection, and fire suppression, with the greatest emphasis on timber.[4] Pinchot's maneuvering led to his dismissal in 1910, but he remained a political presence in Washington and in conservation circles for another thirty-five years.

With support in Congress and the federal bureaucracy, the pugnacious Roosevelt eagerly confronted western politicians and commercial interests (such as feather hunters, a scourge in Florida). Douglas Brinkley has recorded the details in his magisterial *Wilderness Warrior*. In Roosevelt's nearly eight years in office, he created eighteen monuments, fifty-one bird reservations, and four game reserves and was instrumental in the creation or enlargement of 150 national forests and six national parks, including Crater Lake in Oregon and Mesa Verde in Colorado.[5] The thirty-two new national forests he authorized in March 1907 (just before Congress required congressional approval of new national forests) totaled 16 million acres. The Tongass National Forest, established a year later, embraced virtually all of southeast Alaska and became and remained, at 17 million acres, the largest of them all.

Yet Roosevelt's record was not unsullied, at least by later standards. He was always an enthusiastic hunter; championed the Reclamation Service, an Interior agency that proceeded to dam major rivers in the West; supported proposals to drain the Everglades in order to promote economic activity in South Florida; and ultimately sided with Pinchot in supporting the damming of Hetch Hetchy. He also endorsed Pinchot's emphasis on regulated forestry and multiple use.

Many conservationists argued that Pinchot's utilitarian approach was too narrow. Some areas were so valuable because of their natural beauty, unique features, or irreplaceable resources that they should be off-limits to economic exploitation, whatever the mode of management. They found a champion in John Muir, the prominent essayist and naturalist who spent most of his adult lifetime promoting the wonders of the Sierra Nevada and southeast Alaska. In numerous books and essays Muir argued that such areas should be preserved for their aesthetic and spiritual values, and not just for their exotic or monumental features, as early national park proponents had argued.[6] But Muir went further than most of his allies. "Why," he asked, "should man value himself as more than a small part of the one great unit of creation? . . . The universe would be incomplete without man; but it would also be incomplete without the smallest transmicroscopic creature."[7]

Muir and Pinchot were friends until the late 1890s, when the forester's growing prominence in the federal government and his emphasis on so-called "wise use" undermined their relationship. To many later writers their antagonism was symbolic of a larger division in the nascent conservation movement. The historian Stephen Fox has summarized: "The utilitarians were better organized and more intent, with money and livelihoods at stake. They had more political power. The preservationists, though more numerous, made up a relatively inchoate, nebulous bloc, lacking the goal of practical self interest."[8] Yet the distinction can be overstated. Muir's followers opposed commodity production but favored tourism, often citing Switzerland as a model of how mountain scenery could be the basis of a healthy economy. The original motto of the Sierra Club, which Muir founded in 1892 to help protect the Sierra Nevada, was to "explore, enjoy and render accessible the mountain regions of the Pacific Coast."[9] For many years Sierra Club leaders were relatively nonchalant about road building in Yosemite and other parks. During the Hetch Hetchy controversy, Muir's followers insisted that the primary reason for their opposition was the dam's impact on human uses of the valley. No one proposed to close the parks to people or to eliminate the many services that visitors demanded.[10]

Most of the other conservation organizations of the pre–World War II years took a similarly relaxed approach to issues outside their immediate areas of concern. The Izaak Walton League, a midwestern organization of hunters and anglers, devoted little attention to public policy issues; the Audubon societies, concentrated in the East, focused narrowly on birds and bird-watching; the Wilderness Society, organized in 1935 in reaction to the government's aggressive policy of road building on public lands, took a broader approach but made no effort to attract a mass membership. A myriad of local and regional groups, mostly devoted to wildlife and recreation, attracted outdoor enthusiasts and hobbyists.

During those years the Forest Service was the most important force in public land conservation. The Weeks Act of 1911 authorized land purchases by the Forest Service, supposedly to control flooding, and in the succeeding years the agency acquired new national forests in the East: fifteen in the 1910s and 1920s and twenty-two in the 1930s. These were mostly cutover lands in southern Appalachia, northern New England, and the upper Midwest. In those areas and in Alaska, the Forest Service became a de facto economic development agency.[11] Yet it is important not to read the agency's later history into that period. In the West, rangers devoted more time and energy to livestock grazing than to timber.[12] Before World War II timber harvests from public lands never amounted to more than 4 percent of the national total, and often much less, a reflection of abundant supplies on private lands and political pressures to restrict government competition. On one related issue, forest fires, the agency did take a resolute stand. Despite a tradition of "light burning" in some areas, it became increasingly committed to fire prevention and suppression. By the 1940s it was wholly committed and a model for other government agencies.[13] By the 1960s the total acreage burned annually in wildland fires was typically less than one-fifth the average of the 1930s.[14]

Another factor shaping Forest Service policy was the foresters' conception of the agency as an elite organization with high professional standards and lofty aims. For much of the period it sought regulatory authority over private timber lands in order to deter "cut and run" logging. A 1933 agency publication insisted that "practically all of the major problems of American forestry center in or have grown out of private ownership."[15] Forest Service personnel worked closely with conservation groups, which in turn viewed it as one of the most enlightened government agencies.[16] Some of the prewar era's best-known conservationists, including Aldo Leopold, Robert Marshall, and Arthur Carhart, served in the Forest Service.

The other decisive influence was the Forest Service's rivalry with the National Park Service (NPS). Since the NPS had no authority to buy land until the 1960s, its parks had to be assembled from private land donations or carved out of the public domain, which meant, in many areas, Forest Service lands. There were major battles over the creation or expansion of Grand Canyon, Kings Canyon, Olympic, and Grand Teton parks, which the Forest Service lost, and over the expansion of Rocky Mountain and Yellowstone, which it won. To increase its appeal, the Forest Service developed campgrounds and other recreation areas and conducted a highly successful publicity campaign against forest fires. Beginning in 1924, it designated "primitive" areas that were off-limits to most economic activity. The first of these was in the Gila National Forest in New Mexico; the most impressive was the magnificent Boundary Waters Canoe Area in northern Minnesota. William Greeley, the chief of the Forest Service, wrote, in a lightly veiled reference to the NPS: "Let us add [to national parks] if that is where [the land] belongs; but curses on the man who bisects it with roads, plants it with hotels, and sends yellow busses streaking through it with sirens shrieking like souls in torment."[17]

Greeley's complaint was directed at NPS director Stephen Mather and his successors, who aggressively promoted tourism to expose visitors to the wonders of nature and, not coincidentally, to support the agency's demands for additional resources. Mather was particularly interested in creating parks near major eastern population centers. And, as he anticipated, the new national parks of the 1920s, Acadia (Maine), Shenandoah (Virginia), and Great Smoky Mountains (North Carolina, Tennessee), soon attracted more visitors than the iconic western parks. The agency's emphasis on accessibility and recreation encouraged travel, provided low-cost nature education, and built political support for park extensions. But it also led to excesses: a multitude of roads, lodges, and other concessions and at times a carnival atmosphere, epitomized by the infamous "fire fall" at Yosemite.

The Mather strategy paid off handsomely in the 1930s, when the Franklin D. Roosevelt administration embraced conservation as part of its economic recovery program. The NPS was given managerial responsibility for battlefields and government monuments, including much of Washington, DC. It acquired "national recreation areas," lands adjoining the new reservoirs that were appearing in the West, such as Lake Mead on the Colorado River; a host of new western monuments; new prominent parks, including

Olympic (Washington) and the Everglades (Florida); and, with the Civilian Conservation Corps, established or developed a host of state parks. Looking back thirty years later, parks expert F. Fraser Darling wrote that the years 1935–40 were "a peak of both achievement and enjoyment. Morale . . . was very high. . . . and there was a beginning of ecological awareness within the Park Service."[18]

The other federal conservation agency, the Bureau of Biological Survey (BBS), established in 1905 as an Agriculture Department office, administered various wildlife programs, including a growing number of bird refuges. Although the BBS employed leading scientists in field work, it remained little known and largely unappreciated. By the mid-1920s it oversaw eighty refuges, including a handful devoted to "big game." A 1916 treaty with Canada that protected migratory birds was the high point of its early history.[19] The agency's status changed in 1933 with the arrival of a new sympathetic president and administration. In 1934 Congress adopted legislation that established a "duck stamp," a tax on hunters that assured a continuing source of funds. It also obtained relief funds to buy lands from drought-stricken farmers in the Midwest. An energetic young administrator, John Clark Salyer II, drove across the region, spotting likely acquisitions; in six weeks he identified 600,000 acres of prime waterfowl habitat.[20] In the Dakotas, BBS officials shrewdly extended their reach by purchasing conservation easements (development rights) rather than the land itself. This was apparently the first use of what would later become a widely used conservation strategy.[21] In 1939 Interior secretary Harold Ickes engineered the transfer of the BBS to the Interior Department, where he merged it with the Bureau of Fisheries (formerly in the Commerce Department) to create the Fish and Wildlife Service. In 1934 BBS had administered 1.7 million acres in the forty-eight states and 4 million in Alaska. During the following six years it added almost 8 million acres in the states and a quarter million in Alaska. The expansion of the wildlife refuge system was Roosevelt's "most enduring conservation achievement," though most refuges encouraged hunting and in many cases agricultural or even industrial activities.[22]

Yet throughout this period most of the agency's resources were devoted to killing wolves, coyotes, mountain lions, bears, prairie dogs, and other animals that preyed on livestock or were otherwise troublesome to farmers and ranchers. BBS professionals scorned traditional state and county bounty systems as haphazard and ineffective. As one administrator noted, the BBS "promised permanent relief, namely, actual extermination of the pests."[23] By the late 1920s it had killed off virtually all wolves, had rid most areas in the West of grizzly bears, and was aggressively attacking coyotes and prairie dogs. It was so successful that it attracted a growing number of critics, scientists concerned about the extinction of predator species and a handful of landowners who realized that the wholesale elimination of predators inevitably led to an increase in the number of rodents and other genuine pests. BBS leaders responded with soothing assurances but no change in policy.

Despite the many government initiatives, more than half of all publicly owned lands, including most of the desert or semidesert lands of the intermountain West, remained in managerial limbo, neither park, national forest, nor refuge. Technically available to purchasers or homesteaders, in practice these lands were devoted to cattle and sheep grazing. In 1934 Congress passed the Taylor Grazing Act, which introduced a lease system administered by a new Interior agency, the Grazing Service. The Taylor Act helped to clarify the legal status of the land but did nothing to improve the fragile environment. The Grazing Service was weak, underfunded, and necessarily accommodating to ranchers; lease payments were low, rancher influence was high, and overgrazing was common. By the end of the decade the Grazing Service had become a notable example of agency "capture" by the industry it supposedly regulated. In the 1940s opposition to even modest increases in lease payments led to its collapse and left its successor, the Bureau of Land Management (BLM), largely at the beck and call of the livestock industry. The first director of the BLM, Marion Clawson, sought to make it into a multiple-use agency modeled after the Forest Service, but readily acknowledged the challenges that lay ahead.[24] The BLM would remain the "underdog" of land management agencies.[25]

By the post–World War II years, then, the federal conservation agencies emphasized a variety of utilitarian services. The Forest Service promoted timber production, grazing, and mining. The Park Service managed an ever growing road and highway system, hotels and restaurants, campgrounds, gift shops, and a myriad of other commercial establishments. The Fish and Wildlife Service accommodated farmers, ranchers, and hunters. In the meantime, most public lands (together with rivers, lakes, and oceans) remained outside the conservation system, unprotected and susceptible to a multitude of abuses.

State and local park systems, state forests, and other preserves had also proliferated, especially in the eastern and Pacific Coast states. Their overriding mission was public recreation, but a handful, large and strategically located, were also designated or de facto wildlife refuges.[26]

A New Era

If the depressed economy of the 1930s muted concerns about environmental degradation, the economic expansion that dated from the late 1930s and continued with only minor interludes for nearly forty years brought renewed attention to the dangers of air and water pollution as well as the unanticipated effects of new technologies, notably nuclear fallout and pesticide poisoning.[27] No less important were concerns about the reckless exploitation of natural resources: deteriorating parks and natural areas, deforestation, endangered wildlife, the accommodating policies of the conservation agencies toward commercial interests, urban sprawl, and many others. The "most revolutionary element of this new public consciousness," writes Richard N.L. Andrews, was a sense of the environment "as a living system—a 'web of life,' or ecosystem."[28] In their history of the era, G. Calvin MacKenzie and Robert Weisbrot argue that the initial political response came from above. "Congress outpaced public demands for federal protection," they write. Major environmental initiatives came "from the highest levels of government."[29] That may be an accurate description of the campaigns against air and water pollution and the haphazard use of toxic substances, but it is a misleading portrayal of the reinvigorated conservation crusade. More than a decade before the first Earth Day, April 22, 1970, which seemingly marked the emergence of mass support for environmental legislation, conservation leaders had mobilized broad public support for parks, public forests, and a new approach to wilderness.[30]

As early as the mid-1950s there had been signs of change. Spurred by the established conservation organizations, together with a growing number of new groups, a distinctive political force began to emerge. Joseph Voigt, a leader of the Izaak Walton League, the largest postwar conservation society, recalled "how small we were in numbers . . . [a] ragtag little army."[31] But the army quickly expanded. The number of organizations grew at least sixfold in the next twenty years, and the league, which consisted largely of traditional "sportsmen," was soon surpassed by its new and newly militant competitors.[32] Rachel Carson's *Silent Spring* (1962), one of the seminal works of the new environmentalism, documented the irresponsible behavior of chemical manufacturers and the fecklessness of federal and state officials, but it also noted the growing volume of protests—notably from the Audubon Society, in which Carson herself had been active for many years. Interior secretary Stewart Udall's *The Quiet Crisis*, published the following year, captured the new sensitivity among government officials. The word "conservation" now seemed too narrow and tainted by the "wise use" policies and commercial associations of the federal agencies. New and old groups alike embraced the term "environmental" to suggest their broad, seamless concerns and hostility to the status quo.

The first great battle of the postwar era went a long way toward redefining the conservation movement. In the late 1940s the Bureau of Reclamation proposed a series of dams on the Colorado River and its tributaries to provide water and hydropower for the growing cities of the region. The plan had the enthusiastic support of western development interests. Among the proposed dams was one at Echo Park on the Green River in remote northwestern Colorado. The dam would be inside Dinosaur National Monument, a Park Service unit, and would inundate the canyon and its fossil beds, the area's distinctive feature. The parallels with Hetch Hetchy were obvious, including the acquiescence of the NPS staff. The Wilderness Society, the Sierra Club, and other conservation groups organized a nationwide protest campaign that emphasized the sanctity of the national parks. The protests persuaded congressional leaders to delete the Echo Park dam from the legislation in 1956, reaffirming the inviolability of national parks. In later years environmentalists often bemoaned the fact that the defense of Dinosaur led to a tactical decision not to oppose the much larger and more significant dam at Glen Canyon, just north of Grand Canyon.[33]

In any event, the Echo Park campaign proved to be a turning point for the emerging environmental movement. It attracted a new generation of supporters and demonstrated how they could overcome influential and entrenched opponents. In orchestrating the campaign, the Sierra Club's new executive director, David Brower, demonstrated a flair for public relations that would soon make him the best-known environmental leader of that era. Henceforth there would always be a corps of activists that he and other leaders could mobilize for environmental causes.

In the years after the Echo Park battle, the Forest Service increasingly became the issue. The postwar housing boom had increased the demand for lumber, and the timber industry turned to the public forests. The Forest Service responded by dropping its long-standing goal of regulating the industry and became an enthusiastic and increasingly uncritical partner. During the 1950s the national forests' timber harvest tripled; between 1950 and 1960 the aggregate was twice the total of all the years from 1905 to 1950.[34] In 1962 the long-time chief of the Forest Service, Richard McArdle, who had engineered the "rapprochement" with industry, retired and was succeeded by Edward Cliff, an advocate of maximum timber production. Under Cliff the agency became increasingly single-minded: "get out the cut" became its mantra. To unhappy environmentalists as well as many agency veterans, the new policies represented a "profound shift in orientation," a disturbing indication that the Forest Service "had lost its essential integrity."[35] Areas that had been set aside for recreation or wilderness were reclassified, igniting numerous controversies: one notorious example, involving the French Pete Valley in central Oregon, was second only to the Echo Park dam proposal in galvanizing opponents.[36]

No less provocative were qualitative changes in forestry practices, notably the widespread adoption of clear-cutting, which removed all of the trees in a given area and was often indistinguishable from the "cut-and-run" forestry of earlier years. The Forest Service promoted clear-cutting because young Douglas firs, the most commercially desirable trees, required open, sunny spaces. But clear-cutting was widely adopted in other settings as well because it simplified the work and permitted a higher degree of mechanization. The ecological costs were substantial. Clear-cutting not only removed the forest cover but damaged the forest floor, destroyed wildlife habitat, and produced dramatic visual blight. Erosion increased and the land became less fertile.[37] In the words of ecologist Nancy Langston, "short-term economic efficiency" often led to "long-term ecological disaster."[38]

Perhaps the best measure of what had happened to the agency after World War II was the proliferation of below-cost timber sales. In the old-growth areas of Oregon and Washington timber sales were highly profitable to the agency; in the South, moderately profitable; everywhere else, they lost money. Why, critics asked, was the government subsidizing the timber industry when a full accounting, including erosion and habitat loss, would have shown that even the "profits" from the Northwest forests were illusory? In the infamous case of Alaska's Tongass National Forest, the Forest Service became subservient to the wood pulp industry. Logging was ecologically disastrous and harmful to the fishing industry, the area's other principal activity; yet the Forest Service also lost millions.[39]

As the Forest Service became increasingly devoted to timber production, it continued to proclaim its fidelity to the multiple-use ideal. In 1955 agency leaders persuaded Congress to give them the ability to regulate mining claims when "mining" was an obvious pretext for cutting timber. It then lobbied for multiple-use legislation to help deal with competing interests, fend off the more extreme demands of the timber industry, and compete with the NPS. Congress passed the Multiple Use—Sustained Yield Act in 1960, awkwardly restating the purposes of the national forests as "outdoor recreation, range, timber, watershed, wildlife and fish."[40]

The timing of the act could not have been more ironic. The inconsistency between the agency's embrace of multiple use and its commitment to "get out the cut" was hard to conceal and impossible to reconcile: David Clary has observed that the Multiple Use Act "asked an organization that was composed of people inclined to focus on one thing to think equally about several other things, even if at the expense of their principal object."[41] The evident hypocrisy of the Multiple Use Act aroused widespread criticism. To opponents, multiple use and the brand of conservation that it seemed to represent were only slightly different from the free-market forestry that had been a target of Roosevelt, Pinchot, and the other pioneers.

The NPS faced similar pressures. During World War II the agency had lost personnel and revenue; its headquarters was moved to Chicago and nearly all maintenance was postponed. Consequently, the parks were ill equipped to handle the dramatic increase in visitations that coincided with the return of prosperity. NPS director Conrad Wirth, who had a background in landscape architecture and recreation planning, saw opportunity in the onrush. He devised an ambitious plan of infrastructure improvements that he called Mission 66 (i.e., a plan to update and modernize the parks before the fiftieth anniversary of the national park system). New roads, visitor centers, and accommodations would make the parks accessible, convenient, and attractive, appealing to newly affluent travelers.[42] Congress was agreeable and provided additional appropriations, beginning in 1956. Many park supporters soon became critics. Amid all the construction Mission 66 did "compara-tively little for the plants and animals" and "nothing at all for the ecological maintenance of the system."[43] The "single most controversial project" was the upgrading of the Tioga Road, which bisected Yosemite park and opened much of the interior to auto traffic.[44] The road became a symbol, similar to the Colorado River dams and French Pete, of a bureaucracy that had lost its bearings. The Sierra Club, a longtime ally of the Park Service in California, now became a vigorous critic.[45] Wirth's press releases, which emphasized the magnitude of the building program, did not help.

Environmentalists became still more vocal after Steward Udall became sec-retary of the Interior in 1961. Udall was alert to the growing environmental movement and to critics who portrayed the NPS as a glorified tourist bureau. Public outrage over the culling of the large elk population in Yellowstone Park provided an opportunity to introduce changes. Udall recruited A. Starker Leopold, a respected professor of zoology at the University of Cali-fornia (and son of Aldo Leopold, the pioneering forester and wildlife expert whose posthumous *A Sand County Almanac* would become the bible of the environmental movement), to head an investigating committee. An aca-demic diplomat who successfully navigated the interstices between scientific research and public policy for more than two decades and who trained many of the wildlife biologists who would be instrumental in introducing greater ecological sensitivity to the Park Service, Leopold understood the scope of his assignment. His report, finished in early 1963, helped define the new envi-ronmental activism of the 1960s and 1970s and had a lasting impact on the Park Service.[46]

Leopold began with a short section on the history of the Park Service and a long quotation from a report by the recent First World Conference on National Parks, summarizing the latest ideas on park management. Leopold then addressed the state of the Park Service in what would become the report's best-known and most influential section. "As a primary goal," he wrote, "we would recommend that the biotic associations with each park be maintained, or where necessary recreated, as nearly as possible in the con-dition that prevailed when the area was first visited by the white man. A national park should represent a vignette of primitive America."[47] In short, the NPS had wandered far from its goal of preserving the dramatic, "mon-umental" settings that it managed. Biotic associations, not roads, lodges, souvenir shops, or even trails, should be the foremost concern. Leopold acknowledged that such a change of emphasis would have "stupendous" implications, particularly since a century or more of human activity meant that "the biotic associations in many of our parks are artifacts, pure and simple." Restoration would be neither simple nor, in some cases, possible. Yet "a reasonable illustration of primitive America" might be feasible, provided that the Park Service proceeded with "skill, judgment, and ecological sensitivity" and adopted a "diversity of management procedures." Leopold then endorsed what at the time were still relatively novel and often controversial policies: an emphasis on native plants and animals; the controlled use of fire; bans on insecticides and chemical treatments of vegetation; limits on road building, animal feeding, and other tourist-oriented activities; and removal of golf courses, ski lifts, marinas, and similar recreational facilities. The report strongly opposed hunting in parks and reviewed methods of controlling animal populations through natural predation. The Yellowstone situation was only discussed at the end in the commentary on animal populations. "Above all other policies," Leopold concluded, "the maintenance of naturalness should prevail."[48]

The Leopold report was a critique of the contemporary Park Service and, by implication, the practice of conservation. The federal government had set aside some of the most notable scenery in North America, saved animals from extinction, and embraced regulated forestry. But the agencies charged with administering public lands had grown increasingly accommodating to economic interest groups and increasingly indifferent to the actual resources they managed. Leopold called them to account. Yet for all its apparent boldness, the report also reflected assumptions about nature and the North American environment that would come under increasing scrutiny in the following years. His association of "primitive America" and "naturalness" with the conditions existing when the land was "first visited by the white man" was widely criticized, both for neglecting the impact of indigenous Americans (a notable example of the "shifting baselines" problem) and its assumption of an unchanging natural order. The goal of creating "vignettes of primitive America" similarly reflected the idea of a relatively stable, predictable natural setting, captured in a phrase common at the time, the "balance of nature."[49] Ecologists of the 1960s and afterward increasingly insisted that such assumptions were misleading, that storms, fires, droughts, and other natural upheavals constantly created new and unanticipated combinations of plants and animals. One could not simply remove the golf courses, ski lifts, shops, and other extraneous facilities and restore what had existed. A more realistic goal was "historical integrity," preserving the types of plants, animals, and ecological processes that had traditionally characterized an area.[50] These issues would emerge in the future. In the meantime, the Leopold report was enormously influential.

Prompted in part by Leopold's conclusions, Udall soon replaced Wirth with George Hartzog, an activist and "political wheeler-dealer" (in the words of environmental journalist Michael Frome) who was eager to respond to another common complaint, that the park system was not growing fast enough to meet the needs of a growing, mobile population.[51] "I had a simple credo," Hartzog recalled, "take it now, warts and all."[52] Abandoning Wirth's emphasis on recreational planning, he saw his assignment as a "race" against urban sprawl and rural industrialization. "Rounding out" the park system, a traditional theme among park advocates, became "rounding up."[53] Working closely with congressional leaders, he championed new western parks as well as seashores, lakeshores, and urban national parks. During Hartzog's tenure (1964–72), the Park Service added seventy-two units covering 3 million acres and did much of the planning for the anticipated Alaska parks.

Apart from the absolute number of new units, the hallmark of the Hartzog years was the varied character of the new parks. For decades the Park Service had emphasized areas of stunning natural beauty, which usually translated into snow-capped mountains or distinctive geological features. There were exceptions, but the emphasis on "quality" had long been a constant in the discussions of national park administrators and supporters.[54] By the time of Hartzog's arrival, however, many park advocates had concluded that this emphasis was obsolete, if not wrong-headed. Congress characteristically embraced both sides of the debate. At the same time it authorized a half-dozen new parks with distinctive scenery, it also endorsed what President Richard Nixon would later call "parks to the people." In 1961 it created Cape Cod National Seashore, largely because of the interest of President Kennedy. Point Reyes, California, and Padre Island, Texas, followed in 1962, and five others by 1972. Beginning in 1966 it authorized a series of midwestern lakeshores: Pictured Rocks, Michigan, and Indiana Dunes, Indiana, in 1966; Apostle Islands, Wisconsin, and Sleeping Bear Dunes, Michigan, in 1970. Six national recreation areas in or adjacent to large cities were added in the early 1970s. In the late 1970s, thanks largely to Representative Philip Burton (D-CA), the pace accelerated, provoking jokes about "park barrel" bills. Burton's goal supposedly was to locate a park unit in every congressional district.[55] In any case there was no pretense of a systematic effort to "round out" the park system with distinctive landscapes. An influential advocate was more important than the setting itself.

An increasingly important hurdle was the cost of park land. The western parks were created by transferring land from the Forest Service or BLM to the Park Service; additional facilities and employees would be required, but the acquisition cost was zero. The seashores and lakeshores were mostly privately owned, as were most lands in the eastern two-thirds of the country. Redwood National Park, in northern California, was by far the most costly of the new parks, especially after the initial purchase in 1968 had to be supplemented with adjacent forest lands to protect the redwoods. "Willing sellers ran the show," concluded one group of historians.[56] Because of high land costs and a reluctance to force residents to leave, the seashores, lakeshores, and national recreation areas included many inholdings, privately owned lands inside park boundaries that totaled nearly 4.5 million acres by 1980.[57] Some of the new parks were "greenline" by design, depending on regulations and cooperation rather than fee purchases.

There were also important qualitative changes. The older parks featured a road system, extensive development around an outstanding natural attraction, perhaps another developed area, and one or more "gateway" communities. The newer rural parks were at least initially roadless, with minimal amenities and only minor recreational features. Canyonlands (1964), Guadalupe Mountains (1966), North Cascades (1968), and Voyageurs (1970) are examples of the more restrained approach. Geographer Thomas Vale has noted that the "reduced emphasis on recreational development . . . expressed a more general trend" of the park system.[58] Visitor services now competed with an effort to preserve as much of the natural landscape as possible.

Spurred by Leopold and his Berkeley colleague, Harold Biswell, an expert on forest and wildland fires, the Park Service also embraced a more positive view of forest fires. They had long been a feature of resource management at Everglades and several other eastern parks, but the breakthrough came at Sequoia and Kings Canyon, where lightning-caused fires were common and years of fire suppression had led to dangerous accumulations of dead trees and woody plants. After 1965 park managers generally allowed backcountry fires to burn themselves out and experimented with prescribed burns. In 1968 the NPS explicitly endorsed the new approach, although it proceeded warily and did not even announce the change in policy to the public for another six years.[59] The new NPS policies, however, were a major victory for what fire historian Stephen J. Pyne has called the "fire counterculture."[60] They marked yet another important break with the past.

CONGRESS LEADS

By the mid-1960s the environmental movement had become a powerful political force, with a growing cadre of lobbyists and extensive grassroots support. Civil rights campaigns and exposés of environmental abuses, such as *Silent Spring*, helped pave the way for an extraordinary series of environmental laws, which increased the regulatory responsibilities of the federal government and transformed the management of public lands. In the 1960s a group of western liberal senators, including Lee Metcalf (D-MT), Frank Church (D-ID), Clinton Anderson (D-NM), and Henry "Scoop" Jackson (D-WA), took the lead. In the 1970s, as western commodity producers mobilized against additional conservation legislation, the House of Representative played a larger role, especially after Morris Udall (D-AZ) became chair of the Interior Committee in 1973. Responding to public pressures, Presidents Kennedy, Johnson, Nixon, Ford, and Carter were generally supportive, and Carter played a major role in the passage of ANILCA. This unusual combination marked this decade and a half as an uncommonly productive and atypical chapter in the history of American conservation.

Congress passed twenty-two major environmental laws between 1964 and 1980, half of which dealt with public lands and wildlife. Seven were of particular importance in the following years:

The Land and Water Conservation Act (1964) established a fund with revenues from offshore oil leases to finance land purchases by federal, state, and local governments. It facilitated the expansion of the national park system and later included money for historic preservation.

The Wilderness Act (1964) authorized Congress to designate "untrammeled" federal lands as part of a National Wilderness Preservation System, permanently excluding roads, structures, and commercial activities. Wilderness became the highest form of land protection. Nine million acres of national forest land that the Forest Service had administratively classified in several wilderness categories became the foundation for the new system. The Forest Service, NPS, and FWS were to review their roadless lands in the following decade and recommend additions.

The National Environmental Policy Act (NEPA, 1969) required federal agencies to prepare "environmental impact statements" for projects with environmental implications and invite public comment. Later judicial decisions required evaluations with explicit alternatives.

The Endangered Species Act (1973) was the capstone to a series of wildlife measures designed to protect endangered species and prevent extinctions. The FWS and the Commerce Department's National Marine Fisheries Service were to maintain lists of "threatened" and "endangered" species, which required protective measures, and to designate "critical habitats" necessary for recovery. The law applied to private and public property but emphasized single species.

The Federal Land Policy and Management Act (FLPMA, 1976), the long-delayed organic act for the Bureau of Land Management, gave it and the vast areas it administered in the West and Alaska a permanent role in public land management. It upgraded the low-status grazing service into a multiple-use agency and required wilderness reviews of all BLM lands.

The National Forest Management Act (NFMA, 1976) required periodic detailed plans for each forest and invited public comments on the plans. It restricted clear-cutting in some situations and required protection of wildlife "diversity." The act became fundamental to Forest Service operations.

The Alaska National Interest Lands Conservation Act (ANILCA, 1980) authorized ten new national parks and enlarged three existing parks in Alaska. It also greatly expanded the wildlife refuge system, designated huge wilderness areas, and accelerated land transfers to Native corporations. The new parks and refuges were based largely on natural boundaries. Altogether 104 million acres were transferred from the BLM to other agencies. The legislation also included controversial provisions that subsidized logging in the Tongass National Forest and provided a mechanism for opening the new Arctic National Wildlife Refuge to oil drilling.

Other laws provided for the designation of rivers or parts of rivers as "wild and scenic," limiting development and prohibiting dams (1968); authorized a series of long-distance hiking trails (1968); and regulated strip mining and required the reclamation of mined areas (1977).[61] Other regulatory measures, such as the federal water pollution control acts of 1965 and 1972, also influenced conservation policy.

The large majorities by which most of these measures passed were often misleading. Public opinion may have dictated the final votes, but that was after the most controversial proposals had been eliminated or diluted. Most conservation bills attracted strong and persistent opposition. Liberals, usually Democrats, typically sponsored the legislation; Republicans were the usual opponents. But party affiliation was less important than geography. Representatives and senators typically defended home state or hometown business interests, which meant that most opposition came from the West, notably the rural West. By the 1970s western liberals were well aware of the growing opposition to parks and especially wilderness legislation and became more cautious. Symptomatic of this change was the behavior of Senator Henry Jackson. As the powerful head of the Senate Interior Committee, he authored the National Environmental Policy Act and guided other measures through his committee. A decade later, in response to the concerns of Seattle business and labor interests, he repeatedly delayed the ANILCA legislation. The most influential Republican senator on conservation issues, Mark Hatfield (R-OR), was generally a friend of the environment but a vigorous opponent of restrictions on public land logging.

A critical political event during these years was the defeat of Wayne Aspinall (D-CO) in the 1972 Democratic primary by a coalition of environmentalists.[62] Aspinall, the longtime chair of the House Interior Committee, was a vigorous defender of traditional western commodity interests. His defeat created an opening for Udall, a leader of the House liberals and an environmentalist. At the same time Philip Burton, the most influential congressional liberal, and John Seiberling (D-OH), a champion of parks and wilderness, joined the committee. This triumvirate made the Interior Committee a source of innovative environmental legislation for more than a decade.

The Wilderness Act had its origins in the mid-1950s as conservationists worried about rampant development, Mission 66, and the apparent transformation of the Forest Service. The agency's practice of setting aside roadless areas had slowed in the 1940s and was now gradually being reversed as it became increasingly preoccupied with timber cutting.[63] Howard Zahniser, the executive director of the Wilderness Society, and other environmental leaders responded with a plan for a "wilderness preservation system" that would permanently restrict the Forest Service, the Park Service, and the Fish and Wildlife Service. Zahniser, the principal author, defined wilderness as an "area where the earth and its community of life are untrammeled by man, where man himself is a visitor who does not remain." The proposed law would apply to federally owned lands "without permanent improvements or human habitation" and where the "imprint of man's work" was "substantially unnoticeable." It preserved existing Forest Service wilderness areas and provided for additions from the national parks and wildlife refuges (BLM lands became eligible after 1976). In 1956 Zahniser persuaded Senator Hubert Humphrey (D-MN) to introduce the initial bill. The proposed legislation went through numerous revisions but made little progress until the early 1960s, when Senator Clinton Anderson (D-NM), the chair of the Senate Interior Committee, became its champion. Anderson secured passage of the Senate bill in 1961, but it remained stalled in the House Interior Committee. Aspinall's price for approval was a series of weakening amendments: each addition to the wilderness system would require an act of Congress, and mining claims in wilderness areas would be allowed for another twenty years.[64] The final legislation made the 9.1 million acres of existing national forest wilderness the starting point for the new system and required the Forest Service, Park Service, and Fish and Wildlife Service to review their holdings over the next decade for possible additions. President Johnson signed the Wilderness Act on September 3, 1964, at the same time he signed the legislation creating the Land and Water Conservation Fund. More than any other measure, the Wilderness Act reflected the growing public antipathy toward the Forest Service and other federal agencies that had capitulated to commercial interests and the likely legacy of their policies, a rural landscape bereft of trees and other natural features.

One of Aspinall's hurdles, the requirement of congressional action on each addition to the wilderness system, soon backfired on opponents. It effectively politicized the process of designating wilderness and became, in the words of political scientist Christopher Klyza, "the first successful challenge to the privilege of technocratic utilitarianism."[65] By requiring demonstrations of public support, it gave environmental organizations a large, often critical role in drafting legislation and mobilizing public sentiment, and it ultimately speeded the expansion of the system.[66] Many areas that the agencies never would have recommended now received serious consideration.

The Wilderness Act was dramatically unsuccessful in one regard: it had little or no impact on the Forest Service's ability to "get out the cut." Timber harvest totals remained at historically unprecedented levels through the mid-1970s, and the conflict between the agency and the environmental organizations intensified, with the Bitterroot National Forest in Idaho and Montana the single most important battleground.[67] In 1973 the Izaak Walton League scored a major victory when a judge ruled, in a suit involving West Virginia's Monongahela National Forest, that clear-cutting was not permitted under the agency's 1905 organic act. A similar decision in an Alaska suit the following year shocked the Forest Service and the timber industry. When their lobbyists asked Congress to overturn those decisions, environmentalists responded with legislation that severely limited clear-cutting and imposed other restrictions on the Forest Service. A final compromise, the National Forest Management Act (1976), legalized clear-cutting with some qualifications. It also required the Forest Service to protect wildlife and to prepare detailed plans for each forest and solicit public comment on those plans. The hearings, comment periods, and administrative appeals—with lawsuits a possibility—underlined the prevailing distrust of the agency and the multiple-use doctrine. The first seventy-five plans produced over 600 lawsuits.[68]

The Fish and Wildlife Service also received greater scrutiny in the 1960s and 1970s. One obvious target was the predator control program. Responding to complaints from environmentalists, Secretary Udall in 1963 asked members of the Leopold committee to examine the program and make recommendations. The committee's 1964 report was as critical of the wildlife managers as it had been of the NPS but did not call for abolition of the program or suggest sweeping changes. Criticism of the agency continued to grow in the following years as the plight of endangered species received more attention, and it became a target of Representative John Dingell (D-MI), the emerging congressional expert on wildlife issues. In 1971 the secretary of the Interior appointed a new study committee. It repeated the criticisms of 1964 but this time called for an end to predator controls. Dingell proposed restrictive legislation, but before Congress could act, President Nixon, in a bid for public support, issued a sweeping executive order ending the control program except for rodents. The executive order temporarily halted the attacks on predators and gave Congress an excuse not to act.[69] As a result, Presidents Ford and Reagan were able to backtrack, essentially canceling Nixon's order with little fanfare or publicity.

A parallel campaign to protect endangered species did lead to the passage of major legislation. A series of exposés on the fate of dolphins, seals, and whales, together with accumulating evidence of the glaring ineffectiveness of the International Whaling Commission, spurred Congress to adopt the Marine Mammal Protection Act of 1972. The new law gave the federal government exclusive jurisdiction over marine mammals, divided enforcement between the Commerce Department's National Marine Fisheries Service (whales, porpoises) and the Fish and Wildlife Service (polar bears, sea otters, manatees, walruses, etc.), and defined the objective of regulation as the "health and stability of the marine ecosystem." The law's provisions grew ever more complex in the following years as Congress attempted to reconcile the marine mammal law with the demands of the commercial fishing industry. A major controversy over the incidental killing of dolphins by fishing crews demonstrated the difficulty of treating each species separately.[70]

In the meantime, Nixon's executive order on predator controls gave new impetus to the movement for a comprehensive endangered species act. The possible extinction of large, familiar animals, such as bison, grizzly bears, and bald eagles, had spurred several remedial measures in earlier years, but federal initiatives on behalf of endangered species (in contrast to the animal control effort) was sporadic and unsystematic. Secretary Udall made endangered species a priority and helped persuade Congress to adopt legislation applying to animals on public lands in 1966 and 1969. Environmentalists demanded a broader approach, similar to the Marine Mammal Act, and Nixon's endorsement in 1972 removed the last major obstacle. Legislation introduced by Representative Dingell and Senator Hatfield encountered virtually no opposition.[71] The final votes, in July and December of 1973, were overwhelmingly favorable. Under the Endangered Species Act, the Fish and Wildlife Service and the National Marine Fisheries Service were to list threatened or endangered animals and plants and use the authority granted under the law to prevent their extinction. Citizens could sue to compel enforcement. The law was unusually broad and prescriptive and covered public and private land. Despite its sweeping language, many members of Congress supported it because they assumed it would have little practical effect.

In later years, as the law became more central to conservation campaigns, it was often criticized for its emphasis on single species. An equally serious problem, as many environmentalists had anticipated, was its reliance on the Fish and Wildlife Service (not to mention the Marine Fisheries Service, which was largely overlooked). Traditionally weak and underfunded, the Fish and Wildlife Service had little standing in the Washington bureaucratic world and little appetite for confronting powerful interest groups. Saving plants and animals from extinction would be a challenging assignment under the best of conditions. As enforcement efforts became more extensive and controversial, the agency gradually emerged from bureaucratic obscurity. In the 1990s, when the act arguably became the single most influential legacy of the legislative avalanche of the 1960s and 1970s, the Fish and Wildlife Service at last became a full-fledged partner of the other conservation agencies.

By the 1970s environmentalists had concluded that that the Bureau of Land Management also could play a meaningful role in preserving western landscapes. At that time, the BLM administered twice as many acres as the other agencies together, with most of its land in the lower forty-eight states devoted to grazing, under the highly permissive system established by the Taylor Grazing Act. The BLM role in Alaska was largely custodial. Nevertheless, the agency gradually became more assertive. In the 1950s and 1960s it conducted range surveys to determine the "carrying capacity" of the land. This seemingly modest initiative was "a local level manifestation of the professional maturation of the BLM" and had some impact on land utilization.[72] Secretary Udall and his BLM directors accelerated this process by emphasizing "professional, scientific management."[73] An important change came in 1974, when the National Resources Defense Council, one of the new activist organizations of the 1960s, successfully sued the BLM for violations of the National Environmental Policy Act. The court required the agency to prepare separate environmental impact statements for each of its 144 grazing districts. This process, which took more than a decade, resulted in substantial reductions in the number of animals on leased lands.[74] The 1974 decision marked "the beginning of modern rangeland management."[75]

Finally, in 1976, Congress completed the process of converting the BLM into a multiple-use agency with the Federal Land Policy and Management Act (FLPMA). The law provided for the permanent retention and management of BLM lands, affirmed the BLM's managerial role and authority, and committed it to multiple use. The law also ordered the BLM to review its lands for possible wilderness designations and created a large "desert conservation area" in southeastern California. Only the second such conservation area, the California Desert National Conservation Area symbolized the evolving character of the agency and its mission.[76] FLPMA did not address another controversial issue, grazing fees. Two years later, in another compromise measure, Congress adopted a rancher-sponsored formula that kept rates low but reemphasized the need to improve range quality, which meant further reductions in livestock numbers.[77]

ANILCA

The capstone to the legislative achievements of the 1960s and 1970s was the Alaska National Interest Lands Conservation Act. The Alaska lands act was avowedly preservationist and ecologically informed, designed in part to protect the habitat of wildlife characteristic of arctic and subarctic landscapes. It explicitly recognized the interests of the substantial Native population and emphasized the compatibility of conservation with local economic interests. ANILCA was the single best example of the effects of an activist Congress and the ability of environmentalists to mobilize the public. Opponents charged that it would "lock up" exploitable resources, which was both untrue and ironic; the lands with the most obvious potential were deliberately excluded from the legislation, and ANILCA provided the foundation for a new tourism-based economy. In the words of Dave Foreman, an outspoken critic of the Washington-oriented environmental organizations of that era, ANILCA "remains the highest point for visionary protected area designation."[78]

The roots of ANILCA went back more than a decade to the discovery of a huge and long-sought oil field off Alaska's Arctic coast at Prudhoe Bay. The field was more than a thousand miles from the nearest refineries, and a proposal to build a pipeline 800 miles south to Prince William Sound, on the Pacific Coast, encountered strenuous objections from two groups: Alaska's Natives, whose long-neglected land claims had received scant attention before the Prudhoe Bay discoveries, and environmentalists, who worried about the hazards of shipping oil through the treacherous sound and down the Pacific Coast. After extended debates, mostly over the amount of land and money to settle the Natives' claims, Congress proved to be remarkably generous.[79]

Eager to accommodate the petroleum industry and not far removed from the civil rights crusade of the 1960s, it passed the Alaska Native Claims Settlement Act (ANCSA) of 1971. The law vacated the land claims, awarded a total of 44 million acres (12 percent of Alaska) and a billion dollars to a series of new Native corporations, reaffirmed the spirit of the civil rights movement, and removed the most important legal obstacles to the pipeline. Alaska historian Stephen Haycox has described ANCSA as "monumental, landmark legislation," probably the "most generous settlement" of Native land claims in American history.[80] To mollify environmentalists as well as the federal conservation agencies, which had cast wistful looks at Alaska's magnificent scenery and bountiful wildlife, Congress added Section 17d(2), authorizing the secretary of the Interior to reserve as much as 80 million acres of Alaska for possible national parks and wildlife refuges. Section 17d(2) had a five-year time limit. In the meantime, the passage of ANSCA set off an extended battle between environmentalists and the Nixon and Ford administrations over the exact route of the pipeline. The environmentalists held out for an overland route through Canada, but Congress again deferred to the industry, approving a pipeline to Valdez on Prince William Sound. Completed in 1977, the pipeline became "a paradigm of 1980's greed."[81]

That left the issue of new or expanded parks still unresolved. Alaska already had Glacier Bay, Mt. McKinley, and Katmai National Parks, Tongass and Chugach National Forests, and more than twenty wildlife refuges.[82] But 200 million additional acres of federally owned land, embracing vast mountain ranges, large lakes, and free-flowing rivers, were wholly unprotected. Section 17(d)2 temporarily restricted the most aesthetically and ecologically desirable lands, but there was nothing to prevent Congress from designating 100 or 200 million acres of parks and refuges.

On the other hand, there was also no guarantee that Congress would do anything. The battle over the pipeline had resulted in a narrow victory for the oil industry and a strong aversion among congressional leaders to additional Alaska legislation. To many, the area was too remote and the hostility of local industrial interests too intense. Despite bipartisan support for environmental legislation, it appeared that five years would not be enough time and that a single omnibus bill would be impossible before the expiration of the 17d(2) withdrawals in 1978 (the terminal date, as the secretary of the Interior had made the final selections in 1973).

Two developments of 1976–77 radically altered the prospects for an Alaska lands act. The first was political: the election of President Jimmy Carter, who supported an Alaska settlement. The second was a decision by leaders of the environmental movement to mount a nationwide campaign for an Alaska bill. The pipeline act had revealed the limits of their influence; another defeat on Alaska lands would be devastating. The Alaska campaign was thus a high-stakes gamble even with the support of Carter and Morris Udall, who agreed to sponsor the legislation. By 1976 the leaders of Alaska's burgeoning environmental movement, with the assistance of local representatives of the Park Service and the Fish and Wildlife Service, had identified the most desirable 17d(2) areas. But they also insisted that the proposed legislation include millions of acres of wilderness in the Tongass National Forest, a longtime goal of Alaska environmentalists. By early 1977 the Sierra Club, Wilderness Society, and Friends of the Earth had enlisted other national environmental organizations, plus dozens of related groups, in an Alaska Coalition and began to mount the most ambitious campaign of the decade. The coalition soon had organizations in most states and a Washington headquarters filled with youthful activists and headed by two Sierra Club staffers, Chuck Clusen and Doug Scott.[83]

The bill that Udall introduced in 1977 provided for nearly 160 million acres of parks and wildlife refuges, with more than 100 million acres designated as wilderness. The most important features were the expansion of the three Alaskan national parks and the creation of ten other parks, monuments, and preserves, all administered by the NPS. To win the support of Alaska's Natives and fulfill the promise of ANCSA, the legislation provided for traditional subsistence activities (hunting, trapping, fishing, collecting edible plants) in the parks and the use of vehicles such as snowmobiles in some wilderness areas. No one would be able to argue that land conservation was achieved at the expense of racial minorities or the rural poor. Since Alaska's elected leaders opposed the legislation, success depended on demonstrating widespread popular support. During the spring and summer of 1977 a special House subcommittee on Alaska lands, chaired by Representative Seiberling, held a series of widely publicized hearings in western cities and in Alaska, most of which became rallies for the legislation. The opposition came mostly from the timber industry and focused on the Tongass wilderness provisions. This pattern continued as the House and then the Senate considered the bill.

With the backing of Udall and Seiberling, the House passed the bill by an overwhelming margin in May 1978. The Senate proved to be less enthusiastic, largely because Senator Jackson delayed action until the end of the congressional session and then unsuccessfully tried to orchestrate a last-minute deal. With the 17d(2) withdrawals about to expire and the state government prepared to press its land claims, Carter used his authority under the 1906 Antiquities Act to create 54 million acres of national monuments, essentially the proposed national parks.

Thanks to Carter, the bill's supporters had at least two more years to win Senate approval for a lands act. The Alaska Coalition continued its campaign, and Udall introduced a similar bill in the new Congress. The House passed Udall's bill, again by a large margin, and the Senate again stalled until the end of the session. As late as mid-July 1980, many insiders believed the bill would fail. The Senate finally acted just before the presidential election, adopting a weakened version of the Udall bill. If Carter had won, Udall would have insisted on additional concessions. But the victory of Ronald Reagan and the election of a Republican majority in the Senate meant that the only option was to accept the Senate bill. The House passed ANILCA on December 2.[84]

Despite this imperfect ending, ANILCA generally reflected the plan that Alaska environmentalists had formulated five years earlier. The major park and refuge units remained intact, and the total acreage, 104 million, was generous compared with the 80 million acres reserved in ANCSA. The outpouring of public support had indeed proven decisive. The concessions were in the details of the legislation. ANILCA substantially reduced the amount of wilderness and added liberal provisions for public access and subsistence activities in protected areas. There were also two troubling additions to the bill that became sources of continuing controversies. The Alaska senators had won a mandate for a continued high level of logging in the Tongass and a generous government subsidy to the local timber industry. Together with a provision in ANCSA that allowed some Native corporations to select Tongass lands, this concession led to record levels of timber cutting in the following years, denuding many of the coastal islands. The second important concession was the treatment of the new Arctic National Wildlife Refuge, a vast reserve of 18 million acres in the northeast corner of the state. Although much of the refuge was designated as wilderness, a 1.5 million-acre area adjacent to the state-owned Prudhoe Bay oil field was placed in a separate category, to be studied as a possible addition to the Prudhoe Bay field. The area could be opened to commercial drilling by an act of Congress.[85]

ANILCA was thus the product of prolonged political maneuvering, extended negotiations, and the leadership of Udall, Carter, and others, but the indispensable ingredient had been the Alaska Coalition and the many groups and volunteers it represented. Similar collaborative efforts had been a hallmark of the environmental movement for many years and had repeatedly succeeded in forcing politicians to act. Yet the Alaska Coalition stood out, both for its size and the sophistication of its methods. Its success inspired envy and emulation. Opponents had tried unsuccessfully to create their own version of the Alaska Coalition, but they, and groups hostile to environmental legislation and regulation in general, found a public champion in Reagan, who had handily triumphed over Carter in November 1980. The increasingly militant opposition, symbolized by the campaigns against ANILCA and a parallel effort in the western states against the federal government and the Bureau of Land Management—the so-called sagebrush rebellion—ensured that there would be no easy victories in the foreseeable future.

❧

In spite of its shortcomings, ANILCA was a fitting end to the legislative achievements of the previous decade and a half, during which land and wildlife conservation, in the form of new protected areas, restraints on managerial prerogatives, and restrictions on commercial activities was among the most important and most successful aspects of contemporary environmentalism. Activists could look back on those years with considerable satisfaction, regardless of what the future might hold. Yet even they had to admit that the new laws and regulations did not tell the whole story. The parks, refuges, and wilderness areas were highly concentrated in the West and in places notable mostly for their visual appeal. Lakes, rivers, and oceans had received comparatively little attention, and the effort to protect wildlife was of uncertain value. The campaign to reform the Forest Service had been only partially successful and had little impact on the agency's timber policies. ANILCA illustrated both the breadth of public support for conservation and the ability of entrenched interests to affect the outcome of political campaigns. The influence of such groups would play a far larger role in shaping the course of conservation activism in the following years.

NOTES

1. Robert W. Righter, *The Battle over Hetch Hetchy: America's Most Controversial Dam and the Birth of Modern Environmentalism* (New York: Oxford University Press, 2005), 130.

2. Alfred Runte, *National Parks: The American Experience,* 3rd ed. (Lincoln: University of Nebraska Press, 1987), 98–104.

3. Douglas Brinkley, *Wilderness Warrior: Theodore Roosevelt and the Crusade for America* (New York: Harper Collins, 2009), 642–47.

4. Char Miller, *Gifford Pinchot and the Making of Modern Environmentalism* (Washington, DC: Island Press, 2000), 147–76.

5. Brinkley *Wilderness Warrior,* 828–30.

6. Runte, *National Parks,* chaps. 1–3; Donald Worster, *A Passion for Nature: The Life of John Muir* (New York: Oxford University Press, 2008).

7. John Muir, *Nature Writings* (New York: Library of America, 1997), 826.

8. Stephen Fox, *The American Conservation Movement: John Muir and His Legacy* (Madison: University of Wisconsin Press, 1985), 121; Samuel P. Hays, *Conservation and the Gospel of Efficiency: The Progressive Conservation Movement, 1890–1920* (Cambridge, MA: Harvard University Press, 1959), 141–45, 189–98.

9. Righter, *Battle over Hetch Hetchy,* 208.

10. Ibid., 211.

11. Daniel Nelson, *A Passion for the Land: John F. Seiberling and the Environmental Movement* (Kent, OH: Kent State University Press, 2009), 23–31.

12. Samuel P. Hays, *War in the Woods: The Rise of Ecological Forestry in America* (Pittsburgh: University of Pittsburgh Press, 2007), 27–30.

13. Stephen J. Pyne, *Fire in America: A Cultural History of Wildland and Rural Fire* (Seattle: University of Washington Press, 1997).

14. Mark Hudson, *Fire Management in the American West: Forest Policies and the Rise of Megafires* (Boulder: University Press of Colorado, 2011), 17.

15. Christopher McGrory Klyza, *Who Controls Public Lands? Mining, Forestry, and Grazing Policies, 1970–1990* (Chapel Hill: University of North Carolina Press, 1996), 18; Samuel P. Hays, *The American People and the National Forests: The First Century of the U.S. Forest Service* (Pittsburgh: University of Pittsburgh Press, 2009), 8.

16. Susan R. Schrepfer, "Establishing Administrative 'Standing': The Sierra Club and the Forest Service," in *American Forests: Nature, Culture, and Politics,* ed. Char Miller (Lawrence: University of Kansas Press, 1997), 130–37.

17. Craig W. Allin, "Wilderness Preservation as a Bureaucratic Tool," in *Federal Lands Policy,* ed. Philip O. Foss (New York: Greenwood Press, 1987), 132.

18. F. Fraser Darling and Noel D. Eichhorn, *Man and Nature in the National Parks*, 2nd ed. (Washington, DC: The Conservation Foundation, 1969), 26.

19. Thomas R. Dunlap, *Saving America's Wildlife* (Princeton: Princeton University Press, 1988), 38; Charles C. Chester, *Conservation across Borders: Biodiversity in an Interdependent World* (Washington, DC: Island Press, 2006), 19–20.

20. Joe Roman, *Listed: Dispatches from America's Endangered Species Act* (Cambridge, MA: Harvard University Press, 2011), 96–97; Fox, *American Conservation Movement*, 194; Douglas Brinkley, *Rightful Heritage: Franklin D. Roosevelt and the Land of America* (New York: Harper Collins, 2016), 293–95.

21. Sally K. Fairfax et al., *Buying Nature: The Limits of Land Acquisition as a Conservation Strategy, 1780–2004* (Cambridge, MA: MIT Press, 2005), 113.

22. Brinkley, *Rightful Heritage*, 497; also Fairfax et al., *Buying Nature*, 116.

23. Michael J. Robinson, *Predatory Bureaucracy: The Extermination of Wolves and the Transformation of the West* (Boulder: University Press of Colorado, 2005), 187.

24. William Voight Jr., *Public Grazing Lands: Use and Misuse by Industry and Government* (New Brunswick: Rutgers University Press, 1976), 299–303.

25. James R. Skillen, *The Nation's Largest Landlord: The Bureau of Land Management in the American West* (Lawrence: University Press of Kansas, 2009), xi.

26. See, e.g., Thomas R. Cox, *The Park Builders: A History of State Parks in the Pacific Northwest* (Seattle: University of Washington Press, 1988).

27. Mark V. Barrow, *Nature's Ghosts: Confronting Extinction from the Age of Jefferson to the Age of Ecology* (Chicago: University of Chicago Press, 2009), 308–18; Hal K. Rothman, *The Greening of a Nation? Environmentalism in the United States since 1945* (Fort Worth: Harcourt Brace College Publishers, 1998), 8–20.

28. Richard N.L. Andrews, *Managing the Environment, Managing Ourselves: A History of American Environmental Policy* (New Haven: Yale University Press, 1999), 202. Also Adam Rome, *The Bulldozer in the Countryside: Suburban Sprawl and the Rise of American Environmentalism* (Cambridge: Cambridge University Press, 2001), 139–65.

29. G. Calvin MacKenzie and Robert Weisbrot, *The Liberal Hour: Washington and the Politics of Change in the 1960's* (New York: Penguin Press, 2008), 217, 219.

30. Adam Rome, *The Genius of Earth Day: How a 1970 Teach-In Unexpectedly Made the First Green Generation* (New York: Hill and Wang, 2013).

31. Voight, *Public Grazing Lands*, 102.

32. Dunlap, *Saving America's Wildlife*, 109.

33. Mark W.T. Harvey, *A Symbol of Wilderness: Echo Park and the American Conservation Movement* (Albuquerque: University of New Mexico Press, 1994), 51–285.

34. Charles F. Wilkinson, *Crossing the Next Meridian: Land, Water, and the Future of the West* (Washington, DC: Island Press, 1992), 137; Paul W. Hirt, *A Conspiracy of Optimism: Management of the National Forests since World War II* (Lincoln: University

of Nebraska Press, 1994), 131; Dennis Roth, "The National Forests and the Campaign for Wilderness Legislation," in *American Forests*, ed. Miller, 235.

35. Frederick H. Swanson, *The Bitterroot and Mr. Brandborg* (Provo: University of Utah Press, 2011), 252; also Hays, *American People*, 58; Hirt, *Conspiracy of Optimism*, 221.

36. Kevin M. Marsh, "'Save French Pete': Evolution of Wilderness Protests in Oregon," in *Natural Protest: Essays on the History of Environmentalism*, ed. Michael Egan and Jeff Crane (New York: Routledge, 2008), 228. For additional background, see Frederick H. Swanson, *Where Roads Will Never Reach: Wilderness and Its Visionaries in the Northern Rockies* (Salt Lake City: University of Utah Press, 2015).

37. Curt D. Meine, "The Oldest Task in Human History," in *A New Century for Natural Resources Management*, ed. Richard L. Knight and Sarah F. Bates (Washington, DC: Island Press, 1995), 28–29.

38. Nancy Langston, *Forest Dreams, Forest Nightmares: The Paradox of Old Growth in the Inland West* (Seattle: University of Washington Press, 1995), 292.

39. Lawrence Rakestraw, *A History of the Limited States Forest Service in Alaska*, Tongass Centennial Special Edition (Washington, DC: US Department of Agriculture, 2002); Daniel Nelson, *Northern Landscapes: The Struggle for Wilderness Alaska* (Washington, DC: Resources for the Future, 2004), 28–30, 82–90.

40. Paul J. Culhane, *Public Lands Politics: Interest Group Influence on the Forest Service and the Bureau of Land Management* (Baltimore: Resources for the Future, 1981), 52–53.

41. David A. Clary, *Timber and the Forest Service* (Lawrence: University Press of Kansas, 1986), 156.

42. Ethan Carr, *Mission 66: Modernism and the National Park Dilemma* (Amherst: University of Massachusetts Press, 2007), 43, 123.

43. Jeanne Neinaber Clarke and Daniel McCool, *Staking Out the Terrain: Power Differentials among Natural Resource Management Agencies* (Albany: SUNY Press, 1985), 51.

44. Carr, *Mission 66*, 257.

45. Michael P. Cohen *The History of the Sierra Club, 1892–1970* (San Francisco: Sierra Club Books, 1988), 134–42.

46. George A. Cevasco and Richard P. Harmond, eds., *Modern American Environmentalists; A Biographical Encyclopedia* (Baltimore: Johns Hopkins University Press, 2009), 250–55; Richard West Sellers, *Preserving Nature in the National Parks: A History* (New Haven: Yale University Press, 1997), 213–15; Hal K. Rothman, *Blazing Heritage: A History of Wildland Fire in the National Parks* (New York: Oxford University Press, 2007), 103.

47. Lary M. Dilsaver, *America's National Parks System: The Critical Documents* (Lanham, MD: Rowman & Littlefield, 1994), 239.

48. Ibid., 240, 242.

49. John Kricher, *The Balance of Nature: Ecology's Enduring Myth* (Princeton: Princeton University Press, 2009), 159.

50. David N. Cole, Eric S. Higgs and Peter S. White, "History Fidelity: Maintaining Legacy and Connection to Heritage," in *Beyond Naturalness: Rethinking Park and Wilderness Stewardship in an Era of Rapid Change*, ed. David N. Cole and Laurie Yung (Washington, DC: Island Press, 2010), 137.

51. Michael Frome, *Rebel on the Road and Why I Was Never Neutral* (Kirksville, MO: Truman State University Press, 2007), 161.

52. George B. Hartzog Jr., *Battling for the National Parks* (Mt. Kisco, NY: Moyer Bell Limited, 1988), 205.

53. Kathy Mengak, *Reshaping Our National Parks and Their Guardians: The Legacy of George B. Hartzog, Jr.* (Albuquerque: University of New Mexico Press, 2012), 127.

54. Paul S. Sutter, *Driven Wild: How the Fight against Automobiles Launched the Modern Wilderness Movement* (Seattle: University of Washington Press, 2002), 116–39; John C. Miles, *Guardians of the Parks: A History of the National Parks and Conservation Association* (Washington, DC: Taylor and Frances, 1995), 71–75.

55. John Jacobs, *A Rage for Justice: The Passion and Politics of Philip Burton* (Berkeley: University of California Press, 1995), 345–71.

56. Fairfax et al., *Buying Nature*, 163–66.

57. Ronald A. Foresta, *America's National Parks and Their Keepers* (Washington, DC: Resources for the Future, 1984), 250.

58. Thomas R. Vale, *The American Wilderness: Reflections on Nature Protection in the United States* (Charlottesville: University of Virginia Press, 2005), 113–15.

59. Rothman, *Blazing Heritage*, 124.

60. Stephen J. Pyne, *Between Two Fires: A Fire History of Contemporary America* (Tucson: University of Arizona Press, 2015), 60.

61. Christopher McGrory Klyza and David Sousa, *America's Environmental Policy, 1990–2006: Beyond Gridlock* (Cambridge, MA: MIT Press, 2008), 36–37.

62. Steven C. Schulte, *Wayne Aspinall and the Shaping of the American West* (Boulder: University Press of Colorado, 2002), 272–79.

63. Chad P. Dawson and John C. Hendee, *Wilderness Management: Stewardship and Protection of Resources and Values,* 4th ed. (Golden, CO: Fulcrum Publishing, 2009), 91–92; Mark W.T. Harvey, *Wilderness Forever: Howard Zahnizer and the Path to the Wilderness Act* (Seattle: University of Washington Press, 2005), 152–55, 165–67, 194–95.

64. Harvey, *Wilderness Forever*, 186–209, 229–38; Schulte, *Wayne Aspinall*, 132–58; Dawson and Hendee, *Wilderness Management*, 196–97; Klyza, *Who Controls Public Lands*, 92.

65. Klyza, *Who Controls Public Lands?*, 92.

66. Doug Scott, *The Enduring Wilderness* (Golden, CO: Fulcrum Publishing, 2004), 63–64; Kevin R. Marsh, *Drawing Lines in the Forest: Creating Wilderness Areas in the Pacific Northwest* (Seattle: University of Washington Press, 2007), 88–89, 94–96, 115–17.

67. Swanson, *The Bitterroot*, 158–242.

68. Peter Duinker, Gary Bull, and Bruce A. Shindler, "Sustainable Forestry in Canada and the United States: Developments and Prospects," in *Two Paths Toward Sustainable Forests: Public Values in Canada and the United States*, ed. Bruce A. Shindler, Thomas M. Beckley, and Mary Carmel Finley (Corvallis: Oregon State University Press, 2003), 53.

69. Robinson, *Predatory Bureaucracy*, 316–20; Dunlap, *Saving America's Wildlife*, 127–40.

70. Michael J. Bean and Melanie J. Rowland, *The Evolution of National Wildlife Law*, 3rd ed. (Westport: Praeger, 1997), 110–23.

71. Barrow, *Nature's Ghosts*, 319–39; Charles C. Mann and Mark L. Plummer, *Noah's Choice: The Future of Endangered Species* (New York: Alfred A. Knopf, 1995), 156–61.

72. Culhane, *Public Lands Politics*, 92.

73. Skillen, *Nation's Largest Landlord*, 70.

74. R. McGregor Cawley, *Federal Land, Western Anger: The Sagebrush Rebellion and Environmental Politics* (Lawrence: University Press of Kansas, 1993), 51–52.

75. Wilkinson, *Crossing the Next Meridian*, 98.

76. Jeffrey O. Durrant, *Struggle Over Utah's San Rafael Swell: Wilderness, National Conservation Areas, and National Monuments* (Tucson: University of Arizona Press, 2007), 72–73.

77. Wilkinson, *Crossing the Next Meridian*, 98–99; Klyza, *Who Controls Public Lands?*, 118–24.

78. Dave Foreman, *Rewilding North America: A Vision for Conservation in the 21st Century* (Washington, DC: Island Press, 2004), 156.

79. Donald Craig Mitchell, *Take My Land, Take My Life: The Story of Congress's Historic Settlement of Alaska Native Land Claims, 1960–1971* (Fairbanks: University of Alaska Press, 2001).

80. Stephen Haycox, *Frigid Embrace: Politics, Economics, and Environment in Alaska* (Corvallis: Oregon State University Press, 2002), 97.

81. Sara Wheeler, *The Magnetic North: Notes from the Arctic Circle* (New York: Farrar, Straus and Giroux, 2009), 67.

82. See Roger Kaye, *Last Great Wilderness: The Campaign to Establish the Arctic National Wildlife Refuge* (Fairbanks: University of Alaska Press, 2006).

83. Nelson, *Northern Landscapes*, 169–85.

84. Ibid., 185–248.

85. Ibid., 245–46, 256–57.

2

Origins of Gridlock

THE REAGAN YEARS

The golden age of political environmentalism came to an abrupt end in January 1981 with the inauguration of Ronald Reagan as Carter's successor and the seating of twelve new Republican senators, which gave the GOP control of the Senate. In earlier years a change of administration would have had little impact and virtually no immediate effect on conservation legislation or policy. But Reagan was different; he had won by mobilizing opponents of activist government, including the western interest groups that had been on the defensive as Congress and the federal conservation agencies chipped away at their favored status.[1] Reagan himself was as inattentive to conservation issues as he was to many other matters, but he delegated appointments and policy to vocal western supporters who sought to sabotage the changes of the previous quarter century. Their campaign was short-lived and generally unsuccessful. Yet it had enduring effects. It drove many environmentalists out of the Republican Party, made the environment a partisan cause, and rallied the opponents of restrictions on resource exploitation. At the same time, the Reagan initiatives forced the environmental movement to

DOI: 10.7330/9781607325703.c002

become more systematic and creative. This chapter examines developments in Congress and the federal government. Chapter 3 traces the evolution of environmental organizations in the 1980s.

THE WATT YEARS

When Reagan took office in 1981, conservation issues were far down on his agenda. As governor of California in the late 1960s and early 1970s, he had done little to reduce the state's role and had even supported the creation of Redwood National Park, a highly contentious issue at the time.[2] As a presidential candidate, he had indicated his support for the "sagebrush rebellion," which had emerged in opposition to federal land management in the West. But apart from his general antiregulatory posture, Reagan was personally no more hostile to conservation than, say, Nixon had been.

His appointees were a different matter, however. John B. Crowell, a lobbyist for the timber industry, was named assistant secretary of agriculture with responsibility for the Forest Service; Robert Burford, a rancher and public land lease holder, was appointed to head the BLM; James Harris, who had fought the federal regulation of strip mining, took charge of the new Office of Surface Mining; and because no prominent western politician or Republican environmentalist could be enticed to take the Interior secretaryship, that key post went to an obscure right-wing activist, James Watt. A Wyoming lawyer who had served in several appointed positions, Watt was known as a champion of states' rights and deregulation. In the mid-1970s he had become the head of the Mountain States Legal Foundation (MSLF), an organization modeled after the highly successful Sierra Club Legal Defense Fund, except that it represented the opposite perspective. Financed by the Colorado Coors family and other right-wing business interests, MSLF represented corporations in environmental lawsuits. Joseph Coors, the Colorado brewer, later boasted that he had made Watt secretary of the Interior. After an interview with the president-elect, Watt reported that Reagan agreed with his plans to promote mining and energy exploration, open more public lands to multiple use, give concessionaires a larger role in the management of national parks, and reduce the influence of environmental activists. Watt believed he had a mandate to roll back the environmental initiatives of the 1960s and 1970s.[3]

The easy part was dealing with the BLM, which was just beginning to adapt to the new order created by FLPMA. Watt's assistants negotiated sweetheart deals with coal companies to mine BLM lands in Wyoming and New Mexico, faked environment impact statements, and demoted or fired professional employees who insisted on the truth.[4] They were equally accommodating to ranchers, the largest and most vocal commodity group. Reacting to the Carter administration's attempts to implement FLPMA, five western state legislatures, led by Nevada, had adopted legislation claiming BLM lands within their boundaries. Rather than try to persuade Congress to accommodate them, Watt proposed a "good neighbor policy," the centerpiece of which was a "cooperative management agreement" allowing "exemplary" ranchers to run their operations for ten years without BLM oversight. When the courts struck down that ploy, the BLM reverted to what one historian has characterized as "benign neglect. . . . BLM officials . . . continued the time-honored system of deferring to the ranching industry."[5]

Above all, this meant not interfering with existing grazing fees, which were well below market prices and had become an embarrassing symbol of BLM subservience. Western senators had foiled a concerted effort to raise grazing fees in 1979, but the issue persisted. Environmentalists argued that higher fees would lead to the abandonment of marginal lands, those most likely to be degraded, and they were joined by political conservatives and free market economists who opposed subsidies and profligate spending. In 1985–86 Congress debated several bills but deadlocked. Reagan's subsequent executive order continuing the existing fee system essentially killed the reform effort.[6] The failure of that campaign was symptomatic of the more general paralysis of the BLM in the 1980s. Despite the promise of FLPMA, the initial impact of the law on BLM operations was minuscule.

Watt's second campaign was to open more public lands to extractive industries. Under his direction, BLM director Burford shifted funds from planning, recreation, and wilderness studies to oil leasing and reclassified large areas to allow mining. Watt forced the Park Service to open its national recreation areas to mining claims. Some national forest areas were also opened. The most controversial initiative, however, was Watt's campaign to encouraging mining claims in wilderness areas before the expiration of the twenty-year window in 1983. Since the passage of the Wilderness Act, the Interior Department had refused to process the miners' claims. Responding to pressures from the industry, Watt hoped to speed up the processing of claims or persuade Congress to extend the deadline. His proposals set off an avalanche of protests. The House Interior Committee invoked an obscure provision of FLPMA to stop leasing in Montana's Bob Marshall Wilderness and sponsored a rider to an Interior appropriations bill that banned the use of funds for processing leases. The entire California delegation and other western representatives sponsored legislation to keep wilderness areas inviolate.[7] Watt then tried to finesse congressional opposition with what became known as the "Watt drop." In 1982 he released 800,000 BLM roadless acres from the wilderness reviews required by FLPMA, opening them to immediate mineral leasing. Environmental groups responded with a lawsuit that effectively cancelled the "drop." The actual changes in policy were "lilliputian compared to the sound and fury."[8]

That was not the case in Watt's dealings with the National Park Service. By definition the park system was devoted to the preservation of resources, and despite a long history of promoting tourism and slighting science, the NPS had an unambiguous mission. Watt's hostility to the NPS was the best measure of his and his allies' attitude toward conservation. It was also the feature of his administration that evoked the fiercest criticism. A secretary of the Interior who had little regard for the glories of the national parks was an affront to millions of people who had only a passing interest in grazing or the Wilderness Act.

The NPS was particularly vulnerable in the 1980s. It had been battered by criticism of its traditional managerial priorities, especially its emphasis on tourism, at the same time as it had been asked to manage a diverse array of new units, including national recreation areas, seashores, lakeshores, and urban parks, plus the new Alaskan parks. To make matters worse, the top level of the NPS had become highly politicized. Since Nixon had discharged George Hartzog in 1972, there had been four directors, and the position was increasingly viewed as a political appointment. The revolving door, coupled with increasing interference by political appointees, "had a paralyzing effect on the once unshakable commitment and high morale of park people."[9] Watt surprised friends and foes alike by retaining the recently appointed Russell Dickenson, who for the next two years would serve as a buffer between Watt and the service's professional staff. Otherwise, Watt's approach was consistent with his larger plan. He replaced the assistant director with a political appointee whose job was to review budgetary and personnel decisions and force reductions. He also merged the NPS and the Heritage Conservation and Recreation Service, which administered grant programs for state and federal land purchases, saddling the Park Service with hundreds of high-level administrators when it badly needed rangers, biologists, and technicians. In his autobiography Hartzog recalls the conclusion of a prominent NPS official: "It seemed as though [Watt] was intent on destroying two of the best professional bureaus in the department."[10]

In April 1981 Watt encouraged rumors that he wanted to abolish some NPS units. He wrote Representative John Seiberling, the chair of the House Public Lands Subcommittee, that he had no plan "for deauthorizing any of the parks" but that his newly appointed advisory committee had concluded that "there had been too many recent additions" to the park system, including "city parks . . . in the federal system."[11] As the sponsor of northern Ohio's Cuyahoga Valley National Recreation Area, a prime example of what critics viewed as a glorified city park, Seiberling could not have mistaken Watt's meaning. Several days later the assistant secretary, Ray Arnett, ordered Dickenson to determine "what is necessary for divestiture of the Cuyahoga Valley NRA to state ownership." He wanted similar information about the Santa Monica NRA in southern California. Seiberling and his allies on the Public Lands Committee were furious. At a subsequent hearing Watt insisted that he had no plan, and Arnett denied that he had even sent the offending memo.[12]

Watt's next step was a systematic effort to discredit Seiberling. In May the secretary announced an investigation of suspected "criminal activities" involving land acquisitions in the Cuyahoga Valley and in three other parks. Ostensibly, this was a response to the fanciful charges of Charles Cushman, a Californian who had made a career of attacking the NPS (and who had been appointed to Watt's advisory committee). Cushman had charged that Seiberling, an inholder in the Cuyahoga Valley recreation area, had profited from the creation of the park. The ensuing investigation examined and largely discredited Cushman's allegations. In 1982 the Interior Department's inspector general reported there had been no irregularities, much less "criminal activities" in the establishment of any of the parks. The lesson, presumably, was that Watt and his associates were as unscrupulous as they were hostile. In the end no parks were "decommissioned," and Seiberling was vindicated.[13]

But there were other, less dramatic policy changes. The administration refused to support legislation for new parks; diverted money from offshore oil leases that was supposed to go to the Land and Water Conservation Fund; gave sympathetic hearings to concessionaires' complaints about park regulations; undermined a campaign to emphasize science and natural history in interpretative programs; refused to support prescribed burning, making the 1980s a "long, lost decade" in fire management; and downplayed external threats to parks, such as urban sprawl and industrial activities.[14] Funding and staffing, especially for the new parks in Alaska, were woefully inadequate. The constant upheavals severely affected morale. Park professionals looked back with nostalgia at the 1970s. One park superintendent bemoaned that "Watt set us back thirty years."[15] Nathaniel Reed, the assistant secretary of the Interior under Nixon and Ford, described Watt as "appalling."[16] Political scientist William R. Lowry concluded that "when the NPS needed consistent leadership and support the most, it received just the opposite."[17]

By 1982 Watt's activities and insensitive public statements had generated a strong political backlash. Like the Reagan appointees at the EPA, Watt and his staff had become a serious political liability to the administration. In September 1983 he was replaced by William C. Clark, a personal friend of Reagan, whose job was to put out, or at least tamp down, the fires Watt had ignited. After the election Clark stepped down in favor of Donald Hodel, Reagan's energy secretary, who had no particular ambition for himself or the department. Hodel recruited William Penn Mott, Reagan's former California state parks director and a respected environmentalist, to succeed Dickenson and publicly called for the removal of the Hetch Hetchy dam in Yosemite, a surprise to nearly everyone. Otherwise he was a caretaker. To replace Arnett he chose William Horn, an Alaskan of the Watt school who was, in effect, an in-house representative of the industrial groups that had promoted Watt and his allies. Horn clashed repeatedly with Mott. By 1987 morale within the conservation agencies was "at rock bottom."[18] Manuel Lujan, who became secretary of the Interior in 1989, and James Ridenour, who succeeded Mott, did little to alter the situation. Lujan became best known for refusing to buy land adjacent to Yellowstone Park owned by a development-minded religious group and for demoting a NPS regional director who urged greater protection for the Yellowstone ecosystem.

Acutely aware of these controversies, the other land management agencies sought to do as little as possible. The Fish and Wildlife Service, already wary of the Endangered Species Act, now avoided conflicts with industry by not listing new endangered species. Congress changed the listing regulations in 1982 to end the foot-dragging, but the backlog continued to mount. By the end of the decade it was apparent that only concerted outside pressures would force the agency to act.[19] The regulation of strip mining, introduced in 1978, was an even better example of studied inaction. Watt's staff first tried to reorganize the Office of Surface Mining (OSM) out of existence and to delegate as much responsibility as possible to the states, which in most cases also tried to do as little as possible. The situation became so embarrassing and the criticism so intense that Watt's successors felt compelled to act. As one student of the law notes, "The new agency strategy was to try competence." By the mid-1980s the OSM actually "began to implement the law."[20]

The changes proposed in 1981 and afterward were, then, abrupt and dramatic. Watt and the other Reagan appointees took particular aim at the most important innovations of the preceding years—the Wilderness Act, the new parks, the grazing reforms, the Endangered Species Act, and the regulation of strip mining. Politically Watt and his associates represented the special-interest groups that had lost access to public resources, faced the prospect of losing taxpayer-financed subsidies, or were subject to regulation. Initially the administration had included advocates of a free market economy, but they quickly lost out to other, more powerful interests that simply wanted a more accommodating government role.

The vast disparity between the conservation policies of the 1960s and 1970s and those of the 1980s was nowhere more apparent than in the operation of the Forest Service. The national forests had been the focus of some of the most significant legislative initiatives of that period, including the Wilderness Act. The effectiveness of those measures was uncertain because of the political clout of the forest products industry and the insular culture of the Forest Service. The result, in a political sense, was a standoff: environmentalists successfully defended the wilderness system and agitated for additions, but logging in nonwilderness areas also rose to an all-time high.

THE WILDERNESS SYSTEM TAKES SHAPE

The Wilderness Act of 1964 reflected a growing public interest in protecting some areas against commercial exploitation and intrusive management, an effort to preserve opportunities for solitude and immersion in nature, and hostility to the Forest Service's timber-first orientation. The act itself opened the door to other possibilities, such as the preservation of biological diversity, but that possibility was still a tangential concern to most environmental activists and politicians of the 1970s and early 1980s.[21] Regardless of the ultimate goal, the immediate issue was the establishment of an actual wilderness system since the price exacted by Wayne Aspinall and other opponents had been a series of procedural hurdles, notably the requirement of congressional action on every proposal. Yet by 1980 wilderness advocates had recorded major victories and, in ANILCA, ensured that the wilderness system was indeed viable and important. But opposition had also grown, and in the following years the Reagan appointees to Forest Service leadership positions would expose the limitations of the wilderness system.

The act itself designated only 9.1 million acres of national forest land as wilderness—land that had already been administratively designated as wilderness but had not been permanently protected. The Forest Service was to study other "primitive" areas in the national forests for wilderness suitability, and the Park Service and Fish and Wildlife Service were to conduct similar studies of their roadless areas of 5,000 acres or more. All the agencies were to complete their studies within ten years and make recommendations to the president, who would transmit them to Congress. Thus, barring some unforeseen initiative, prospects for immediate additions to the system were remote. The Park Service, for example, did not begin its reviews until 1966.[22] The Forest Service was equally slow to act. The Fish and Wildlife Service was more energetic but had much less land to review. By the end of 1974, the original deadline, the Wilderness Preservation System had grown to 12.6 million acres (a net addition of 3.5 million acres), 11.9 million of which were in national forests.[23] Since the de facto wilderness lands of 1964 (land managed as wilderness, with or without a specific administrative designation) had totaled more than 100 million acres, the results of the first decade of wilderness legislation were meager.

The Forest Service and the NPS were both guilty of foot-dragging but for different reasons. NPS officials saw themselves as wilderness managers and resented the congressional mandate. Director Hartzog initially dismissed promoters of wilderness as "nuisances."[24] He and his staff complained about the enormity of the job they were expected to tackle, the lack of funds to pay for it, and the need to combine wilderness reviews with other planning activities. Their first thorough study, of Great Smoky Mountains Park, resulted in extended controversy. A pattern soon emerged. The agency proposed as little as possible; environmental groups demanded more; and the Park Service revised the plan upward, but not enough to satisfy critics.[25] Rather reluctantly, the NPS completed its reviews in the late 1970s, identifying 26 million acres of potential wilderness in thirty-six units. The parks would manage these lands as wilderness pending congressional action. Since wilderness legislation often required concessions to opponents, there was little incentive to take the final step. With few exceptions these lands remained "orphaned" for the next third of a century.[26]

Many Forest Service managers had more fundamental objections. After passage of the Wilderness Act, the Forest Service assembled a top-level committee to devise guidelines for wilderness areas. The committee was given "a free hand and not subject to any external pressures."[27] After nine weeks of supposedly grueling study, the members announced what became known as the "purity" doctrine: only the most pristine areas, with no evidence of human activity, would be considered. This approach, which had some support from dedicated activists outside the agency, would limit the amount of wilderness and keep it far away from the commercially valuable valleys that the Forest Service was busy converting into tree farms. It would also exclude second-growth forests, including all the eastern national forests. The purity doctrine guided the Forest Service in its original wilderness studies.

Environmental groups responded by bypassing the agencies and going directly to Congress with their own plans. A series of confrontations over wilderness proposals gradually discredited the purity doctrine, and in the Eastern Wilderness Areas Act of 1975 Congress designated a series of wilderness areas in eastern national forests, explicitly rejecting the purity doctrine.[28] The 1975 legislation reiterated the original language of the Wilderness Act, namely that wilderness lands only had to be "untrammeled," not necessarily pristine or undisturbed. The Endangered American Wilderness Act of 1978 added more "instant" wilderness in western national forests. ANILCA, which accounted for three-quarters of the wilderness designated before 1981, became the ultimate example of the congressional approach.

A second avenue was the courts, which proved receptive to lawsuits charging the agencies with violations of the National Environmental Policy Act or (after 1976) the National Forest Management Act. Lawsuits against

Forest Service logging plans for roadless areas became so common that in 1971 the agency, in frustration, proposed a Roadless Area Review and Evaluation (RARE) with the goal of systematically identifying potential wilderness areas and segregating them from other roadless lands, which would be available for multiple use. At stake were 1,449 roadless areas totaling 55.9 million acres. The agency held 300 public meetings in communities near national forests and received more than 50,000 comments. The result, at least to environmentalists, was more inaction. Only 274 areas, covering 12.3 million acres, were identified for additional study. After the Sierra Club sued again to stop logging in a roadless area that had not been on the RARE list, the chief of the Forest Service conceded defeat and ordered an environmental impact study for each roadless area scheduled for logging. Now everything would be on the table.

Five years later, after more appeals and lawsuits, the new assistant secretary of agriculture, Rupert Cutler, announced a second Roadless Area Review (RARE II) to correct the errors of the earlier review and reestablish the credibility of the Forest Service.[29] This time the agency examined lands covering 62 million acres, held countless public meetings, solicited letters and statements, and came up with a final report that was only slightly different. Cutler had promised critics that only noncontroversial lands would be assigned to the wilderness or nonwilderness categories; everything else would be relegated to "further planning." But he underestimated the agency's bias. The RARE II report (January 1979) recommended 15 million acres of wilderness, including 5 million in the Tongass National Forest that were included in the ANILCA legislation, 36 million acres of nonwilderness, and only 11 million acres for "further planning," very little of which was likely to be considered for wilderness designation. Environmentalists were outraged. In Oregon and Washington the report recommended less than 12 percent of roadless acreage as potential wilderness. An Oregon Sierra Club leader wrote: "There are a lot of unhappy people here in the Northwest. . . . These folks are coming out swinging and they're not going to take the Forest Service decision lying down."[30]

Their complaints found a receptive audience in California, where the industry was less influential and the environmental movement was committed to additional wilderness. Responding to criticism of RARE II, Huey Johnson, the state natural resources director, sued the Forest Service, charging that the California RARE study did not fulfill the agency's responsibilities under

NEPA. A judge agreed and in January 1980 issued an injunction that stopped logging in all roadless areas of California's national forests. Lobbyists for the national environmental organizations were more anxious than pleased: they feared that the injunction would lead to precipitous action by Congress and a result even worse than RARE II.[31] In fact, the California injunction, and the possibility of injunctions in other states, proved to be the spur that finally forced the Forest Service and the industry to embrace the wilderness system.

In the four-plus years of political maneuvering that followed, there were several possible outcomes. Industry leaders and the Forest Service wanted an omnibus bill that included most or all of the RARE II wilderness recommendations and the "release" of the nonwilderness lands for multiple-use planning. Timber companies in particular favored a "hard" release that would preclude consideration of potential wilderness areas when new forest plans were drawn up; RARE II would be a "once and for all" review of national forest lands. Environmentalists opposed an omnibus bill based on RARE II and insisted on the "soft" release of nonwilderness land, which would permit reconsideration in later forest plans. The legislative decisions of the early 1980s would thus be only one step in the growth of the Wilderness Preservation System.

Reconciling these conflicting views was principally the job of the Public Lands Subcommittee of the House Interior Committee, which had jurisdiction over wilderness legislation. Closely identified with the activist leadership of the Interior Committee, Representative Seiberling, the chair, was skeptical of RARE II and the rush for an omnibus bill. He favored a state-by-state approach and soft releases. He and his staff worked out the details in negotiating bills for California, Colorado, and New Mexico, all of which passed the House in 1980. (The California bill failed in the Senate.) Starting with the environmentalists' proposals, Seiberling conducted a personal inspection of each area, held at least one hearing, and brought the contending sides together. In the meantime his staff and lobbyists for the environmental organizations drew up "soft" release language, which was included in all the legislation. By the end of the congressional session national forest wilderness acreage had increased by 4.4 million acres (including an unrelated Idaho bill) or 25 percent.[32]

In the nearly twenty separate bills that followed, the subcommittee adopted the same procedure. Staff members would meet with environmental groups, timber industry representatives, and local officials, searching for common ground. Then Seiberling would visit the area, tour the most important or most controversial parts of it, hold one or more public hearings, and meet with leaders of the opposing groups. Back in Washington he would negotiate with senators from the state. Since Seiberling's staff now knew as much as or more than the industry representatives and their political allies about the areas in question, they were often able to reach advantageous agreements. The full Interior Committee and the House of Representatives typically rubber-stamped the subcommittee's bills. The Senate Energy Committee, chaired by Senator James E. McClure (R-ID), a timber industry ally, stalled until 1984, when appeals from western Republican senators, fearful of more injunctions, forced McClure to act. Reagan signed every wilderness bill. An industry lobby-ist complained that "they just turned Ronald Reagan into Teddy Roosevelt."[33]

Several of the campaigns illustrate these themes. The California effort was an example of how torturous and prolonged the negotiations could become even in a generally supportive state. Seiberling and his California colleague, Philip Burton, cajoled and coerced their fellow representatives, only to encounter the implacable opposition of Senator S. I. Hayakawa (until his retirement in 1983) and the more nuanced opposition of his successor, Pete Wilson. The final bill designated 1.8 million acres of wilderness, in contrast to the 5 million acres that environmentalists wanted and the 2-plus million in the House-passed bills. In other western states, where there was less public interest in wilderness, the negotiations became even more heated and pro-longed. The Wyoming contest lasted more than two years and resulted in a million acres of wilderness, about half of what the Wyoming Wilderness Association originally proposed. The Oregon campaign featured the usual conflicts between industry representatives and environmentalists as well as divisions among wilderness proponents. Operating independently of the Sierra Club and other national lobbying groups, the Oregon Natural Resources Council urged a more militant approach and greater emphasis on old-growth forests. The council may or may not have influenced the final Oregon bill, but it almost certainly persuaded Oregon senator Mark Hatfield that a settlement was imperative.[34] In Idaho and Montana industry hostility was so intense that a compromise was impossible.

There were similar conflicts in eastern states. National forests in Pennsyl-vania, Indiana, and Illinois were located in areas where nonfarm employment opportunities were limited and there was little tourism. Wilderness designations threatened jobs in logging and gas and oil exploration. The battle over Pennsylvania's Allegheny National Forest was particularly bitter and disappointing to wilderness advocates. It resulted in the designation of one 10,000-acre area and several small islands in the Allegheny River, together with a legacy of conflict that would persist for many years.[35]

Every negotiation involved a trade-off between wilderness and nonwilderness lands. Although soft releases meant that nonwilderness land could be reconsidered a decade or more later, some roadless land almost certainly would be opened to logging in the intervening years. In California, for example, the law designated 1.8 million acres of wilderness and 1.6 million acres for multiple-use planning. In other states, such as Wyoming, the released lands exceeded the proposed wilderness total. Activists criticized these arrangements, but it is questionable whether a different course would have produced a more desirable outcome. Additional lawsuits might have halted logging, at least for a time, but they would have also increased the likelihood of a congressional backlash. The reality was that western politicians of both parties favored the status quo, which meant large-scale logging. Seiberling's efforts resulted in a 50 percent increase in wilderness lands over the Forest Service's RARE II recommendations and held out the possibility of additional wilderness designations in the 1990s. At that time a combination of lawsuits, more scientific data, and a more accommodating president resulted in greater protection for western national forests as a whole but no substantial additions to the wilderness system.

Still, the trade-offs were bitter pills for many environmentalists and became a stimulus to new wilderness campaigns in the following years. The modest Utah Wilderness Act (only 10 percent of Utah's national forest land) was a factor in the emergence of the Southern Utah Wilderness Alliance, which would spearhead later battles for BLM wilderness designations.[36] Earth First!, the most colorful and militant of the new environmental groups, was another expression of disillusionment with the legislative process.

Apart from the compromises, the most serious shortcomings of the new wilderness laws were the conditions, directions, and loopholes that crept into the legislation. Most were designed to "grandfather" existing activities, many of which seemed fairly innocuous. Yet each concession was a challenge to the spirit of the Wilderness Act. The process began with the Colorado legislation. The House version permitted grazing where it had been a customary activity, and the Senate bill added more loopholes, such as allowing ranchers to use vehicles to manage their herds. These concessions in turn became precedents in subsequent negotiations. A quarter of a century after the Colorado act, a total of nineteen wilderness acts permitted grazing. The 1980 New Mexico act prohibited buffer zones around wilderness areas, which led to the inclusion of similar language in twenty-nine other acts.[37] Until Seiberling ordered his staff to oppose such provisions, it appeared that every state would have a slightly different wilderness system. As it was, the Forest Service was handed a host of special situations to manage. As the historian Craig Allin notes, Congressional "micro management" was a predictable accompaniment of the shift from "distributive" (where no one lost, as in the case of mountaintops and "rock and ice") to "regulatory" designations (which involved opportunity costs for ranchers and timber and mining companies).[38]

By the time of its twentieth birthday, the Wilderness Preservation System had become a prominent feature of public lands management. The agencies had discarded the purity idea and other rationales for inaction or minimal action. The commodity producers had grudgingly accepted larger wilderness areas than they had anticipated as well as the possibility of substantial future additions. Yet most "untrammeled" public lands, especially the vast areas managed by the Bureau of Land Management, remained outside the system. Several studies reported that no more than half of all ecoregions were adequately represented.[39]

The limitations of the wilderness system could be attributed to its youth and restriction to federal lands, disproportionately located in western states. Yet another shortcoming, also apparent by the end of the wilderness system's second decade, was more fundamental. Environmentalists had long viewed the wilderness system as a critical weapon, perhaps the single most important weapon, in their attack on the Forest Service's postwar timber policy. Most of the battles over provisions of the act, and then over their implementation, reflected an assumption by both sides that wilderness designations would restrict the agency's logging plans. The RARE II evaluations had cast doubt on that assumption. The Reagan appointees, together with their allies in the Forest Service bureaucracy and the Congress, soon demonstrated that there wasn't any necessary connection at all.

Between 1950 and the mid-1960s, the timber harvest, measured in millions of board feet per year, had tripled and remained at that level through the early

1970s. It declined in the mid-1970s as a result of a recession, lawsuits, attacks on clear-cutting, and the beginning of more comprehensive planning, and then declined precipitously from 1978 to 1982, as the most severe recession since World War II reduced the demand for wood products. Logging fell to the level of the mid-1950s in the Pacific Northwest, and employment in wood products fell by one-third. The economic distress of the early 1980s led Forest Service managers to shift their attention to road building and other preparatory activities in the roadless areas assigned to multiple use. After 1982 more and more of those areas were opened and the timber harvest increased rapidly, reaching an all-time high in 1987.

Given the agency's recent history and the economic distress in many areas of the Northwest, the Reagan appointees had little trouble redefining multiple use as de facto single use. The Forest Service budget became "wholly politicized." Appropriations for logging grew while everything else—recreation, wildlife, even grazing—fell. Washington bureaucrats "often nullified local management decisions," disregarded other agency goals, and circumvented planning requirements designed to ensure sustainability. Historian Paul W. Hirt reports that "faulty yield tables and erroneous inventories showed up all over the country."[40] Despite protests, local officials applauded the revival of the industry, and Washington and Oregon congressional representatives raised the logging totals even more with riders on appropriation bills.

Proponents of increased logging often argued that it would create new jobs and a healthy economy throughout the region. In reality, technological innovations meant that employment never returned to pre-1980 levels. In the Pacific Northwest wood products employment in 1987, the record harvest year, was 35,000 less than it had been in 1978. Timber-dependent towns, which were typically among the poorest of the region, remained depressed. In contrast, communities with more diversified economies, which usually meant recreation and tourism, enjoyed rapid growth. By the end of the decade the evidence was indisputable: timber was rarely, if ever, a spur to employment and economic growth. Continued mechanization, high accident rates, and worker turnover made the industry more often associated with instability and economic decline.[41]

By the late 1980s, a full-scale rebellion against Forest Service policy was underway. Within the agency itself, an organization of dissident employees, Forest Service Employees for Environmental Ethics, mobilized opposition to the political appointees and the Washington bureaucracy. Environmental groups devoted more attention to forestry, particularly in the Pacific Northwest, and recruited numerous allies. The resulting battle soon escalated into the single most significant environmental conflict of the era, distinctive for its length, intensity, and complexity, but also for the central role that biological science and scientific investigations played in shaping the issues and the eventual outcome.

Post-ANILCA Alaska

Despite its importance, ANILCA was flawed by the compromises that emerged from the prolonged legislative battle, the administrative powers granted to the Interior and Agriculture Departments, and the continuing opposition of Alaska's elected officials. A Sierra Club newsletter summarized the situation succinctly: "The chief weaknesses of ANILCA during the 1980s were with its implementation."[42] The decade featured numerous federal and state-sponsored development schemes aimed at the new parks and refuges; a high-profile battle over new wilderness designations that evolved into an extended conflict over oil drilling on the Arctic coast; and a concerted and ultimately successful campaign to reorient the management of the Tongass National Forest. Nowhere was the continuity between Watt and his successors more obvious. But nowhere else were environmentalists more successful in thwarting the Reagan and Bush administrations and consolidating the achievements of the 1970s. Alaska remained on the frontline in the battle over American parks and forests.

Predictably, Watt attempted to use the discretionary powers granted to the secretary of the Interior to undermine the legislation. He ordered the BLM not to evaluate its remaining Alaska lands for additional wilderness designations (which ANILCA encouraged but did not require), refused to consult Canada on measures to protect migrating caribou, and slowed NPS studies of its nonwilderness lands, all contrary to the letter or spirit of ANILCA. A lawsuit prevented him from transferring the mandated petroleum survey of the Arctic coast from the Fish and Wildlife Service to the more industry-friendly US Geological Survey. Most serious was his opposition to expenditures for the new parks and refuges. Only twenty-four additional NPS rangers were initially assigned to Alaska, each one having charge of an area comparable to

Yellowstone.[43] Katmai, which had been a national monument since 1918, had a staff of three permanent and fourteen seasonal staff in 1979; by 1983 the park, now four times as large, had six permanent and twenty seasonal staff. The handful of rangers who were assigned to the new parks often encountered hostile local people, who viewed them as agents of a faraway bureaucracy intent on "locking up" the area. By overlooking violations of park regulations and hiring locals whenever possible, they were able to neutralize some of the opposition and stop the vandalism that had initially threatened their safety.[44]

Watt's overriding goal was to open the Arctic National Wildlife Refuge to oil drilling. The critical area was 1.5 million acres of the coastal plain adjacent to the Prudhoe Bay oil fields, which the Fish and Wildlife Service was to study for possible drilling; Congress would make the final decision. Even before the agency study was completed, Watt and Bill Horn, his assistant for Alaskan issues, concocted a plan to trade parts of the area to Native corporations in exchange for Native inholdings in other refuges, presumably to preempt adverse congressional action. Lawsuits stopped the initial effort in 1981 but were unable to thwart a 1983 deal that allowed the Chevron Corporation to drill a test well in the refuge near the town of Kaktovik. In 1986 Horn initiated negotiations with nineteen Native corporations on the premise that Congress would open the area if it knew that most of the royalties would go to Native corporations rather than to the state. Horn's so-called "megatrade" set off a storm of protests in Congress as well as in Alaska, including complaints from state officials and oil companies that had not been invited to participate. Amid the objections and recriminations, the publicly stated rationale for opening the refuge—that it was essential for national security or energy independence— became less and less persuasive. By 1987 the Horn plan was dead.[45]

There were many other efforts to compromise ANILCA or to take advantage of provisions intended to accommodate inholders and rural residents. They reflected indifference or hostility to national parks and wildlife refuges, but also an approach to economic activity that had long characterized the state's politics. When Senator Frank Murkowski (R-AK) spoke to a 1991 conference marking the first decade of ANILCA, he urged "conservation not preservation" because "preservation denies man's place in nature and the right to use natural resources."[46] No one in the audience doubted that in Murkowski's mind, "conservation" was a synonym for "development" or "exploitation." But it was also clear that Murkowski's views resonated with a large number of politically influential Alaskans. Walter Hickel, a flamboyant former governor and, briefly, Nixon's secretary of the Interior, had recently won the Alaska governorship as a third-party candidate. Charging that neither the Republicans nor Democrats were sufficiently committed to resource development, Hickel pledged a no-holds-barred effort to promote oil and gas exploration, mining, and commercial forestry.

In this setting, wilderness was the single most unpopular feature of ANILCA. Because only Congress could create or eliminate wilderness and was unlikely to reverse itself, Watt, Horn, and their successors had to be content with preventing additional designations. Although Watt could prevent the BLM from reviewing its Alaska holdings, ANILCA explicitly charged the NPS and the Fish and Wildlife Service with conducting wilderness reviews. In addition, environmentalists viewed the coastal area of the Arctic Wildlife Refuge as unfinished business. The result was continuing conflict, with the national government now an opponent, rather than an advocate, of wilderness.

Alaska's park superintendents conducted wilderness suitability reviews in the mid-1980s. Those evaluations left little doubt about their views: the Alaska parks were huge, mostly remote, and largely undisturbed; they would be excellent laboratories for the development of wilderness management. The superintendents recommended wilderness designations for 18.4 million of the 21.7 million acres of nonwilderness parkland, including more than 90 percent of the five new parks that had had no designated wilderness. Horn systematically vetoed virtually every recommendation. As Boyd Evison, the NPS regional parks director observed, "The 'recommended' alternatives were imposed directly by Bill Horn . . . [using] some phony criteria."[47] He cut the total by more than half, to 7 million acres, and then to a mere 4.7 million acres. The Wrangell–St. Elias superintendent had called for 3.2 million acres of new wilderness; Horn revised that number downward until the official recommendation was for a net reduction.[48] As a result the proposals that he finally sent to Congress went nowhere. For the next thirty years, Alaska's proposed wilderness areas would constitute the bulk of the park system's "orphaned" wilderness lands.

The story of the wildlife refuges was similar, except that the Fish and Wildlife Service, instructed to do as little as possible, largely complied, saving time and frustration.

Given the hostility of the political appointees at Interior and Agriculture and their allies in the Congress, was it realistic to campaign for an Arctic coast wilderness? Not if the environmentalists' goal had been an immediate designation for the remainder of the Arctic Wildlife Refuge. Their effort, however, was a way to mobilize public support and prepare for a more accommodating Congress. Spearheaded by a reconstituted Alaska Coalition, their campaign revived interest in Alaska and thwarted a congressional compromise that might have opened the refuge in exchange for a face-saving quid pro quo, such as inholdings in other wilderness areas.

After the Reagan administration finally released the report on the Arctic Wildlife Refuge, recommending drilling, Representative Morris Udall introduced a wilderness bill for the area, and his longtime antagonist, Representative Don Young (R-AK), introduced a bill to open the area to drilling. By the summer of 1987 Udall had 79 cosponsors; Young 144. The Senate Energy Committee, headed by the pro-drilling senator J. Bennett Johnston (D-LA), worked on a drilling bill in the fall but deadlocked when opponents refused to compromise. The House was similarly stymied.

In 1989 the new George H.W. Bush administration sought to take advantage of the president's "honeymoon" to push a drilling bill through Congress. That effort might well have succeeded; certainly the wilderness bill faced an uphill battle. But in March 1989 the oil tanker *Exxon Valdez* collided with a reef in Prince William Sound, causing the largest oil spill in American history and recalling the warnings of environmental groups, dating from the mid-1970s, that shipping oil via Prince William Sound posed unacceptable risks. Amid reports of dying animals and blighted shores, public revulsion against the industry made the passage of drilling legislation impossible, although the crisis did not translate into meaningful support for the wilderness bill.[49]

A parallel effort to close the other glaring loophole in ANICA, the Tongass subsidy plan, was more promising. The Tongass National Forest had long epitomized the Forest Service's post–World War II commitment to timber cutting, and its long-term contracts with pulp mills in Sitka and Ketchikan, guaranteeing a supply of wood under extremely favorable conditions, had been the original stimulus for the Tongass wilderness campaign. Thanks to ANILCA, the Tongass now had more than twice as much wilderness as any other national forest, although with the exception of Admiralty Island, at the northern end of the forest, most of the new wilderness was "rock and ice," with little commercially desirable timber. On the other hand, ANILCA also required the Forest Service to offer 450 million board feet of timber for sale annually, regardless of demand, and required Congress to provide $40 million per year for road building and other preparatory measures. By almost any measure it was an environmentally disastrous trade-off.

The effects of the Tongass subsidy plan was greatly magnified by a provision of the Native Claims Act that allowed several of the new Native corporations to select Tongass lands. By 1980 these selections totaled a half-million acres, about a quarter of the old-growth area. The Native corporations committed themselves to expensive timber operations just in time for the recession to devastate the market. Faced with huge losses, they disposed of the trees at fire-sale prices. The purchasers, freed from even the modest restrictions of the Forest Service, clear-cut the land as rapidly as possible. From 1982 to 1987 the annual harvest from Native-owned lands greatly exceeded even the most inflated prerecession estimates.[50] The combination of Forest Service road building and Native mismanagement promised to obliterate the remaining lowland forests of the Tongass. Yet the devastation also spurred the revival of the Southeast Alaska Conservation Council (SEACC), the environmental organization that had long spearheaded opposition to the Forest Service in the Tongass.

Under a new and aggressive executive director, Bart Koehler, SEACC planned a legislative campaign for 1987 against the timber subsidy. Clearly the wilderness designations had not and would not preserve the remaining forest in its natural state; a more direct approach was necessary. Compared to the Arctic wilderness campaign, which faced powerful corporate opponents and had national implications, the Tongass effort was relatively simple. The legislated subsidy was an embarrassment, even to the Forest Service, and the pulp mills had few backers outside the immediate area. The House of Representatives passed a bill in 1989 that terminated the subsidy and the long-term contracts. The Senate bill died in committee. A new House bill in 1990 added 1.7 million acres of wilderness and buffer zones along salmon streams, an important concession to the fishing industry. The Senate passed a more modest bill, and the final legislation retained the long-term contracts and reduced the amount of wilderness. The Tongass Timber Reform Act of 1990 ended the subsidy and sales quota, required stream buffers, designated 300,000 acres of additional wilderness, and restricted logging on another

200,000 acres.[51] More bitter battles followed, but it can be argued, at least in retrospect, that the management of the nation's largest national forest had turned a critical corner. New vegetation soon had obscured many of the clear cuts that had been a hallmark of the Forest Service's postwar preoccupation with "getting out the cut," though the forest ecosystem would take much longer to heal.

❧

The 1980s and early 1990s thus witnessed far-reaching changes in government policy. The statistics are revealing. From 1964 through 1980 Congress set aside 83 million acres, 3.5 percent of the United States, as wilderness, reaffirming the US position as a world leader in land and wildlife conservation. In the following decade it added only 15 million acres, mostly a result of Seiberling's national forest legislation. Between 1961 and 1980 Congress created seventy-seven national park units, excluding historical sites; between 1981 and 1990, only thirteen units, again excluding historical sites. The numbers do not tell the whole story, but they do suggest the end of one distinctive era and the beginning of a very different time, when legislative activity would be less important and other public and private initiatives would increasingly determine the character of American conservation.

NOTES

1. Charles F. Wilkinson, *Crossing the Next Meridian: Land Water, and the Future of the West* (Washington, DC: Island Press, 1992), chap. 1.

2. Alfred Runte, *National Parks: The American Experience*, 3rd ed. (Lincoln: University of Nebraska Press, 1987), 147–53; Susan R. Schrepfer, *The Fight to Save the Redwoods: A History of Environmental Reform, 1917–78* (Madison: University of Wisconsin Press, 1983), 149–52.

3. Daniel Nelson, *A Passion for the Land: John F. Seiberling and the Environmental Movement* (Kent, OH: Kent State University Press, 2009), 178–86.

4. Michael Frome, *Regreening the National Parks* (Tucson: University of Arizona Press, 1992), 40–41.

5. Wilkinson, *Crossing the Next Meridian*, 100.

6. Christopher McGrory Klyza, *Who Controls Public Lands? Mining, Forestry, and Grazing Policies, 1870–1990* (Chapel Hill: University of North Carolina Press, 1996), 134–39.

7. Paul J. Culhane, *Public Lands Politics: Interest Group Influence on the Forest Service and the Bureau of Land Management* (Baltimore: Resources for the Future, 1981), 300–302.

8. Robert F. Durrant, *The Administrative Presidency Revisited: Public Lands, the BLM, and the Reagan Revolution* (Albany: SUNY Press, 1992), 193.

9. William C. Everhart, *The National Park Service* (Boulder: Westview Press, 1983), 29.

10. George B. Hartzog Jr., *Battling for the National Parks* (Mt. Kisco, NY: Moyer Bell Limited, 1988), 267.

11. Daniel Nelson, *Northern Landscapes: The Struggle for Wilderness Alaska* (Washington, DC: Resources for the Future, 2004), 182.

12. Ibid., 182–83.

13. Ibid., 183–84.

14. Stephen J. Pyne, *Between Two Fires: A Fire History of Contemporary America* (Tucson: University of Arizona Press, 2015), 182.

15. William R. Lowry, *The Capacity for Wonder: Preserving National Parks* (Washington, DC: Brookings Institution, 1994), 66.

16. Frome, *Regreening the National Parks*, 42.

17. Lowry, *Capacity for Wonder*, 32.

18. Hartzog, *Battling for the National Parks*, 262.

19. Douglas Bevington, *The Rebirth of Environmentalism: Grassroots Activism from the Spotted Owl to the Polar Bear* (Washington, DC: Island Press, 2009), 167–68.

20. David Howard Davis, "Energy on Federal Lands," in *Western Public Lands and Environmental Politics*, ed. Charles Davis (Boulder: Westview Press, 2001), 157.

21. Samuel P. Hays, *War in the Woods: The Rise of Ecological Forestry in America* (Pittsburgh: University of Pittsburgh Press, 2007), 2–3.

22. John C. Miles, *Wilderness in National Parks: Playground or Preserve* (Seattle: University of Washington Press, 2009), 169.

23. "Wilderness Data Search," 1964–74, http://www.wilderness.net/NWPS/adv Search.

24. Kathy Mengak, *Reshaping Our National Parks and Their Guardians: The Legacy of George B. Hartzog, Jr.* (Albuquerque: University of New Mexico Press, 2012), 131.

25. Miles, *Wilderness in National Parks*, 175–201.

26. National Park Service, *National Parks: Our Treasured Landscapes*, June 2009, 2, https://wilderness.org/resource/national-parks-our-treasured-landscapes.

27. Dennis M. Roth, *The Wilderness Movement and the National Forests* (College Station, TX: Intaglio Press, 1988), 19–45.

28. Ibid., 16; Doug Scott, *The Enduring Wilderness* (Golden, CO: Fulcrum Publishing, 2004), 66–71.

29. M. Rupert Cutler, "The Evolution of a Wilderness Conservationist," *International Journal of Wilderness* 17 (December 2011): 17–23.

30. Roth, *Wilderness Movement*, 52–53.

31. Susan Zakin, *Coyotes and Town Dogs: Earth First! and the Environmental Movement* (New York: Viking, 1993), 95–96.

32. Nelson, *Passion for the Land*, 168–76; Frederick H. Swanson, *Where Roads Will Never Reach: Wilderness and Its Visionaries in the Northern Rockies* (Salt Lake City: University of Utah Press, 2015), 242–45.

33. Nelson, *Passion for the Land*, 184–204; Kevin R. Marsh, *Drawing Lines in the Forest: Creating Wilderness Areas in the Pacific Northwest* (Seattle: University of Washington Press, 2007), 138.

34. Marsh, *Drawing Lines in the Forest*, 235–38.

35. Samuel A. MacDonald, *The Agony of an American Wilderness: Loggers, Environmentalists, and the Struggle for Control of a Forgotten Forest* (Lanham, MD: Rowman & Littlefield, 2005), 139–46.

36. Jeffrey O. Durrant, *Struggle over Utah's San Rafael Swell: Wilderness, National Conservation Areas, and National Monuments* (Tucson: University of Arizona Press, 2007) 67.

37. Chad P. Dawson, Blake Propst, and John C. Hendee, "Special Provisions of Wilderness Legislation in the United States, 1964 to 2009," *International Journal of Wilderness* 16 (2010): 33.

38. Craig W. Allin, "Wilderness Policy," in *Western Public Lands and Environmental Politics*, ed. Charles Davis (Boulder: Westview Press, 2001), 202–13.

39. Ibid., 209.

40. Paul W. Hirt, *A Conspiracy of Optimism: Management of the National Forests since World War II* (Lincoln: University of Nebraska Press, 1994), 271, 278.

41. Thomas Michael Power, *Lost Landscapes and Failed Economies: The Search for a Value of Place* (Washington, DC: Island Press, 1996), 140–47.

42. *Alaska Report*, 16 (December 12, 1990): 3.

43. William C. Everhart, *The National Park Service* (Boulder: Westview Press, 1983), 138.

44. Miles, *Wilderness in National Parks*, 227–32.

45. Nelson, *Northern Landscapes*, 251–54.

46. *Alaska Report* 17 (March 1991): 4.

47. Miles, *Wilderness in National Parks*, 246.

48. Ibid., 247.

49. Nelson, *Northern Landscapes*, 254–56.

50. Martin Nie, *The Governance of Western Public Lands: Mapping Its Present and Future* (Lawrence: University Press of Kansas, 2008), 133.

51. Nelson, *Passion for the Land*, 256–61.

3

Upheaval

THE ENVIRONMENTAL MOVEMENT IN TRANSITION

The dramatic changes associated with Reagan, Watt, and their acolytes marked the beginning of a new political era marked by public confrontations and high-stakes battles over the legacy of the 1960s and 1970s. The enemies of conservation were no longer intimidated. And if political gridlock was the result, that was largely due to the ability of the environmental movement to operate as an effective lobby. This strategy, however valuable in the political realm, had obvious costs: resources devoted to defending past successes were not available to confront new problems. That in turn led many groups to search for new approaches and techniques. The diverse pattern that emerged was possible only because public support for environmental protection remained high, despite Reagan's electoral success. If the congressional approach to land and resource protection was no longer productive, other avenues beckoned.

One notable individual conveniently captured the changing strands of conservation activism in these years. Dave Foreman personified the restless rebel of western legend. A New Mexican who took his native land seriously

DOI: 10.7330/9781607325703.c003

(not just as a bundle of opportunities for money making), he had been one of the scruffy young environmental activists of the 1970s. Rebelling against the RARE II wilderness legislation and the transformation of the Wilderness Society into a conventional Washington lobby, he emerged in the 1980s as an articulate exponent of aggressive action to save the West from its enemies, in and out of the government. Dismissing public officials as feckless and ineffectual, he became a champion of direct action in the form of public protests and "ecotage" or "monkey-wrenching"—disabling machinery used in logging and road construction and other potentially destructive activities. Foreman was also instrumental in the emergence of Earth First!, an avowedly radical collective that proclaimed "No compromise in defense of Mother Earth" and stirred the imaginations of a new generation of activists. After nearly a decade of agitation, with Earth First! fragmented and in turmoil, Foreman turned his considerable literary skills to the cause of conservation biology, joining a group of activist scientists to plot a network of "wildlands" in response to the looming extinction crisis. Still restless, impatient, appalled at the seeming complacency of many of his colleagues, he continued to call for "true blue" environmentalists to "take back the conservation movement."[1]

A Movement under Fire

Reagan and his followers had attacked the leaders of the Sierra Club, the Wilderness Society, and other organizations as "environmental extremists" and pledged a return to the post–World War II multiple-use philosophy. Looking back, several historians of the Reagan presidency have concluded that Reagan was largely successful in implementing his admittedly limited agenda. That may have been true in some cases, such as foreign policy, but it is not an accurate description of his environmental policies. The administration's initial problem was overreach, but Watt's successors had no greater success in turning back the clock. Their failures were the result of what Sierra Club executive director Michael McCloskey described as "the tremendous gap between what the public wanted and what it was getting" and the community of environmental organizations working to close that gap.[2] Political scientist Christopher J. Bosso lists five major national organizations in the early 1960s, twelve in the early 1970s, and twenty-five in the early 1990s. Memberships in those organizations grew from 125,000 at the beginning of the 1960s to 1 million in the early 1970s and 8.6 million in the early 1990s.[3]

That listing does not account for important qualitative changes. The Sierra Club evolved from a California-based outings club into a "full-service" national organization, with vastly more clout. Other old-line groups, including the National Audubon Society, National Wildlife Federation, and the National Parks Association (which became the National Parks and Conservation Association in 1970), also substantially extended their reach. The Wilderness Society underwent a wrenching shakeup in the 1970s and emerged as an aggressive lobbying force.[4] That was also true for many of the regional groups. The Appalachian Mountain Club, Adirondack Mountain Club, and Green Mountain Club, which had large memberships in the Northeast, became more politically active. There were many new statewide wilderness groups, some of which, like the Southern Utah Wilderness Alliance and the Oregon Natural Resources Council (Oregon Wild after 2006), became formidable organizations. In the 1980s, Montana, a mostly rural state with less than a million citizens, boasted "a dozen homegrown environmental groups with full-time, paid staff . . . a very active corps of national environmental group members; a host of highly active and effective chapters of the Sierra Club, the Audubon Society, and other national organizations; and several professional staff and field offices of major national organizations."[5] Alaska had at least ninety-five environmental organizations by 1992, an extraordinary total given the state's tiny population and reactionary political culture.[6] Many state and local groups were ephemeral and short-lived, but their presence suggested a broad-based movement that extended far beyond the better-known national organizations.

Bosso divides the nationals into three categories: "keystones," "sectoral players," and "niche players." The keystones—Sierra Club, National Wildlife Federation, and three relative newcomers, Natural Resources Defense Council, Environmental Defense Fund, and World Wildlife Fund—were organizations "around which all others within an advocacy sector orient themselves in one way or another, consciously or not."[7] They were not necessarily the largest in terms of membership and support: Greenpeace temporarily overshadowed all of the keystone organizations in the late 1980s, and the Nature Conservancy would in the 1990s and after. But the keystones defined their missions broadly and embraced a variety of tactics. The sectoral players were somewhat narrower, and the niche players were more specialized still, often the products of NIMBY ("not in my backyard") protests or concern for a single species, such as wolves or whales. Air or water pollution issues often prompted activity at the local level, but wildlife and land conservation continued to attract the most dedicated, long-term supporters. Recalling his own experiences with the Sierra Club, McCloskey reported that "the issues that captured the hearts of members were protecting wilderness, defending Alaska's wildlife, saving old-growth forests and 'keeping the money changers out of the temples.'"[8] Yet many issues overlapped. The gradual transformation of the National Wildlife Federation, an umbrella organization of hunting and fishing clubs and traditionally among the most conservative of the national groups, into a broader organization with an emphasis on habitat preservation, suggested the larger trend of the 1980s.

Significant distinctions remained, especially over the appropriate role of government, the importance of market incentives, litigation, and political endorsements, but there was general agreement that the days of the small elite organization and the all-volunteer society were past. To confront complex problems, especially in a hostile political climate, a better-organized, more professional and bureaucratic presence seemed essential. The major national organizations employed approximately 2,400 staff members in 1987 and more than 4,600 in 1995.[9] Officers were increasingly perceived as executives and fundraisers. In 1981 the Henry Kendall Foundation sponsored the formation of an informal association of environmental executives, the Group of Ten, to develop coordinated responses to the Reagan administration. The Group of Ten came to symbolize a more general pattern, whereby environmental organizations "became more self-sufficient, broader, more mass based, and more professional."[10]

The Conservation Foundation conducted a survey of the environmental community in 1988 that reached the same conclusion but also contrasted the comparative well-being of the national organizations with the haphazard organization and poverty of many niche groups, most of which were "perpetual management experiments." Their meager memberships and budgets severely limited their effectiveness, but they often refused to cooperate with competitors for fear of losing their identity. Consequently, they failed to reach potential members, including "people of color, the rural poor, the politically and economically disenfranchised."[11] These shortcomings were most evident in the Southeast and Great Plains, where the combination of poverty and powerful extractive industries severely limited opportunities. "For most practical purposes," the report concluded, there were "two distinct branches" of the environmental movement.[12]

The Conservation Foundation study was a valuable snapshot of the environmental movement at the end of the decade, but it also raised questions about the appropriate yardstick for measuring progress. If the baseline was the 1950s, then the membership gains, legislative achievements, and political influence of the movement in the 1980s and early 1990s made it one of the great social phenomena of American history. On the other hand, if the measure was success in addressing contemporary environmental challenges (and the report cited scientists' warnings of global warming and mass extinctions as well as more immediate threats), the record was far less impressive. However the survey data is interpreted, the critical issue was whether environmentalism, for all its strengths and weaknesses, had created a foundation for continuing activism.

Viewed from that perspective, the patterns gleaned from public opinion polls are revealing. They indicate that most Americans became aware of environmental issues in the late 1960s. Environmental awareness peaked around the first Earth Day, 1970, then gradually declined through the 1970s as economic issues and energy shortages diverted attention and persuaded many people that environmental protection required unacceptable sacrifices. (A similar pattern was evident after 2001, as anxiety about terrorist attacks and war once again diverted attention.)[13] Watt's polarizing behavior reversed this pattern: by the mid-1980s the environment rated as highly as it had at any time in the 1970s. Support continued to grow through the decade, and by 1990 approximately three-quarters of the people questioned responded affirmatively to the query "Are you an environmentalist?"[14]

What accounted for this persistent pattern, especially after the departure of the incendiary Watt? One obvious factor was a continuing series of exposés and crises, headed by the *Exxon Valdez* disaster, which provided stark evidence of the tolerance of supposedly responsible institutions for irresponsible, risky behavior. A second reason was the environmental organizations themselves, which, having been tested in the early 1980s, now applied their communications and lobbying skills with greater effectiveness. A third factor was the emerging scientific rationale for environmental activism. Riley

E. Dunlap, who gathered the polling data, concluded that "the growing seriousness of ecological problems" was probably the "critical force in driving public opinion."[15]

By the end of the decade, then, the environmental groups that had emerged or taken on a more aggressively political character in the 1970s had become much more powerful and organizationally mature. The Reagan administration may have been bad for the environment, but it was a boon to the environmental movement, forcing the national organizations to become more assertive, more resourceful, and more like other powerful Washington lobbies. For the moment the ability to thwart the president's initiatives was invigorating, even satisfying. But given the growing backlog of problems yet to be addressed, as well as the "ecological problems" that promised to command greater attention in the future, the movement's expanding legion of followers were unlikely to be content with Washington gridlock.

DISSIDENTS

As the national organizations mobilized to consolidate their role in Washington, they also faced challenges from dissidents within their own ranks. There had always been internal conflicts and schisms in the conservation movement, and it would be unrealistic to believe that the number would not grow with the proliferation of organizations and members. One well-known case became a model. In 1970, after David Brower left the Sierra Club in a dispute over management and finances, he founded a competing entity, Friends of the Earth (FOE), as an institutional home for his supporters. FOE was supposed to be different: broader in scope, international in its reach, less bureaucratic, better able to respond to the challenges of the age. Whether it lived up to its promise is almost beside the point; it forced the Sierra Club and others to reexamine their policies and operations. A similar dynamic operated in the following decades. Activists would conclude that a particular organization, or the movement as a whole, was out of touch, compromised by political associations, elitist, or simply ineffectual. They would then form a new organization that was "purer" or more focused and compete with the older ones for members and influence. The national forests and the policies of the Forest Service accounted for the largest number of dissident groups, as recent studies by Samuel Hays (2007) and Douglas Bevington (2009) have indicated. The new organizations usually struggled and often failed, but, like FOE in the 1970s, they forced the established groups to be address grassroots concerns even as they adapted to the uncertainties of Washington politics. Intramural conflicts, like Watt and his colleagues, could be a stimulus to organizational vitality.

The best-known challenges of the 1980s came from radical groups that rejected the structure and tactics of the mainline organizations, scorned lobbying and politics, and spurned the compromises that were the hallmark of the legislative process. Rooted in the counterculture of the 1960s and 1970s, they drew their inspiration from John Muir, Aldo Leopold, Edward Abbey (a participant in some early activities), and the proponents of "deep ecology." Above all, they were committed to direct action, ranging from civil disobedience to "monkey-wrenching" (from Abbey's 1975 novel, *The Monkey Wrench Gang*). In most cases, their immediate goal was to thwart a particular activity, generating as much publicity as possible. A longer-term goal, in Dave Foreman's words, was to "demonstrate that the Sierra Club and its allies were raging moderates, believers in the system, and to refute the Reagan/ Watt contention that they were 'environmental extremists.'"[16]

Certainly there were reasons for criticism and protest. Although the national organizations could boast of their successes in confronting Watt and the other Reagan appointees, they had not added to the number of national parks, reformed the grazing system, or, most notably, reduced the timber harvest in national forests. The California, Oregon, and Washington wilderness bills had been among the most impressive achievements of the early 1980s, but at the same time those states had became the target of an accelerated logging program aimed at the last remaining old-growth forests. The problems, it seemed, were multiplying faster than the environmental organizations could address them.

A number of radical groups emerged and enjoyed at least a brief vogue during the 1980s. Greenpeace, which dated from 1970 and was known for its efforts to disrupt environmentally destructive activities, notably whaling, became prominent for a few years but declined just as rapidly; by 1990 it operated mostly outside the United States. Sea Shepherds Conservation Society, an offshoot that concentrated on marine problems, had an equally colorful history and limited impact. Earth First!, which emphasized forestry issues, proved to be more durable and influential. It played an important role in the defense of the old-growth forests in the Pacific Northwest, reemphasized the value of grassroots activism, and served as a bridge between the growing community of activist scientists and the mainstream environmental movement. It was, in the words of biologist R. Edward Grumbine, "the strong arm of the fight for biodiversity protection."[17]

In many respects, Earth First! was a throwback to an earlier time, when environmental organizations had been based on popular enthusiasm and charismatic individuals. David Brower and Stewart Brandborg, who headed the Wilderness Society in the 1960s and early 1970s, had epitomized that era. Like Brower, Brandborg was impatient with organizational details like fundraising and financial management. Mounting economic woes led to his ouster in 1976 and the recruitment of William Turnage, a skillful manager similar to Brower's successor, Michael McCloskey. Yet Turnage, unlike McCloskey, was also insensitive, even hostile, to the society's organizational culture. As he turned the society into a Washington lobby, his relations with the staff deteriorated; most of the employees recruited by Brandborg resigned or were fired, to be replaced by lawyers, economists, and researchers.[18] The discarded staffers became the core of Earth First! Joined by other disgruntled individuals, such as Howie Wolke, who left Friends of the Earth, and Mike Roselle, who had been involved in various countercultural groups, they sought to recapture the crusading ardor of the 1960s without the bureaucratic apparatus they associated with Turnage and the national organizations.

Second only to Turnage as an object of the insurgents' antipathy was Doug Scott, the conservation director of the Sierra Club. Originally a TWS staffer, Scott was an informal advisor to Turnage in the late 1970s and then attained near legendary stature as the chief lobbyist for the Alaska Coalition during the ANILCA campaign. Confident of his ability to negotiate, cut deals, and produce immediate results, Scott was a vigorous and articulate proponent of access, negotiation, and compromise. To the dissidents his willingness to work with enemies such as Senator Mark Hatfield, the timber industry's wily and powerful defender, was an indication of confusion if not outright capitulation to the enemy.[19] Disagreements over perspectives and tactics became inseparable from personal and professional animosities.

Earth First! coalesced in the summer of 1980 during a camping trip to Mexico and a gathering of Foreman and other Wilderness Society veterans in Wyoming. From the beginning it was deliberately informal, with no membership lists, headquarters, staff, budget, or platform. The slogan "No compromise in defense of Mother Earth" was as close as the founders came to a mission statement. Most revenue came from unsolicited donations, the sale of the *Earth First! Journal*, edited mostly by Foreman, and other donations from road trips, featuring Foreman and Bart Koehler, a songwriter and folk singer who would later shepherd the Tongass Timber Reform Act through Congress. In the early 1980s Foreman and Koehler traveled from campus to campus, galvanizing college students and activists throughout the West. They emphasized the commitment of Earth First! to direct action, which resonated with those who recalled the civil rights campaigns of the 1960s and had grown impatient and frustrated with the delays and compromises of the congressional campaigns. Nearly as important was their insistence on biocentrism, which recognized the value of plants and animals apart from human uses, an idea still novel to anthropocentric environmentalists. Also appealing was their funky, irreverent, countercultural style. Foreman proposed to bring "vigor, joy, and enthusiasm to the tired, unimaginative environmental movement."[20] Journalist Susan Zakin reported that Earth Firsters "were doing everything from bicycle-locking their necks to bulldozers . . . to parading down Wall Street dressed as spotted owls." On the television news their appearances were "like *Wild Kingdom* on LSD."[21]

No one could accuse Earth First! of lacking imagination. Its first and most famous stunt, in March 1981, involved dropping a huge plastic sheet depicting an enormous crack from the top of Glen Canyon Dam, which had become a symbol of misguided government policy. In the following years Earth First! activists blocked roads and work sites in western forests. In 1983 they began to advocate the spiking of trees in forests slated for cutting. The amount of actual spiking was negligible, but the idea struck most people as a kind of Luddite terrorism, especially after a mill worker was injured in 1987 (though not as a result of spiking by Earth First! activists). Most western states passed laws against tree spiking.

In the meantime Earth First! added more effective tactics to its antilogging repertoire. In 1985 it began to promote tree sitting, whereby one or more protesters would construct a platform high in a tree scheduled for cutting and live there as long as necessary to save it. Tree sitting did not endanger workers or property; the considerable risks were all borne by the protestors. And it created abundant and irresistible opportunities for newspaper and television coverage. Finally there was "monkey-wrenching," which Foreman spelled out at length in a best-selling 1985 manual, *Ecodefense: A Field Guide to Monkeywrenching*. While he insisted that he did not want to injure people, he was powerless to prevent less scrupulous individuals from using his methods in careless or indiscriminate ways.

As Foreman predicted, Earth First! made the mainstream environmental organizations seem more responsible and acceptable. A five-month protest against the construction of a forest road in the Siskiyou Mountains of southern Oregon halted logging in that area and energized the Sierra Club–led campaign for the Oregon Wilderness Act. In subsequent years Earth First! protests aided the statewide organizations that were campaigning to preserve Oregon's old-growth forests. Another Earth First! campaign, to preserve the Headwaters redwood forest of northern California, became one of the most bitterly contested environmental battles of that era and generated years of publicity for the old-growth cause. If Earth First! saved only a handful of trees, it provided invaluable assistance to the "raging moderates."

By the mid-1980s the notoriety of Earth First! began to attract frustrated activists far and wide. A British version, founded in 1987, became active in blocking proposed highways.[22] But success and growth brought new challenges, including many problems familiar to conventional organizations. Particularly perplexing was a large influx of activists from California university communities, many of whom had at best a passing interest in biocentrism and deep ecology. The immediate fight was only one phase of a larger struggle for social justice; feminism and, for some, anarchism were no less important than biodiversity. They rallied around Roselle, who had become involved in civil disobedience campaigns as a Greenpeace organizer, and Judi Bari, an outspoken labor organizer and feminist. Bari summarized their perspective when she wrote that "Earth First! is not just a conservation movement, it is also a social change movement."[23] By 1987 or 1988, there were distinct Earth First! factions, notably the original group, centered around Foreman, and the Roselle-Bari-California contingent.[24] An unhappy Foreman, weary, harassed, and uncomfortable with the newcomers, began to distance himself from Earth First![25] His arrest in connection with a plot to destroy power lines in Arizona, concocted by a handful of radicals and one or more FBI agent provocateurs, was the last straw. Coupled with the other controversies, that incident led him and several other close associates to abandon

Earth First! By that time most Earth First! veterans had become involved in the broader campaign to preserve old-growth forests, with increasingly violent splinter groups devoted to animal rights and other fringe causes.[26]

For a few years, then, Earth First! dramatized the limitations of the mainstream environmental movement, the tactical potential of more imaginative forms of protest, and the growing importance of forestry issues in California and the Pacific Northwest. But were Earth First! and the other direct-action groups really a radical alternative to the established organizations? They shared many perspectives: the environmental crisis was worsening; government was largely unhelpful; the prospects for meaningful solutions were uncertain. Most environmentalists, including many Earth First! supporters, also agreed that the answer to the many challenges they faced was greater environmental activism, not ecotage, a "green" political party, or a broad assault on society's ills. Judy Bari supposedly embraced a broader agenda, but her most important initiative was to disavow ecotage as a tactic in order to enlist the support of organized labor. A famous 1989 debate between Foreman and Murray Bookchin, a veteran left-wing polemicist, underlined both the divisions within Earth First! and the gulf that separated most environmentalists from more traditional radical groups.[27]

The reluctance of many environmentalists to embrace a broader critique of contemporary society was also consistent with another manifestation of the activism of the 1980s. Although poles apart from the environmental radicals in many respects, the land trust movement also avoided political entanglements. With a focus on land conservation and direct action (though rarely the kind of direct action associated with Earth First!), it was able to take advantage of a reasonably prosperous economy, the availability of foundation financing, and the perquisites of property ownership to expand rapidly in terms of memberships, financial support, and influence.

LAND TRUSTS AND ENVIRONMENTAL ACTIVISM

Within a remarkably short period, the land trust movement emerged as a prominent feature of American conservation. It included the largest and richest conservation organization (the Nature Conservancy), a critical intermediary in the acquisition of park lands (the Trust for Public Land), and hundreds of local and regional organizations. Unlike Earth First! or even the mainstream environmental groups, land trusts did not seek controversy or thrive on confrontation. Largely apolitical (though not adverse to government grants or to campaigns for conservation bond issues), they relied on private donations and the operation of the tax code, which allowed deductions for easement donations. Like the other groups, they were a reaction to population growth, urban sprawl, the threat of species extinctions, and other signs of environment degradation. As Richard Brewer observes in his history of the movement, their growth "was fueled by the realization that the government had not just abdicated leadership in the conservation wars but had defected to the enemy."[28]

By the time Reagan and Watt arrived in Washington in 1981, the Nature Conservancy (TNC) was a flourishing organization with an increasingly distinctive mission. Organized in 1950 to acquire property that was biologically or aesthetically distinctive, its membership, finances, and land holdings had all grown rapidly. It attracted many wealthy individuals, both as land donors and as contributors—the heiress Katharine Ordway alone gave more than $60 million—and used its resources to purchase sensitive and threatened lands, including coastal islands and the core of Virginia's Dismal Swamp.[29] Many of its purchases, however, were opportunistic: "Some were bought as good opportunities to study ecological succession. . . . Others were bought simply to show local groups how to carry out land conservation. Yet others were acquired to win the gratitude of donors or neighbors."[30]

In 1970 TNC hired biologist Robert E. Jenkins as a science advisor, and in the following years he became increasingly influential. The focus, Jenkins insisted, should be on species diversity, threatened or endangered plants and animals in particular. And since not every place could or should be preserved, TNC should be selective and patient, acquiring only the most biologically sensitive and vital lands and in large enough quantities to achieve its goals. In contrast to its customary procedure, TNC should take the initiative in identifying desirable lands, seeking out owners, and starting negotiations. Donated lands that did not meet TNC's criteria for preservation should be sold to finance other, more worthy acquisitions. Jenkins's ideas, which anticipated the biodiversity campaign of the following decade, were radical and disruptive, particularly for the staff. Yet in 1972 the TNC board embraced his proposal to focus on "the vanishing heritage of wild plant and animal species, their habitats, natural vegetation associations, biotic communities, and other features."[31]

The new approach to land acquisition became the foundation for other innovations. To acquire the information necessary to make his system work, Jenkins sponsored state Natural Heritage programs, starting with South Carolina in the mid-1970s. TNC paid the initial costs, with state governments gradually taking over. The result was a natural resource inventory that would, among other things, guide TNC's search for distinctive flora and fauna. By 1976, twenty-five states had signed on; by 1989, all of the states were involved. The acquisition of Nags Head Woods, on North Carolina's Outer Banks, was the first result of this process.

To take advantage of such opportunities, TNC opened state offices across the country. All of this activity required a larger budget, and the TNC president in the 1970s, Patrick Noonan, was an aggressive fundraiser. He soon turned to corporations, including those with large land holdings, and by 1980 he had signed up more than 200 as contributors. Participation became a badge of good citizenship (or, in some cases, a smoke screen to obscure less savory activities). To critics he had a disarming reply: "The problem with tainted money is there taint enough."[32]

By that time Noonan and his staff could count 70,000 members, nearly a million and a half acres preserved, the new state Natural Heritage programs, and a robust endowment. The advent of Reagan and Watt did not directly affect TNC, but it made property owners more concerned about the threat of uncontrolled development and the dangers of species extinctions. By 1990 TNC had more than 600,000 members and a commensurately larger budget.

As property values rose in the 1980s, TNC found that even its substantial resources were inadequate. Its solution was to emphasize conservation easements rather than fee purchases. Easements had been used for many years but became more attractive after Congress (in 1976 and 1980) voted to allow tax deductions for easement donations. They typically involved the gift or sale of development rights; the owner agreed to limit his or her use of the property, spelled out in an agreement with the land trust. In most cases this meant the property could not be subdivided, and forests, streams, lakes, and ponds had to be preserved. These restrictions reduced the market value of the property; the amount of the reduction qualified as a charitable contribution in calculating income, estate, and sometimes property taxes. By 1980 nearly all state legal codes permitted conservation easements. By lessening the costs of fighting sprawl and preserving sensitive landscapes, they became the principal tool of the local and regional land trusts that proliferated in the 1990s and after.

The growing emphasis on conservation easements also raised troubling questions about private conservation efforts. Easements usually did not allow public access to protected properties and were particularly valuable to landowners with large incomes who could take maximum advantage of the tax deductions. The actual conservation value of a protected property could be an issue as well. The most serious problem, however, was enforcement. Easements were supposed to be permanent, but in practice they were only as good as the organization that backed them. Many local land trusts were shoestring operations, with a handful of active members and meager budgets. If the organization collapsed or could not afford to bring legal action against violators, the easement was essentially meaningless. Yet the appeal of easements was so great that most land trusts found them irresistible and worked to overcome their disadvantages.

Other national land trusts followed in TNC's wake. They included the Trust for Public Land (TPL, 1974), the American Farmland Trust (1980), the Rails-to-Trails Conservancy (1986), and almost twenty others. TPL was especially important, both for its work as an intermediary in the expansion of state and local park systems and its role as a midwife to a host of local land conservancies in California. (While serving as California's natural resources director, TPL's founder, Huey Johnson, had initiated the lawsuit against the Forest Service that ignited the campaign for wilderness legislation.) Basically, TPL's method was to buy land, often at a discounted or conservation price, and resell it to public parks. As a private organization it had greater flexibility than government agencies and could accept charitable donations from property owners. In the early 1980s, when the Reagan administration reduced Land and Water Conservation Fund outlays, TPL faced a crisis, forcing it to raise private funds. By the mid-1980s it had successfully adjusted, borne on the swelling tide of environmental activism.

By that time there were also a large and growing number of local land trusts, devoted to preserving green space and what remained of the natural world in their immediate areas. Two events in 1981 greatly assisted their maturation. In Boston a prominent lawyer, Kingsbury Browne, organized a meeting of New England organizations, and a short time later a Montana land trust hosted a similar gathering of western leaders in San Francisco.

The goal in both cases was to encourage cooperation and find ways to counter the organizational hazards of all-volunteer groups. The conclusions of both conferences were also similar: the desirability of regional coordinating bodies that would preserve the autonomy of the local organizations, provide a mechanism for sharing experiences, and help individual land trusts enlist professional assistance. The New England group took the lead in forming a national coordinating body, the Land Trust Exchange (after 1990, the Land Trust Alliance). The exchange began publishing a magazine and worked on standards and best practices for local organizations.[33] In 1985 it held the first of what became an annual national meeting of land trusts. Suddenly fashionable, local trusts spread rapidly on both coasts and the upper Midwest. In terms of acreage, they had comparatively little to show for their efforts before 1990, but their sheer numbers and popularity were impressive signs of public sensitivity to conservation issues, regardless of what happened in Washington.

∾

Contrary to much of the journalism and some of the polemical writing of the era, the defining characteristics of environmental activism in the 1980s were growth and diversity. If the best-known national organizations had become defensive and reactive, there was no shortage of other options, ranging from radical to conservative, political to apolitical, and national to local. The one obvious omission was the absence of an independent political movement, comparable to the European Green parties. Most environmentalists were well aware of the dismal history of American third parties and the influence of anti-environmental interests in the Republican Party; protest votes would only make the situation worse. In other respects, the proliferation of groups did not denote the splintering of a formerly cohesive movement; rather it signified the continuing growth of an environmental consciousness that increasingly reflected the variety and complexity of nature and the many challenges that emerged as individuals and groups sought to protect parts of it. As more people became involved, the range of causes and objectives multiplied. What had seemed relatively simple and straightforward in earlier years became more complicated and, in many cases, elusive.

What, then, was the purpose of conservation? Was it simply to advance a series of loosely related efforts aimed at preserving features of the natural world? Activists often became embarrassingly vague when they tried to explain what they hoped to achieve beyond their immediate, often narrow goals. That problem would greatly diminish in the following years as a growing number of scientists, who generally worked and published outside the environmental community, advanced a powerful unifying rationale for a host of conservation causes. Their work became a decisive step in the reorientation of American conservation that had accelerated and taken on new and often unfamiliar features with the changing of the political landscape.

NOTES

1. Dave Foreman, "Take Back the Conservation Movement," *International Journal of Wilderness* 12 (April 2006): 6.

2. Michael McCloskey, "Twenty Years of Change in the Environmental Movement: An Insider's View," in *American Environmentalism: The U.S. Environmental Movement, 1970–1990*, ed. Riley E. Dunlap and Angela G. Mertig (Washington, DC: Taylor and Francis, 1992), 31.

3. Christopher J. Bosso, *Environment, Inc.: From Grassroots to Beltway* (Lawrence: University Press of Kansas, 2005), 54–55.

4. James Morton Turner, *The Promise of Wilderness: American Environmental Politics since 1964* (Seattle: University of Washington Press, 2012), 202–9.

5. Donald Snow, *Inside the Environmental Movement: Meeting the Leadership Challenge* (Washington, DC: Island Press, 1992), 174.

6. Ken Ross, *Environmental Conflict in Alaska* (Boulder: University Press of Colorado, 2000), 308–9.

7. Bosso, *Environment, Inc.*, 76.

8. McCloskey, "Twenty Years of Change," 80.

9. Bosso, *Environment, Inc.*, 92.

10. Ibid., 163.

11. Snow, *Inside the Environmental Movement*, xxxii–xxxiii.

12. Ibid., 163.

13. Christopher J. Bosso and Deborah Lynn Guber, "Maintaining Presence: Environmental Advocacy and the Permanent Campaign," in *Environmental Policy: New Directions for the Twenty-First Century*, 6th ed., ed. Norman J. Vig and Michael E. Kraft (Washington, DC: Congressional Quarterly Press, 2007), 82.

14. Riley E. Dunlap, "Trends in Public Opinion toward Environmental Issues," in *American Environmentalism*, ed. Dunlap and Mertig, 92–104.

15. Ibid., 106.

16. Dave Foreman, *Confessions of an Eco-Warrior* (New York: Harmony Books, 1991), 18.

17. R. Edward Grumbine, *Ghost Bears: Exploring the Biodiversity Crisis* (Washington, DC: Island Press, 1992), 222.

18. Turner, *Promise of Wilderness*, 131–33.

19. Susan Zakin, *Coyotes and Town Dogs: Earth First! and the Environmental Movement* (New York: Viking, 1993), 38, 68–69, 77–81.

20. Foreman, *Confessions of an Eco-Warrior*, 18.

21. Zakin, *Coyotes and Town Dogs*, 83.

22. Derek Wall, *Earth First! and the Anti-Roads Movement: Radical Environmentalism and Comparative Social Movements* (London: Routledge, 1999), 45–46.

23. Judi Bari, *Timber Wars* (Monroe, ME: Common Courage Press, 1994), 57.

24. Martha F. Lee, *Earth First! Environmental Apocalypse* (Syracuse: Syracuse University Press, 1995), 90, 96–97, 112–14.

25. Foreman, *Confessions of an Eco-Warrior*, 216–18.

26. Rik Scarce, *Eco-Warriors: Understanding the Radical Environmental Movement* (Walnut Creek, CA: Left Coast Press, 2006), 88–89.

27. Carolyn Merchant, *Radical Ecology: The Search for a Liveable World*, 2nd ed. (New York: Routledge, 2005), 148–52; Murray Bookchin, Dave Foreman, and Steve Chase, *Defending the Earth: A Dialogue between Murray Bookchin and Dave Foreman* (Boston: South End Press, 1991).

28. Richard Brewer, *Conservancy: The Land Trust Movement in America* (Hanover, NH: University Press of New England, 2003), 37.

29. Ibid., 194.

30. Bill Birchard, *Nature's Keepers: The Remarkable Story of How the Nature Conservancy Became the Largest Environmental Organization in the World* (San Francisco: Jossey-Bass, 2005), 43.

31. Ibid., 39.

32. Ibid., 72.

33. Brewer, *Conservancy*, 34–36.

4

An Intellectual Revolution

Since the nineteenth century the most common and compelling arguments for conserving natural resources had been their unique features, aesthetic appeal, or recreational potential. Few people were so hard-hearted that they could not appreciate the beauty of the western national parks or of Acadia, Great Smoky Mountains, Isle Royale, or the new Alaska parks. "Monumentalism" had defined the park system in its early years and remained an important key to mobilizing public sentiment. Preserving wildlife, especially birds, was nearly as important. Recreation enjoyed an upsurge of popularity with the post–World War II generation, many of whose members took affluence for granted and looked to nature for inspiration and excitement. Activists increasingly distanced themselves from "resourcism," the old association of conservation with the "wise use" of natural resources, and embraced a variety of new or newly popular ideas, from "deep ecology" to the protection of whales, eagles, or other wildlife. But few of them could explain how all of these causes fit together, if indeed they did, or contributed to some coherent larger objective.

DOI: 10.7330/9781607325703.c004

But in the 1980s a much more precise and detailed rationale for conservation emerged, and from a different, unanticipated source. A growing number of scientists began to argue that much of what had been done was misguided, even harmful. They proposed a more rigorous, biocentric view that made biological diversity (typically shortened to biodiversity after the mid-1980s) the most important concern of the conservation movement and species extinctions the most telling measure of failure. "A revolution in conservation thinking," wrote the prominent biologist Edward O. Wilson in 1992, "has led to this perception of the practical value of wild species."[1] Attacking the incremental approach of the environmental organizations, they called for far-ranging changes in resource management. Their arguments, which were impossible to ignore and broadly influential by the 1990s, had far-reaching implications for resource managers as well as environmentalists. Case studies of Yellowstone National Park, which was emerging as a vital, preeminent center for wildlife research; the vast western rangelands, where the old "resourcism" was still largely unchallenged; and a movement among scientists and a few allies to show that it was still possible to establish a connected group of wildlands with great remedial potential suggest the changes that were underway by the 1990s.

THE NEW PARADIGM

The last two centuries have seen a dramatic increase in human population and an even more rapid increase in industrial and agricultural production, raising living standards in many countries but also taxing the world's resource base. The possible exhaustion of nonrenewable resources such as minerals or petroleum has been a cause for concern and anxiety. Perhaps more threatening has been the abuse of renewable resources due to urban sprawl, deforestation, and other forms of habitat destruction; the intentional or unintentional spread of nonnative species; air and water pollution; unsustainable levels of fishing; and other activities that emphasize immediate profit at the expense of long-term resource health. One vital measure of these abuses has been the rising extinction rate of plant and animal species. For millions of years speciation exceeded extinctions, and the world grew more varied. That process has now reversed, with extinctions worldwide accelerating to possibly a thousand times the earlier rate.[2] One-third of the plants and animals found in the United States are threatened.[3] Projecting this trend into the future, scientists warn of an impending sixth extinction crisis, comparable to others that have occurred over the past four-plus billion years. Unlike earlier extinctions, which resulted from vulcanism, meteor collisions, and other random, unpreventable events, the present-day extinction crisis is wholly the product of human agency.[4]

What should be done to head off this disaster? The challenge was not just to prevent the extinction of specific plants and animals but also to halt activities that degraded the natural environment to the point where vulnerable species could not survive. Relatively few animals have been hunted to extinction in the modern era. A much larger number have disappeared due to alterations in their physical environment or habitat. In most cases people are not aware of what is happening until the process is advanced and often irreversible.

There are various reasons for interceding, even when the immediate financial costs are substantial. One is ethical because plants and animals have intrinsic value apart from their contributions to human society. A second argument, more appealing to many people, emphasizes the ecosystem services that plants and animals provide. They clean the air and water, thwart floods, provide foods and drugs, and in a myriad of ways make human existence possible and pleasurable. The most compelling case for preserving as much of the natural world as possible, however, is the prospect of a biologically impoverished world overrun by invasive species. Under those circumstances would human life as we know it be possible? The prudent approach was suggested by the environmentalist Aldo Leopold, who famously warned that "the first precaution of intelligent tinkering" is "to keep every cog and wheel."[5]

Congress had addressed the extinction issue in 1973 with the landmark Endangered Species Act, notable for the sweeping powers it conferred on the Fish and Wildlife Service and the National Marine Fisheries Service. Yet the law and the procedures it created were deeply flawed: listings were limited to individual species and did not occur until extinction was a possibility; the agencies were underfunded and timid, especially when it came to protecting habitat; and bureaucratic procedures resulted in long, often disastrous delays. Relatively few species were ever removed from the list, and many continued to decline. Despite its modest dimensions, the program became a lightning rod for developers and other opponents, whose influence helped to ensure that it never overcame its original defects. Still, for all its deficiencies, "it prevented the extinction of some animals and plants" and "slowed or reversed the downward trend of many others."[6] To Edward O. Wilson, it was "easily the most important piece of conservation legislation in the nation's history."[7] To many scientists, the successes of the program were an indication of how desperate the situation had become.

The scientists who devised the most compelling response to the extinction crisis had little interest in the Endangered Species Act per se. They explicitly rejected the single species approach, viewed habitat as all-important, and emphasized the inadequacies of public lands management. They called for a broader and infinitely more ambitious strategy.

That approach reflected their background in ecology, the area of biology that examines the relationships between living things and their role in the larger ("abiotic") environment. Ecology had long been associated with environmental activism: the Ecological Society of America, for example, had been the original parent of the Nature Conservancy.[8] In the 1960s the environmental movement had appropriated much of the scientists' terminology, and words such as "ecology" and "ecosystem" became commonplace. In the meantime the science of ecology was becoming more theoretical, reflecting its place in university curricula and, at least to some practitioners, less associated with the practical and politically troubled real world of conservation.[9] Nevertheless, major revisionist insights of that period had a lasting impact on activists and public officials.

One of the foundations of ecological theory was the idea of a natural succession of plant species, leading eventually to a semipermanent climax state that would persist for decades or even centuries, until some dramatic event, such as a violent storm, earthquake, volcanic eruption, or insect infestation, destroyed or significantly altered the climax state and restarted the succession process. This theory grew out of forestry research, notably the work of a pioneering ecologist, Frederic E. Clements, and had profound implications for industries based on renewable resources. Many different tree species would grow initially in a given area, but the eventual climax forest was predictable, given the climate and topography of the area. Predictability had sweeping practical implications, including the assumption of a "sustainable yield"; in effect, the supply of prudently managed timber (or fish, deer, or other wildlife) would last indefinitely. "Maximum sustainable yield" became the industry standard for calculating harvest levels.

Yet there were complications. The process itself was easily manipulated for economic ends, as the Forest Service vividly demonstrated during the Reagan-Bush years. But there was another, more serious problem. The historical record was filled with exceptions, situations in which succession had not occurred as the theory suggested. The fate of a fifty-acre forest, set aside in 1891 and managed by the New York Botanical Society, was symptomatic of the larger pattern. Called the Hemlock Grove "because of its fine, towering trees," the hemlocks gradually declined; by 1936 they were only 36 percent of the total. "By 1985 they were only 17 percent. Then . . . a hurricane blew in an Asian insect that destroyed all but a few of the remaining specimens." Chestnuts, elms, and others were also permanently lost to insects and disease.[10] Even where succession occurred more or less as predicted, the results varied. For example, the forests of Appalachia, devastated by logging in the early twentieth century, "regained most of their natural qualities" after decades of "benign neglect" but were still markedly different from their predecessors.[11] Likewise, decades of cattle and sheep grazing in the Southwest led millions of acres to "flip" from grass to shrubs, and no one knew "how to run the process backward."[12]

Ecologists of the 1960s and 1970s increasingly questioned the succession theory and its corollary, the "balance of nature." On the contrary, they argued, nature was unpredictable, perhaps increasingly so. Unforeseen, destructive events often interrupted the process and produced an entirely different mix of species. Moreover, once they began to look for change, they found it everywhere. "Regime shifts have been observed in hundreds of different ecosystems, including marine, freshwater, and terrestrial."[13] Over the following decades a "nonequilibrium" model became the dominant paradigm. The nonequilibrium model not only challenged established ecological theory but the policies of the Forest Service, BLM, and other federal and state agencies.[14]

Another casualty of the new ecology was the assumption that preservation meant a return to the historical past. The 1963 Leopold report's casual reference to recapturing "primitive America" was a notorious example of this assumption. The scientists of the 1980s and 1990s dismissed such notions as illusory and fatuous. "It would be nice if there were a simple management plan that could reinstate the prehuman condition of biological evolution," wrote Michael Soulé and a coauthor. "But science is not able to provide such a prescription."[15] A leading ecologist wrote that "there is no original condition for an ecosystem in any meaningful sense; one cannot fix a specific point in time."[16] Preserving ecological processes, and especially biodiversity, was more important than trying to mimic an earlier setting. Where historical fidelity mattered, as in some national parks, it had to be addressed tentatively, adopting "a relative rather than an absolute perspective," emphasizing the "historical range of variability" rather than a given date or point, and attempting to "restore ecological trajectories rather than specific conditions."[17] The goal was to recover "a natural range of variation of composition, energy flow, and change" in order to "optimize adaptability, resilience, and productivity."[18]

As the reassuring belief in the "balance of nature" gave way to the new emphasis on disturbances and "patchiness," it seemed that nothing could be taken for granted; the whole world was subject to irreversible "regime shifts." As a prominent marine biologist warned in a memorable metaphor, the continued abuse of the oceans would ultimately leave only "slime": jellyfish and other aquatic creatures that had no economic value and were repellent to humans.[19] The imagery was arresting. Out of such insights emerged a new activist discipline, conservation biology.

The first major step in this progression was an obscure theoretical debate over the biological diversity of islands. It began with the publication in 1967 of *The Theory of Island Biogeography*, by Edward O. Wilson and Robert H. McArthur. Wilson and McArthur argued that the number of plant and animal species living on an island depended on a relatively small number of variables. The location, size, and shape of the island and distance from the mainland were critical. Large islands near the mainland were most diverse. Small, isolated islands would have fewer species, more of them endemic. The details differed, but the pattern was consistent and predictable. It explained, for example, why Hawaii had more endemic species and more endangered species than any other state. As Wilson recalled, they sought to give ecology "new intellectual rigor and originality."[20] David Quammen has observed that Wilson and McArthur "succeeded [in] . . . transforming biogeography from a descriptive endeavor into one that could articulate some of nature's governing rules."[21]

Wilson and McArthur's work may have been a theoretical breakthrough, but its real value lay in its applicability to metaphorical islands, the parks, wilderness areas, and roadless areas that were increasingly surrounded by agricultural or suburban "seas." Would a proposed national park preserve the biological diversity of the area, regardless of other features? The answer depended on the same variables that applied to actual islands. Jared Diamond, another biologist, made the connection explicit in a famous 1968 paper, "The Island Dilemma: Lessons of Modern Biogeographic Studies for the Design of Natural Reserves." In it he proposed that diversity would best be served by large "reserves" or parks, close to other parks, preferably as large as possible, connected, and shaped as blocks or circles, as opposed to thin or elongated areas. Diamond and his colleagues were primarily interested in African and Asian countries, but their insights came at a propitious time in the history of American conservation as well.

One of Diamond's principles, that a single large reserve was biologically superior to several small ones with the same total acreage, proved to be highly controversial. Other scientists, citing examples of small, unusually rich areas (comparable to the kinds of acquisitions the Nature Conservancy was beginning to emphasize) insisted that he was misguided. The academic controversy, known as SLOSS—single large or several small—continued for years and resulted in a standoff, or perhaps mutual exhaustion. Critics of the dispute noted that it was wholly theoretical; park planners seldom if ever had such a choice. In the real world opportunism was the rule: large areas were preferable, but small ones were better than nothing and, in some cases, valuable, even indispensable.[22]

Regardless of the results, the assumption of an explicit link between the size or shape of a park or wildlife preserve and its value for species preservation piqued the interest of other scientists. They soon adopted a new label. Biological diversity became biodiversity—a term that had been used sporadically in earlier years, was adopted by the president's Council on Environmental Quality in 1980, and then popularized by a 1986 conference, the National Forum on BioDiversity, a "watershed event."[23] The term could refer to genes, species, or ecosystems, but it also encompassed diversity between ecosystems, diversity within species, and other measures. A survey identified eight distinct applications.[24]

At the same time, a graduate student at the University of Michigan, William Newmark, was extending the debate over reserve sizes in ways that nonscientists could not disregard. Operating on a shoestring, Newmark traveled through the West, visiting fourteen iconic national parks and comparing lists of mammals compiled when the parks were created with more contemporary lists. He found that in every case some species had disappeared. The most obvious cause was the size of the park. Zion, Bryce Canyon, and Lassen Volcanic were the smallest parks in his sample, and they suffered the greatest losses. Yellowstone, the largest, had the fewest. He did not test the SLOSS hypothesis directly, but his conclusions were striking: size mattered and probably mattered more than any other feature of the park environment.[25]

The implications for conservation were far-reaching. Most American national parks (and wilderness areas) were apparently too small to preserve biodiversity, at least mammalian diversity. Since the establishment of Yellowstone, conservationists had labored to create what they considered the world's premier park system and supplement it with wilderness areas, wildlife refuges, and other public lands devoted to conservation. They had fought numerous battles with developers and industrialists who complained that they wanted too much, that they were "locking up" economically useful resources. Yet it appeared that they had done too little; they had only delayed, not prevented, the loss of much of the natural world. If they were serious about preserving biodiversity, they would have to go back to the drawing board and reconsider their approach.

An important step in that process was to think of parks and wilderness areas as "cores," an idea that had gained currency since the 1970s. Cores, in general, were relatively undisturbed and untrammeled areas that had suffered comparatively little species loss. As Newmark had demonstrated, most core areas were too small by themselves to be self-sustaining. They had to be enlarged or, if that was impossible, to be surrounded by "buffer" areas, such as multiple-use zones where many features of the core remained but protections were less rigorous. More important still were connections between cores to facilitate migration corridors, which could take a multitude of forms and were the key to resilience, the ability of plant and animal species to withstand and adapt to natural and anthropogenic changes. They received increasing attention in the 1990s and after as a warming climate added new urgency to the threat of mass extinctions.[26]

Size and connectivity were related to another issue that had emerged by the 1980s and would generate more immediate controversy. What determined the level of biodiversity within a given ecosystem? Biologists distinguished between "bottom up" regulation, primarily the availability of food, and "top down" regulation, meaning predation. Conservationists, together with most wildlife officials, traditionally emphasized food supplies. More food meant more animals and more species. Clearly this view made sense. Predation was more controversial, and government policy had long been devoted to curtailing or eliminating the most notable mammalian predators—wolves, coyotes, and bears. But a growing number of researchers had concluded that "top down" was as vital to the health of the ecosystem as "bottom up" regulation. For several decades biologists had systematically studied the relationships between wolves, moose, and the local flora, notably on Isle Royale, and found them to be highly interdependent. In studies of starfish and sea otters, ecologist Robert Paine emphasized the roles of "keystone" species. By the 1970s many ecologists were convinced that "predators could control community structure."[27] In the 1970s and 1980s James Brown and Diane Davidson conducted a series of experiments in southeastern Arizona that focused on this issue. They found that "manipulation of a guild of consumers" (rodents and ants in this case) "resulted in large and often unanticipated changes in the composition of the plant community."[28] Each component played a role, and the elimination of any one of them brought major changes. Thus, the elimination of animals at the top of the food chain—wolves, bears, mountain lions, sharks, sea otters, and sea lions—affected lesser predators, such as coyotes and seals, their prey, especially ungulates (deer, elk, moose), and the plants they in turn consumed. Removing wolves led to an increase in the ungulate population, which in turn led to a reduction in vegetation.[29]

To preserve or restore a functioning ecosystem, then, it was necessary to have both top-down and bottom-up regulation. In practical terms, this meant that long-standing predator control activities would have to stop and where they had succeeded (in the case of wolves, virtually everywhere) the animals would have to be reintroduced. The pressure for predator controls came primarily from the domestic livestock industry, which remained a powerful interest group. The biologists' proposals for reintroducing wolves in national parks and wilderness areas would be among their most controversial proposals.

Just as the elimination of "keystone" predators had led to an abundance of ungulates, other human activities had resulted in invasions of exotic, invasive plants and animals. Native fish had disappeared from many rivers and from lakes everywhere. Poor management of grazing lands had encouraged the spread of woody bushes and invasive grasses. Wetlands were particularly threatened. Even the oceans, seemingly inexhaustible in their bounty, were at risk from overfishing. The problem was large and growing.

There were antidotes, which fell under the general heading of "rewilding."[30] Scientists argued that the reintroduction of predators such as wolves and bears, which frequently had to be imported from other areas or bred in captivity, would go a long way toward ending problems caused by herbivore populations. Allowing rivers to flow freely and protecting stream banks would restore freshwater fish populations. Ending or aggressively regulating certain kinds of fishing and establishing no fishing zones would have similar effects in the seas. Curtailing the most destructive assaults on habitat, such as clear-cutting and public land grazing, were other vital steps toward preserving biodiversity. Recognizing the value of fire in many settings and reintroducing it as a natural ecosystem function would reduce catastrophic fires and be a boon to many plant and animal species. Removal of invasive plants and animals was another essential step. These were obviously not trivial reforms. Together with the demand for much larger natural areas (cores, buffers, and corridors), rewilding promised to alter the face of the continent, not to mention the meaning of "conservation."

The first efforts to draw together the emerging work on the loss of biodiversity and its implications for human society came in the 1970s. The key figure at that time, and for many years thereafter, was Michael Soulé, a biologist who taught at the University of California, San Diego, and later at the University of Michigan and the University of California, Santa Cruz. An early adherent of Arne Naess, whose "deep ecology" emphasized the inherent value of plants and animals, Soulé brought passion and worldly commitment to his research. At one point, disgusted with the parochialism of academic biology, he left his university position to live at a Zen Buddhist center in Los Angeles. Yet troubled by mounting evidence of human assaults on nature, he reversed course and dedicated himself to applying biological research to the environmentalists' agenda. In 1978 he organized a conference in San Diego on "conservation biology," designed to bring together individuals who had been working separately and largely in isolation and to encourage other scientists to become involved. In the introduction to the conference proceedings, he and a coeditor described the problem they faced: "There is no escaping the conclusion that in our lifetimes, this planet will see a suspension, if not an

end, to many ecological and evolutionary processes which have been unin-
terrupted since the beginnings of paleontological time."[31] To cope with this
threat they proposed a "mission-oriented discipline comprising both pure
and applied science."[32] Other scholars referred to it as a "crisis discipline."[33]

In a 1980 book, coauthored with O. H. Frankel, Soulé provided an outline
of what needed to be done. He also began to gather like-minded scientists
in periodic conferences devoted to conservation issues. Five volumes of conference proceedings emerged over the next twenty years. The contributions
were largely technical, and it was not until 1994 that Reed F. Noss and Allen
Y. Cooperrider published a synthetic work, *Saving Nature's Legacy*, aimed at
nonscientists. In the meantime, there was sufficient interest to warrant a formal organization. At a 1985 conference at the University of Michigan, Soulé
and his colleagues launched the Society for Conservation Biology, together
with a scholarly journal, also called *Conservation Biology*. The society grew
rapidly in the following years, as more and more scientists became alarmed
at the loss of biodiversity. Another milestone occurred in 1991, when Soulé
and Dave Foreman, who had recently abandoned Earth First!, organized the
Wildlands Project to promote a network of large North American nature
preserves.[34] Conservation biology was thus at once a scholarly discipline, a
campaign to shape public policy, and an educational program that sought to
revise traditional ideas about the goals of conservation. Other related groups,
devoted to landscape ecology and restoration ecology, provided additional
impetus to the rewilding campaign.

By the end of the 1980s activist scientists had issued a call to arms that
complemented, and in many ways transcended, the now familiar complaints
of the environmental community. The scientists had a different starting
point and clearly defined measures of success and failure, were proactive
and explicit about what needed to be done, and were unequivocal about
the effects of inaction. In their book Noss and Cooperrider wrote that "a
proper philosophy for management of public lands is that all actions must
have ultimately positive or at least neutral effects on global, national, and
regional biodiversity. Globally negative management should no longer be tol-
erated anywhere."[35] Whereas the environmental movement had long called
for additional parks and wildlife preserves, fought the commodity and real
estate industries, and proposed managerial reforms such as the Wilderness
Preservation System, the scientists raised the bar substantially. "Conservation

now means so much more than the protection of endangered species or the creation of wildlife sanctuaries," wrote one prominent scientist. "It now deals with the entire breadth of land and seascapes."[36] Preserving biodiversity required more preserves, more curbs on traditional economic activities, and more dramatic changes in managerial philosophy and technique. The scientists' books and articles provided compelling rationales for these actions. But as veteran environmentalists were quick to point out, logic and data alone were no match for vested economic interests, political maneuvering, and bureaucratic inertia. The defense of biodiversity would require more conflict, no less intense than the battles of earlier years.

In this effort the scientists initially remained aloof from their allies in the environmental mainstream. In a 1995 exchange on the value of wilderness areas, Reed Noss, the editor of *Conservation Biology*, and Michael McCloskey, the now retired executive director of the Sierra Club, explained some of their differences. McCloskey complained that the scientists were one-dimensional in their preoccupation with biodiversity and irresponsible in calling for intrusive management practices, such as prescribed burns in wilderness areas. "I felt that such well-intended but amateurish meddlers in the political process of wilderness designation might do more harm than good," he explained.[37] In response, Noss noted their many common goals, the "bigger is better" idea in designing reserves, for example. But "traditional conservationists" such as McCloskey also had unhelpful biases, especially in the attention they gave to formal wilderness designations. Scientists "are uncomfortable with the wilderness idea because it seems so subjective, soft, and non-quantifiable." They would "just as soon leave wilderness to the backpackers, poets, and treehuggers." Noss personally believed that wilderness areas were "among the most important components of a conservation network," but if they were only to be "public playgrounds" with little attention to their scientific value and compromised by loopholes that permitted grazing or fish stocking, "it is perhaps frivolous to spend much time trying to protect" them.[38]

These statements underscored distinctions in emphasis and perspective that activists in both camps readily acknowledged. After more than twenty years of political activity, McCloskey knew that appeals based on science alone would fall on deaf ears. Public officials were highly receptive to "backpackers, poets, and tree-huggers," provided there were enough of them. Compromises, even honest compromises, providing for prescribed burns or tree thinning, for example, could open the door to precisely the types of abuses that Noss bemoaned. On the other hand, environmentalists had paid too little attention to the extinction problem, had been too casual and opportunistic in setting priorities for parks and wilderness areas, and had often allowed recreational opportunities to limit their perspectives. Yet if both groups were to have any chance of significantly expanding the number of parks and protected areas, they had no choice but to work together.

YELLOWSTONE

The emergence of conservation biology in the 1980s had special significance for the national parks. Maintaining biodiversity had always been one of their goals even before the word became popular, and the prohibition of commodity production made them ideal "core" areas. The new Alaska parks, which combined the familiar (Denali, with its emphasis on majestic scenery and world-class recreational opportunities) and the novel (three parks were accessible only by bush plane), were the outstanding examples. The NPS had earlier abandoned predator controls, the automatic suppression of forest fires, and tourist lures such as the Yosemite "fire fall," anticipating, in effect, many of the biologists' prescriptions. Thus, the parks appeared to be perfectly positioned: they would play a major role in preserving biodiversity and in interpreting the value of biodiversity to the public. The Reagan and Bush administrations were unsympathetic but essentially uninvolved; the important park initiatives would occur within the agency and, even more, within individual parks. More than ever before, they would become educational institutions, embracing scientific research and disseminating the latest and most vital insights.

A key to the success of this role was the park managers' receptivity to ongoing scientific research, since the resources of each park were different and ever changing. Research had never been the NPS's strong suit, as expert reports had emphasized for more than thirty years. The pressures of ever-growing numbers of summer visitors, difficult relations with concessionaires, and intensifying political pressures too often pushed the agency's scientists to the periphery. A study undertaken during the early 1990s was unequivocal: "Faced with having [to increase] science expenditures from 1% to 20% of their budgets to meet the challenges of science-based management, they have largely given up in frustration."[39] Shenandoah, Isle Royale, Channel Islands, and

Great Smoky Mountains were notable exceptions, but Yellowstone, which had vast and varied resources and many eager scientists knocking at its doors, best exemplified the possibilities and pitfalls of the new role.

Not only the first national park but until 1994 the largest in the lower forty-eight states, Yellowstone had a transcendent role as a model for the rest of the world. Whatever happened in Yellowstone would be influential everywhere.[40] Unlike the obscure species whose defense evoked derisive comments from critics of the Endangered Species Act, Yellowstone's characteristic fauna—grizzly bears, bison, elk, and ultimately wolves—were large, easily recognizable, and immensely appealing to the public. Together with the geysers and hot springs, they made Yellowstone one of the most popular parks despite its remoteness from major population centers.

A turning point in Yellowstone management occurred in the late 1960s, when a public uproar over the culling of the ever-growing elk herd prompted Yellowstone officials to embrace a largely passive, hands-off approach, an exclusively bottom-up response that they called "natural regulation." Park biologists argued that without human intervention two natural factors would control the elk population. One was "self regulation (the result of some combination of behavior, physiology, and genetics) which might work to keep the population at some level lower than the food supply would allow." The second was the local environment, which featured severe winters and limited food supplies.[41] Natural regulation did not rely on predation, although elk hunting was popular on public and private lands north of the park. Essentially it combined bottom-up regulation with wishful thinking. Natural regulation was acknowledged to be experimental, an effort "to find out how a large ungulate population interacts with its environment." It would make Yellowstone "a prominent ground for theoretical exercises . . . as well as a continuing forum for debate."[42] By embracing the "naturalness" theme, park officials also held off two politically influential groups: animal welfare advocates, who were appalled at the shootings, and state wildlife officials, who wanted to open the park to hunting.

What they did not fully anticipate was the stridency of the biologists who looked upon Yellowstone as "a prominent ground for theoretical exercises." The fate of the elk herd would command the greatest attention over the next half century, but the first major conflict was an outgrowth of another feature of natural regulation, a decision to stop feeding grizzly bears at garbage dumps. That decision resulted from the recommendations of the famous Leopold committee, which had been asked to consider a number of specific problems after its initial report. The committee did not recommend an immediate closure of all the dumps, but the park administrators read between the lines and ordered immediate closings, completed in 1970.

That decision brought to a head a long-simmering dispute between the park managers and John and Frank Craighead, grizzly experts who had been studying the Yellowstone bears for a decade. The Craigheads were eminent authorities on grizzlies, pioneers in devising new research tools, such as radio tracking collars for wildlife, and among the first scientists to perceive that the Greater Yellowstone Ecosystem (as it was later designated) rather than the park per se was the relevant unit for most wildlife.[43] Their relations with the park staff had deteriorated in the late 1960s, and the failure of the Yellowstone authorities to follow their advice and close the dumps gradually was the last straw. The park's chief naturalist asked: "Do we really need intensive management . . . or is there some way we can get off the road we seem to be on which leads to manipulative management of more and more species . . . ?"[44] In response, the Craigheads suspended their work in the park and devoted much of the next quarter century to attacking the dump closings, the natural regulation idea, the park administrators responsible for those decisions, and the Interagency Grizzly Bear Study Team, which resumed their studies in the mid–1970s. In the mid–1960s they had estimated the grizzly population at more than 300 bears. By the early 1980s the total was perhaps half that many because of reduced food supplies, the loss of customary "ecocenters," and the killing of animals that invaded campgrounds (notably the Fishing Bridge campground, which the Park Service closed in the mid-1980s, partly as a result of the bear problem) and surrounding areas in search of food. The Craigheads viewed the decline in the bear population as vindication of their arguments for gradual change.[45]

Grizzly policy after the Craigheads' departure was largely determined by the bears' listing as an endangered species in 1975. This change of status required Park Service (and Forest Service) officials to try to prevent additional losses. By the early 1980s Yellowstone managers had devised detailed plans to preserve grizzly habitat in the park and in adjoining national forest lands and to minimize confrontations between grizzlies and humans. This effort gradually healed the rift between the park managers and the outside experts—apart from the Craigheads. Beginning in 1983, the grizzly population began to increase again; it would continue to rise over the next thirty years to around 600. Increasingly the problems were outside the park. The Interagency Team's research documented the bears' tendency to travel over large areas well outside the park boundaries where they were likely to encounter humans. By the turn of the century, one-third to one-half of the "Yellowstone" bears lived outside the park. Even Yellowstone was too small to house its most famous inhabitants without artificial constraints.[46] In the meantime, the protected status of the grizzly enabled the population in and around Glacier National Park to increase from about 300 to 1,000 and smaller populations to emerge in northern Idaho and Washington.[47]

The conflict over the grizzlies was, however, only a prelude to a growing controversy over the elk herd. The total number of elk in Yellowstone grew rapidly in the 1970s and 1980s to nearly 20,000 (from about 3,000 when natural regulation was introduced), and critics, including biologists who studied park flora as well as ranchers outside the park, complained about the impact of the growing herd on the grasslands, forests, and food supplies of mammals such as beaver and white-tailed deer. These criticisms reached a popular audience in 1986, when a journalist, Alston Chase, published a scathing exposé, *Playing God in Yellowstone: The Destruction of America's First National Park*. In lively prose Chase summarized the scientists' data and attributed the park's "destruction" to managerial incompetence and a countercultural 1960s aura that lingered over the Park Service.[48] Though savaged in reviews, Chase's account was widely read and became the foundation for his subsequent career as an anti-environmental crusader.[49] A 1985 congressional oversight hearing had already raised concerns about the management of the park and the adjacent national forest lands, including the northern range where the elk spent the winters. Chase's accusations reinforced the demand for more information. Through this indirect process, natural regulation ultimately inspired the type of research that Leopold and the other experts had called for two decades earlier.

The most telling complaint from critics had been the lack of long-term systematic studies of the effects of park policies. Because of personnel changes and budgetary constraints, the Park Service had no research effort devoted to the northern range. The parks' scientific staff had been in the process of mounting a campaign for additional funds at the time when the critics first attracted attention. The ensuing controversy led to additional appropriations and sympathetic responses from private foundations. For the next decade Yellowstone's formerly neglected elk population would be the object of dozens of studies. By the end of the decade more than 300 scientists were busy on projects related to the elk and other features of the Yellowstone environment.[50] In 1988 the park began to host regular meetings where researchers presented their work and debated the meaning of their data.[51]

The research helped fill the information void but did not resolve the underlying issue. Critics, whose work was summarized in books by Utah State University ecologist Frederick Wagner, pointed to the decline of aspens and willows, favorite elk foods, and the disappearance of beaver, whose diet was similar. Other scientists were more positive, arguing that grazing and browsing resulted in only temporary losses of vegetation and no decline in biodiversity. Yellowstone officials insisted that the preponderance of evidence supported natural regulation.[52]

Three additional developments during that period profoundly affected the park and the debates over park management. First, the grazing controversy led the Elk Foundation and the Forest Service to acquire and set aside large areas north of the park as a winter range for the elk herd. With this extra food supply, the park could accommodate a larger number of elk, and the problem of overgrazing receded, at least temporarily.

The second change, wholly unanticipated due to a decade or more of abnormally wet years and the many controversies that absorbed the attention of park managers, was the series of dramatic forest fires that burned almost one-half of Yellowstone in the hot, dry summer of 1988. The magnitude of the destruction shocked even veteran fire professionals, but media coverage of the fires, with their inevitable emphasis on the dramatic and spectacular, exaggerated the losses and their significance for the future of the park. The search for a scapegoat focused attention on the "natural" fire policy, in effect since the 1970s, that allowed backcountry fires to burn. Political pressures became so great that the Park Service temporarily suspended its fire policy, to the scientists' consternation. Subsequent investigations concluded that Yellowstone officials had failed to update what had been, in the 1970s, an enlightened policy; yet as the historian Hal K. Rothman has observed, the principal lesson of the Yellowstone experience was the "fundamental ineffectiveness of all human counter measures."[53] Later evaluations shifted the focus from Park Service policy to the effort to extinguish the fires, largely in response to the growing public outcry. The $120 million that the government spent on "the greatest concentration of fire fighting power in history" may have saved a few buildings; otherwise the money was essentially wasted, perhaps worse than wasted, because some firefighting activities, such as the construction of fire breaks, caused additional, unnecessary damage.[54] Within a year the burned areas were green again and most wildlife had successfully adjusted; indeed, by destroying dense lodgepole pine forests, the fires had created additional food supplies in areas newly open to sunlight. On balance the 1988 fires strengthened the arguments by scientists in favor of the Park Service's wary but tolerant approach to forest fires.[55] Still, four years passed before the Park Service resumed prescribed burns in the western parks.

The third development, accentuated by the drought, the fires, and the severe winter that followed, was a growing bison problem, as more and more members of an expanding herd sought food and shelter outside the park. Like the elk, bison had traditionally moved to lower pastures in winter. Yet neither the park nor the larger Yellowstone ecosystem included all the areas they customarily occupied.[56] Moving onto private property, they broke fences and consumed grass supposedly reserved for cattle. Many of them also carried a disease, brucellosis, which could spread to cattle. The actual threat was relatively slight (infection could and did result from contacts with elk, which were not considered a threat), but it led to extended conflict between park officials, state wildlife managers, and agents of the federal veterinary service. The real issue, or so it seemed to many observers, was de facto control of the park borders.[57] In any case, Yellowstone rangers attempted, usually unsuccessfully, to stop the migration. In 1985 Montana instituted a bison hunting season outside the park; and in 1988–89, with the bison herd numbering nearly 3,000, hunters killed nearly 600 animals. In 1996–97, another severe winter, officials captured more than 1,000 and sent them to slaughterhouses, and in 2007–08 they dispatched another 1,200, despite public outcries and an extended protest by Buffalo Field Campaign, an animal rights group that "infused the conflict with moral and spiritual feeling" and attracted thousands of volunteers.[58] By 2010, a long-term solution had begun to emerge. It included conservation easements on private lands near the park, agreements with Forest Service managers to create more buffer zones on national forest land and with Native Americans to move some bison to reservations, and an easing of brucellosis regulations.[59]

The most important and controversial Yellowstone innovation and the most important experiment in rewilding to date was the reintroduction of gray wolves in 1995, after a quarter century of debate and study. For scientists, the wolf had special significance as the preeminent terrestrial keystone species, with the potential to initiate "trophic cascades" that would reverberate through the food chain. For livestock owners, on the other hand, they were dangerous animals, hunted to extinction for good reason. For NPS officials they were a political hot potato. Strict adherence to natural regulation meant allowing Canadian wolves gradually to reoccupy the Yellowstone backcountry. But park officials knew that an artificial reintroduction would greatly accelerate the process, facilitate top-down regulation, and possibly control the growth of the elk herd. Long experience with wolves, notably in Alaska and on Isle Royale, where they had appeared in the late 1940s and had been the subject of landmark studies, indicated that the fears of ranchers were exaggerated but that wolves would rapidly disperse. Yellowstone officials had discussed the possibility of reintroducing wolves after the gray wolf was placed on the endangered species list in 1974, but had not taken any specific action. Yellowstone was already immersed in political controversy, and the ranchers seemed implacable.

By the 1980s the wolf had attracted influential champions in the environmental movement. A romantic interest in recreating primeval forest conditions together with scientific studies of the significance of predation stirred the interest of Defenders of Wildlife and the National Wildlife Federation. Park Service director William Penn Mott enthusiastically backed reintroduction, despite the hostility of Wyoming's Republican office holders and the opposition of the Reagan administration. At Mott's suggestion, Hank Fischer of Defenders of Wildlife organized a fund to compensate ranchers who could document losses to predation. The fund would neutralize the economic argument for opposing wolves.[60] Another influential individual was a young scientist-turned-activist, Renee Askins, whose Wolf Fund, formed in the late 1980s to promote the reintroduction of wolves in Yellowstone, financed a high-profile public relations campaign, with many celebrity endorsers. In 1988 Fischer, Askins, and their allies decided to test the waters. They proposed a modest beginning, a congressionally sponsored environmental impact statement (EIS) that would highlight the scientific research. They went to Senator James McClure (R-ID), chair of the Senate Resources

Committee and a leading opponent of conservation legislation. McClure and the two Wyoming senators, defenders of ranching interests, were predictably unsympathetic. But the environmentalists persisted, arguing that an EIS might well support the ranchers' position and, in any case, would clarify the issues.[61]

This strategy had two effects. It eventually persuaded McClure and, indirectly, the Wyoming senators that a more flexible approach would be the best defense of livestock interests. In 1990 McClure introduced a bill for the EIS, which resulted in a series of investigations and studies that paved the way to the actual reintroduction. Local environmental leaders agreed to support the reintroduction under an "experimental population" provision of the Endangered Species Act, which allowed ranchers to kill wolves that attacked livestock. When the Sierra Club, Audubon, and the Sierra Club Legal Defense Fund initially opposed this concession, they responded that the western senators would never support the reintroduction without safeguards for their constituents. By taking a moderate position they would be able to cast the issue as a conflict between reasonable environmentalists and intransigent ranchers and politicians. And indeed this contrast was a critical ingredient in generating public support for the wolf reintroduction during the many hearings and comment periods that followed.

In 1991 Congress authorized an EIS on wolf reintroduction. Over the next year the NPS held twenty-seven "scoping sessions"—public meetings inviting public comment—in towns near Yellowstone, and when the livestock supporters, outmaneuvered and overwhelmed, still complained, they conducted an additional twenty-seven hearings in the same towns, with exactly the same result. By the summer of 1993 the NPS had prepared a preliminary, or draft, EIS supporting the reintroduction. More hearings followed. A total of 160,000 written public comments, with approximately 100,000 supporting the reintroduction, demonstrated the scope and effectiveness of the pro-wolf campaign. The final environmental impact statement, in July 1994, proposed to reintroduce wolves to Yellowstone and wilderness areas of central Idaho under the "experimental population" rule. The plan was adopted in November 1994. Several groups sued, and in December 1997 a judge, responding to local objections, ordered the government to remove the wolves, then numbering nearly 200, in Yellowstone and Idaho. That remarkable decision was reversed on appeal.[62]

The wolves, imported from Canada, readily adapted to their new homes. The population grew to more than 480 in thirty-four packs by 2001 and to 1,000 by 2010. The area occupied by the packs expanded just as rapidly and soon extended far beyond the park boundaries. Attacks on domestic livestock became more common. Defenders of Wildlife paid more than $215,000 in the first five years of the program and a total of $542,000 between 1995 and 2010, when the federal government took over the compensation program.[63] As many scientists predicted and hoped, the wolves had a marked effect on the park ecosystem. They attacked and killed old, young, and sick elk and frightened the others, who were less inclined to gather in the most desirable areas. Reduced browsing had a positive effect on vegetation in many areas of the park, allowing other animals, such as beaver, to multiply. The carrion from wolf kills provided food for a host of other animals, from grizzlies to songbirds. The wolves also drove away coyotes, which resulted in larger populations of small mammals. "Ultimately," noted one scientist, "wolves will touch almost everything in Yellowstone." By the end of the century, the park "had all the [wildlife] species it did when Columbus first stepped ashore."[64]

Wolves also had great popular appeal and became one of the park's principal attractions. That popularity translated into economic opportunities for service providers in and out of the park; by 2000 the extra income attributed to wolves vastly overshadowed the costs of the wolf program, including the value of lost livestock. The wolves' economic benefits underlined the bizarre disconnect between their actual impact and the continued hostility of Wyoming and Montana politicians, supposedly devoted to their constituents' economic welfare. Some observers suggested that the very success of the reintroduction, underlining the ability of the federal government, and outsiders, to deal effectively with seemingly intractable problems accounted for the hostility. "More than anything, [it] really polarized the issue here in the West," explained Bob Ream of the Wolf Ecology Project at the University of Montana. The sociologist Justin Farrell agreed. Wolves were "a symbol of deeper cultural anxieties."[65]

There were at least two additional lessons from the Yellowstone experience. The first was the importance of a true sanctuary—an area such as a national park where the wolves would not be molested. When the Fish and Wildlife Service tried to introduce the Mexican gray wolf in the national forests of southern Arizona and New Mexico, which permitted widespread cattle grazing and hunting, the results were quite different; few of the animals survived the first year.[66] The second was the need for relatively undeveloped land outside the sanctuary to serve as habitat for the expanding wolf (and bear and bison) populations. This realization helped to promote the idea of a Greater Yellowstone Ecosystem, embracing the park and the seven national forests that surrounded it, and the introduction of "ecosystem management," which called for the relaxation of traditional bureaucratic boundaries and more collaboration between agencies. A private environmental group, the Greater Yellowstone Coalition, also promoted the ecosystem concept.

Representatives of the park and the surrounding national forests formed a coordinating committee to exchange ideas and develop compatible policies. At first this was little more than a public relations gesture. The national forests all were considering various development plans, and the park administrators were preoccupied with the controversies over natural regulation. A critical report by the Congressional Research Service (part of the broader examination of the area in the mid-1980s) made the government's "stewardship . . . look very bad indeed." Nevertheless, the report proved to be a "breakthrough" that made the land managers take the ecosystem idea seriously.[67] They began to address the conflicting perspectives of the NPS and Forest Service, the diverse plans of the different management entities, and the constant criticism of commodity producers and environmentalists. Some forest managers embraced ecosystem management and worked closely with the Park Service; others persisted in encouraging gas and oil leasing and clear-cutting. Still, by the end of the decade, as Robert B. Keiter and Mark S. Boyce have written, "traditional economic interests are giving way—albeit grudgingly—to the ecological imperatives of modern natural resource management."[68] Keiter believed that "a revised preservationist ethic is displacing the ethic of consumption" and was indeed "rising to a dominant position" in the Greater Yellowstone area.[69]

The best examples of the new spirit of cooperation were two jointly produced documents of the late 1980s, an "Aggregation" of Park Service and Forest Service management plans (1987), which "showed the incompatibility of goals, information, and activities," and a "Vision Statement" (1990), which outlined a model for interagency cooperation.[70] The vision statement did not propose any major changes, but it did emphasize the need for greater environmental sensitivity in national forest planning and for restrictions on geothermal drilling and gold mining on the park's border. The document, released in July 1990, was sufficiently innocuous that environmental groups did not mobilize supporters to speak at the three public hearings scheduled for nearby towns. On the other hand, a coalition of commodity interests, mobilized under the "Wise Use" banner and financed in this case by mining companies, prepared wildly exaggerated analyses of the statement, portraying it as evidence of a conspiracy to create vast wilderness areas. Gullible local people packed the hearings and shouted down the federal officials. After a particularly raucous hearing in Bozeman in January 1991, the Department of the Interior cancelled other hearings, withdrew the vision statement, and issued an abbreviated substitute that did not include the words "vision" or "biodiversity" or emphasize the value of ecosystem management. The regional NPS director, Lorraine Mintzmyer, who had had responsibility for the project, later testified that a political appointee had prepared the final draft. The goal was "to retain the appearance" of a "professional and scientific effort" when in reality it reflected "political concerns."[71] Mintzmyer was then summarily demoted and transferred. Park Service officials were shocked, both by the brazenness of the politicians and the meager support they received from the environmental community.[72]

A congressional study in 1992 provided additional details. The protests against the vision statement were anything but spontaneous reactions to oppressive government. Shortly after the vision statement was released, commodity interests had orchestrated a series of meetings between their representatives, Wyoming's senators, political appointees in the Interior and Agriculture Departments, and the president's chief of staff. The protests and demonstrations emerged from these discussions, and compliant Interior Department officials then canceled the remaining hearings before the environmental groups could mobilize their supporters.[73] The episode revealed more about the disruptive potential of hostile political groups than it did about public attitudes toward wolves and grizzlies or interagency cooperation.

It nevertheless had a lasting effect. The uproar was "more than [NPS and Forest Service officials] could cope with." They "made virtually no credible attempt to defend the 'Vision' or push forward an active program to address criticisms." A decade and a half later political scientist Susan Clark reported that those events "still live actively in [their] cultural memory. . . . the consensus has been to avoid similar exercises at all costs." Consequently, they confined their joint activities to information gathering and small-scale, non-controversial projects. Within these limits they operated more effectively, conditioned perhaps by the shared memory of their earlier experiences as well as their modest agenda.[74]

A somewhat different perspective on the Yellowstone experience was provided by Karl Hess, a former Park Service biologist who attacked the management of Rocky Mountain National Park in a 1993 book. In terms reminiscent of Alston Chase, he argued that Rocky Mountain Park was "experiencing rocky times, relentlessly moving toward an ecological Armageddon."[75] The problems were familiar: too many elk, years of fire suppression, briefly abandoned in the 1970 but then resumed after a 1978 blaze threatened local communities, and the liberal use of pesticides in areas where insect infestations might offend visitors. "Mismanagement and bureaucratic ineptitude" thus threatened the park. Yet apart from the purple prose, Hess had little in common with Chase. He acknowledged that the park was too small to reintroduce wolves successfully on its own and too close to population centers to allow fires to burn unchecked. He reviewed and criticized a variety of recommendations by various groups and individuals, but his call for a new management agency was no more realistic or satisfactory. Hess's study confirmed the point that William Newmark and other biologists emphasized. Given the real-world constraints that confronted even the most enlightened park managers, not to mention the inherent tensions between preserving biodiversity and accommodating millions of visitors, the role of national parks in the campaign to preserve biodiversity would not be easy or automatic. Thirteen years later, with an ever-growing surfeit of elk, perhaps three times the optimum number, Rocky Mountain park officials resumed culling animals and fencing sensitive areas.[76]

RANGE LANDS AND BIODIVERSITY

The obstacles to a more science-based management in the other public lands agencies were no less formidable. The Fish and Wildlife Service continued some predator control activities, though Wildlife Services in the Department of Agriculture and various state agencies were responsible for most of the killing.[77] The wildlife refuge system itself continued to be an administrative hodgepodge, ranging from enormous areas in Alaska where de facto natural regulation prevailed, to many small refuges committed to preserving single species, usually ducks or other waterfowl. The bulk of western public lands, under the aegis of the BLM, suffered from a combination of passivity and deference to commodity producers. The Federal Land Policy and Management Act of 1976 had encouraged efforts to emulate the Forest Service, but the inertia of a century and a half of neglect was impossible to overcome in a single decade. Very little had changed.[78]

Still, by the late 1980s North America's vast semiarid and arid rangelands had begun to command the attention of scientists who were not associated with livestock production. A huge area was involved, more than half of the land west of the 100th meridian. Too dry for conventional agriculture, much of it flat and unattractive, it typically remained the de facto property of nearby lessees whose political clout in the western states and the US Senate prevented meaningful regulation. Overgrazing and fire suppression had taken their toll, and nearly all rangelands showed signs of desertification.[79] Until the 1990s most critics of the supine BLM had attacked below-market leasing fees. That campaign failed most dramatically in the early 1990s, when the House of Representatives repeatedly passed bills raising fees but the Senate refused to act.[80] The fee issue then gave way to more fundamental questions of ecological integrity.

This contest pitted environmentalists and biologists against ranchers, the BLM, and their allies in the state agricultural agencies and western state universities. Like the BLM and the state agencies, the academic departments were products of an era when the viability of the dominant regional industry was a critical public concern. By the 1980s and 1990s their utilitarian approach and narrow emphasis on livestock forage had become outmoded. As the proceedings of the Society for Range Management demonstrated, they were not utterly hidebound.[81] But changes occurred slowly at the local level.

In the meantime the ranchers' prospects suffered a slow, relentless decline. The rationale for federal subsidies and state assistance had been the contributions of the livestock industry to the food supply. By the late twentieth century, however, the cattle "frontier" had shifted eastward to Texas and the Gulf states; western public rangelands (i.e., 170 million acres of BLM lands and nearly 100 million acres of national forest) produced only 2–3 percent of US livestock and employed less than 1 percent of the regional labor force.[82] Eliminating all public grazing would have had only a slight, temporary impact, perhaps a week of lost economic growth in the eleven western states.[83] In fact, the number of ranches with public land leases was rapidly declining, as more and more ranchers conceded the truth of historian Paul F. Starrs's observation that ranching was not a business but "an elaborate form of conspicuous consumption."[84] Those with the smallest herds gave up the struggle and found other employment. For the survivors, the preservation of rural lifestyles and open spaces increasingly became the justification for BLM leases, other forms of government assistance, and, in a growing number of cases, the organizational and managerial reforms associated with conservation biology. Without leased public lands, proponents argued, many ranches would cease to be economically viable; the land would be sold and subdivided into 50- to 100-acre "ranchettes" or into five- to ten-acre building lots. Forget about preserving endangered species or using fire to restore the land. "No matter how bad you think cows are, condos are worse," wrote critic George Wuerthner.[85]

The test (since ranchers retained sufficient political power to preserve the lease system) was whether they were actually serious about preserving the natural environment. Would they embrace the idea of a "working wilderness"?[86] There were encouraging examples, such as the Theodore Roosevelt Memorial Ranch in northern Montana. Created by the Boone and Crockett Club in 1986, the 10,000-acre ranch was devoted to the idea that cattle and wildlife, including wolves and grizzlies, could coexist. It was, however, a "demonstration" ranch that reflected the convictions of its well-heeled backers that "public lands alone could not sustain the full array of large mammals in the West."[87] Another notable example was the Sun Ranch, adjacent to Yellowstone's northern range, which provided habitat for both cattle and elk. Cattle grazed sections of the ranch during the summer and then were moved in time to allow new growth before the elk arrived for the winter.[88] Ted Turner's Flying D Ranch, the largest in the Greater Yellowstone Ecosystem, was home to a variety of wildlife, including the area's largest wolf pack.[89] However, the preeminent example of a private effort to address the grazing problem was the Malpai Borderlands Group and the 300,00-acre Gray Ranch in southwestern New Mexico, strategically located east of the Chiricahua Mountains in one of the most biologically diverse areas of North America.

Through the 1980s it appeared that the Gray Ranch would eventually become a national wildlife refuge. It was high on the Fish and Wildlife Service's list of possible acquisitions until 1981, when another large ranch became available;

it was acquired and rechristened the Buenos Aires National Wildlife Refuge in order to preserve the habitat of the endangered masked bobwhite and other grassland species. With the federal government temporarily preoccupied, the likelihood that the Gray Ranch would be sold and probably divided prompted the Nature Conservancy to intervene, purchasing it in 1990, in the largest and most expensive purchase in TNC history. Nature Conservancy officials planned to hold it only until the Fish and Wildlife Service was able to buy it, but vociferous local opposition to yet another government land purchase and the refusal of Interior secretary Lujan to authorize the acquisition led TNC to change its plan and look for an acceptable private buyer. Turner was a possibility; when he backed out, TNC turned to another wealthy local rancher, Drummond Hadley. Hadley had a good record of land stewardship and was working with his neighbors in what would soon emerge as the Malpai Borderlands Group. After extended negotiations TNC sold the ranch to Hadley's family foundation, together with a conservation easement that prevented subdivision and preserved a role for TNC in the ranch's operation. By the mid-1990s, Hadley and his neighbors owned or leased lands totaling 800,000 acres and were embracing many of the scientists' proposed reforms.[90]

A lightning-caused fire on Forest Service land in July 1991 was the initial stimulus to organization. Over the objections of the local lease holders, Forest Service firefighters put out the fire before it had any effect on the parched landscape. In response the unhappy and frustrated ranchers began to meet, inviting others in the area who shared their concerns. In 1992 they drew up a "Malpai Agenda for Grazing" (named after the ranch where the fire had started), which spelled out their conservation agenda. In 1993 they persuaded Forest Service and state officials to reverse their usual practice and introduce prescribed burns. Two large fires in the following years helped to restore more than 15,000 acres of grazing land. A plan for a third, even larger fire led to an extended dispute with Fish and Wildlife Service biologists, who were concerned that a fire of that magnitude would wipe out the endangered ridge-nosed rattlesnake. An agreement was finally concluded in 2003 allowing the ranchers to proceed; the fire burned 46,000 acres, the largest prescribed burn to date.[91]

Working in concert, the Malpai Group gradually undertook other cooperative projects. They agreed to protect endangered species, such as the leopard frog and the jaguar, and sought to anticipate the impact of periodic droughts with a "grass bank." Under this plan, which Hadley originally introduced in 1992, participating ranchers would move their herds to parts of the Gray Ranch for several years while their lands revived. In exchange they had to agree to easements limiting development of their properties. Borderlands Group members also worked closely with the Forest Service, Fish and Wildlife Service, and state agencies on collaborative programs to stop erosion.[92]

Granted the importance and distinctiveness of the Gray Ranch and a hand-ful of others, what about the remainder? In the 1990s the number of collab-orative plans multiplied, spurred by economic pressures and the accelerat-ing growth of urban and suburban populations in much of the West. There were common ingredients: rancher anxieties, the presence of sympathetic federal and state officials, and the willingness of the Nature Conservancy and local land trusts to supply organizational expertise and useful contacts when fund-raising was required. A prime example was the Altar Valley Conservation Alliance in southern Arizona, founded in 1995. For many years hostilities between ranchers, officials of Tucson and the surrounding county, and environmentalists, led by the Center for Biological Diversity, had pre-vented any thought of collaborative activity; a participant recalls "polariza-tion, paranoia and interest group politics."[93] The Conservation Alliance was at first an act of faith. In the late 1990s, however, TNC began to sponsor activities aimed at resolving some of the conflicts, and relations between the antagonistic groups gradually improved. Collaborative projects increased in the following years; by 2010 the managers of the nearby Buenos Aires Refuge and Conservation Alliance members, former antagonists, were working har-moniously on several major gully restoration projects.[94]

But basic differences remained. Many environmentalists continued to call for a permanent cessation of public land leasing. At the other extreme were disciples of Allan Savory, a South African rangeland theorist and consultant who insisted that grazing—trampling the land and eating the plants—was essential to good land management.[95] Somewhere in the middle were propo-nents of "grazing optimization," who were highly critical of the prevailing practice of leaving cattle to cluster in riparian areas, damaging stream banks and polluting the water. Systematically moving herds, they argued, would eliminate many of the ill effects of overgrazing.[96] Critics were unpersuaded, emphasizing the variability of conditions.[97]

In any case there was no way to compel any of these changes, apart from the self-interest of the owner or leaseholder. With profits low and prospects for recovery problematic, many ranchers did not have the capital, interest, or skill to introduce changes that would pay financial and ecological dividends only in the relatively remote future. Systematically moving cattle from pasture to pasture, for example, required more labor and managerial perspective than many hard-pressed ranchers possessed. And there remained the question of whether, even under the best of conditions, restoration was possible in many regions. After reviewing the literature, Noss and Cooperrider were not optimistic: "In light of the many detrimental effects of livestock and the difficult challenge of grazing an area sustainably, livestock will need to be removed from many areas where they are now grazed. . . . A policy such as this may require removal of livestock from over 50 percent of the West."[98] Was ranching compatible with the preservation of native flora and fauna, particularly in an era of persistent drought? This question would continue to inspire, and haunt, land conservation in the West.

BIODIVERSITY PLANNING

By the 1990s the importance of biodiversity and the essentials of restoration—including cores, connectivity, and carnivores—were widely acknowledged in the scientific and conservation communities and among a handful of public lands managers. But how were these ideas to be transferred from the drawing boards of scientists to the real world of forests, farms, and wetlands? The experiences of Yellowstone and the ranchers underlined the potential, as well as the many obstacles that lay ahead. The job of selling the new ideas to public lands managers, who had careers based on different and often conflicting ideas, would be a formidable undertaking in itself; enlisting private property owners, many of whom viewed their holdings as resources to be exploited, was an infinitely greater undertaking. Many environmentalists concluded that the best way to overcome these barriers was to think big, to avoid the parochial conflicts that had beset the Yellowstone effort and made progressive ranching an impossibly idealistic notion to many. If people could see what was at stake and how restoration would ultimately benefit them as well as nature, rapid advances might be possible.

From this perception emerged an unusual alliance of activist scientists and environmentalists. Several of the founders of Earth First!, notably Foreman and Howie Wolke, insisted that neither RARE II nor the wilderness legislation that followed was adequate and began their own study of roadless areas.[99] Their efforts, which reflected personal familiarity with many of the areas, attracted attention and inspired other collaborative activities. Reed Noss contributed an article to *Earth First! Journal* in 1983, and Foreman, as editor, offered the first of Michael Soulé's edited volumes for sale through the *Journal*. In 1985 Noss published a detailed proposal for interconnected conservation areas in Florida in both an academic journal and in *Earth First! Journal*. It suggested that the benefits associated with wilderness were also possible in highly developed areas, given careful planning. No region should be automatically written off. A flurry of planning efforts followed over the next decade.

By 1990 the ties between the Earth First! activists and biologists were close enough to warrant a more formal collaborative approach. At the suggestion of Soulé, and with financing from Douglas Tompkins, a wealthy supporter, they met for several days in San Francisco in late 1991 and inaugurated the Wildlands Project, a systematic effort to design and promote a "wildlands network."[100] Existing protected areas were "too small, too isolated," and included "too few types of ecosystems to perpetuate the biodiversity of the continent." Building on existing "cores," the Wildlands Project sought to connect them to multiple-use areas, state and local parks, and other conservation lands to create corridors for wildlife movement.[101] They had no illusions that such a network could be assembled quickly. Soulé urged "a long-term vision, a 22nd century vision."[102] *Wild Earth*, the Wildlands Project's journal, devoted an issue to proposals for the Adirondacks, Appalachians, Rockies, and others. Noss himself prepared detailed plans for the Oregon coast and the Greater Yellowstone region. Foreman helped draw up a Sky Islands Wildlands Network (southern Arizona and northern Mexico) and a New Mexico Highlands network. Other groups prepared a variety of regional plans.

The regional plans in turn led to more expansive proposals. By the turn of the century there were four proposed North American corridors, two based on the Appalachians and the Pacific coastal range; a "Spine of the Continent Wildway," which extended from Alaska to Central America; and a "Boreal

Wildway," which ran east and west across northern Canada.[103] The most important and promising of these was the "Spine of the Continent" plan, prepared by the Alliance for the Northern Rockies. Drawn up in the early 1990s and incorporated in a congressional bill called the Northern Rockies Ecosystem Protection Act, it seemed to demonstrate the potential of conservation biology for real-world political activity, and it inspired an influential offshoot, the Yellowstone to Yukon initiative (Y2Y), in 1993. The product of collaboration between the Wildlands Project and the Canadian Parks and Wilderness Society and its influential leader, Harvey Locke, Y2Y quickly "seeped out of conservation circles into the popular culture."[104] It enlisted hundreds of local cooperating groups and influenced the Canadian government in planning additional parks and refuges in the northern Rockies and in less ambitious ways, such as building overpasses in Banff National Park to facilitate wildlife movements.[105]

Y2Y, the Wildlands Project, and the other scientifically informed conservation projects of the late 1980s and early 1990s soon encountered the same obstacles that traditionally limited and frustrated environmental initiatives. Interest-group opposition, timid politicians, and the difficulty of sustaining public attention meant that what had seemed so obvious in theory was much more difficult to achieve in practice. Although the authors of the connectivity plans readily acknowledged that their proposals were long-term guides and did not depend on the success of any single legislative campaign or policy change, they must have been disappointed at the meager results of their work. They had successfully recast the intellectual foundations of conservation activism, but would have to depend on the mainstream environmental movement, laboring over a much longer period, to translate their ideas into meaningful changes in perception and policy.

൭

The emergence of conservation biology marked the culmination of a process that began decades before and at first had little impact on the practice of conservation. By the late 1980s, however, it was no longer creditable to argue that the earth would heal itself (except over periods so long that they had no meaning for human society) or that renewable resources could be taken for granted. The celebrated achievements of the environmental movement also looked less impressive. Amid their many successes activists and politicians had inadvertently answered the question posed by SLOSS; they had opted for a multitude of small, attractive, frequently inspiring but ecologically compromised parks and refuges. Even more serious challenges were directed against the prevailing managerial orthodoxy, including much of what had been acceptable to conservationists in the first half of the twentieth century. Universal fire suppression had been a monumental mistake; dam building had huge unanticipated environmental costs; predator controls, together with clear-cutting and overfishing, wreaked havoc on nature; invasive species were serious threats; and the endangered species program was too little and often too late. Remedial activities invariably led to clashes with defenders of the status quo and were, in any case, hugely expensive.

On the assumption that defining a problem was the first step toward a solution, environmental activists of the late twentieth century now had a clear, sobering assessment of the challenges that lay ahead. But it was also obvious that scientists had comparatively little influence in the rough-and-tumble world of public policy, and even that tended to be sporadic, dependent on the issues of the moment. The biodiversity plans of that era assumed that informed, rational planning would lead to constructive action. In fact, highly organized political campaigns, comparable to the most ambitious efforts of the 1960s and 1970s, would be necessary to advance virtually every feature of the new conservation agenda.

NOTES

1. Edward O. Wilson, *The Diversity of Life* (Cambridge, MA: Harvard University Press, 1992), 282.

2. Georgina M. Mace et al., "Assessment and Management of Species at Risk," in *Conservation Biology: Research Priorities for the Next Decade*, ed. Michael E. Soulé and Gordon H. Orians (Washington, DC: Island Press, 2001), 13; David S. Wilcove, *The Condor's Shadow: The Loss and Recovery of Wildlife in America* (New York: W. H. Freeman and Co., 1999), 8.

3. Christina Eisenberg, *The Wolf's Tooth: Keystone Predators, Trophic Cascades, and Biodiversity* (Washington, DC: Island Press, 2010) 152.

4. Anthony D. Barnosky et al., "Has the Earth's Sixth Mass Extinction Already Arrived?" *Nature* 471, no. 7336 (March 3, 2011): 51–57.

5. Roderick Frazier Nash, *The Rights of Nature: A History of Environmental Ethics* (Madison: University of Wisconsin Press, 1989), 259.

6. James D. Williams and Ronald M. Nowak, "Vanishing Species in Our Own Backyard: Extinct Fish and Wildlife of the United States and Canada," in *The Last Extinction*, 2nd ed., ed. Les Kaufman and Kenneth Mallory (Cambridge, MA: MIT Press, 1993), 140.

7. Edward O. Wilson, "Afterword," in *Silent Spring*, by Rachel Carson (Boston: Houghton Mifflin, 2002), 362.

8. Mark V. Barrow, *Nature's Ghosts: Confronting Extinction from the Age of Jefferson to the Age of Ecology* (Chicago: University of Chicago Press, 2009), 232–33.

9. Donald Worster, *The Wealth of Nature: Environmental History and the Ecological Imagination* (New York: Oxford University Press, 1993), 164–66; Peggy L. Fielder, Peter S. White, and Robert A. Leidy, "The Paradigm Shift in Ecology and Its Implications for Conservation," in *The Ecological Basis of Conservation: Heterogeneity, Ecosystems, and Biodiversity*, ed. S.T.A. Pickett et al., (New York: Chapman and Hall, 1997), 84. Also see Sharon E. Kingsland, *The Evolution of American Ecology, 1890–2000* (Baltimore: Johns Hopkins University Press, 2005).

10. Edward Rothstein, "Preserving a Wilderness Where the Lenape Trod," *New York Times*, November 4, 2011; David Ehrenfeld, "Life in the Next Millennium: Who Will Be Left in Earth's Community?" in *Last Extinction*, ed. Kaufman and Mallory, 201.

11. Reed F. Noss and Allen Y. Cooperrider, *Saving Nature's Legacy: Protecting and Restoring Biodiversity* (Washington, DC: Island Press, 1994), 189–90.

12. William DeBuys, *A Great Aridness: Climate Change and the Future of the American Southwest* (New York: Oxford University Press, 2011), 98; Carl Zimmer, "Ecosystems on the Brink," *Scientific American* 307, no. 4 (October 2012): 60–65.

13. Lance H. Gunderson and Craig R. Allen, "Introduction," in *Foundations of Ecological Resilience*, ed. Lance H. Gunderson, Craig R. Allen, and C. S. Holling (Washington, DC: Island Press, 2010), xvii.

14. Nels E. Barrett and Juliana P. Barrett, "Reserve Design and the New Conservation Theory," in *Ecological Basis of Conservation*, ed. Pickett et al., 238.

15. Michael E. Soulé and John Terborgh, eds., *Continental Conservation: Scientific Foundations of Regional Reserve Networks* (Washington, DC: Island Press, 1999), 117.

16. Robert W. Adler, *Restoring Colorado River Ecosystems: A Troubled Sense of Immensity* (Washington, DC: Island Press, 2007), 11.

17. David N. Cole, Eric S. Higgs and Peter S. White, "Historical Fidelity: Maintaining Legacy and Connection to Heritage," in *Beyond Naturalness: Rethinking Park and Wilderness Stewardship*, ed. David N. Cole and Laurie Yung (Washington, DC: Island Press, 2010), 133.

18. Eisenberg, *Wolf's Tooth*, 166.

19. Jeremy B.C. Jackson, "Ecological Extinction and Evolution in the Brave New Ocean," *Proceedings of the National Academy of Sciences of the United States of America* 105, suppl. 1 (2008): 11458–65.

20. Edward O. Wilson, "Island Biogeography in the 1960's: Theory and Experiment," in *The Theory of Island Biogeography Revisited*, ed. Jonathan B. Losos and Robert E. Rickles (Princeton: Princeton University Press, 2010), 5.

21. David Quammen, *The Song of the Dodo: Island Biogeography in an Age of Extinctions* (New York: Scribner, 1996), 444.

22. Eisenberg, *Wolf's Tooth*, 152; Jodi A. Hilty, William Z. Lidicker Jr., and Adina M. Merenlender, *Corridor Ecology: The Science and Practice of Linking Landscapes for Biodiversity Conservation* (Washington, DC: Island Press, 2006), 54–55.

23. Timothy J. Farnham, *Saving Nature's Legacy: Origins of the Idea of Biological Diversity* (New Haven: Yale University Press, 2007), 16–18, 22, 275–76; Charles C. Chester, *Conservation across Borders: Biodiversity in an Interdependent World* (Washington, DC: Island Press, 2006), 6; Barrow, *Nature's Ghosts*, 353; Eisenberg, *Wolf's Tooth*, 147.

24. Farnham, *Saving Nature's Legacy*, 6–9; Ian J. Harrison, Melina Flaverty, and Eleanor J. Sterling, "What Is Biodiversity?" in *Life on Earth: An Encyclopedia of Biodiversity, Ecology, and Evolution*, vol. 1, ed. Niles Eldridge (Santa Barbara: ABC Clio, 2002), 6–19.

25. William D. Newmark, "Extinction of Mammal Populations in Western North American National Parks," *Conservation Biology* 9, no. 3 (June 1995): 518–19; R. Edward Grumbine, *Ghost Bears: Exploring the Biodiversity Crisis* (Washington, DC: Island Press, 1992), 42–43.

26. Daniel Simberloff et al., "Movement Corridors: Conservation Bargains or Poor Investments?" *Conservation Biology* 6, no. 4 (1992): 493–504.

27. Robert S. Steneck," An Ecological Context for the Role of Large Carnivorous Animals in Conserving Biodiversity," in *Large Carnivores and the Conservation of Biodiversity*, ed. Justina C. Ray et al. (Washington, DC: Island Press, 2005), 13.

28. Soulé and Terborgh, *Continental Conservation*, 54.

29. See the essays in Ray et al., *Large Carnivores*.

30. Caroline Fraser, *Rewilding the World: Dispatches from the Conservation Revolution* (New York: Metropolitan Books, 2009).

31. Michael E. Soulé and Bruce A. Wilcox, "Conservation Biology: Its Scope and Its Challenge," in *Conservation Biology: An Evolutionary-Ecological Perspective*, ed. Soulé and Wilcox (Sunderland, MA: Sinauer Associates, 1980), 8.

32. Quammen, *Song of the Dodo*, 529–30.

33. Reed R. Noss and Allen Y. Cooperrider, *Saving Nature's Legacy: Protecting and Restoring Biodiversity* (Washington, DC: Island Press, 1994), 86.

34. Dave Foreman, *Rewilding North America: A Vision for Conservation in the 21st Century* (Washington, DC: Island Press 2004), 4–5, 114.

35. Noss and Cooperrider, *Saving Nature's Legacy*, 89.

36. John Kricher, *The Balance of Nature: Ecology's Enduring Myth* (Princeton: Princeton University Press, 2009), 192.

37. Michael McCloskey, *In the Thick of It: My Life in the Sierra Club* (Washington, DC: Island Press, 2005), 258.

38. Reed F. Noss, "Biodiversity, Ecological Integrity, and Wilderness," *International Journal of Wilderness* 2 (August 1996): 5–8.

39. Gary E. Davis and William L. Halvorson, "Long-Term Research in National Parks: From Beliefs to Knowledge," in *Science and Ecosystem Management in the National Parks*, ed. Halvorson and Davis (Tucson: University of Arizona Press, 1996), 7.

40. Jessica Brown, Nora Mitchell, and Michael Beresford, "Protected Landscapes: A Conservation Approach That Links Nature, Culture, and Community," in *The Protected Landscape Approach: Linking Nature, Culture, and Community* ed. Brown, Mitchell, and Beresford, (Gland, Switzerland: IUCN—The World Conservation Union, 2005), 7.

41. Yellowstone National Park, *Yellowstone's Northern Range: Complexity & Change in a Wildland Ecosystem* (Mammoth Hot Springs: Yellowstone National Park, 1997), 11.

42. Ibid., 10–11.

43. Etienne Benson, *Wired Wilderness: Technologies of Tracking and the Making of Modern Wildlife* (Baltimore: Johns Hopkins University Press, 2010), 54–59; Paul Schullery, *Searching for Yellowstone: Ecology and Wonder in the Last Wilderness* (Boston: Houghton Mifflin, 1997), 196.

44. James A. Pritchard, *Preserving Yellowstone's Natural Conditions: Science and the Perception of Nature* (Lincoln: University of Nebraska Press, 1999), 244.

45. John J. Craighead, Jay S. Sumer, and John A. Mitchell, *The Grizzly Bears of Yellowstone: Their Ecology in the Yellowstone Ecosystem, 1959–1992* (Washington, DC: Island Press, 1995); Benson, *Wired Wilderness*, 68–69; Michael J. Yochim, *Protecting Yellowstone: Science and the Politics of National Park Management* (Albuquerque: University of New, Mexico Press, 2013), 37–42.

46. Tony Prato and Dan Fagre, *National Parks and Protected Areas: Approaches for Balancing Social, Economic, and Ecological Values* (Ames, IA: Blackwell Publishing, 2005), 328.

47. Pritchard, *Preserving Yellowstone's Natural Conditions*, 254–55, 326.

48. Alston Chase, *Playing God in Yellowstone: The Destruction of America's First National Park* (New York: Harcourt Brace Jovanovich, 1987).

49. Samuel P. Hays, *War in the Woods: The Rise of Ecological Forestry in America* (Pittsburgh: University of Pittsburgh Press, 2007), 57.

50. Jim Robbins, *Last Refuge: The Environmental Showdown in Yellowstone and the American West* (New York: William Morrow & Co., 1993), 198–99.

51. Yellowstone National Park, *Yellowstone's Northern Range*, 13; Frederick H. Wagner, *Yellowstone's Destabilized Ecosystem: Elk Effects, Science, and the Policy Conflict* (New York: Oxford University Press, 2006); Pritchard, *Preserving Yellowstone's Natural Conditions*, 272–75.

52. Pritchard, *Preserving Yellowstone's Natural Conditions*, 274–75.

53. Hal K. Rothman, *Blazing Heritage: A History of Wildland Fire in the National Parks* (New York: Oxford University Press, 2007), 164.

54. Dennis H. Knight, "The Yellowstone Fire Controversy," in *The Greater Yellowstone Ecosystem: Refining America's Wilderness Heritage*, ed. Robert B. Keiter and Mark S. Boyce (New Haven: Yale University Press, 1991), 88–91; John D. Varley and Paul Schullery, "Reality and Opportunity in the Yellowstone Fires of 1988," in *Greater Yellowstone Ecosystem*, ed. Keiter and Boyce, 111–14; Stephen J. Pyne, *Between Two Fires: A Fire History of Contemporary America* (Tucson: University of Arizona Press, 2015), 234–35.

55. Yochim, *Protecting Yellowstone*, 58–77.

56. David S. Wilcove, *No Way Home: The Decline of the World's Great Animal Migrations* (Washington, DC: Island Press, 2008), 120–21.

57. Mary Ann Franke, *To Save the Wild Bison: Life on the Edge of Yellowstone* (Norman: University of Oklahoma Press, 2005), 135.

58. Yochim, *Protecting Yellowstone*, 152–53; Franke, *To Save the Wild Bison*, 172; E. Tom Thorne, Mary Meagher, and Robert Hillman, "Brucellosis in Free-Ranging Bison: Three Perspectives," in *Greater Yellowstone Ecosystem*, ed. Keiter and Boyce, 282.

59. Yochim, *Protecting Yellowstone*, 152–63. Also Molly Loomis, "Bison and Boundaries," *Sierra*, November/December 2013, 28–31, 70; "The Latest," *High Country News* 48 (January 28, 2016): 9

60. Hank Fischer, *Wolf Wars: The Remarkable Inside Story of the Restoration of Wolves to Yellowstone* (Helena, MT: Falcon Press, 1995), 103–8.

61. Thomas McNamee, *The Return of the Wolf to Yellowstone* (New York: Henry Holt & Co., 1997), 189–90.

62. Ibid., 37–51; Fischer, *Wolf Wars*, 146–53.

63. Robert B. Keiter, *Keeping Faith with Nature: Ecosystems, Democracy, and America's Public Lands* (New Haven: Yale University Press, 2003), 134–35; Yochim, *Protecting Yellowstone*, 128.

64. Bruce H. Campbell, Bob Altman, Edward E. Bangs, Doug W. Smith, Blair Csuti, David W. Hays, Frank Slavens, Kate Slavens, Cheryl Schultz, and Robert W.

Butler, "Restoring Wildlife Populations," in *Restoring the Pacific Northwest: The Art and Science of Ecological Restoration in Cascadia*, ed. Dean Apostol and Marcia Sinclair (Washington, DC: Island Press, 2006), 362–63.

65. Elliott D. Woods, "Wolflandia," *Outside*, February 2015, 74; William R. Lowry, *Repairing Paradise: The Restoration of Nature in America's National Parks* (Washington, DC: Brookings Institution Press, 2009), 47, 54–56; Justin Farrell, *The Battle for Yellowstone: Morality and the Sacred Roots of Environmental Conflict* (Princeton: Princeton University Press, 2015), 194.

66. Michael J. Robinson, *Predatory Bureaucracy: The Extermination of Wolves and the Transformation of the West* (Boulder: University Press of Colorado, 2005), 351–61; Christina Eisenberg, *The Carnivore Way: Coexisting with and Conserving North America's Predators* (Washington, DC: Island Press, 2014), 127–29.

67. McNamee, *The Return of the Wolf*, 219.

68. Robert B. Keiter and Mark S. Boyce, "Greater Yellowstone's Future: Ecosystem Management in a Wilderness Environment," in *Greater Yellowstone Ecosystem*, ed. Keiter and Boyce, 308.

69. Keiter, *Keeping the Faith*, 13.

70. Susan G. Clark, *Ensuring Greater Yellowstone's Future: Choices for Leaders and Citizens* (New Haven: Yale University Press, 2008), 73.

71. Grumbine, *Ghost Bears*, 165.

72. Ibid., 226.

73. David Helvarg, *The War against the Greens: The "Wise-Use" Movement, the New Right, and Anti-Environmental Violence* (San Francisco: Sierra Club Books, 1994), 79–82; Robbins, *Last Refuge*, 263–65.

74. Clark, *Ensuring Greater Yellowstone's Future*, 74.

75. Karl Hess Jr., *Rocky Times in Rocky Mountain National Park: An Unnatural History* (Boulder: University Press of Colorado, 1993), 10.

76. David Pettibone, "Rocky Mountain National Park: Wilderness after 35 Years," *International Journal of Wilderness* 19 (April 2013): 12; Jerry J. Frank, *Making Rocky Mountain National Park: The Environmental History of an American Treasure* (Lawrence: University Press of Kansas, 2013), 113, 137–42.

77. John A. Shivik, *The Predator Paradox: Ending the War with Wolves, Bears, Cougars, and Coyotes* (Boston: Beacon Press, 2014), 9–10.

78. Debra L. Donahue, *The Western Range Revisited: Removing Livestock from Public Lands to Conserve Native Biodiversity* (Norman: University of Oklahoma Press, 1999), 4.

79. Reed Noss and Allen Y. Cooperrider, *Saving Nature's Legacy: Protecting and Restoring Biodiversity* (Washington, DC: Island Press, 1994), 221.

80. Craig W. Allin, "Wilderness Policy," in *Western Public Lands and Environmental Politics*, ed. Charles Davis (Boulder: Westview, 2001), 197, 201.

81. Donahue, *Western Range Revisited*, 81–82.

82. Ibid., 252; Howard G. Wilshire, Jane E. Nielson, Richard W. Hazlett, *The American West at Risk: Science, Myths, and Politics of Land Abuse and Recovery* (New York: Oxford University Press 2008), 79.

83. Thomas Michael Power, *Lost Landscapes and Failed Economies: The Search for a Value of Place* (Washington, DC: Island Press, 1996), 186.

84. Paul F. Starrs, *Let the Cowboy Ride: Cattle Ranching in the American West* (Baltimore: Johns Hopkins University Press, 1998), 73.

85. Donahue, *Western Range Revisited*, 274.

86. Nathan F. Sayre, *Working Wilderness: The Malpai Borderlands Group and the Future of the Western Range* (Tucson: Rio Nuevo Publishers, 2005).

87. Eisenberg, *Wolf's Tooth*, 176, 178.

88. Courtney White, *Resolution on the Range: The Rise of a New Ranch in the American West* (Washington, DC: Island Press, 2009), 55–56.

89. Tony Hiss, "The Wildest Idea on Earth," *Smithsonian* 45 (September 2015): 76–77.

90. Dan Dagget, *Beyond the Rangeland Conflict: Toward a West That Works* (Flagstaff: Good Stewards Project, 1998), 14–23; Sayre, *Working Wilderness;* Kelly Cash, "Malpai Borderlands: The Search for Common Ground," in *Across the Great Divide: Explorations in Collaborative Conservation and the American West*, ed. Philip Brick, Donald Snow, and Sarah Van de Wetering (Washington, DC: Island Press, 2001), 114–21.

91. For another TNC grassbank, see Scott McMillion, "Ranching Rebooted," *Nature Conservancy Magazine*, November–December 2013, 35–36, 42.

92. Sayre, *Working Wilderness;* Scott McMillion, "New Life in the Badlands," *Nature Conservancy Magazine*, October–November 2015, 32–43.

93. Thomas E. Sheridan, Nathan F. Sayre, and David Seibert, "Beyond 'Stakeholders' and the Zero-Sum Game: Toward Community-Based Collaborative Conservation in the American West" in *Stitching the West Back Together: Conservation of Working Landscapes*, ed. Susan Charnley, Thomas E. Sheridan, and Gary P. Nabhan (Chicago: University of Chicago Press, 2014), 59.

94. Ibid., 59–60.

95. Donahue, *Western Range Revisited*, 141–42; Allan Savory, "Re-Creating the West . . . One Decision at a Time," in *Ranching West of the 100th Meridian: Culture, Ecology, and Economics*, ed. Richard L. Knight, Wendell C. Gilbert, and Ed Marston (Washington, DC: Island Press, 2002), 158–63.

96. Dagget, *Beyond the Rangeland Conflict*, 33–39.

97. Donahue, *Western Range Revisited*, 140–41.

98. Noss and Cooperrider, *Saving Nature's Legacy*, 25.

99. Dave Foreman and Howie Wolke, *The Big Outside: A Descriptive Inventory of the Big Wilderness Areas of the United States*, rev. ed. (New York: Harmony Books, 1992).

100. Dave Foreman, *Rewilding North America: A Vision for Conservation in the 21st Century* (Washington, DC: Island Press, 2004), 163–64.

101. Dave Foreman et al.," The Wildlands Project Mission Statement," *Wild Earth*, Special Issue (1992): 3.

102. Michael Soulé, "A Vision for the Meantime," *Wild Earth*, Special Issue: The Wildlands Project (1992): 7.

103. Eisenberg, *Wolf's Tooth*, 191–92.

104. Fraser, *Rewilding the World*, 34.

105. Chester, *Conservation across Borders*, 137–216.

5

Forests and Owls

The new emphasis on biodiversity may have been applauded in scientific and environmental circles by the late 1980s, but it raised troubling questions and concerns in other quarters. The federal and state agencies devoted to natural resource management typically reacted with curiosity, skepticism, and a wariness of fundamental changes. Commodity producers were aggressively hostile to ideas that threatened familiar business practices. Progressive ranchers were a tiny minority; most of their neighbors opposed any changes in their operations or in the government policies they had come to rely on. Y2Y and other regional biodiversity plans inspired heated opposition as well as enthusiastic support. At Yellowstone a quarter century passed between the public uproar over the culling of elk and the introduction of wolves.

These examples help to explain the intensity of the conflict that emerged in the Pacific Northwest in the late 1980s and became a preview of the political confrontations that would mark the following years. The timber industry had escaped largely unscathed from the environmental turmoil of the 1970s. Despite the growth of the Wilderness Preservation System, logging, usually

DOI: 10.7330/9781607325703.c005

clear-cutting, had rapidly increased. The Reagan and Bush administrations abandoned any pretense of sustainability, raising the total timber harvest to record levels and precipitating the crisis of the late 1980s. Environmentalists counterattacked, demonstrating the political value of the 1973 Endangered Species Act. A campaign to protect an obscure bird quickly evolved into a landmark battle to preserve diversity in western forests and ultimately to change Forest Service and BLM policies that many local residents and officials considered essential and sacrosanct. A 1989 timber rider sponsored by Senator Mark Hatfield was a symbolic turning point, the demarcation line between the post–World War II history of the national forests and the very different era that lay ahead.

FORESTRY AND WILDLIFE

For most of the twentieth century there had been no apparent conflict between the Forest Service's commitment to timber and its simultaneous obligation, under the multiple-use formula, to preserve wildlife. Just as trees were thought of as timber, wildlife was assumed to be game, and especially the ungulates that flourished in the "edge" areas that logging created. That happy association came under attack in the 1970s as environmentalists challenged the status quo. Two laws, classic expressions of hostility to prevailing policies, struck at the simplistic assumptions of earlier years. The first was the Endangered Species Act of 1973. The second was the National Forest Management Act of 1976, which, among other things, made the preservation of species "diversity" a feature of the multiple-use formula.

The Endangered Species Act (ESA) was "one of the last pieces of symbolic environmental legislation passed to satisfy a powerful environmental lobby"[1] Yet it was one thing to decree that animals and plants should be preserved, and something quite different to save them as they approached extinction. The first obstacle was the administrative authority. The Fish and Wildlife Service remained a backwater in the Interior Department and many FWS employees, like many state wildlife officials, were "game" specialists. From the beginning environmentalists complained that the agency provided minimal support for the small endangered species staff. The National Maritime Fisheries Service was even less enthusiastic about enforcing the law. Out of place in the Commerce Department, subject to continued harassment by the commercial fishing industry, deprived of adequate resources, it only "reluctantly implemented" the Endangered Species Act.[2] Even Fish and Wildlife Service officials complained that "NMFS just sits on its ass and bitches."[3]

A second, more critical problem was the real-world consequences of listings. There had been little opposition in 1973 because most politicians viewed the ESA as a largely meaningless gesture. That quickly changed as the potentially disruptive impact of species listings became clear. Uncomfortable with their new responsibilities, the agencies tried to accommodate critics. The grizzly bear listing in 1975 permitted the killing of up to twenty-five bears per year in northwestern Montana, a concession to trophy hunters. Congress was no less sensitive. In 1978, when the listing of an obscure fish, the snail darter, jeopardized a nearly completed dam on the Little Tennessee River, it amended the law to allow economic factors to be considered in critical habitat designations and to authorize a "god squad" of government officials with the power to overrule the biologists on economic grounds. (Ironically, in this case, the god squad ruled in favor of the snail darter; a congressional rider ultimately overruled the god squad.) Nevertheless, the lesson was clear: if the costs were too great, Congress would eviscerate or even repeal the law.

The third difficulty was the program's fundamental approach, which received increasing attention as it became apparent that it was having at best a marginal effect on survival rates. The law provided only for the consideration of individual species and then only when they approached extinction. It was a last-ditch, emergency room strategy that did nothing to prevent the emergency from occurring. In the first forty years of the law's application, only 28 of more than 2,000 listed species recovered sufficiently to be delisted. Later studies concluded that most endangered species were "conservation reliant" and would survive only with continuous, often intricate and expensive human assistance.[4] In contrast, conservation biology proposed an affirmative approach, preserving habitats that would accommodate a variety of species in a natural setting.

By 1980 the Endangered Species Act had become a political football, the subject of endless, highly symbolic conflicts between developers and their government allies on the one side and environmental groups on the other. The most contentious disputes involved proposed dams. The 1978 amendments required the designation of critical habitats at the time of listing, which slowed the listing process. The Reagan appointees tried to use this requirement as an excuse to halt it altogether. Environmentalists counter-attacked in 1982 with amendments that permitted delays in the naming of critical habitats and required that listings be based solely on biological considerations. During the following years the grizzly and wolf listings became particularly controversial because of the animals' threats to domestic livestock, but environmentalists successfully resisted efforts to weaken the law; amendments adopted by Congress in 1988 actually strengthened it. Yet, as one student of the endangered species process observed, the conflict "shows no signs of abating."[5]

Until the 1980s, wildlife, including endangered wildlife, were at best a marginal concern in Forest Service Region 6, embracing California, Oregon, and Washington. This was the economic and political heart of the national forest system, an area of stunning physical beauty and the largest, most commercially valuable trees. Whereas most national forests lost money on timber sales, Region 6 was highly profitable, at least on paper. The timber industry greeted even the most modest suggestions for reduced logging with protests and political appeals, a major factor in the Forest Service's reluctance to act on endangered species. During the Reagan years, when political appointees in the Agriculture Department constantly pushed for more cutting, pressures on the national forest managers in the Northwest were particularly severe.

Yet there were also countervailing forces that became more important and visible as timber harvests increased. The environmental movement in the Northwest, centered in Portland, Eugene, Seattle, and other urban areas, became an important political force in Oregon and Washington during the campaigns for the state wilderness acts, and many of the local groups continued to be active afterward. The largest of these, the Oregon Natural Resources Council, increasingly relied on litigation to restrict logging. Earth First! also had an active following in Oregon and Washington. Another important influence was the Sierra Club Legal Defense Fund (SCLDF), which opened an office in Seattle in early 1987. The Seattle lawyers soon launched "one of the most successful legal campaigns in the history of American environmental law."[6] Northwest environmentalists were also buoyed by the release of the 1987 Brundtland Report by the United Nations World Commission on Environment and Development, which argued that forest preserves enhanced local economic activity and resulted in "sustainable development." The report had a marked effect on government policy in western Canada and helped alleviate anxieties in the Pacific Northwest that reduced logging would inevitably sound the death knell for timber-dependent communities.[7]

Finally, the Forest Service was less monolithic than it appeared to critics. Although traditional foresters occupied the top positions, a growing number of biologists and other scientists, hired in response to the NFMA planning process and other environmental regulations, did not necessarily share their perspectives. One notable example of this divergence was the development of "new forestry" by the Forest Service staff at the H. J. Andrews Experimental Forest in west-central Oregon. "New forestry" sought to reconcile logging with the scientists' emphasis on preserving biodiversity. Forest ecologist Jerry Franklin, the leader of the Andrews group, argued that old growth (generally, trees that were at least eighty years old) was not simply old; it was also different and distinctive. Replacing old "decadent" trees with younger, more vigorous ones—a long-standing Forest Service rationale for clear-cutting—had a profound, deleterious effect on the entire ecosystem. "New forestry" called instead for the careful selection of harvest areas to avoid fragmentation and minimize road building, as well as the retention of dead trees, snags, and debris. It sought to mimic the impact of fires and storms.[8] In practice, Franklin, the "guru of old growth," and his allies were calling for greater attention to nontimber values, including biodiversity.[9]

By the late 1980s dissatisfaction with the Forest Service had spread beyond top-level scientists like Franklin. Public opinion surveys found growing hostility to timber cutting and increased interest in wildlife and recreation. A "new resource management paradigm" seemed to be emerging.[10] A tangible expression of this change was the formation of the Association of Forest Service Employees for Environmental Ethics (FSEEE) at a meeting in Tucson in November 1989. The dissidents' first step was to send a scathing critique of the Forest Service to Chief Dale Robertson. They attacked the agency's preoccupation with timber, its relentless demands for timber cutting, and the influence of the Washington bureaucracy. Robertson responded with promises to lessen the emphasis on commodity production and in 1990 named influential biologist Hal Salwasser to head a "New Perspectives" campaign, which promoted environmental sensitivity. Employees who attended Salwasser's presentations were reported to be "cynically optimistic."[11] Academics such as Reed Noss were less kind, dismissing "New Perspectives" as a public relations gesture "to disguise the negative effects of logging and road building in old growth and roadless areas."[12] Salwasser's colleagues had another complaint. "New Perspectives" was "too ethereal and touchy-feely." They preferred a different name, "ecosystem management," which had "substance and heft."[13]

Despite the divisions within the Forest Service, the "New Perspectives" effort, and a growing body of scientific research that emphasized the value of old growth forests, the agency was still accountable to political appointees and congressional representatives who reflected industry concerns and interests. Largely oblivious to the growing army of critics, the timber lobby was as relentless as ever. And regardless of Robertson's rhetoric, the Washington office of the Forest Service was as attentive as ever to demands for more cutting. If there was any doubt, it disappeared in 1991, when John Mumma, regional forester for the Forest Service's Northern Region, proposed to reduce the timber harvest in the northern Rockies. In response to the predictable outcry from Congress, Robertson fired Mumma, sparking a congressional investigation, which highlighted the travails of Mumma and other employees who embraced something similar to "New Perspectives."[14]

THE SPOTTED OWL CONTROVERSY

All of these developments—the tortured endangered species program, the mounting concern about old growth, the conflicted Forest Service, the growing influence of conservation biology, and the role of the timber industry in the Pacific Northwest—came to a head at the end of the decade in a controversy over the fate of the northern spotted owl, a bird that lived only in old-growth forests and faced likely extinction as those forests disappeared. The owl had long been considered an "indicator species," whose welfare was assumed to be indicative of the welfare of other forest creatures. That designation is the best way to understand its role in the controversy. The possible extinction of the owl was an issue, but the larger question was the fate of a host of plants and animals, at least 1,100 species, that lived in and depended on old-growth forests.[15] The Endangered Species Act became a mechanism for holding off the Forest Service and its local allies until an aroused public forced Washington to defend the forests. The danger was that if the campaign to list the owl succeeded, Congress might amend or even repeal the Endangered Species Act in a reprise of the 1978 experience.

Was this the best way to defend old-growth forests and their inhabitants? The owl had no economic value, while other threatened species, notably the salmon that spawned in the Northwest's unsullied forest streams, supported an industry that was a major contributor to the regional economy. Several species of salmon were later listed as endangered and inspired elaborate and costly recovery efforts; in the meantime timber companies were able to cast the dispute as "owls" versus "jobs." "Salmon jobs" versus "timber jobs" might have better captured the complexity of the issue. The biologist Carl Safina has emphasized this distinction: "Hyping the protections . . . for the owl, the companies were able to dodge responsibility for job losses due to mechanization and exports, and pin the blame on environmentalists. Using owls instead of salmon as the flagship species . . . might be the largest single tactical error the conservation community has ever made."[16] Safina probably overstates his case. It is worth noting that the commercial fishing industry in the Great Lakes was largely obliterated in the 1950s and 1960s at great social and economic cost, but without extended controversy, and that belated efforts to save the Pacific salmon resulted in many of the same divisions and arguments that marked the spotted owl controversy.[17]

The spotted owl had been an issue for more than a decade before the environmental community became committed to its survival. In the early 1970s an Oregon State graduate student, Eric Forsman, had written a thesis on the owl, establishing its link to old-growth forests. In 1973 the Oregon State Game Commission created an interagency committee, including representatives of the Forest Service, Fish and Wildlife Service, and BLM, to establish guidelines for managing endangered species; the spotted owl topped its list of concerns. The scientists continued to emphasize the seriousness of the problem, but their warnings had no effect. Foreman recalled that "the Forest Service and BLM attitude from the beginning has been stall."[18] Federal officials tried to finesse the issue by proposing small owl reserves, insisting that all decisions were temporary, making enough concessions to prevent the owl's listing as an endangered species, and pretending that their planned timber harvests were unrelated to the owl's fate.[19] They may have prevented the owl from being declared a threatened or endangered species, but they still faced a major legal hurtle, the diversity requirement of the NFMA. That was sufficient to keep the issue alive through the 1980s.

The shortcomings of the Forest Service approach became apparent in 1984, when the agency published a forest plan for the Pacific Northwest, and in 1986, when it added an environment impact statement (EIS) devoted to owl habitat. Both documents brought protests and appeals from environmental groups; the draft EIS drew more than 40,000 responses, nearly all of which attacked the plan. Two years later the agency issued its final version, largely unchanged. Environmentalists appealed to the chief of the Forest Service, emphasizing the inadequacy of the owl reserves. The timber companies also appealed. Chief Robertson rejected the appeals but promised larger reserves and an interagency committee to propose additional measures. The environmental organizations then sued the agency for failure to comply with the diversity requirements of the NFMA. In March 1989 federal district judge William Dwyer agreed and issued an injunction stopping national forest timber sales in western Oregon and Washington. A shock to the Forest Service and the industry, the Dwyer injunction was a turning point in the debate over old growth.

The failure of the Forest Service to adopt a satisfactory forest plan also raised the possibility of an endangered species listing. The environmental community was divided on the wisdom of such a request because of the likely political backlash. However, in late 1986 a small Boston-based group submitted a petition to list the spotted owl, ultimately forcing the issue. Recognizing that a decision was now inevitable, the Sierra Club Legal Defense Fund sought to strengthen the case for a listing by submitting its own petition on behalf of twenty-nine environmental groups. Fish and Wildlife Service experts reviewed the petitions, consulted several biologists, and concluded that the owl should be listed. The agency's director, a political appointee, turned down the recommendation and tried to suppress the scientists' data.[20] The Government Accounting Office later concluded that he had "substantially changed the body of scientific evidence . . . after it had been reviewed and adjusted by outside experts."[21] The SCLDF appealed and helped to mobilize government scientists. By 1988 Fish and Wildlife Service biologists had joined the revolt against the agency's leaders.[22] In November a federal judge ordered a new evaluation. The FWS reversed itself and agreed to proceed.

The Dwyer injunction and the prospect of an endangered species listing had immediate and dramatic effects. The stall had backfired, endangering the timber industry. The timber companies responded with protests reminiscent of earlier campaigns against ANILCA and the RARE II wilderness legislation. Soon-to-be unemployed loggers and mill workers wore yellow ribbons, complained about "owls vs. jobs," and pressured local politicians. Environmental groups formed an Ancient Forest Alliance in an effort to counter the industry effort, but in the short term, at least, the contest was one-sided. Oregon officials organized a "timber summit" in June and agreed that the injunction had to be overturned. Their preferred mechanism was no surprise. Since 1985 Senator Hatfield had added timber "riders" to several unrelated bills, most recently overturning a 1988 injunction against a BLM spotted owl plan for its Oregon timberlands. Representative Les AuCoin (D-OR) made sure that the riders were not derailed in the House. The proposed 1989 rider mandated continued timber sales in 1989 and 1990 and barred judicial interference. Senator Brock Adams (D-WA) agreed to cosponsor the rider.

If the success of the rider was a foregone conclusion, some of the details were negotiable. Hatfield sought to preserve his reputation as a centrist and was willing to listen to Doug Scott of the Sierra Club and others from the Wilderness Society and Audubon. Given the certainty of a Hatfield victory, they fared reasonably well. The legislation acknowledged the value of old growth and described the rider as a "last resort" that would not be repeated. The law also authorized a citizen review panel for each national forest and BLM district, a seemingly empty gesture that in fact proved to be surprisingly effective in educating the public to the value of old-growth forests. Finally, and most importantly, the legislation created an expert panel of scientists who were given a twelve-month deadline for submitting a plan to preserve the spotted owl.[23] The "rider from hell," as environmentalists labeled it, preserved the status quo for another year, but it also maintained the pressure on the Forest Service to come up with a permanent solution under ever more trying circumstances.

STANDOFF

The next three years featured virtually nonstop confrontations over old-growth forests in the Northwest, with the spotted owl the central point of contention. The timber industry, Bush administration officials, and Forest Service and BLM administrators were insistent that the logging should continue, regardless of the owl's fate, and that the Endangered Species Act should be revised. On the other side were the environmental groups, the scientists, including most of those who worked for the Forest Service and BLM, and finally the judges who were supposed to uphold the law regardless of political consequences. Environmentalists pointed out that market fluctuations and technological innovations had already cost many jobs, that the depletion of old-growth forests would eliminate many additional positions in the near future, and that the region was shifting to a service economy, with overall employment gains outpacing job losses. However compelling, these arguments did not lend themselves to dramatic television coverage or appealing slogans. Public discussions only occasionally rose above the level of "owls vs. jobs."

Yet because it was the judges who made most of the meaningful decisions, the scientists, working behind the scenes, had more influence than their numbers or public visibility might suggest. And they, in turn, were influenced by contemporary work in conservation biology, especially studies of the relationships between habitat, biodiversity, and extinctions. Their conclusions repeatedly shocked politicians and agency leaders, who focused almost exclusively on economic issues and privately dismissed statements about the ecological value of old-growth forests.

In this context the formation of the Interagency Scientific Committee (ISC) in the summer of 1989 took on special significance. The committee, authorized in the timber rider, was assigned to devise a permanent solution to the owl issue by the summer of 1990. Clearly it was an important assignment, and Robertson and his advisors were committed to recruiting able and knowledgeable individuals. Yet as Eric Forsman, one of the appointees, recalled: "I don't think the higher-ups in the agencies had any idea what they were doing."[24] To head the committee Robertson selected Jack Ward Thomas, a Forest Service biologist whose research specialty was elk habitat. Well known, respected, and politically astute, Thomas was given a free hand to select the other members and to organize the study. In addition to Forsman, he chose one BLM and three Forest Service biologists; five of the six had PhDs. An advisory committee of scientists from universities, environmental organizations, and the timber industry aided them. As Thomas confided to his journal, the interagency study was likely to be the "trigger" that initiated the "conservation debate" of the decade. "The outcome will, quite likely, determine if there is any chance for sustaining biodiversity. . . . We are, simply and irrevocably, at the end of an era."[25]

Beginning in October, the committee members gathered in Portland, Oregon, worked long hours, visited a number of old-growth areas, and rigorously studied the scientific literature on spotted owl habitat and behavior. Barry Noon, a committee member whose specialty was modeling bird populations, recalled that Thomas and Forsman, traditional field researchers, were initially uncomfortable with the theoretical scientists, especially when they began to project the minimum size of old-growth "islands" necessary to insure that the birds could sustain themselves indefinitely. But the literature was compelling, and everyone eventually agreed that large reserves, as large as the politicians would conceivably agree to, were necessary. By February 1990, there was unanimity on that point. "We finally made a decision," Forsman recalled. "From that point on, there was never any discussion of starting over." Thomas supposedly told the group: "We've crossed the Rubicon. The die is cast."[26] Meeting with the advisory committee, they began drawing lines on maps and set aside lands that included cut-over and second-growth areas to provide connections between old-growth reserves. After more discussions they decided they had to restrict logging on the connecting lands as well. The final recommendations would reduce logging by 25 percent on national forest land and as much as 40 percent on BLM land, numbers that seemed shockingly large at the time.[27]

The Thomas report of April 1990 jolted the agency leaders and politicians who still believed that the environmentalists' lawsuit and the likely endangered species listing required only superficial, symbolic concessions. Thomas had private sessions with agency leaders in March and with members of the Northwest congressional delegation in early April; in both cases his report produced expressions of surprise and concern and, from the politicians, reminders that they had the power to alter the plan. Shortly thereafter, Thomas was summoned to Washington and interrogated, first by administration staffers and economists, then by members of the Senate Energy Committee, whose questions in many cases were prepared by timber industry lobbyists. The agriculture secretary announced the appointment of a peer review panel to evaluate the report, presumably with the intention of discrediting it. That tactic failed when the panel praised the report for its careful and thorough analysis. Still, the administration's position was captured in an unexpectedly candid statement by Secretary of the Interior Manual Lujan: "No bunch of biologists are going to determine policy for the United States government."[28] The Forest Service also received a message from the president's chief of staff: "Don't adopt ISC."[29] Its hands tied, the Forest Service simply announced in September that it would proceed "in a manner not inconsistent" with the Thomas plan.

Environmental groups attacked the Forest Service again for its reluctance to embrace the Thomas plan or prepare an environmental impact statement. The agency's response, that the official listing of the owl as a threatened species (June 1990) relieved it of its obligations under NFMA, elicited a caustic response from Judge Dwyer, who granted a new injunction and demanded a satisfactory forest management plan and environmental impact statement by March 1992. The Forest Service then announced that it had adopted the ISC recommendations. This belated gesture did not help. Environmentalists obtained another injunction on the grounds that the Forest Service had not prepared an adequate environmental impact statement.[30]

The ISC report marked the emergence of an authoritative scientific voice in the debate. It announced, in effect, that the scientists would no longer be passive observers of whatever action the agency heads or Congress decided to take. By mobilizing data and presenting information in a persuasive fashion, they successfully redefined the issue. As political scientist Stephen Yaffee notes, after the ISC report, "The debate was about what kind of balance . . . was appropriate, and less about the scientific justification for owl protection."[31]

The designation of the spotted owl as a threatened species reinforced that effect. The Bush administration reluctantly appointed an interagency task force to devise a forest plan for 1991 and threatened to invoke the god squad proviso if that plan, presumably less restrictive than the ISC proposals, was not acceptable. The task force proved to be a public relations disaster. After several months of fruitless deliberations, it called for more timber cutting than the ISC did, but did not indicate where the additional trees were located. When the Forest Service tried to implement the plan, by proposing to sell timber in areas that were restricted in the ISC plan, another outcry ensued. For the SCLDF it was almost too easy. Judge Dwyer issued a new injunction halting all timber sales until a satisfactory forest plan was completed. In May 1991 he made the injunction permanent, noting a "deliberate and systematic refusal by the Forest Service and the FWS to comply with the laws protecting wildlife." He added that the agency's behavior "reflects decisions made by the higher authorities in the executive branch of government."[32]

When the Fish and Wildlife Service also refused to approve the BLM's 1991 plan for its Oregon lands, the administration turned to its fall-back position, the god squad. Most observers saw this maneuver as the first step in a campaign to persuade Congress to revise the Endangered Species Act. In any case, it soon backfired. The rationale for the god squad was suspect, since the BLM lands were only a small part of the affected area. Even the members, all Bush appointees, were skeptical. Despite arm-twisting by Secretary Lujan, the god squad only approved an exemption for the BLM lands on the condition that the agency follow the Thomas plan until it came up with a different, scientifically credible plan. Thwarted again, Lujan's last initiative was a stripped-down owl recovery plan that preserved almost nothing, in the hope that Congress would embrace it as an alternative to the existing paralysis in the Northwest. It too went nowhere.

By mid-1992, the portion of the Northwest timber industry that depended on the national forests and BLM lands was paralyzed. That was far more than the ISC had proposed, indeed, more than all but the most extreme environmental groups had had the temerity to suggest. This remarkable result was the consequence of a situation summarized by Donald Knowles, one of Lujan's assistants: "Everyone wanted the same thing, a scientifically credible plan with no impacts."[33]

The spotted owl controversy had two other effects that would complicate the search for a "solution." The first was a proliferation of grassroots environmental groups devoted to the preservation of old-growth timber. They embraced a variety of objectives; some favored litigation and political negotiations; others, like the Native Forest Council, called for "zero cut," or an end to all logging in national forests. Regardless of approach, they made the prospect of a politically acceptable consensus even more elusive, especially after they discovered that several large foundations would finance litigation against the Forest Service and BLM.[34]

The second effect was a belated emphasis on fish in the development of an acceptable forest plan. As the pace of old-growth logging accelerated in the 1980s, the impact on water runoff, stream flow, and fish habitat had attracted more attention. Alarmed, a coalition of local Oregon groups and the Sierra Club persuaded Senator Hatfield to sponsor the Oregon Omnibus Wild and

Scenic Rivers Act of 1988, the most sweeping act in the statute's twenty-year history. Still, the law depended on the Forest Service and the BLM for implementation, and for the next two years the agencies did nothing to update their meager river protection plans. When several activists organized a workshop to explore policy options at the H. J. Andrews Forest and invited biologists from universities and government agencies, the response was overwhelming. One of the mildly surprised organizers recalled that the scientists "said . . . no one had asked them to help put their research into policy form before."[35] The conference, in October 1990, proved to be a seminal event, similar to the deliberations of the ISC. The scientists pointed to the plight of salmon and other fish that depended on wild rivers and called for the protection of their habitat and adjacent riparian areas.

In the following months several alarming reports on the decline of Pacific salmon suggested that they would soon join the spotted owl on the endangered list. In 1991, as the forestry subcommittee of the House Agriculture Committee began to consider various bills related to the spotted owl and old-growth controversies, it enlisted a four-member expert committee, including Jack Ward Thomas and Jerry Franklin, to assess its options. When this so-called Gang of Four became aware of the reports from the Andrews workshop, they added several Forest Service fishery experts to their team. Comparing maps of spotted owl habitat and watersheds vital to salmon reproduction, they realized that they were looking at the same areas. Old growth was vital to fish as well as birds. The Gang of Four reported in July that salmon protection would require additional reductions in the timber harvest.[36] Hardly a surprise to anyone familiar with the salmon issue or old-growth forestry, this statement was included in the subcommittee's report and suggested that timber lobbyists could no longer take congressional support for granted.

The logging controversy inevitably became an issue in the 1992 presidential election. In his campaign statements President Bush sided with the timber industry and endorsed legislation to overrule Judge Dwyer and directly or indirectly weaken the Endangered Species Act. The Democratic candidate, Bill Clinton, rejected the industry's simplistic dichotomy between "owls" and "jobs" and pledged to hold a "forestry summit" in the Northwest soon after taking office to find a solution that would reconcile the disparate views of the contending sides. The voters agreed, and Clinton carried both Washington and Oregon. His success in the Northwest was testimony to the popularity of his proposal but also to the changing character of the regional economy and the persuasiveness of the environmentalists' arguments.

CALIFORNIA CONFLICTS

The spotted owl confrontation in the Pacific Northwest was the best-known battle over public land forestry in the early 1990s, but it was only one example of a more general backlash against timber harvests. In eastern Washington, where the environmental movement had limited public support, the Forest Service and its political allies were able to resist demands for change. In northern California, where political alignments were more dynamic, the outcome was more complex. A campaign to restrict logging on privately owned lands in Humboldt County, spearheaded by the California wing of Earth First!, produced what one observer recalled as the "most intense and long-running conflict over old-growth forestry."[37] On the other hand, in the Sierra Nevada, state and local officials took the lead in negotiating a compromise that avoided the legal and political confrontations characteristic of Humboldt County and the Pacific Northwest.

From the beginning the Humboldt campaign had elements of melodrama. It originated with the 1986 takeover of Pacific Lumber Company, which owned half of the remaining privately owned redwoods in California, by a notorious corporate raider, Charles Hurwitz, and his Maxxam Corporation. To pay for the acquisition, Hurwitz accelerated logging in Pacific Lumber's forests and plunged, perhaps unwittingly, into the emerging old-growth controversy. Confronting Maxxam was Earth First!, which delighted in emphasizing the link between corporate rapacity and the logging of northern California's majestic trees. By 1987 Earth First! sympathizers in Humboldt County had identified the Headwaters forest, a large, mostly pristine area, as the most vulnerable Maxxam property. Working through a local activist group, the Environmental Protection Information Center (EPIC), they sued Maxxam and the California Department of Forestry for failing to follow required logging procedures. The Sierra Club soon joined them in a series of lawsuits. The escalating conflict led to two major forestry initiatives in 1990. The first was a statewide referendum to revise logging regulations for privately owned lands and to create a fund to purchase areas of special significance, such as Headwaters. The second was an extended demonstration against Maxxam called "Redwood Summer."[38]

From the beginning Redwood Summer was controversial, even within EarthFirst! Mike Roselle explained: "We were running out of steam. Most of our activists had been arrested, many of them several times. We had been hit with lawsuits, there was increasing violence by loggers . . . and we simply could not recruit enough people,"[39] Judi Bari, the principal organizer of Redwood Summer, saw it as a way to revive Earth First! as well as save Headwaters. She took the civil rights movement of the early 1960s as her model and planned marches, mass arrests, and other activities at the company's Humboldt County facilities. To show solidarity with loggers, she disavowed tree spiking and monkey-wrenching. Her pronouncements widened the division in EarthFirst![40]

Hurvitz wanted no part of Earth First! in any form. He allied Maxxam with the "Wise Use" movement, the industry-inspired campaign to mobilize rural westerners against environmental regulations, and launched an aggressive media campaign to portray Earth First! as a radical group seeking to advance its own agenda. That interpretation drew support from an ongoing FBI investigation of Earth First!, which many activists believed was aimed at Redwood Summer.[41]

In May 1990, Bari and Darryl Cherney, a musician, activist, and close friend, began a series of rallies aimed at recruiting California college students for the Headwaters demonstrations. On May 24, as they drove through Oakland on their way to an event, a blast inside the car caused extensive damage to the vehicle and severely injured Bari. Rushing to the scene, local police and FBI agents arrested Bari and Cherney for supposedly transporting a bomb. The case against them quickly collapsed (Cherney and Bari's estate—she died in 1997 from an unrelated illness—eventually won a large financial settlement), but it delayed the investigation and probably contributed to the authorities' failure to identify or apprehend the actual culprit. Their later suspects included several local men with histories of violent behavior, including Bari's former husband.[42] Although the bombing and investigation generated extensive news coverage and sympathy for Bari, they were critical blows to the summer campaign.

In Bari's absence, Redwood Summer was at best a partial success. The Humboldt County demonstrations attracted at least 3,000 participants, far more than any other Earth First! protest, and were widely reported in news-papers and on television. But they had no apparent effect on Maxxam's oper-ations or logging in other California forests and probably hurt the forestry referendum, which lost by a narrow margin.[43]

The old-growth issue in the Sierra Nevada emerged overnight with the publication of a series of revelatory investigative reports in the *Sacramento Bee* in June 1991. The newspaper accounts told a familiar story of environmen-tal decline and of state and federal agencies unwilling or unable to intervene. In response to the exposés, the California Natural Resources secretary called a "Sierra-Summit" to discuss the situation in November 1991, followed by regional workshops in 1992. Environmental groups had their own conference in August 1992 and formed a lobbying organization modeled after the Greater Yellowstone Coalition. Wise Use and local business groups set up a separate, antagonistic organization. The most pressing issue was the likely addition of the California spotted owl (a separate species from the northern spotted owl) to the endangered species list and the reductions in logging that would follow. The Forest Service had struggled with this prospect for several years, but it had not come up with a satisfactory remedial plan. Aware of the situation in the Pacific Northwest, most participants in the 1991 summit meeting and the 1992 workshops acknowledged the severity of the challenge and the desirabil-ity of a negotiated solution, even if it required reductions in logging. Federal and state officials then appointed a California Spotted Owl Assessment and Planning Team, which spent the next two years preparing a forestry plan that went into effect with relatively little fanfare or controversy. By the mid-1990s logging in the Sierra Nevada had declined to a fraction of the earlier level and timber-dependent communities were adjusting, often painfully, to the new restrictions. The Sierra Nevada conflict had once more demonstrated the power of the Endangered Species Act and its value to the conservation effort.[44]

❧

Between 1987 and 1992, public land forestry was suddenly and often convul-sively transformed, the Endangered Species Act became a formidable weapon, and biodiversity emerged as a popular and compelling rationale for conserva-tion activism. But was this the harbinger of more sweeping changes in pub-lic policy or simply a successful attack on a vulnerable industry? Certainly the northwestern timber industry was easy to cast as a villain. Despite the profitability of the industry, employment continued to decline, timber-dependent towns struggled, the region's magnificent large trees disappeared at an accelerating pace, and the denuded hillsides were an ecological disaster. Forest Service officials readily admitted that the supply of the largest, most desirable trees was nearing an end.[45] Even if there had been no owls or no Endangered Species Act, major changes were inevitable; the only question was how much, if any, of the original forest would survive. This was the point at which conservation biology, with its insistence on large cores and connectivity, became an invaluable aid to environmental activists. Although the controversy continued well beyond 1992, the scientists' analyses set the bar at a higher level than would have been possible in earlier years.

It did not require an overly vivid imagination, then, to foresee similar progress in dealing with other resource issues, such as public land grazing and ocean fishing. Furthermore, the election of Bill Clinton in 1992 promised to alter the political climate and the role of the federal government. Together with the scientists' compelling arguments and continuing evidence of broad public support for environmental initiatives, the coming changes in Washington, DC, gave environmentalists good reason to believe that the 1990s would be a new and more productive era for conservation.

NOTES

1. Stephen Lewis Yaffee, *Prohibitive Policy: Implementing the Federal Endangered Species Act* (Cambridge, MA: MIT Press, 1982), 47, 57.

2. Michael L. Weber, *From Abundance to Scarcity: A History of U.S. Marine Fisheries Policy* (Washington, DC: Island Press, 2002), 149.

3. Ibid., 114.

4. J. Michael Scott et al., "Conservation-Reliant Species and the Future of Conservation," *Conservation Letters* 3, no. 2 (2010): 91. Also see Peter Kareiva and Michelle Marvier, *Conservation Science; Balancing the Needs of People and Nature* (Greenwood Village, CO: Roberts and Company, 2011), 97, 99–100.

5. Debra A. Rose, "Implementing Endangered Species Policy" in *American Fish and Wildlife Policy: The Human Dimension*, ed. William R. Mangun (Carbondale: Southern Illinois University Press, 1992), 109.

6. George Hoberg, "The Emerging Triumph of Ecosystem Management: The Transformation of Federal Forest Policy," in *Western Public Lands and Environmental Politics*, ed. Charles Davis (Boulder: Westview, 2001), 67.

7. Peter Duinker, Gary Bull, and Bruce A. Shindler, "Sustainable Forestry in Canada and the United States: Developments and Prospects, in *Two Paths toward Sustainable Forests: Public Values in Canada and the United States*, ed. Bruce A. Shindler, Thomas M. Beckley, and Mary Carmel Finley (Corvallis: Oregon State University Press, 2003), 36–37.

8. Reed F. Noss and Allen Y. Cooperrider, *Saving Nature's Legacy: Protecting and Restoring Biodiversity* (Washington, DC: Island Press, 1994), 210.

9. Cristina Eisenberg, *The Wolf's Tooth: Keystone Predators, Trophic Cascade, and Biodiversity* (Washington, DC: Island Press, 2010), 115–23.

10. Paul W. Hirt, *A Conspiracy of Optimism: Management of the National Forests since World War II* (Lincoln: University of Nebraska Press, 1994), 253.

11. Ibid., 285; Richard Freeman, "The EcoFactory: The United States Forest Service and the Political Construction of Ecosystem Management," *Environmental History* 7, no. 4 (October 2002): 636, 639–40.

12. Noss and Cooperrider, *Saving Nature's Legacy*, 213.

13. Jim Furnish, *Toward a Natural Forest: The Forest Service in Transition* (Corvallis: Oregon State University Press, 2015), 92.

14. Hirt, *Conspiracy of Optimism*, 286–87; R. Edward Grumbine, *Ghost Bears: Exploring the Biodiversity Crisis* (Washington, DC: Island Press, 1992), 174.

15. Dean Apostol and Marcia Sinclair, "Conclusions: The Status and Future of Restoration in the Pacific Northwest," in *Restoring the Pacific Northwest: The Art and Science of Ecological Restoration in Cascadia*, ed. Apostol and Sinclair (Washington, DC: Island Press, 2006), 428.

16. Carl Safina, *Song for the Blue Ocean: Encounters along the World's Coasts and beneath the Seas* (New York: Henry Holt, 1998), 173.

17. James D. Williams and Ronald M. Nowak, "Vanishing Species in Our Own Backyard: Extinct Fish and Wildlife in the United States and Canada," in *The Last Extinction*, 2nd ed., ed. Les Kaufman and Kenneth Mallory (Cambridge, MA: MIT Press, 1993), 131–32. Also see Kristin M. Szylvian, "Transforming Lake Michigan into the 'World's Greatest Fishing Hole': The Environmental Politics of Michigan's Great Lakes Sport Fishing, 1965–1985," *Environmental History* 9, no. 1 (January 2004): 102–27.

18. Stephen Lewis Yaffee, *The Wisdom of the Spotted Owl: Policy Lessons for a New Century* (Washington, DC: Island Press, 1994), 29.

19. Ibid., 40; Grumbine, *Ghost Bears*, 145.

20. Kathie Durbin, *Tree Huggers: Victory, Defeat, and Renewal in the Northwest Ancient Forest Campaign* (Seattle: The Mountaineers, 1996), 92.

21. Grumbine, *Ghost Bears*, 146

22. Yaffee, *Wisdom of the Spotted Owl*, 111.

23. Durbin, *Tree Huggers*, 106–8.

24. Ibid., 112.

25. Jack Ward Thomas, *The Journals of a Forest Service Chief* (Seattle: University of Washington Press, 2004), 16–17.

26. Durbin, *Tree Huggers*, 115–16.

27. Ibid., 116.

28. Thomas, *Journals*, 30.

29. Durbin, *Tree Huggers*, 121.

30. Michael J. Bean and Melanie J. Rowland, *The Evolution of National Wildlife Law*, 3rd ed. (Westport: Praeger, 1997), 360–64.

31. Yaffee, *Wisdom of the Spotted Owl*, 125.

32. Ibid., 134.

33. Durbin, *Tree Huggers*, 134.

34. Douglas Bevington, *The Rebirth of Environmentalism: Grassroots Activism from the Spotted Owl to the Polar Bear* (Washington, DC: Island Press, 2009), 34–38.

35. Durbin, *Tree Huggers*, 167.

36. Ibid., 168–70.

37. Richard Widick, *Trouble in the Forest: California's Redwood Timber Wars* (Minneapolis: University of Minnesota Press, 2009), 228.

38. Bevington, *Rebirth of Environmentalism*, 46–50.

39. Mike Roselle with Josh Mahan, *Tree Spiker: From Earth First! to Lowbagging: My Struggles in Radical Environmental Action* (New York: St. Martin's Press, 2009), 129.

40. Martha F. Lee, *Earth First!: Environmental Apocalypse* (Syracuse: Syracuse University Press, 1995), 134–35.

41. Kate Coleman, *The Secret Wars of Judi Bari: A Car Bomb, the Fight for the Redwoods, and the End of Earth First!* (San Francisco: Encounter Books, 2005), 138–40.

42. Ibid., 167–77.

43. Bevington, *Rebirth of Environmentalism*, 41–53; David Helvarg, *The War against the Greens: The "Wise-Use" Movement, the New Right, and Anti-Environmental Violence* (San Francisco: Sierra Club Books, 1994), 2–6; Susan Zakin, *Coyotes and Town Dogs: Earth First! and the Environmental Movement* (New York: Viking Press, 1993), 386–89.

44. Timothy P. Duane, *Shaping the Sierra: Nature, Culture, and Conflict in the Changing West* (Berkeley: University of California Press, 1999), 23–30.

45. Joe Roman, *Listed: Dispatches from America's Endangered Species Act* (Cambridge, MA: Harvard University Press, 2011), 86.

6

Conservation on Trial

THE CLINTON YEARS

By 1993, the major elements of a new, more rigorous approach to natural resource conservation were in place. As the biologist Edward Gumbine noted, environmentalists were beginning to see "ecosystems instead of endangered species and biodiversity instead of parks and forests."[1] In the scientific world the intellectual revolution of the previous decade had led to calls for "cores, corridors, and carnivores." In the more cautious world of government administration it was reflected in "ecosystem management," which called for managers to take into account the full spectrum of resources they managed and, at minimum, to consider the long-term, not just the immediate, well-being of their human constituents. The spotted owl controversy had underlined the potential of the new conservation. In the following years, the Clinton administration would include a commitment to biodiversity in its approach to resource management. It would also quickly confront an aroused timber industry and other commodity producers. The consequences of these battles varied, depending on the issue, but by 2001 it was possible to look back at the preceding years as a time of significant but hardly irreversible changes.

DOI: 10.7330/9781607325703.c006

THE NORTHWEST FOREST PLAN

As a candidate Clinton had sought to diffuse the polarized, confrontational environment that had resulted from nearly five years of conflict over Forest Service plans to cut the last of the old-growth forests of the Pacific Northwest. His solution was a "timber summit," which would bring together the competing interest groups and hammer out an agreement they could all accept. He pledged to hold the summit shortly after taking office. It would be the first test of the new administration's approach to conservation issues.

The timber summit was scheduled for April 2, 1993, in Portland, Oregon. The night before, 50,000 partisans of old-growth forests gathered for a concert under a banner that read "Stumps Don't Lie." They chanted: "Clinton and Gore, Cut No More." In opposition, timber companies ran pro-logging ads on local television and organized a counterdemonstration that attracted 10,000.[2] The president's staff invited fifty-three speakers, but no top Forest Service administrators or elected officials. The panel discussions, attended by President Clinton, Vice President Albert Gore, and half the Cabinet, continued for eight hours. Industry officials, local environmentalists, scientists, and workers spoke, generally repeating familiar arguments. Jack Ward Thomas, the Forest Service biologist who had played a large role in the government's response to the dispute and who soon would be Clinton's choice to head the agency, "explained that environmental laws and court decisions had altered the agency's mission, making biodiversity its foremost concern."[3] At the end of the day Clinton called on the participants to end the bickering and to "keep trying to find common ground." He promised a new administrative arrangement that would emphasize that "common ground."[4] Later Clinton announced that a top-level committee, the Forest Ecosystem Management Assessment Team (FEMAT), headed by Thomas, would prepare a list of options within ninety days. He would choose from the list, and that choice would become the basis for new Forest Service and BLM forest plans.

For three years Thomas and his colleagues had battled politicians who thought they were saving too many trees. Now they had to satisfy politicians who were concerned about saving too few, thereby inviting new rounds of litigation, injunctions, and layoffs. Apart from the owls and marbled murrelets (another old-growth-dependent bird added to the endangered species list in 1992), they were supposed to preserve salmon and salmon streams, safeguard riparian areas, and anticipate the discovery of other endangered or potentially endangered species. They were also supposed to come up with a plan that avoided more litigation, removed the Endangered Species Act from the headlines, muted the controversy in the Northwest, and allowed the president to move on to other issues. Operating within these constraints, the FEMAT scientists struggled to find an acceptable formula. They soon realized that they had little choice but to reduce logging well below the levels projected in earlier studies.

For three months Thomas and the other scientists worked virtually non-stop to assemble a satisfactory proposal. To guard against leaks to the media and political pressures, they required visitors, including agency managers, to wear orange vests, making them easily visible.[5] Their deliberations were extended and often heated. At one point Thomas supposedly pleaded with his colleagues: "We have to do better, guys. . . . Who will help me try one more time?"[6] Jerry Franklin, one of the FEMAT participants, came up with a plan for cutting younger trees in old-growth forests, what he called "restoration forestry." He argued that removing the smaller trees would accelerate the maturation of the others, presumably making them more attractive to owls and other old-growth-dependent wildlife. Whether Franklin's plan would have the desired effect was uncertain and essentially irrelevant; it would permit an increase in logging and became an important feature of "Option 9" in their report. They assumed Clinton would select that option because it included the largest timber harvest.[7]

The eventual report listed ten options, differing largely in the size and configuration of the old-growth reserves. Option 9 included "aquatic protection measures" partly because they allowed more land to be designated for conventional forestry.[8] It also included a new feature called "Survey and Manage," an "intense fine-filter approach" for identifying additional threatened or endangered species. In areas that remained open to logging, teams of investigators would search for any of 400 possible rare or threatened plants or animals and would cancel the planned harvest if they found one or more of them. Survey and Manage was "one of the more complex, expensive, and controversial parts of the plan" and proved to be as effective as the spotted owl restrictions in reducing the timber harvest.[9]

The plan covered 23 million acres of national forest and BLM land, basically the western slopes of the Cascade range extending from the Canadian border to northern California. The region was divided into seven new categories, the largest of which were Late Succession/Old Growth Reserves (43 percent), Riparian Reserves (23 percent), Adaptive Management (8 percent), and Matrix (23 percent). Old Growth Reserves were off-limits to logging. Adaptive Management and Matrix were traditional multiple-use areas, where logging would continue, assuming Survey and Manage did not find evidence of endangered species. In Adaptive Management the Forest Service would experiment with new techniques, such as Franklin's "restoration" forestry. It could also cut young trees in some Late Succession Reserves in order to accelerate the transition to old growth. In Riparian zones the agency would undertake various remedial activities to protect and, if possible, increase fish stocks. The many reserves meant that only 31 percent of the total acreage would be available for conventional logging, The FEMAT scientists estimated that the timber harvest would shrink to about 25 percent of the 1980s average, a drastic reduction from the 75 percent that the ISC had forecast in 1990.[10] To deflect industry criticism, Clinton proposed large expenditures for retraining and other job-creating activities in communities where there would be layoffs.

As the details of the plan became known, environmentalists and their allies complained that the reserves were too small while industry leaders and their congressional representatives insisted that they were too large. Scientists were among the most outspoken critics. They believed the plan "posed unacceptable risks to salmon and marbled murrelets, and might not even insure the recovery of spotted owls."[11] The controversy continued as the president submitted Option 9 as his Northwest Forest Plan to Judge Dwyer, who ruled it acceptable six months later. By that time many western representatives and senators had signed on to a congressional rider (ultimately unsuccessful) designed to undermine it.

Despite the criticism of environmentalists and scientists, the Clinton plan marked a substantial break with the past. Thomas called it the "biggest, boldest plan for forestland management ever put into action in this or any other country."[12] A later scholarly evaluation labeled it a "global model in biodiversity protection."[13] By ultimately reducing the timber harvest by 90 prevent, it addressed one of the notable failures of American conservation in the previous quarter century. It also "planted seeds of change in management agency culture," facilitating the shift to "biodiversity conservation."[14] But the course of change would be erratic, with numerous stops, starts, and detours along the way.

Some features of the plan failed or were never implemented. There were few efforts at riparian restoration or at introducing innovative logging practices. FEMET leaders later complained of a "general lack of flexibility and adaptability" among Forest Service and BLM managers.[15] University of Utah law professor Robert Keiter concluded that the conservation agencies "are still finding it difficult to reconcile their new ecological responsibilities with countervailing political and economic pressures."[16] A notable exception to this "disappointing" pattern was the Siuslaw National Forest in Oregon, where an aggressive forest supervisor, Jim Furnish, worked effectively with community groups to develop one of the first "forest stewardship" projects. He won support for forest thinning, prescribed burns, vegetation removal, and related activities.[17]

In any case, the Northwest Plan led to huge reductions in logging. Some of the decline was due to depressed economic conditions and to continued litigation. Most of it, however, resulted from the spotted owl reserves and the Survey and Manage program, both aimed at safeguarding endangered species. Because the decline in logging greatly exceeded expectations, the effort to preserve jobs largely failed. The more isolated and timber-dependent towns in the region continued to lose residents, in some cases most of those associated with the timber industry. Federal grants, concluded one report, "have helped in some small ways, but not nearly at a scale that compensate" for the lost jobs. The anticipated restoration work was only marginally more helpful. As receipts from timber sales fell, the Forest Service slashed budgets and laid off employees.[18]

There were also unexpected results. Many residents of the area, as opposed to timber company managers, took a surprisingly realistic, positive view of the changes. They believed that the industry's behavior had "undermined the health of the forest." and they faulted the Forest Service for lack of "active forest management," the restoration effort in particular, and only sporadic efforts to inform and work with them.[19] A wholly unanticipated consequence was the continued decline of the spotted owl and the marbled murrelet. Ongoing logging on state and privately owned lands was partly responsible. But the owls also suffered from an influx of barred owls, larger and more aggressive birds with a similar diet. When the Fish and Wildlife Service reviewed the spotted owl program in 2004, it concluded that the birds were still endangered. And their number continued to fall in the following years.[20]

Yet they were, after all, only the tip of the proverbial iceberg. Nearly two decades after the plan went into effect, environmentalists protested when the Forest Service proposed boundary revisions, supposedly in response to changes in the beleaguered birds' nesting patterns. Eliminating clear reserve boundaries "says 'Danger' to me," explained one Oregon leader, "because science doesn't rule here—politics rule."[21]

Apart from the forests, the Northwest Forest Plan became a catalyst in the emergence and spread of ecosystem management. FEMAT's immediate goal, as the committee's name implied, was to view the forests as ecosystems and to determine what that meant within existing political constraints. After 1993 ecosystem management became the touchstone of a wide-ranging effort to modernize the federal conservation agencies and to bring greater coherence to conservation policy. The term itself defied precise definition. A week-long conference of Forest Service and Park Service officials, two-thirds of whom were science PhDs, became an extended argument over definitions, with the multiple-use veterans clearly on the defensive. After reviewing these and other attempts to define ecosystem management, biologist Thomas R. Stanley identified two distinctive approaches, the biocentric and the anthropocentric, with government officials, regardless of bureaucratic affiliation, in agreement that "protecting [biological] integrity does not take priority over human use."[22] Grumbine complained that "the insights of conservation biology propel their ideas [but]. . . theirs is a 'process' ecosystem management."[23] Federal officials agreed to take a broader view of their responsibilities, pay less attention to traditional institutional boundaries, and collaborate. Beyond that, they were uncertain and in many cases unconvinced. But even in this limited sense, ecosystem management served an important political role, especially after the Republicans gained control of Congress in 1995. Judith Layzer has concluded that it typically "perpetuate[d], rather than mitigate[d] the existing imbalance of power between development and environmental interests."[24] But it also helped to blunt the move to return to the 1950s. Above all, it reflected the scientists' success in injecting ideas about environmental processes and species preservation into management deliberations and forcing the agencies to modify their traditional, narrower goals. Despite continued, often intense, opposition from commodity interests, numerous setbacks, and compromises, ecosystem management made rapid progress in the 1990s. The unanswered question remained: was that sufficient to address the many challenges that the agencies faced?

Congressional Stalemate

As the story of Clinton's Northwest Forest Plan implies, the new science-based conservation had at best a limited impact on Congress in the 1990s. Debates over public lands and forest policy revolved around familiar themes, with subsidies to special interest groups the principal concern. Two general factors were at play. First was a growing tendency, especially among Republicans, to simply dismiss science as biased and partisan and insist that the threat to biodiversity was exaggerated or even falsified. Second was the continuing pull of special interest lobbying, reinforced by political campaign contributions. Thus, Senator Hatfield continued to champion the timber policies of the 1980s, which favored an important Oregon constituency. Western Democratic senators were no less determined proponents of below-cost timber sales. California's large environmental community created different alignments there, but interest group lobbying was no less intense or influential. The result was a business-as-usual setting, which, together with the intense partisan bickering, meant that relatively little was accomplished.

Influenced by Vice President Gore and Secretary Bruce Babbitt of the Interior, both of whom had close ties to the environmental movement, Clinton initially proposed a number of policy innovations to modify long-standing but widely discredited features of public land management. At the top of his list were proposals to raise grazing fees on BLM lands and repeal an 1872 mining law that amounted to a giveaway to mining companies. Neither proposal made much headway in Congress. The president abandoned the fee increase in budget negotiations and was no more successful in introducing it through regulatory action. The mining reform bill passed both houses in 1994 but died in conference committee.[25] Environmentalists complained bitterly that the administration had not invested sufficient political capital in either cause. A major reason for the president's apparent reluctance to push harder had been the opposition of western Democratic senators. Amid many issues demanding attention, grazing and mining reform were relatively unappealing. But Congress also failed to act on a variety of other environmental issues, including some, such as the elevation of the

EPA to Cabinet status, which had bipartisan backing and priority status. The League of Conservation Voters judged the 103rd Congress the worst in a quarter century.[26]

One particularly embarrassing expression of this situation was the fate of the Convention on Biological Diversity, an international agreement concluded at the Rio Earth Summit of 1992. Each signatory pledged to take meaningful steps to preserve native flora and fauna. The convention also included language calling for wealthy nations to compensate poorer nations for resources they imported. The actual language was vague and even contradictory, but the US biotechnology industry and others that might be affected by the compensation provision strongly objected.[27] In the past such complaints had usually been disregarded. The Reagan administration, for example, had embraced the Ramsar Convention, which encouraged wetland preservation, and the North American Waterfowl Management Act, which protected waterfowl habitat.[28] Responding to industry lobbying, however, President Bush had refused to sign the Convention on Biological Diversity, making the United States the lone major holdout. Clinton immediately signed the convention and sent it to the Senate for ratification. The Senate refused to act, reaffirming its reputation as a "virtual grave yard of unapproved environmental treaties."[29]

There was one notable exception to this pattern, the landmark California Desert Protection Act, passed at the end of the 1994 congressional session. The most significant national park and wilderness measure since ANILCA, the Desert Protection Act embraced nearly 7 million acres of neglected but ecologically and culturally rich desert landscape. It expanded Death Valley and Joshua Tree National Monuments, elevating them to National Park status, and created the Mojave National Preserve, an area of extinct volcanoes and rare Joshua trees. The Preserve designation permitted the continued hunting of deer and mountain goats. Nearly 4 million acres of park and preserve land and an additional 3.6 million acres of BLM land were designated as wilderness. The legislation reflected contemporary concerns: the scientists' emphasis on larger park units, capable of protecting a variety of species; the value of less than "iconic" landscapes, even seeming "wastelands" like much of eastern California; and the potential of the much-derided BLM as a conservation agency. Yet the law was, in fact, the product of several decades of often frustrating work.

The area's distinctive flora and fauna—such as the Joshua tree, a member of the lily family found nowhere else—had initially attracted the attention of conservationists. A variety of threats, including the famous motorcycle races from Barstow, California, to Las Vegas, had spurred a long and tortured effort to protect the area. The first meaningful victory came in 1976, when FLPMA authorized a special wilderness review and management plan for the California desert, to be completed by 1980. The review led the BLM to designate a large "national conservation area" and several wilderness study areas and to admit—a judgment judiciously omitted from its final report—that the Mojave region would probably be best managed as a national park.[30]

The Sierra Club pressured the BLM to take a more active role in protecting the desert and was instrumental in the formation of Citizens for Mojave National Park, an influential local lobbying group. When the BLM failed to introduce additional protective measures, the citizens organization aggressively publicized the national park alternative. The last straw was the campaign by Interior secretary James Watt to open more BLM land to commercial uses. Frank Wheat, the historian of the desert legislation, writes that Watt's effort persuaded environmentalists "that the Desert Plan under BLM management had failed . . . the Plan seemed to have no stability. Attempt after attempt was made to weaken it. . . . It would be necessary to resort to legislation to protect the desert."[31]

That campaign began in late 1984, immediately after the passage of the California Wilderness Act. The Sierra Club, Wilderness Society, and California Wilderness Coalition took the lead in forming the California Desert Protection League, an umbrella group that ultimately enlisted more than 100 California environmental and community organizations. With the crucial assistance of Edgar Wayburn, the former president of the Sierra Club and the state's best-known environmentalist, the Desert Protection League persuaded Senator Alan Cranston (D-CA) to introduce its bill in early 1986. That bill failed, but Cranston continued to champion the desert plan until his retirement in 1993. The opposition included mining and grazing interests, off-road vehicle groups, the Reagan and Bush administrations, and the mostly Republican representatives from eastern California districts. The BLM covertly and sometimes overtly fought the bill. As much as anything, publicity about the plight of the endangered desert tortoise swayed public opinion toward greater protection. Significant concessions, such as making Mojave a preserve and permitting grazing to continue in areas where it was an established activity, satisfied some critics. Still, opponents were able to stall the legislation until 1992, when California elected two Democratic senators. It finally passed on the last day of the session in October 1994, ten years after the beginning of the legislative effort and a quarter century after the broader educational campaign had begun.[32]

A little-noticed bonus was a commitment to ecosystem management by NPS and BLM officials, who now had large adjoining wilderness holdings. Their collaborative efforts became "a model for federal land management in the twenty-first century."[33]

The next important congressional initiative, after Clinton's reelection in 1996 had temporarily halted Republican attacks on the environment, was a reaction to the haphazard management of the wildlife refuge system. The "timid character" of the Fish and Wildlife Service, the "dim public awareness" of the refuges, and the absence of an organic act comparable to those of the Park Service, Forest Service, and BLM, made the refuges dependent on executive authority, which could result in forceful action but more often led to neglect or deference to commercial and recreational interests.[34] A 1964 law had given local governments a share of proceeds from commercial activities on refuge lands, and a 1966 act specifically authorized "compatible" uses, opening the door even wider to commodity production, hunting and fishing, and other activities.[35]

Environmental and wildlife organizations became increasingly alarmed as secondary uses of the refuges overshadowed wildlife preservation. A 1989 Government Accounting Office report included a detailed description of the Fish and Wildlife Service's seeming inability to eliminate incompatible activities and became a catalyst for reform. Congressional hearings and legislative proposals followed, including a 1992 bill by Senator Bob Graham (D-FL) that made "ecological integrity" the basis of refuge management. Yet Congress failed to act and the Fish and Wildlife Service made no progress on its own. Audubon, the Wilderness Society, and Defenders of Wildlife sued in 1992 and negotiated an agreement with Secretary Babbitt to eliminate some activities. A 1995 study reported some success in reducing incompatible activities.[36] In an effort to sidetrack Republican legislation that would have given hunting even greater prominence in the refuges,

Clinton then issued an executive order that emphasized the system's eco-logical mission and established a hierarchy of compatible uses. Hunting and fishing were included in a list of "priority general public uses," but commodity production was not.[37]

The culminating step in this extended reform campaign was the 1997 National Wildlife Refuge Improvement Act, the Fish and Wildlife Service's long-delayed organic act. Modeled after the National Forest Management Act and the Federal Land Policy and Management Act, the Refuge Improvement Act required unit-level planning with public participation. It also followed the precedent of ANILCA, which had required unit plans for the new and old Alaska refuges (which included 85 percent of total refuge system lands), and specified a hierarchy of compatible uses. ANILCA had also given a group of refuge managers the kinds of experiences with land management plans that had become routine in the other conservation agencies.

Apart from these procedures, the most important and innovative feature of the act was its emphasis on maintaining the "biological integrity, diversity, and environmental health" of the refuges. The language, which had been anticipated in Graham's 1992 bill and in Clinton's executive order, reflected the impact of the new science-based conservation. In the words of one scholar, it "catapults the Refuge System to the front lines of conservation biology."[38] Given the tortured history of the refuges and the many conflicts over compatible activities, it was a surprising affirmation of public responsi-bility. Together with the expansion of the refuge system—twenty-eight were added in the 1990s—and the growing importance of the endangered species program, the 1997 act marked the belated emergence of the FWS as a con-servation agency comparable, at least in theory and statute, to the NPS and Forest Service.

That role was reflected in the Wildlife Conservation and Restoration Program of 2000, which provided the Fish and Wildlife Service with a mod-est budget to help state wildlife agencies protect threatened species.

Congress also authorized two symbolically important land purchases in the 1990s. One was the proposed New World gold mine, just outside Yellowstone National Park. A local citizens group, the Beartooth Alliance, and the Greater Yellowstone Coalition had mobilized opposition to the mine, arguing that it would threaten the park's wildlife, water quality, and even the geothermal activity that was one of the area's most distinctive and popular features. They enlisted the support of the national environmental organizations, sued the mining company for Clean Water Act violations (the result of earlier mining on the company's property), and gradually won the support of Wyoming and Montana politicians. Clinton visited the area in 1995, partly to emphasize the importance of the issue. In 1996, with the miners on the defensive and park officials now actively opposing the mine, Congress authorized $65 million to buy the land and mineral rights. The mining company accepted this arrangement, but a recalcitrant part-owner of the mineral rights delayed the final settlement for more than a decade. Finally in 2009–10, the Trust for Public Land acquired the remaining mineral rights and resold them to the Forest Service. The disputed area was added to the Gallatin and Custer National Forests.[39]

The second purchase was the Headwaters forest in northern California. After Redwood Summer, Earth First! and other groups continued to mobilize protestors against Maxxam; in 1996 and 1997 as many as 8,000 people rallied outside the company's mill in tiny Carlotta, California. EPIC, the local litigation group, and the Sierra Club also kept up their legal attacks on the company. In 1994 the district's congressional representative sponsored a bill to purchase Headwaters that passed the House but failed in the Senate.

Two years later, with ever-larger demonstrations planned for Humboldt County, Senator Diane Feinstein (D-CA) proposed another settlement with Maxxam. The federal and state governments would pay $380 million for 7,500 acres, half of which was old growth, if the company agreed to a plan that restricted logging on an additional 200,000 acres of its property. Widespread criticism of the comparatively small amount of old growth and some features of the forestry plan led California lawmakers, who were to provide $130 million of the total, to ask Carl Pope, the executive secretary of the Sierra Club, to review the deal. Pope called for additional restrictions, and the legislature reluctantly accepted the revised plan in August 1998. No one was entirely satisfied with the outcome, and the litigation against Maxxam continued for another decade. Finally, in 2007, Maxxam's Pacific Lumber operation declared bankruptcy and sold its California properties to Mendocino Redwood, which had operated successfully under a similar forestry plan and was publicly committed to sustainable logging.[40] If the resolution of the major issues demonstrated that it was possible for Congress to cooperate on small projects, the prolonged final phase of the conflict suggested the continuing, often tortured association between the nation's forests and the spread of the new conservation.

LOGGING WITHOUT LAWS

If Congress was largely indifferent to conservation in 1993–94, the new Republican-dominated Congress that took over in 1995 was aggressively hostile. The most popular target was the Endangered Species Act; a close second was the Northwest Forest Plan. But given the role of the courts, Clinton's personal association with the Forest Plan, and the mounting evidence of the harm that large-scale logging did to the forest environment, attacking either of them directly was not likely to be successful. Still, there was another option, albeit a temporary one. A series of drought-induced forest fires during the summer of 1994 provided the pretext for a "salvage" logging campaign. Just as environmentalists had used the spotted owl to defend old-growth forests, timber companies sought to use the fires to circumvent legal and political restrictions on logging.

By 1994 the national forests of eastern Washington, Oregon, and Idaho faced many of the same problems as their neighbors to the west. With rapidly accumulating evidence that several species of salmon were no better off than the spotted owl, the Forest Service and BLM reduced logging and grazing in a vain effort to avoid even greater reductions. When the National Marine Fisheries Service listed the chinook salmon as endangered, the courts halted logging in two national forests and seemed poised to extend their injunctions to others. The administration's response was to preserve as much flexibility as possible with an ecosystem management plan covering eastern Washington and Oregon, Idaho, and parts of Montana and other nearby states. This effort did little to placate local interests, and the presence of antigovernment extremists in Idaho and Montana further complicated the situation. Drought and forest fires in the summer and early fall of 1994, followed by the Republican victories in November, tipped the scales against the administration. By 1995 Congress was committed to a salvage logging plan that would supersede ecosystem management east of the Cascades; depending on the exact provisions, it might also nullify parts of the Northwest Forest Plan.[41]

In June Congress adopted a salvage rider that defined "salvage" broadly and included lands in Washington and Oregon that were covered by the

Forest Plan. The rider also prohibited appeals to the agencies or courts. Environmental groups termed it "logging without laws" and mounted a nationwide campaign for a presidential veto. Clinton responded with veto in June, but then signed a largely unchanged version in late July over the opposition of his environmental advisors (because of other unrelated provisions that he strongly supported). The timber industry immediately and successfully sued to win the broadest possible application of the rider.

There followed a year of legal challenges, civil disobedience, political protests, and intense lobbying that ended with the congressional Republicans in retreat. Logging increased, and some old-growth areas that had been set aside in western Washington and Oregon were reopened. It is impossible to tell how much of the additional cutting was authentic salvage logging, but it was soon obvious that the salvage campaign was primarily a smoke screen for increased logging in areas that had not burned. The new activity was a blow to old-growth forests and a setback for other ecologically sensitive areas—as witnessed by the large number of landslides in clear-cut areas during the extremely wet spring of 1996—but the overall total represented only a slight increase over what the Forest Service had planned for 1995–96.[42] In any case, the protests were sufficiently widespread to prevent the extension of salvage logging after mid-1996.

Most of the other effects were political. The Forest Service's receptivity to the salvage effort, even when dead and dying trees were not involved, reminded critics that the agency was still comfortable with the old ways. During the same period it largely scrapped the "Adaptive" management provisions of the Northwest Forest Plan.[43] In this atmosphere, Jack Ward Thomas, who had headed the Forest Service since 1993, felt increasingly uncomfortable. Although a loyal Forest Service veteran, he was a champion of the policy innovations of the previous decade and was committed to reforming the agency. As chief, Thomas promoted conservation biology and ecosystem management, often against entrenched opposition. A reorganization plan that emphasizing ecoregions rather than state boundaries won little support in the agency or in Congress. On other issues he encountered similar roadblocks. By 1995 he was tired and disheartened. During the salvage logging controversy he made little effort to blunt the congressional effort even though it contradicted everything he had emphasized for more than a decade. Facing growing criticism, he resigned in frustration in late 1996.[44]

The environmental movement was also affected. During the spotted owl conflict, the new militant groups, with little patience for the give-and-take of congressional deliberations and agency appeals, attracted a growing number of adherents. A group calling itself Sierra Club Members for Environmental Ethics (after the dissident Forest Service employees organization), and later the John Muir Sierrans, began a campaign to change the policies and leadership of that venerable organization. Viewing the club's leaders as weak and unprincipled, too willing to compromise with timber lobbyists, the Sierrans called for the adoption of a "zero cut" policy. A club referendum on zero cut failed in 1993 but succeeded the following year. For the next decade the John Muir Sierrans would contest establishment candidates for seats on the club's executive committee; on more than one occasion they came within a few votes of dominating it.[45] There were similar upheavals in other national organizations.

With the Republican takeover of Congress, however, the situation changed. Opponents of environmental regulation headed most of the relevant congressional committees and demanded capitulation, not compromise. The environmental groups were soon working together again to pressure President Clinton to veto the salvage timber bill and other anti-environmental initiatives. They persuaded him to veto a 1996 Interior appropriations bill that had numerous offensive provisions, and another bill that would have opened the Arctic Wildlife Refuge to oil drilling. Their insistent defense of the Endangered Species Act helped undermine another prominent feature of the Republican agenda. Clinton's election had led many environmentalists to turn their attention to other causes. The Republican assault was a reminder that nothing could be taken for granted.

The salvage logging dispute also had a galvanizing effect on Clinton. He had taken only a cursory interest in environmental legislation after the completion of the Northwest Forest Plan and was widely faulted by environmental groups for his "sporadic leadership."[46] However, the protests against "logging without laws" were impossible to disregard. Together with ebbing of public support for the Republican cause, Clinton's renewed interest in natural resource issues made possible modest victories, such as the Refuge Improvement Act, and prevented the Republicans from realizing any major goals after 1995.

Managerial Initiatives

The congressional stalemate largely explained the absence of new national parks, the meager additions to the Wilderness Preservation System, and the seemingly interminable battles over logging that marked the years after 1994. Whereas Congress had played a leading role in the environmental activism of the late 1960s and 1970s, it now became a laggard, an outlier, as leadership shifted to the Clinton administration, state governments, and private conservation groups. Public support for environmental initiatives was reflected in the popularity of science-based approaches to conservation, opposition to salvage logging and opening the Arctic Wildlife Refuge, and an increasingly hostile reception to other efforts to roll back the environmental initiatives of the previous quarter century.

Clinton had appointed a number of leading environmentalists to important posts in his administration. Of these Bruce Babbitt, the former governor of Arizona and president of the League of Conservation Voters and now secretary of the Interior, had the greatest impact. Babbitt was well aware of the biodiversity crisis and the growth of conservation biology; he was also familiar with the commodity orientation of the BLM, the plight of the wildlife refuges, and the challenges of managing tourism in many of the parks. Like many leaders of environmental organizations, he originally assumed that it would be relatively easy to remedy the most glaring deficiencies in federal land management. Embarrassing setbacks in 1993 and 1994 led him to shift his attention to internal reforms. Under his aegis, the Interior agencies continued their gradual shift to ecosystem management, with an emphasis on interagency cooperation, ecological restoration, and protection of biodiversity. One of the first examples of this change was his successful effort, aided by assistant secretary Douglas Frampton, to persuade the Alaska Oil Spill Trustee Council to devote the bulk of the fines from the *Exxon Valdez* disaster to habitat restoration. With the Exxon money, the council was able to protect, through fee purchase or conservation easement, nearly 650,000 acres of coastal timberland that had been slated for logging.[47]

Babbitt also promoted ecosystem management as a way to bring coherence to national resource management without a wholesale overhaul. The Forest Service announced its commitment in 1992, followed by the other agencies. A 1993 Clinton executive order supposedly completed the process.[48] Despite the uncertainty and skepticism noted earlier, an interagency task force developed a basic outline; an interagency conference in late 1995 went further in setting goals for the agencies. The participants agreed to strive for consistency where they had similar responsibilities, as in wilderness management, and to undertake more cooperative activities where they worked side by side, as in Yellowstone, the Columbia Basin, the Sierra Nevada, the California desert, and other locations.[49] They had long cooperated in managing wildlands fires. Now they foresaw a "variety of cooperative arrangements over ecosystem-wide resource problems."[50]

Ecosystem management also suggested new approaches to the politically sensitive endangered species program. Although the Reagan and Bush administrations had tried to slow the listing of new species, environmental groups had not backed down. Ninety percent of new listings in the following years resulted from lawsuits.[51] With each new controversial listing, however, the fate of the entire program became more tenuous. Congressional Republicans were committed to major revisions of the law, though divisions in their ranks gave Clinton and Babbitt time to respond.[52] In 1982 Congress had created a loophole, the Habitat Conservation Plan (HCP), which allowed the Fish and Wildlife Service to approve development projects in sensitive areas, even if they led to the "incidental" killing of protected wildlife, provided the developer set aside enough land to sustain the plants or animals and monitored the results. Only a handful of HCPs were approved in the following decade, but in 1993, when the listing of the California gnatcatcher promised to halt building in many areas of Orange County, California, Babbitt seized on the HCP as a way to deflect the impending conflict by shifting the focus from the gnatcatcher to the habitat where it and other desirable animals and plants lived. Using the Endangered Species Act as a club, the Fish and Wildlife Service staff quickly negotiated an HCP with the Irvine company, the principal Orange County developer, which agreed to set aside 30,000 acres for the gnatcatcher and thirty-two other "species of concern." Babbitt recalled that the settlement was a "defining moment in the emergence of the Endangered Species Act as a land use planning statute."[53] Biologist Joe Roman concurs: "Essentially prohibitive in its original form," the act "was transformed into a permitting statute. 'No' became 'if' or 'maybe.'"[54]

HCPs were no less important in Washington. Secretary Babbitt, recalled an officer of the World Wildlife Fund, "very consciously, very cynically, but I think, also very brilliantly, said the only way we're going to survive with the

[Endangered Species] Act intact was to divide and conquer the people on the Hill who were pushing to gut it."[55] Babbitt effectively defused the grass-roots campaign for revision or repeal by making it easy for landowners and developers to cooperate. HCPs included a "no surprises" provision, which meant that later revelations about the number or distribution of endangered species or "unforeseen circumstances" that adversely affected the recovery effort would not derail an existing plan. A related innovation, "Safe Harbor" agreements that the Fish and Wildlife Service negotiated with landowners, encouraged habitat preservation, limited the number of protected animals or plants, and entitled landowners to financial assistance for costs incurred in implementing the agreement. The new measures not only helped save the red-cockaded woodpecker in the pine forests of Virginia and North Carolina but had landowners in the area clamoring to be included in the recovery plan.[56] In later years, the sagebrush lizard, the Oregon chub, and, ultimately, the greater sage grouse would be notable beneficiaries of agreements covering millions of acres of western land.[57]

In the 1990s the Fish and Wildlife Service negotiated more than 200 HCPs covering nearly 6 million acres. They included a multiple-species conservation plan for San Diego, a similar plan for the greater Las Vegas area, and an even more expansive habitat and ecosystem protection plan for Tucson and vicinity. HCPs remained controversial, environmentalists frequently complaining that they gave away too much and were unenforceable. Critics cited a 1999 Washington State forest plan as a gift to the timber industry. Other plans for privately owned forests in California and Oregon produced similar objections.[58] Babbitt and his staff replied that half a loaf was better than nothing. By 2010 there were more than 1,600 HCPs.[59]

Babbitt also introduced important changes in BLM operations. Abandoning the fight over grazing fees, he concentrated on the agency itself. His first major opportunity grew out of the continuing struggle over potential wilderness designations in the red rock area of southern Utah. Environmentalists demanded at least 6 million acres of wilderness while Utah's politicians were willing to concede at best 2 million. When Republicans took control of Congress, they introduced an even less generous plan, with numerous loopholes and a "hard" release. Environmental groups attacked the legislation, and the bill failed. In the meantime Clinton was looking for ways to enlist environmentalists in his 1996 reelection campaign. The Interior Department staff had been working on plans for a possible southern Utah national monument, but the decisive influence apparently was Clinton's public opinion pollster, who found widespread public support for a Utah monument. On September 18, 1996, without notifying Utah officials, Clinton used his powers under the Antiquities Act to proclaim 1.9 million acres of southern Utah as Grand Staircase Escalante National Monument. The new conservation area effectively linked Bryce Canyon National Park, Capitol Reef National Park, and the Glen Canyon National Recreation Area and included lands that the state's developers had sought. Utah politicians were outraged, but public opinion was supportive, and the courts ruled for the president.[60]

At Babbitt's insistence the new monument remained under BLM management. His goal was to mollify local interests and force the agency to broaden its approach and perspectives. By assigning the BLM responsibility for a high-profile addition to the roster of national monuments, Babbitt hoped to use Grand Staircase Escalante to create a larger and more forceful BLM role in land conservation. Initially, at least, he must have been disappointed. The BLM made no effort to reduce cattle grazing within the monument boundaries or otherwise alter its leasing policies, even after the Grand Canyon Trust, an environmental organization, bought up leases covering nearly one-half million acres.[61]

Grand Staircase Escalante nevertheless became the prototype for an aggressive campaign during Clinton's last year in office. Inspired by the example of Theodore Roosevelt and the behind-the-scenes politicking of Babbitt and new presidential chief of staff John Podesta, Clinton designated eighteen additional monuments, including Grand Canyon–Parashant (1,014,000 acres), Giant Sequoia (327,769), Craters of the Moon (661,000), Upper Missouri River Breaks (377,346), and Sonoran Desert (481,149). Including Grand Staircase Escalante, they totaled nearly 6 million acres and were the most important applications of the Antiquities Act since 1978. Giant Sequoia was to be managed by the Forest Service; all the others remained under BLM auspices. The BLM monuments represented the "strongest policy change yet" in the agency's evolution.[62] Using the threat of more proclamations, Babbitt successfully pressured congressional leaders for three new BLM conservation areas, an additional monument, and a cooperative protection area.[63] At the urging of environmental groups and Senator Harry Reid (D-NV), Congress also designated more than 800,000 acres of northwest Nevada's mountains and deserts as wilderness, the largest addition to the Wilderness Preservation System since 1994. Together with other BLM conservation holdings, the monuments and wilderness areas became the basis for a new BLM Landscape Conservation Service.

The creation of the Steens Mountain Cooperative Management Area in southeastern Oregon illustrated Babbitt's strategy. In August 1999 the secretary visited the area, announced that he intended to ask the president to protect it, and asked the members of the local BLM resource advisory council to work out the details of an acceptable proposal. When the resource committee balked and the Oregon congressional delegation and the governor were unable to break the deadlock, Babbitt threatened to ask Clinton to act without their approval. Reluctantly, representatives of the ranchers and local environmental organizations patched together a compromise. "It was not what any one of us wanted," recalled Bill Marlett of the Oregon Natural Desert Association. The agreement designated 170,000 acres of wilderness, including 100,000 that would be "cattle free"; three wild and scenic rivers; 425,000 acres devoted to recreation; and restrictions on 900,000 acres to prevent mining or geothermal development. Ranchers received thirty-year leases in exchange for conservation easements. With the support of the Oregon congressional delegation, Congress passed the Steens Mountain bill in 2000.[64]

The Clinton record, then, was one of organizational innovations coupled with new monuments and wilderness areas. The move toward ecosystem management introduced an overarching conservation theme to federal policy, the national monuments protected critical landscapes, the Fish and Wildlife Service's organic act acknowledged that agency's growing importance, and the wilderness designations ended the threat of destructive activities in sensitive BLM areas of California, Nevada, and other states. Together with dramatic and potentially far-reaching innovations in national forest policy, these initiatives set the stage for conservation policy in the twenty-first century.

NATIONAL FORESTS REVISITED

The controversies over the national forests and the salvage rider spurred efforts to find a new approach that would insulate national forest policy from partisan politics and institutionalize ecosystem management. Two prominent examples, which reflected the congressional stalemate, growing concerns about endangered species, and the pressure for "zero cut" or, at minimum, a more ecologically informed approach to national forest operations suggested the range of possibilities.

The first was the community-based collaborative, which brought together local timber industry representatives, forestry officials, and environmentalists to identify common interests and develop nuanced plans, supposedly reflecting the participants' intimate knowledge of the area. Pioneered by the Applegate Partnership in southern Oregon, which dated from the 1980s, the collaborative approach was most closely associated with the Quincy Library Group (after its meeting place in Quincy, California). Concerns about the future of the local industry led to meetings between representatives of timber companies and local environmental organizations in an effort to work out mutually acceptable policies. In 1998 they persuaded Senator Feinstein to sponsor legislation designating 1.5 million acres in three national forests in the northern Sierra Nevada as a special ecosystem management area. It would be managed separately from the surrounding national forests with the goal of safeguarding sensitive areas and endangered species and preserving timber industry jobs.

Over the next thirteen years the Forest Service spent nearly $300 million on a variety of projects, including the removal of underbrush and small trees, the restoration of riparian areas, and the identification and protection of spotted owl nesting locations. Still, an expert panel that visited the area periodically after 2007 was not impressed. The "unprecedented type and level of federal investment" had led to improvements to riparian areas and reduced wildfire damage but had not resulted in "full implementation" of the original plan. There were various obstacles, including litigation (some of the original collaborators had had second thoughts) and the role of the Forest Service. Rapid turnover in personnel and differences in outlook among administrators of the three forests took their toll. Some activities "lacked sufficient input or guidance from either senior scientists or administrators at critical times." In many cases "insufficient scientific and statistical rigor made it impossible to determine if there were adverse impacts" on wildlife, a major objective of the project. But even these deficiencies paled beside the failure to sustain "community stability." That was largely a result of the recession of 2007–9, which devastated the local economy. Forest industry employment during those years fell by 60 percent and total employment by 16 percent as tourism, the other foundation of the economy, also collapsed. During the first decade of the new century the population of the area declined by 43 percent. Adverse technological, institutional, and especially economic developments had simply overwhelmed the collaborative effort. The expert panel concluded that collaboration "cannot yet be considered a model of how institutions and collaborative partnerships achieve the complex outcomes of promoting forest health and economic stability while maintaining environmental values."[65] Many environmentalists, skeptical of the collaborative approach in general and critical of the Quincy Group's logging plans, felt vindicated. Collaborative conservation, from their perspective, was simply a timber industry ruse.[66]

Although the Quincy experience was hardly a definitive test, it did suggest the limits of the collaborative process. Social contacts and cooperative projects were useful in defusing polarized attitudes, but they had little or no impact on the larger economic and political forces driving the controversies. During the same period, more modest experiments based on thinning second-growth forests, stewardship contracts (which permitted a range of activities, including conservation initiatives on privately owned lands), and continuous contacts between environmentalists, industry representatives, and Forest Service officials had happier outcomes in Oregon's Siuslaw and Malheur National Forests.[67]

A second, less innovative but ultimately more meaningful strategy emerged from the fight over the salvage rider. By showing that congressional Republicans were captive to special interest groups, lobbyists for environmental organizations had succeeded in generating a substantial public backlash. They soon realized that they had also created an opportunity to move in the opposite direction, to push the Forest Service toward greater restrictions, if not "zero cut." Initially spurred by the grassroots forestry groups that had emerged in the early 1990s and financed largely by activist foundations, especially the Pew Charitable Trusts, they made the national forests the focus of an extensive new mobilization. Their efforts became a stimulus to the Clinton administration's single most important conservation initiative.

The model for this effort was the Alaska Rainforest Campaign, which began to address managerial abuses in the Tongass National Forest after the passage of the Tongass Timber Reform Act of 1991. The act had addressed the most obvious problems, but it had not disturbed the incestuous relationships between local Forest Service officials, the managers of the large pulp mills at Ketchikan and Sitka, and many local and state politicians. With generous financing from Pew and other foundations, the Rainforest Campaign brought together the national organizations and the Southeast Alaska Conservation Council (SEACC), representing the region's local environmental groups. Through publicity, litigation, and pressure on the EPA and other regulatory agencies, the Rainforest Campaign and SEACC put the mill operators on the defensive. Depressed conditions in the pulp industry and EPA demands for reductions in air and water pollution effectively sealed their fate. The Sitka mill closed in 1994; the Ketchikan mill held out until 1997.[68] To the surprise of many Alaskans, who had been conditioned to equate the mills with regional prosperity, the closures had little effect on the local economy. A boom in tourism, partly in response to the reduction in logging, more than compensated for the loss of pulp mill employment.[69] The key ingredients in the environmentalists' victory had been the mobilization of the large numbers of supporters and moderate goals. It also did not hurt to have unscrupulous opponents, seemingly oblivious to the public interest.

In another effort to exploit criticism of Forest Service policy, environmental lobbyists enlisted two House members, a Democrat and a Republican, to introduce an amendment to the 1996 Forest Service budget canceling the road construction appropriation, which was crucial to the opening of roadless areas in national forests. The amendment passed by a single vote, only to lose after Republican leaders forced a second vote. In 1997 a proposal to reduce the road construction budget passed the House but died in the Senate on a tie vote. In both cases a clear up-or-down vote would almost certainly have passed with a bipartisan majority. Environmentalists remained optimistic.[70]

The congressional votes and the certainty of additional attacks on the agency's construction budget attracted the attention of the new chief of the Forest Service, Mike Dombeck. A Forest Service veteran, biologist, and, most recently, head of the BLM, Dombeck was amenable to change. In 1996 his staff listened to a presentation from the environmental groups on the proposed road legislation. Over the next year Dombeck gave the proposal serious consideration. He was sympathetic to the environmentalists' arguments and concerned about the agency's budget, its huge backlog of road maintenance projects, and the controversy that every roadless-area timber plan inspired. In January 1998 he announced an eighteen-month road building moratorium, during which his staff would continue to study the issue. Northwest politicians reacted angrily, Forest Service traditionalists "felt downright insulted," and environmentalists, while pleased with the announcement, carefully read the fine print. Dombeck's order excluded the Northwest Forest Plan and the Tongass National Forest, which had recently adopted a new forest plan. It also did not address logging that relied on helicopters or other machinery that did not require roads. The moratorium only indirectly protected roadless areas. It was a temporary, partial victory.[71]

At this point the Pew Trusts launched a Heritage Forests Campaign. Unhappy with the endless squabbling of the dissident groups, Pew insisted on a centralized operation and professional leadership. The national environmental organizations, which at first had "scrambled" to influence the reform effort, pledged their cooperation.[72] Ken Rait, a veteran of earlier forestry conflicts, was hired to head a small leadership committee that coordinated the activities of the many participating groups. Together, they mounted the most ambitious and sustained nationwide environmental campaign since ANILCA. Their goal was different, however. Republican control of both houses of Congress meant that meaningful legislation was unlikely, probably impossible. The objective now was to persuade the president to exercise his administrative powers.

The goal of the campaign was to end road building in national forests and protect the 58 million acres of national forests lands that were still roadless. A ban on road building appealed to a wide variety of environmentalists, from "zero-cut" activists to champions of the Northwest Forest Plan, as well as proponents of reduced government spending. The Forest Service was ambivalent. Even traditional foresters acknowledged that roads contributed to erosion, disrupted wildlife, aided the spread of invasive species, and encouraged poaching, the cultivation of illegal drugs, and other criminal activities. Many of them were willing to maintain the existing road system and cut second-growth timber.

For the next two years the Heritage Forest Campaign sought to persuade Clinton to endorse a permanent ban and eliminate the moratorium's loopholes. "The driving force," writes historian James Morton Turner, was the "synergy" between the Heritage Forests Campaign, the president's advisors, and the Forest Service.[73] Of particular importance was Podesta, who became chief of staff in 1998. Working closely with Babbitt on the campaign for new monuments, he also embraced Dombeck's cause.[74] By the fall of 1999 the president and his aides were satisfied that there was sufficient public support for the plan and authorized Domcheck to proceed with a permanent rule. When the Forest Service undertook a "scoping" process to gauge public reactions, the Heritage Forest staff mounted a nationwide campaign; sympathizers flooded the agency with more than 1 million supportive comments. The effects were apparent in the draft environmental impact statement, released in May 2000. It called for a ban on road building in all the national forests except the Tongass. A massive publicity campaign urged the inclusion of the Tongass and more restrictions on extractive activities.

The final environmental impact statement listed four possible choices. The first was a return to the premoratorium status quo, which would result in the construction of 232 miles of new roads per year in roadless areas. The second was a ban on road building with a few exceptions, which would reduce the annual total to about 60 miles. The third choice, the preferred alternative, would ban road building and commercial logging in roadless areas except for "stewardship" logging, which would emphasize thinning and protection of endangered species. The final option was to ban all logging unless it was to protect endangered species. The Tongass National Forest was exempted from all four plans and subject to special rules.

The EIS also provided abundant evidence of the modest economic impact of the proposed rule. Alternative 2 was likely to reduce total employment by 607 jobs, Alternative 3 by 730. Alternative 4 would cost 886 at a time when overall employment in the Northwest, the most critically affected area, was growing by more than 10,000 jobs per year.[75] Even a "zero cut" policy would reduce the region's projected annual job growth by less than 10 percent. This surprisingly modest total was a devastating commentary on the industry's supposed preoccupation with jobs and on the impact of a decade and a half of accelerated logging, which had targeted the most accessible roadless lands. The remaining areas were generally remote, difficult to reach, and, to timber companies, unappealing; almost two-thirds were between 5,000 and 11,000 feet above sea level, and one-third was adjacent to wilderness areas.

The Forest Service estimated that approximately 10 percent of the 58 million acres would eventually be designated as wilderness.[76]

The most controversial feature of the proposed rule was the exclusion of the Tongass National Forest. Despite the closing of the pulp mills, the local superintendent appealed, successfully, for special treatment. The recently adopted Tongass forest plan called for an annual total of fifty-eight miles of road construction and extensive logging. Two-thirds of the timber harvest would come from roadless areas, and the total, assuming the adoption of Alternative 3, would amount to about half of all logging in roadless areas. The cost of including the Tongass under Alternatives 2, 3, or 4 would range from 360 to 380 jobs. The agency was explicit about the reasons for this convoluted arrangement: "The effects of implementing any of the prohibition alternatives would be more dramatic on the Tongass than other national forests. . . . Communities where the timber industry continues to be a cornerstone of the economy and where the Agency has a strong presence would especially be at risk of economic decline."[77] Much of the ensuing controversy would be over the Tongass exclusion and would grow more heated as the toll from the Northwest Forest Plan and the impact of other policy changes made the likely loss of 380 Alaskan jobs seem a remarkably small price to pay for preserving fragments of one of the world's great temperate rain forests.

On January 5, 2001, the president and the secretary of agriculture announced that they had selected Alternative 3. The Roadless Area Conservation Rule, commonly called the roadless rule, would potentially join other landmarks of modern conservation such as the Wilderness Act and ANILCA. It marked the culmination of more than a decade of debate, legal maneuvering, and congressional negotiation that often pushed the experts to the sidelines but could never entirely disregard their ideas. Yet as an agency regulation, the roadless rule was vulnerable. It had been promulgated by Clinton's appointees, and it could be modified or even scrapped by their successors. And it was almost certain that the appointees of the incoming George W. Bush administration would be less supportive. Already the Boise Cascade Company and the state of Idaho had filed lawsuits, initiating what proved to be another extended conflict over the national forests.

ॐ

A conservation scorecard on the Clinton years would record a large number of achievements, several major precedents, a few defeats, and evidence that the science-based conservation of the 1980s had had a large, perhaps surprisingly large, impact. Such an accounting would be incomplete unless it also noted that the achievements were accompanied by great controversy, that many of the innovations resulted from administrative initiatives that could be canceled or reversed, and that economic and employment trends, particularly in the rural West, had played a large role in the president's decision making. Heading the list of accomplishments would be the Northwest Forest Plan and the roadless rule, which directly addressed the most glaring threats to public land conservation. Next would be the BLM monuments, followed by the California Desert Act, the Refuge Improvement Act, and the additions to the wilderness system. The Clinton HCPs helped preserve the Endangered Species Act and may even have helped a few endangered species. The administration's inability to make more than superficial changes in the grazing system was a notable failing, as was its neglect of the looming extinction crisis in rivers, lakes, and oceans. In short, the picture was positive but mixed and, above all, tentative.

Notes

1. R. Edward Grumbine, *Ghost Bears: Exploring the Biodiversity Crisis* (Washington, DC: Island Press, 1992), 155.

2. David Helvarg, *The War against the Greens: The "Wise-Use" Movement, the New Right, and Anti-Environmental Violence* (San Francisco: Sierra Club Books, 1994), 108.

3. Jack Ward Thomas, *The Journals of a Forest Service Chief* (Seattle: University of Washington Press, 2004), 54.

4. Ibid., 111.

5. Elaine Zielinski, "The Northwest Forest Plan," http://www.blm.gov/wo/st/en/info/history/sidebars/ecosystems/Northwest_Forest_Plan.html.

6. Kathie Durbin, *Tree Huggers: Victory, Defeat, and Renewal in the Northwest Ancient Forest Campaign* (Seattle: The Mountaineers, 1996), 203.

7. Jack Ward Thomas et al., "The Northwest Forest Plan: Origins, Components, Implementation Experience, and Suggestions for Change," *Conservation Biology* 20, no. 2 (2006): 281.

8. Ibid.

9. Randy Molina, Bruce G. Marcot, and Robin Lesher, "Protecting Rare, Old-Growth, Forest Associated Species under the Survey and Manage Program

Guidelines of the Northwest Forest Plan," *Conservation Biology* 20, no. 2 (2006): 308; Thomas et al., "Northwest Forest Plan," 281.

10. Thomas et al., "Northwest Forest Plan," 282.

11. Durbin, *Tree Huggers*, 207. Also Steven Lewis Yaffee, *The Wisdom of the Spotted Owl: Policy Lessons for a New Century* (Washington, DC: Island Press, 1994), 147–49.

12. Thomas, *Journals*, 88.

13. Dominick A. DellaSala, "Temperate and Boreal Rainforests of the Pacific Coast of North America," in *Temperate and Boreal Rainforests of the World: Ecology and Conservation*, ed. DellaSala (Washington, DC: Island Press, 2011), 69.

14. Dominick A. DellaSala and Jack E. Williams, "Special Section: The Northwest Forest Plan: A Global Model of Forest Management in Contentious Times," *Conservation Biology* 20, no. 2 (2006): 275.

15. Thomas et al., "Northwest Forest Plan," 283.

16. Robert B. Keiter, *Keeping Faith with Nature: Ecosystems, Democracy, and America's Public Lands* (New Haven: Yale University Press, 2003), 112–13.

17. Shiloh Sundstrom and Johnny Sundstrom, "Stewardship Contracting in the Siuslaw National Forest," in *Stitching the West Back Together: Conservation of Working Landscapes*, ed. Susan Charnley, Thomas E. Sheridan, and Gary P. Nabhan (Chicago: University of Chicago Press, 2014), 166–71; Jim Furnish, *Toward a Natural Forest: The Forest Service in Transition* (Corvallis: Oregon State University Press, 2015), 123–32.

18. Susan Charnley et al., "Northwest Forest Plan—The First Ten Years (1994–2004): Socioeconomic Monitoring of the Klamath National Forest and Their Local Communities," USDA General Technical Report, August 2008, viii, http://www.fs.fed.us/pnw/pubs/pnw_gtr764.pdf.

19. Ibid.

20. Barry R. Noon and Jennifer A. Blakesley, "Conservation of the Northern Spotted Owl under the Northwest Forest Plan," *Conservation Biology* 20, no. 2 (2006): 293; "Spotted Owls in Rapid Decline," *Forest News*, Fall 2015, 7; Ben Goldfarb, "Murrelet Malaise," *High Country News* 47 (December 7, 2015): 6.

21. Nathan Rice, "Bigger Fires and Evolving Threats Force Changes in the Northwest Forest Plan," *High Country News*, April 29, 2013, http://www.hcn.org/issues/45.7/seeking-balance-in-oregons-timber-country/bigger-fires-and-evolving-threats-force-changes-in-the-northwest-forest-plan.

22. Thomas R. Stanley Jr., "Ecosystem Management and the Arrogance of Humanism," *Conservation Biology* 9, no. 2 (April 1995): 155–62; Richard Freeman, "The EcoFactory: The United States Forest Service and the Political Construction of Ecosystem Management," *Environmental History* 7, no. 4 (October 2002): 642.

23. Grumbine, *Ghost Bears*, 156.

24. Judith A. Layzer, *Natural Experiments: Ecosystem-Based Management and the Environment* (Cambridge, MA: MIT Press, 2008), 281.

25. Christopher McGrory Klyza, *Who Controls Public Lands? Mining, Forestry, and Grazing Policies, 1870–1990* (Chapel Hill: University of North Carolina Press, 1996), 151–51; Charles Davis and Sandra Davis, "The Politics of Hard-Rock Mining in the American West," in *Environmental Politics and Policy in the West*, ed. Zachary A. Smith and John C. Freemuth (Boulder: University Press of Colorado, 2007), 140.

26. Christopher McGrory Klyza and David Sousa, *American Environmental Policy, 1990–2006: Beyond Gridlock* (Cambridge, MA: MIT Press, 2008), 52.

27. Michael J. Bean and Melanie J. Rowland, *The Evolution of National Wildlife Law*, 3rd ed. (Westport: Praeger, 1997), 509–12.

28. Ann Vileisis, *Discovering the Unknown Landscape: A History of America's Wetlands* (Washington, DC: Island Press, 1997), 287–89.

29. James Gustave Speth, *Red Sky at Morning: America and the Crisis of the Global Environment* (New Haven: Yale University Press, 2004), 104.

30. Frank Wheat, *California Desert Miracle: The Fight for Desert Parks and Wilderness* (San Diego: Sunbelt Publications, 1999), 53.

31. Ibid., 100.

32. Ibid., 213–94.

33. Hal K. Rothman and Char Miller, *Death Valley National Park: A History* (Reno: University of Nevada Press, 2013), 68.

34. Robert L. Fischman, *National Wildlife Refuges: Coordinating a Conservation System through Law* (Washington, DC: Island Press, 2003), 32–33.

35. Bean and Rowland, *Evolution of National Wildlife Law*, 288.

36. Ibid., 292–93.

37. Fischman, *National Wildlife Refuges*, 62.

38. Ibid., 125.

39. Michael J. Yochim, *Protecting Yellowstone: Science and the Politics of National Park Management* (Albuquerque: University of New Mexico Press, 2013), 87–111; Trust for Public Land, "Final Chapter of New World Mine Controversy Complete," June 15, 2010, https://www.tpl.org/media-room/final-chapter-new-world-mine-controversy-complete.

40. Douglas Bevington, *The Rebirth of Environmentalism: Grassroots Activism from the Spotted Owl to the Polar Bear* (Washington, DC: Island Press, 2009), 53–82.

41. Durbin, *Tree Huggers*, 226–40.

42. Ibid., 284.

43. Peter Duinker, Gary Bull, and Bruce A. Shindler, "Sustainable Forestry in Canada and the United States: Developments and Prospects," in *Two Paths toward Sustainable Forests: Public Values in Canada and the United States*, ed. Bruce A. Shindler,

Thomas M. Beckley, Mary Carmel Finley (Corvallis: Oregon State University Press, 2003), 46–47.

44. Samuel P. Hays, *Wars in the Woods: The Rise of Ecological Forestry in America* (Pittsburgh: University of Pittsburgh Press, 2007), 155–56.

45. Mark Dowie, *Losing Ground: American Environmentalism at the Close of the Twentieth Century* (Cambridge, MA: MIT Press, 1995), 216–18.

46. Michael E. Kraft and Norman J. Vig, "Environmental Policy from the 1970s to the Twenty-First Century," in *Environmental Policy: New Directions for the Twenty-First Century*, 6th ed., ed. Vig and Kraft (Washington, DC: CQ Press, 2007), 15.

47. Joe Hunt, *Mission without A Map: The Politics and Policies of Restoration Following the Exxon Valdez Oil Spill: 1989–2002*, rev. ed. (Anchorage: Exxon Valdez Oil Spill Trustees Council, 2009), 116.

48. Duinker, Bull, and Schindler, "Sustainable Forestry," 30.

49. Keiter, *Keeping Faith with Nature*, 115.

50. Holly Doremus, "Private Property Interests, Wildlife Restoration, and Competing Visions of a Western Eden," in *Reclaiming the Native Home of Hope: Community, Ecology, and the American West*, ed. Robert B. Keiter (Salt Lake City: University of Utah Press, 1998), 80.

51. Joe Roman, *Listed: Dispatches from America's Endangered Species Act* (Cambridge, MA: Harvard University Press, 2011), 182–83.

52. Ronald T. Libby, *Eco-Wars: Political Campaigns and Social Movements* (New York: Columbia University Press, 1998), 189–204.

53. Bruce Babbitt, *Cities in the Wilderness: A New Vision of Land Use in America* (Washington, DC: Island Press, 2005), 73.

54. Roman, *Listed*, 142.

55. Ibid., 143

56. Ibid.

57. Jim Robbins, "On the Life List," *Nature Conservancy Magazine*, no. 1 (2012): 38–43.

58. William R. Mangun, "Wildlife Resource Policy Issues in the West," in *Environmental Politics and Policy*, ed. Smith and Freemuth, 121–22.

59. Richard Primack, *Essentials of Conservation Biology*, 5th ed. (Sunderland, MA: Sinauer Associates, 2010), 476.

60. Klyza and Sousa, *American Environmental Policy*, 114–18; Babbitt, *Cities in the Wilderness*, 103.

61. "A Monumental Tug of War," *High Country News* 47 (February 16, 2015): 16.

62. Jeffrey O. Durrant, *Struggle over Utah's San Rafael Swell: Wilderness, National Conservation Areas, and National Monuments* (Tucson: University of Arizona Press, 2007), 90.

63. Klyza and Sousa, *American Environmental Policy*, 119.

64. Oregon Explorer, "A Monumental Accord: Steens Mountain Cooperative Management Area," http://oregonexplorer.info/content/monumental-accord-steens-mountain-cooperative-management-area?topic=86&ptopic=62; Nancy Langston, *Where Land and Water Meet: A Western Landscape Transformed* (Seattle: University of Washington, 2003), 148–49.

65. Pinchot Institute, *Independent Science Panel Report: Herger-Feinstein Quincy Library Group Forest Recovery Act* (Washington, DC: Pinchot Institute for Conservation, July 31, 2013), 5, 12–20, 31–41. Also USDA, *Status Report to Congress, Fiscal Year 2011, Herger-Feinstein Quincy Library Group Forest Recovery Act Pilot Project*, http://www.fs.fed.us/r5/hfqlg/publications/congress_report/2011/FY2011%20HFQLG%20Report%20Final%20for%20Release.pdf.

66. Ed Marston, "The Quincy Library Group: A Divisive Attempt at Peace," in *Across the Great Divide: Explorations in Collaborative Conservation and the American West*, ed. Philip Brick, Donald Snow, and Sarah Van de Wetering (Washington, DC: Island Press, 2001), 79–90; Andy Stahl, "Ownership, Accountability, and Collaboration," in *Across the Great Divide*, ed. Brick, 195; Edward P. Weber, *Bringing Society Back In: Grassroots Ecosystem Management, Accountability, and Sustainable Communities* (Cambridge, MA: MIT Press, 2003), 6–7; Mangun, "Wildlife Resource Policy Issues," 110.

67. Sundstrom and Sundstrom, "Stewardship Contracting," 159–76; Cassandra Moseley and Emily June Davis, *Stewardship Contracting for Landscape-Scale Projects*, Ecosystem Workforce Program Working Paper, no. 25 (Eugene: University of Oregon, Institute for Sustainable Environment, Summer 2010), 8–10, 12–13.

68. Kathie Durbin, *Tongass: Pulp Politics and the Fight for the Alaska Rain Forest*, 2nd ed. (Corvallis: Oregon State University Press, 2005), 249–86.

69. Ibid., 305.

70. James Morton Turner, *The Promise of Wilderness: American Environmental Politics since 1964* (Seattle: University of Washington Press, 2012), 351–53.

71. Ibid., 324; Furnish, *Toward a Natural Forest*, 152.

72. Turner, *Promise of Wilderness*, 356.

73. Ibid., 355–56.

74. Elizabeth Shogren, "Legacy Maker," *High Country News* 47 (May 25, 2015): 12, 14.

75. USDA, *Forest Service Roadless Area Conservation, Final Environmental Impact Statement*, vol. 1 (Washington, DC: USDA, 2000), ES5–6.

76. Ibid., 3–241.

77. Ibid., ES7.

7

Land Conservation circa 2000

By the end of the century the deceptively simple formula favored by scientists for preserving biodiversity, "cores, corridors, and carnivores," masked the formidable assignment they had proposed. Corridors, the links between core areas, designed to facilitate the movement of plants and animals, were hard to define and even harder to create. The reintroduction of carnivores, even under carefully controlled conditions, often stirred intense local opposition. Suffice it to say that establishing corridors and reintroducing carnivores would be long-term projects. On the other hand, cores, the parks, wilderness areas, wildlife refuges, and in some cases lands owned or controlled by land conservancies, were reasonably abundant and were the principal reason for the sense that progress was possible, that the United States might still serve as a positive example for the world.

Eighty-three million acres of national park land, including 44 million acres of wilderness, an additional 60 million acres of wilderness outside the parks, together with the other lands—totaling, in all, perhaps 260 million acres nationwide—were a meaningful starting point. There were problems

DOI: 10.7330/9781607325703.c007

resulting from the opportunistic way that parks and wilderness areas had been established and the persistent efforts of politicians and outside interests to exploit them for commercial purposes, but the most fundamental problem was geographical. The acreage totals are inflated by vast holdings in Alaska, which had many virtues but contributed relatively little to biodiversity. In addition, the overwhelming majority of national park lands (outside Alaska) and about 95 percent of wilderness lands (again, outside Alaska) were located in eleven western states, a reflection of the history of the public domain, the role of "monumentalism," and the requirements of the wilderness system. Most of the western lands were mountainous or arid, which limited their suitability as biological reserves. Several surveys concluded that US national parks and wilderness areas included less than half of all North American ecoregions.

A survey of park and wilderness lands at the turn of the century emphasizes two themes: the promising but tentative achievements of the 1960s and 1970s in setting aside visually, aesthetically, and in some cases biologically valuable areas, and the struggles of the post-1980 years to expand and consolidate those lands into effective cores. Examinations of the national park system and the Park Service, the critical agency; two large, sprawling, notably threatened core areas, Everglades National Park and Adirondack park and forest preserve; and the evolving Wilderness Preservation System underline the continuing challenges of land conservation.

THE NPS IN BAD TIMES AND GOOD

By the early 1990s, the National Park Service, prestigious and beloved by the public, may have been less well equipped than at any time in its history to manage its sprawling lands and, especially, to reconcile its traditional commitment to visitor services with demands for ecosystem management and ecological integrity. It did not suffer the internal divisions of the Forest Service and BLM: the problem was the politicians' perception of the NPS as a tourist bureau and the individual parks as sources of favors for constituents. From the beginning the NPS had had to wrestle with the often conflicting demands of recreation and resource preservation. James Watt and other Reagan appointees had been determined to tip the balance. Their successors, while less outspoken, were no less partisan. William R. Lowry, a leading student of the national parks during this period, concluded that "the momentum . . . to establish preservation as the primary policy goal had disappeared by 1992."[1] It was precisely at that time that biologists and environmentalists were demanding more emphasis on preservation in the form of restrictions on road building and auto use, limitations on commercial services, more backcountry wilderness, and more attention to wildlife. As the gap between Washington and park professionals and their allies in the scientific and environmental communities widened, the future of the national park system became increasingly uncertain.

One ominous measure of this trend was the growing power of the political appointees in the Interior Department. Lowry documents a consistent pattern, at least to 1993. Reagan and Bush appointees sought to intimidate or eliminate professional employees who objected to their emphasis on commercial activities. The notorious William Horn "harassed into retirement" western regional director Howard Chapman in the mid-1980s, and his successors purged regional director Lorraine Mintzmyer and others who worked on the ill-fated 1991 Yellowstone "vision" report.[2] These celebrated incidents were examples of a pattern of behavior that demoralized many employees. A 1992 internal report acknowledged that "the agency is beset by controversy, concern, weakened morale and declining effectiveness."[3]

Congressional interference also reached new levels. Although appropriations for Park Service operations declined after 1983 and did not reach that level again until 1997, the construction budget, a separate account, doubled during the same period, as members of Congress added funds for specific projects in their districts. Typically two-thirds to three-quarters of the construction budget was designated for such projects, which only coincidentally matched the Park Service's list of needed repairs and improvements. A 1995 General Accounting Office study of a dozen popular national parks reported serious infrastructure problems and much deferred maintenance.[4]

The advent of the Clinton administration reduced, at least temporarily, the tensions of the preceding years. The new administration welcomed additional parks and monuments and recommended increased appropriations for the Park Service. It was also sympathetic to efforts in and out of the Park Service to place greater emphasis on ecosystem integrity. NPS managers responded with relief and enthusiasm and a new emphasis on preservation. Following the publication of a critical study of the Park Service's neglect of scientific research by NPS historian Richard West Sellers in 1997, the director authorized park-by-park inventories of natural resources and more exten-sive collaboration with academic scientists.[5] Given the hostilities that had marked the preceding decade, the post-1993 transition was remarkably rapid and thorough. By the end of the century, the NPS had regained much of its former élan and was more sensitive to the importance of the parks' biologi-cal resources than ever before.

TROUBLED PARKS

The political and bureaucratic relationships that dominated discussions of the national park system often obscured another long-standing problem that com-promised the role of parks as core areas. Most parks were simply too small to assure the protection of animals and plants, which was one of their principal functions. This had not been a serious issue as long as most of them had been surrounded by undeveloped land. But population growth and the continued industrialization of the rural West, together with aggressive timber cutting by the Forest Service in the 1970s and 1980s, eliminated the informal buffers and made many parks seem like isolated islands. Despite efforts to reverse this trend, including the Northwest Forest Plan and the roadless rule, it was certain to become more severe in the absence of continuing efforts to counter it.

The national parks in the eastern half of the United States provided an often distressing preview of the likely future of the park system as a whole. Each park faced a distinctive combination of potentially threatening activi-ties around its periphery, but the common challenge was the spread of real estate developments that brought roads, houses, stores, cars, and more peo-ple to the park boundaries. Since the eastern parks generally did not have national forests or other public lands to serve as buffers, the effects of sprawl were inescapable. The prevalence of privately owned land typically made park expansion prohibitively expensive.

Of the troubled eastern parks—a list that features Shenandoah and Great Smoky Mountains, among others—Everglades, ironically the first park to be authorized (1934) and established (1947) specifically to preserve a distinctive ecosystem, easily topped the list. By any standard, Everglades, at 1.5 mil-lion acres, was not small. In 1974 Congress had added Big Cypress Preserve (700,000 acres) as a buffer, and three state-owned water conservation areas (500,000 acres) added another layer of protection. Florida also had a large and vocal environmental community, epitomized by the legendary Marjory Stoneman Douglas, who remained the public face of the Everglades campaign until her death in 1998. Most Florida politicians gave lip service to the preservation effort, and the federal government repeatedly authorized large expenditures to "save" the Everglades.

Yet the threats persisted, and neither the Everglades ecosystem as a whole nor the park were demonstrably more secure after thirty years of effort and a long list of apparent successes. Rapid population growth on both Florida coasts, endless sprawl, a powerful agricultural lobby, and an ever-increasing demand for fresh water effectively canceled out the so-called victories; no matter how many offending projects were defeated, the day-to-day expansion of residential and commercial areas of both coasts was a constant, escalating threat. David McCally has explained it in terms of the "social epistemology of the Florida dream." Most Floridians, he argues, had implicit faith in three elements: science, negotiated political compromises, and "ever-increasing consumption and continuous growth." In late twentieth-century South Florida, this meant a preference for expensive engineering solutions that minimized any possible threat to the economic status quo.[6]

Regardless of what contemporary residents believed or assumed, protecting the Everglades was a formidable challenge. The vast South Florida wetland had long been recognized as unique, and a large park had been on the federal drawing board as early as the 1930s, when the population of South Florida was less than a half million. In a move fraught with symbolism, the area that would later become Big Cypress National Preserve was deleted from the original park plans because of extensive logging and the discovery of oil in one area.[7] Nevertheless, the creation of the park suggested the possibility that biology "might supersede scenic monumentalism."[8] What was less well understood was the Everglades' dependence on water flowing through Big Cypress, which in turn depended on the area around Lake Okeechobee to the north and ultimately on the Kissimmee River wetlands, which extended to the outskirts of Orlando, more than 150 miles from the park border. Douglas's seminal *River of Grass* (1949) made that point, but few people grasped its significance.

In the following decades extensive growth on the Atlantic Coast led to decisions that would compromise the park's viability. To supply fresh water to the burgeoning cities and to guard against floods, the US Army Corps of Engineers diverted the natural flow of water through the center of the state. Between the late 1940s and the 1970s these projects largely obliterated the natural system.⁹ In the meantime the Cuban revolution and US tariffs on imported sugar spurred the growth of sugar cane farming south of Lake Okeechobee, further complicating the situation. By the 1960s the Everglades was beginning to show the effects of these activities. A 1968 proposal to build a large airport on the edge of the park provoked the first concerted political backlash against development. The airport plan failed, but the other problems became more serious and disruptive. From that time until the present the battle to save the Everglades has been continuous, with most Floridians professing affection for the Everglades but also wary of meaningful restrictions. Douglas summarized the situation nicely when she wrote that "Florida has made great strides, but the degradation of the environment has become institutionalized, embedded in the nature of things."¹⁰

There were significant victories. The creation of Big Cypress Preserve involved the largest purchase of private land in Park Service history. Governor Bob Graham's "Save Our Everglades" plan of 1983 had the unrealistic goal of restoring the Everglades by 2000, but it did begin the reengineering of the Kissimmee River to its natural, meandering course. Beginning in 1988, a federal lawsuit over water pollution from the agricultural area south of Lake Okeechobee led to years of bitter litigation but ultimately a significant reduction in pollution levels. As a US senator, Graham successfully proposed legislation that expanded the park to the east and began the restoration of that area. Yet none of these victories did more than address relatively small parts of the larger problem, and Florida environmentalists remained frustrated. When the legislature passed the Marjory Stoneham Douglas Everglades Forever Act in 1994, largely written by sugar lobbyists, the feisty Douglas, at age 103, indignantly insisted that her name be removed from the law.¹¹

In 1993 a committee of distinguished scientists charged with outlining additional steps came to the commonsense conclusion that the best way to protect the Everglades was to restore it literally, to allow water to flow naturally from Lake Okeechobee through the park to the ocean. This proposal set the stage for another massive restoration plan, "the largest and most expensive attempt at ecological restoration" ever undertaken.¹² In the following years the actual recommendations of the scientists gained little support outside the environmental community, but they helped stimulate interest in a grand gesture that would make the Everglades' problems go away without disrupt-ing the Florida economy. That took the form of an ambitious 1998 Corps of Engineers plan to remove one-third of the dikes and levees in the Everglades, drill hundreds of wells to store water underground and utilize two large quarries for aboveground storage, raise part of the main highway crossing the Everglades to improve water flow, and plant 30,000 acres of sawgrass on the eastern border. The plan would take thirty years to implement and cost $8 billion dollars. It was another attempt to treat "the environmental ills of the region as little more than a problem of engineering."[13]

Although most scientists and environmentalists were deeply skeptical, the Corps' plan became the basis of the Comprehensive Everglades Restoration Plan (CERP), adopted by Congress in 2000. Secretary Babbitt recalled his sur-prise at the broad, bipartisan support for the legislation.[14] Within the state the plan also had wide appeal because it promised more water to South Florida and did not disrupt the sugar industry. Rather than restoring the Everglades to something approaching its original condition, the politicians sought to construct, in the words of one longtime observer, a "Disneyland Everglades," similar in appearance but wholly contrived and artificial.[15]

As CERP was taking shape, the park's scientists studied the plan and con-cluded that it did not "represent a restoration scenario for the south, central and northern Everglades." Robert Johnson, the head of the park's science staff, complained that it "gave the cities and the ag guys all the water they needed. . . . Then they said: Okay, if there's anything left, we'll try to get it to the Everglades someday, as long as nobody gets flooded." What the Corps and the politicians were creating was "an economic boondoggle in environ-mental clothing."[16] CERP's backers were shocked. To quiet the criticism, they revised the plan to supply additional water to the park. However, as the leg-islation worked its way through Congress, the additional water became a target for other interests, and, in the end, the park lost virtually everything it had gained. Despite its name, CERP reflected the interests of real estate developers and city managers, though two late amendments helped blur this reality and mollify critics. The final legislation authorized adaptive manage-ment, whereby managers would make changes as problems emerged and conditions changed, and independent scientific panels were to make periodic evaluations of the project. Still, Friends of the Everglades and other environ-mental groups remained skeptical.[17]

If CERP was reminiscent of earlier Everglades restoration schemes, its aftermath also struck a familiar note. As more and more people read the fine print, disillusionment grew. As critics became more outspoken and the politicians turned their attention to other issues, the appropriations to make CERP a reality fell behind schedule.[18] In 2003 Florida governor Jeb Bush, initially an enthusiastic CERP supporter, persuaded the legislature to renege on its contributions, presumably at the behest of sugar lobbyists. Conflict and litigation followed for nearly a decade until something like the original partnership with the federal government was restored. In the interim large-scale projects gave way to piecemeal efforts "that would permit at least some progress."[19] The National Research Council, assigned to make biennial reports on the progress of CERP, was increasingly pessimistic. Its 2012 report observed that "little progress has been made in restoring the core of the Everglades ecosystem."[20] Or as the historian Jack E. Davis has concluded, "Everglades management seemed as dysfunctional as ever."[21]

An addendum to this story provides still more evidence of the remarkable persistence of the Everglades' problems. The principal criticisms of CERP were that it depended on traditional engineering techniques and did not provide an adequate supply of water to the park. A better and probably cheaper approach was simply to restore the natural movement of surface water between Lake Okeechobee and the park. In June 2008 Florida governor Charlie Crist embraced this idea by proposing to buy 187,000 acres of land, mostly on the southern shore of Lake Okeechobee, for $1.75 billion. The purchase would put one of the large sugar producers, United States Sugar Corporation, out of business and would allow water to move relatively freely through its former fields. The proposal was politically appealing as well: it would enhance Governor Crist's stature and please environmentalists, who had been battling the sugar companies for decades. But like so many previous Everglades plans, this one soon ran into trouble. United States Sugar's employees protested, local officials were outraged at the prospect of lost jobs and tax revenues, and the national recession devastated the state's budget. In November 2008 the governor reduced the plan to 180,000 acres and $1.34 billion; in April 2009 to 72,8000 acres and $536 million; and in 2010 to 26,790 acres and $197 million. The deal included options to buy additional land, but with Florida's economy severely depressed and the legislature increasingly hostile to land purchases, the prospects for additional acquisitions were slim indeed.[22]

What of the park? In 2010 the UN World Heritage Committee reaffirmed the dubious status of Everglades National Park as a World Heritage in Danger, citing "serious and continuing degradation" of its aquatic ecosystem.[23] An ever-increasing list of invasive species promised to complicate an already difficult situation. Thousands of Burmese pythons, one of the most fearsome of the recent additions, have virtually eradicated small mammals from large areas of the park.[24] Thus, the park remains "on life support," despite more than fifty remedial projects funded by CERP. The "number one priority," as Superintendent Dan Kimball explained, is still "to restore the freshwater flows."[25] Like the larger Everglades area, the park can point to gains and losses while it awaits an effective restoration plan. "It's not if we can save it," observes Stephan Davis, a wetlands ecologist for the Everglades Foundation. "It's whether we want to."[26]

FOREVER WILD

The largest park in the lower forty-eight states and one of the few state parks to attract the attention of environmentalists and biologists alike, New York's Adirondack Park (5.9 million acres by the 1970s, including the state-owned Forest Preserve, 40 percent of the total) has faced similar problems, though with a meaningful difference. The Everglades and many other national parks were too small to fulfill their roles as protectors of biodiversity and catalysts for networks of wild lands. The Adirondack Park was big enough, but the "blue line," the boundary that had been extended outward over a century to embrace more and more of the Adirondack region, included large areas of privately owned land. Originally the state planned to buy out inholders, but, as the park grew, that strategy became prohibitively expensive. Until the 1970s the relationship between the park and its inholders was largely unregulated and relaxed, mostly because the area was an economic backwater with fewer than 100,000 permanent residents. Then growth, in the form of a vacation home boom, forced the state to restrict real estate developments, setting off a twenty-year battle to define the character of the park. In Florida most problems arose from activities outside the park; in New York many similar problems arose inside the park's boundaries. At a time when many other eastern parks were attempting to operate without fee title to all of the lands they encompassed, the Adirondacks served as an augury of the future of public land management.

Unlike the Everglades, the Adirondack region is extremely varied with rugged mountains, lakes, rivers, and wetlands. There are fourteen major river systems, 30,000 miles of streams and rivers, and thousands of lakes, marshes, bogs, and fens.[27] These features, together with a short growing season; long, cold, and snowy winters; and thin, infertile soils, inhibited development. Native Americans avoided the area until the fur trade emerged in the early seventeenth century. After they and their European partners had extirpated the beaver and other fur-bearing animals, the Adirondacks returned to its former status, isolated and overlooked. In the second half of the nineteenth century, wealthy New Yorkers bought up huge tracts of land and created elaborate estates, renowned for their distinctive rustic architecture and interior decoration. Every July and August witnessed a remarkable gathering of the nation's financial, political, and intellectual elite.

Along with the vacationers came loggers, who stripped the valleys of conifers and the uplands of hardwoods and whose locomotives spewed sparks and coals, causing numerous fires, some of which destroyed large areas of the forest. Since the Adirondacks include the headwaters of most of the state's major rivers, including the Hudson, the loggers' depredations attracted widespread concern. Fears for the state's water supply led to the establishment of the Forest Preserve in 1885. Ten years later the state constitution specified that the preserve "shall be forever kept as wild forest land." "Forever wild" henceforth became the mantra of the state's conservationists.

For the next three-quarters of a century the Adirondacks remained a remote vacation area, attracting hunters, anglers, hikers, and a diminishing number of magnates. The most important controversies pitted conservationists, who demanded adherence to the literal meaning of the state constitution, against the state's resource managers, who sought to "improve" the forest with dams, salvage logging schemes, and similar initiatives. Thanks to the tireless work of individuals such as Paul Schaefer, who was personally responsible for at least a dozen organizations, the conservationists won more than they lost.[28]

Gradually, however, the nature of the threat changed. A burgeoning postwar population, more affluent and mobile than earlier generations, increasingly looked to the Adirondacks for recreational opportunities, a trend that accelerated with the construction of an interstate highway, the Northway, from Albany to the Canadian border. By the late 1960s, the town of Lake George in the southeast corner of the park had become the "gaudiest, most commercial" place in the Adirondacks with attractions such as Santa's Workshop, Frontier Land, and Animal Land.[29] The completion of the highway also attracted a new wave of real estate speculators, who proposed residential developments, golf courses, shopping centers, and other amenities for affluent second-home purchasers. Their plans threatened to transform the area, making the state land simply a backdrop for extensive commercial operations.

Opponents mobilized to fight this new challenge. Emphasizing the need for action, the prominent conservationist Laurence Rockefeller proposed the creation of a 2 million–acre national park in the center of the Forest Preserve. Other activists agreed that something should be done but preferred to rely on the state government. In 1968 New York governor Nelson Rockefeller appointed a Temporary Study Commission on the Future of the Adirondacks, chaired by prominent Adirondack resident Harold R. Hockschild. The Temporary Study Commission acknowledged the "crisis" and called for the creation of a new authority, the Adirondack Park Agency (APA), which the legislature authorized in 1971. The APA drew up a Master Plan for the Forest Preserve, completed in 1972, and a Private Land Use and Development Plan, completed in 1973. The Master Plan divided the state land into zones with about 40 percent, or 1.1 million acres, designated as wilderness, using the same definition as the federal Wilderness Act. The plan also created categories of private land, with half of the total, mostly land owned by timber and paper companies, in the most restrictive category. The existing towns were largely unregulated.

The Adirondack plan was a pioneering experiment in "sustainable development," an ambitious effort to manage residential and industrial growth. It effectively prohibited the large developments that had been on the architects' drawing boards in the early 1970s, while encouraging new projects in and around existing towns. It also created the largest wilderness system in the East. It was highly controversial, with many Adirondack residents incensed at the private land restrictions (and the often heavy-handed and dilatory actions of the APA in its early years). They had long been suspicious of outsiders, particularly rich outsiders, who paid little attention to them and their interests. Real estate developers, usually wealthy outsiders themselves, manipulated these sentiments. In response to protests, New York's governors began to appoint APA members who were more sympathetic to the residents or at least determined not to provoke them. That approach antagonized the conservation groups that wanted more stringent restrictions in order to preserve open space and biodiversity. The APA was caught in the middle.[30]

By the late 1980s the APA was the object of regular attacks by local government officials, developers, and environmentalists. In addition, several timber companies with vast tracts of Adirondack land began to sell off their holdings, creating additional challenges. Seeking new direction, Governor Mario Cuomo appointed a study group, the Twenty-First Century Commission, chaired by Peter A.A. Berle, a leading environmentalist who would later head the National Audubon Society. The Berle commission took its charge seriously and came up with 245 recommendations. It called for the state to purchase an additional 645,000 acres, increase the APA's powers, do more to safeguard backcountry areas, and declare a one-year moratorium on most development. These were hardly radical proposals, but they set off a firestorm of opposition, including public demonstrations, vandalism, and death threats.[31] Many local government officials were directly or indirectly involved and made no effort to prosecute the vandals. Eventually there was a strong reaction against the protests; some residents supported the commission proposals, others were ambivalent, and even those who sympathized with the protesters began to realize that they were compromising the area's appeal to developers and potential buyers. In any case, the controversy made the report political poison. The governor refused to support the most controversial recommendations, and the legislature declined to act on it.

The reaction to the Berle commission's report was one example of a broader backlash against government activism. In 1990 New York voters turned down a bond issue that would have financed additional land purchases in the Adirondacks, and in 1994 Governor Cuomo, who was associated with big government projects (but not specifically with the Adirondacks or other state parks), lost his reelection campaign to Republican George Pataki, an obscure state senator. As the political scientist Jon D. Erickson reports, "an era of nearly universal top-down planning that began with the APA Act was coming to a close."[32]

But disarray at the top did not necessarily mean less support for the park or for the preservation of open space. Three other factors were also involved. First, by the 1990s it was clear that the APA had not hurt the local economy. On the contrary, employment and incomes had risen faster than in other parts of the state.[33] A major contributor was construction. In the 1970s and 1980s the Adirondacks averaged more than 1,000 new homes per year; in the 1990s the average was closer to 1,500. Most of these were not occupied year round, so the demand for services lagged behind the rise in property tax payments, a boon to local governments. Some school districts were able to spend far more per pupil than the state average.[34] By deterring large-scale developments, the APA had also created an aura of stability attractive to outsiders. Second was the more accommodating approach of the APA, which diffused much of the local opposition. Public opinion polls showed overwhelming support for preserving the area's rural character and ambivalence about the proliferation of second homes since rising property values often priced local purchasers out of the real estate market.[35] While the old conflicts did not end, new, more cooperative relationships emerged in the late 1990s.

The final and most important element in the new political environment was the conservation easement, the principal mechanism for preserving open space in the 1990s and after. Although the Temporary Study Commission of the 1960s had called for the formation of a regional land conservancy, nothing happened until the late 1980s, when George Davis of the Adirondack Council, an umbrella group of the area's environmental organizations, prepared an influential series of reports on the future of the Forest Preserve. Davis was also instrumental in forming the Adirondack Land Trust, which became a local partner of the Nature Conservancy in 1988. The land trust benefited from the increasing popularity of land conservancies and conservation easements in the fight against urban sprawl. During the next fifteen years the Adirondack Land Trust would be involved in more than 200 deals, preserving 600,000 acres. As the first executive director explained, "More by accident than design, [we] operated at the landscape scale."[36]

One other, initially surprising development of the mid-1990s was the emergence of Governor Pataki as a "remarkably strong supporter of environmental protection."[37] In 1993 the legislature had finally authorized an Environmental Protection Fund to finance land acquisitions. Pataki used the money to buy new park lands and easements; two-thirds of the acreage acquired by 2007, nearly 700,000 acres, was in the Adirondacks.[38] The governor's willingness to spend state money, coupled with the work of the land trust and the desire of the Adirondacks' largest land owners, the timber and paper companies, to reduce their holdings or sell out altogether, combined to produce an unprecedented wave of land transactions. Some of the land was added to the Forest Preserve. Most of it, however, was sold to new buyers as "working forests," with restrictions to ensure sustainability. The easements thus reduced the cost of land conservation and preserved jobs in timber-dependent communities. The local head of the Sierra Club acknowledged that "it just shows what a difference a governor makes."[39]

The success of the softer, less confrontational approach of Pataki and the Adirondack Land Trust had a profound impact. Philip Terrie, a leading histo-rian, argues that there are now two Adirondacks. "The Forest Preserve is get-ting better and bigger through major additions, and other extensive portions of the backcountry are protected by easements, while significant parts of our private land, subdivided and developed, slowly degrade."[40]

The increase in protected acreage has also had a positive impact on the bio-logical health of the area. The forests have made a remarkable recovery from the early twentieth century, when they were ravaged by careless logging and fires. They now approximate presettlement conditions. Forest expert Charles Canham writes that the Adirondacks includes "the largest expanses of old-growth forest" in the eastern United States and probably "the largest remaining tracts of old-growth temperate deciduous forest anywhere in the world."[41] Wildlife has also flourished. Beaver and moose, which had been extirpated or nearly extirpated by the late nineteenth century, are now as numerous as they were 200 years ago.[42] A comparison of the Adirondack Park with several large national parks—Acadia, Great Smoky Mountains, Shenandoah, and Yellowstone—concluded that it is comparable in the num-ber of amphibians, fish, mammals, and reptiles, but had fewer bird species.[43] The most serious deficiency is the lack of well-defined wildlife corridors, a result of the haphazard, opportunistic approach to land acquisition.

The problems and challenges are also great. Extensive property develop-ment around some of the lakes, Lake George being the most notable example, is a persistent issue, and there is the possibility that one or more of the remain-ing large landowners could sell out to developers or develop the land them-selves, as the Whitney family threatened to do in the 1990s. Thanks to more stringent restrictions on the coal-burning utilities of the Midwest, the prob-lem of acid rain, which for decades had killed trees and fish in the Northeast, has diminished, but the longer-term problems of carbon emissions and cli-mate change may well have even greater, potentially catastrophic effects.

WILDERNESS CHALLENGES

The other important core areas were the nearly 600 (by the year 2000) separate parts of the National Wilderness Preservation System, consisting of "untrammeled" land that had "outstanding opportunities for solitude" and primitive recreation as well as "ecological, geological," or other features. The system's potential became apparent in the early 1980s with ANILCA, the national forest wilderness acts, and FLPMA. While the need for solitude and primitive recreation did not diminish, it was the ecological value of wilderness, originally almost an afterthought, that excited the greatest interest after the mid-1980s and that in turn highlighted the role of wilderness management, at first blush an oxymoron. Yet as scientists and many government officials were quick to point out, a "hands off" policy promised to accelerate the loss of biodiversity and healthy ecosystems. "The ideal future may be one where management is no longer needed," observed Reed Noss and Allen Y. Cooperrider in the mid-1990s, but "letting things be is not a safe option . . . in the near future."[44] Michael Soulé was even more emphatic: "management is the only viable alternative to massive attrition of living nature."[45] But if the need for human intervention seemed obvious, what restraints would preserve both the "untrammeled" character of the land and its role in preserving biodiversity? Wilderness advocates bemoaned the tendency of government officials and scientists to become "gardeners" rather than "guardians" of wilderness.[46]

If the wilderness system had become a notable feature of American land conservation by the mid-1980s, its future expansion—and expansion had been the overriding concern of proponents—was less certain than at any time since the 1960s. One obvious obstacle was the success of earlier campaigns. Eighty-five percent of national park land was now wilderness or proposed wilderness; most national forest lands had been reviewed in the process of drafting the wilderness legislation of the 1980s; and the wildlife refuges were either small, de facto wilderness areas (in the case of many islands) or mostly wilderness (in the case of the Alaskan refuges). Most important, the federal management agencies had little interest in enlarging the system. The historian John C. Miles and a dissident federal employees organization, Public Employees for Environmental Responsibility (PEER), have documented the reluctance of the NPS, the agency with the greatest wilderness holdings, to work actively to add to its total. Part of the problem was inertia: once the initial wilderness evaluations were completed in the 1970s, park officials turned to other more immediate issues. There is also controversy, especially where wilderness designations are likely to restrict recreational activities. The battle over motorized rafts on the Colorado River has stalled the designation of wilderness areas in Grand Canyon National Park for more than thirty years.[47] Nor were the environmental organizations, which typically mobilized congressional support for wilderness legislation, entirely blameless. Facing serious challenges on other fronts, they were content to allow the Park Service, and in some cases other agencies, to manage the backcountry as quasi wilderness, without formal designations.

The recent history of the wildlife refuge system provides more dramatic examples of political and bureaucratic resistance. The 1997 Improvement Act required each refuge to prepare a Comprehensive Conservation Plan, which was to include a wilderness review and recommendations to Congress. The agency's response was a prolonged stall; ten years later 40 percent of the refugees still had not completed the plans or wilderness reviews. Apart from the delays, a 2008 evaluation of refuge management reported "a lack of systems for managing or tracking wilderness lands system-wide . . . no central repository of Wilderness Management Plans, no documentation on threats and violations to wilderness areas, and no information available on minimum requirements analysis."[48] The Alaska refuges had been assigned to prepare similar plans under ANILCA, with wilderness recommendations due by 1985. Interior secretary James Watt and his successors sabotaged this process, and the deadline passed with no action. In 2003 Interior secretary Gale Norton decided that it was too late to submit recommendations. The Wilderness Society estimated that at least 57 million acres deserved consideration.[49]

The continuing opposition of commodity producers was another potent factor in the wilderness slowdown. The mining, timber, and grazing interests that originally led the opposition to the Wilderness Act, augmented in recent decades by oil and gas producers and off-road vehicle groups, coalesced to form the anticonservation Wise Use movement of the 1990s and have continued to be influential in western states. Montana and Idaho politicians had been among the earliest and most enthusiastic backers of wilderness legislation. By the 1980s a newer generation of public officials from those states included many of the most determined opponents. The long fight over a Montana national forest wilderness act, which ended in stalemate and inaction, was a measure of this change.[50]

A final factor has been a sense among traditional proponents that wilderness designations may not be as useful as originally imagined. They had not stopped the clear-cutting of western national forests or had much effect on federal land managers. Their value for outdoor recreation diminished as the number of parks, recreation areas, and state and local preserves increased. Many scientists considered them only tangentially relevant to the biodiversity campaign. This skepticism was at least indirectly reflected in an academic debate over the role of wilderness in American culture that generated a flood of polemical writing in the 1990s and after. Critics attacked the use of the term in works like the 1963 Leopold report and in Roderick Nash's classic, *Wilderness and the American Mind* (1969), which portrayed undeveloped (or seemingly undeveloped) land as an abiding influence in American history. Traditional wilderness proponents were incredulous; the author Kenneth Brower referred scornfully to the "myth of the myth of wilderness."[51] Apart from the often florid rhetoric, there was the issue of perspective. Whatever their limitations, writers and activists had played a critical role in warning the public about the many threats to the natural environment. And the Wilderness Preservation System, which received remarkably little attention in the so-called debate, had emerged by the turn of the century as an indispensable feature of the campaign to preserve wildlands and wildlife and slow the pace of climate change.

The story of wilderness expansion in the 1990s is marked by continuing conflict, punctuated by occasional successes as wilderness campaigns found sympathetic congressional backers. The wilderness reviews authorized by FLPMA resulted in 745 wilderness study areas, totaling 25 million acres (14 percent of all BLM lands), a scandalously small number given the remoteness of most BLM holdings. The agency had adopted a procedure reminiscent of the Forest Service's purity doctrine. In this case the critical test was not whether the area was "pristine," but whether any commercial activity could possibly occur there.[52] The resulting wilderness study areas consequently consisted mostly of rugged mountains and deserts. Still, there were several important additions to the wilderness system. The 1990 Arizona Wilderness Act designated 1.1 million acres; the 1994 California Desert Act another 3.6 million acres; and between 1995 and 2000 another million acres were added, three-quarters of it in Nevada. What was not done was also impressive. In Utah, for example, the BLM grudgingly identified 3.2 million acres of potential wilderness, mostly in the sparsely populated southern half of the state, then recommended less than 2 million acres for congressional action. The Utah Wilderness Coalition insisted on more than twice as much, including lands that might conceivably be valuable to the mining or oil industries. The result was a political stalemate that lasted through the 1990s and beyond.[53]

The consequences of such conflicts were not only delays and frustrations, but a continuing failure to close the gap between what ecologists said was needed to preserve biodiversity and the actual pattern of land conservation. The most authoritative survey of the late 1980s found only 157 of 261 "ecotypes" or ecological regions represented in the wilderness system. The legislation of the 1990s added large areas of desert to the "rock and ice" that dominated the national forest lands and Alaskan parks, but notable omissions remained, especially grasslands, eastern hardwoods, and coastal lowlands. Many of these landscapes were present mostly in areas with few public lands, limiting the prospects for compensatory actions in the western states.[54]

Despite its shortcomings, the wilderness system had preserved much ecologically valuable public land by the turn of the century. Most intriguing were areas where wilderness, together with national parks and other conservation lands, had created relatively large de facto preserves. Northwest Arizona, a series of conservation areas north of Las Vegas, Death Valley National Park and the Mojave National Preserve, the Sierra Nevada national parks, and the neighboring BLM wilderness areas were one example. The Yellowstone to Yukon complex, embracing the Yellowstone ecosystem, wilderness areas in Idaho and Montana, Glacier and Waterton National Parks, Canadian provincial parks, large preserves in British Columbus, Alberta, and the Yukon, and the parks and wildlife refuges that spanned the Alaska-Yukon border, was another. The northwest coast, from British Columbia north and west around the great arc of Alaskan coastal lands, included a variety of wilderness, park, and wildlife refuge lands. Another similar east-west band embraced the Brooks Range in northern Alaska. The Boundary Waters Canoe Area, Quetico Provincial Park, Voyageurs National Park, Apostle Islands and Pictured Rocks National Lakeshores, Isle Royale National Park, and nearby national and state forests preserved a large lake and wetland area in the Midwest; and the Adirondack preserve, wilderness areas in the Green and White Mountains, and large areas of privately preserved land in northwestern Maine, coupled with Baxter State Park, created a northeastern core. Great Sand Dune National Park, an adjacent national forest and wildlife refuge, and private conservation lands protected a large area of south-central Colorado. Great Smoky Mountains National Park was potentially the basis for a large preserve in the southern Appalachians; the parks and "sky islands" of southern Arizona and northern Mexico had similar possibilities; and Everglades National Park, Big Cypress National Preserve, and nearby state-owned lands could conceivably play that role in South Florida. In no case were all the lands contiguous, making connectivity a challenge. But given the haphazard process by which public lands were preserved and the pressures of urban sprawl, the results were surprisingly positive.

The Wilderness Preservation System had also become a stimulus to conservation planning in other countries. By the first decade of the twenty-first century at least nine countries, including Canada, had legally designated wilderness areas, and ten others had adopted administrative procedures for creating wilderness.[55] Biennial conferences, sponsored by the United States' WILD Foundation among others, brought together experts on wilderness management. Development pressures and a growing concern for biodiversity were potent reasons for exchanging ideas on the day-to-day operations of wilderness systems.

Wilderness management in the United States dated from the late 1930s, when the Sierra Club formed a committee to advise the Forest Service, then in the process of making semipermanent administrative wilderness designations. An extensive correspondence between the committee members and Robert Marshall, the famous forester who was instrumental in the formulation of Forest Service wilderness policy, started a process of identifying acceptable activities in wilderness areas. Sierra Club wilderness conferences in the 1950s continued that effort and built support for the movement that produced the 1964 Wilderness Act.[56] For the next thirty years most of the activists' energies went into expanding the Wilderness Preservation System, and agency managers, implicitly subscribing to the notion—"draw a line around it and leave it alone"—devoted relatively little attention to the actual management of wilderness lands. They did begin to calculate the "carrying capacity" of given areas, the number of people who could hike or camp or otherwise utilize an area without degrading it. When demand exceeded that limit, it would be necessary to restrict access to the area. A related concept was minimum impact camping, institutionalized as Leave No Trace in the 1970s. Leave No Trace was a reaction to the traditional practice of cutting trees for firewood and shelter materials. The simultaneous development of compact, lightweight camp stoves, lanterns, tents, and mattresses meant that Leave No Trace required campers to make only minimal sacrifices of comfort and convenience.[57]

As the number and variety of wilderness areas increased, more complex management issues emerged. Most wilderness laws grandfathered existing activities, notably grazing and water diversions, compromising the supposed naturalness of the area. The Colorado Wilderness Act of 1980 spelled out the rights of ranchers, and most subsequent legislation included the Colorado grazing provisions. By the end of the century one-third of all wilderness lands were legally available for grazing, although the amount actually used was considerably less. More loopholes pertained to water development: in practice, dams and reservoirs that predated the legislation were rarely disturbed. ANILCA had added many additional exceptions to accommodate the relatively large number of Alaska's residents who lived in remote areas and depended on motorboats, snowmobiles, and airplanes. More generally, the "subsistence" provisions of ANILCA were a source of continuing challenges for NPS officials in Alaska.[58] And then there was the tendency of some officials to disregard the letter of the law in order to avoid conflicts. The Forest Service in the late 1980s and 1990s fell into what one agency veteran termed the "'reasonable, practical and flexible quagmire.'"[59]

To hold the line as much as possible, wilderness managers adopted the "nondegradation" principle common to water and air pollution legislation. Regulations tailored to one area did not create precedents for other areas. Regardless of local conditions, the goal was to adhere to the letter and spirit of the Wilderness Act, avoid conditions that would degrade an area, and eliminate exceptions wherever and whenever possible. To take an obvious example, the many special provisions included in the Alaska wilderness legislation were treated as responses to a distinctive, atypical situation.

In an effort to create more uniform management and a cadre of trained managers, the four agencies with wilderness lands established the Arthur Carhart Wilderness Training Center in Missoula, Montana, in 1993. (The Aldo Leopold Wilderness Research Center, established at the same time, also in Missoula, became its research arm.) The Carhart Center provided a variety of courses for agency employees involved in wilderness management. Apart from technical subjects, the program emphasized flexibility and accommodation within a framework consistent with the Wilderness Act. Key managerial principles included the "historical range of variation" or HRV, to help gauge the significance of changes in the environment, and "limits of acceptable change" or LAC, an important refinement of the carrying capacity concept.[60] LAC shifted the emphasis from numerical totals to their impact and became the basis for managing popular hiking and camping areas. Rather than arbitrary limits on the number of people, LAC meant that the number of campers could vary and probably be substantially larger if Leave No Trace principles were widely embraced. Used successfully to resolve conflicts between user groups and to improve backcountry camping areas in Montana's popular Bob Marshall Wilderness, LAC soon became an accepted management tool.[61]

The most sensitive managerial issues involved the larger public rather than wilderness users. The reintroduction of predators and efforts to eradicate invasive species generated controversy, but the most common problems involved wildfires, underlined most dramatically by the Yellowstone fires of 1988. By the 1990s the new, more flexible approach to fires was widely accepted and the subject of interagency planning. A handful of disasters, notably the 2000 Cerro Grande fire in New Mexico's Bandelier National Monument, when a prescribed burn raged out of control and required the most expensive suppression effort to that time, emphasized the need for caution.[62] Yet even greater challenges were emerging with the proliferation of resorts and vacation homes in many areas of the rural West. Although officials readily conceded the desirability of allowing lightning-caused fires to burn, the presence of so many people in formerly remote areas, now the "wildland-urban interface," made the new approach problematic. According to one study, only in the most remote areas of Idaho's national forests "has such a program been able to restore some semblance of the historical fire regime." In other areas, even in national parks such as Yellowstone, "restoration efforts have been significantly constrained by the need to protect resorts and other facilities."[63] Throughout the West, prescribed burns, the only real antidote to large, costly fires, including "megafires," became a "niche enterprise."[64] A warming climate and increasingly erratic weather patterns virtually guaranteed that fires would be a persistent challenge for land managers.

The inescapable conclusion is that wilderness areas might be remote and largely empty of human beings, but they are not isolated from the effects of human activity. This fact alone meant that Wilderness Watch, the organization founded in 1989 in reaction to the Forest Service's "reasonable, practical and flexible" approach, never ran out of projects.[65] By 2000, however, most wilderness advocates accepted the need for managerial intervention and, in some cases, restoration activities. The critical distinction was between managerial initiatives that made the area more natural, by whatever yardstick, and activities that served immediate human needs, including the convenience of wilderness managers.

∾

By the beginning of the twenty-first century the United States had a large number of untrammeled lands that met the scientists' definition of core areas. The distribution was highly skewed toward the West and Alaska and toward mountaintops and deserts, and far too many parks and wilderness areas were isolated "islands." Yet the total was impressive, certainly a meaningful step toward the goal of preserving biodiversity. The other notable feature of this achievement was how little of it was directly attributable to the scientists' critiques and proposals. Environmentalists were most successful when they emphasized the natural beauty of an area, the possibilities for outdoor recreation, and the value of wildlands as antidotes to the stresses of everyday life. These arguments, especially when combined with efforts to preserve the economic status quo, notably the retention of grazing leases, had broad appeal. It was not that environmentalists were indifferent to the biodiversity argument, but they recognized its limitations in the political realm. This pragmatic approach was costly, notably in blurring the long-term consequences of the compromised measures that typically emerged from legislative bodies, but its effectiveness made it difficult, indeed impossible, to disregard.

NOTES

1. William R. Lowry, "National Parks Policy," in *Western Public Lands and Environmental Politics*, ed. Charles Davis (Boulder: Westview, 2001), 183.

2. William R. Lowry, *The Capacity for Wonder: Preserving National Parks* (Washington, DC: Brookings Institution, 1994), 56–57.

3. Jim Robbins, *Last Refuge: The Environmental Showdown in Yellowstone and the American West* (New York: William Morrow and Co., 1993), 183.

4. Gary C. Bryner, *U.S. Land and Natural Resources Policy: A Public Issues Handbook* (Westport: Greenwood Press, 1998), 4.

5. Richard West Sellers, *Preserving Nature in the National Parks: A History* (New Haven: Yale University Press, 1997); Michael J. Yochim, *Protecting Yellowstone: Science and the Politics of National Park Management* (Albuquerque: University of New Mexico Press, 2013), 177–78.

6. David McCally, "The Everglades and the Florida Dream," in *Paradise Lost? The Environmental History of Florida*, ed. Jack E. Davis and Raymond Arsenault (Gainesville: University Press of Florida, 2005), 142–43.

7. Gordon E. Harvey, "'We Must Free Ourselves . . . From the Tattered Fetters of the Booster Mentality': Big Cypress Swamp and the Politics of Environmental Protection in 1970s Florida," in *Paradise Lost?*, ed. Davis and Arsenault, 355.

8. Jack E. Davis, *An Everglades Providence: Marjory Stoneman Douglas and the American Environmental Century* (Athens: University of Georgia Press, 2009), 370.

9. Terrence "Rock" Salt, Stuart Langton, and Mary Doyle, "The Challenges of Restoring the Everglades Ecosystem," in *Large-Scale Ecosystem Restoration: Five Case Studies from the United States*, ed. Mary Doyle and Cynthia A. Drew (Washington, DC: Island Press, 2008), 9–10.

10. Davis, *Everglades Providence*, 25.

11. Ibid., 588; Michael Grunwald, *The Swamp: The Everglades, Florida, and the Politics of Paradise* (New York: Simon and Schuster, 2006), 301; Gail M. Hollander, *Raising Cane in the Glades: The Global Sugar Trade and the Transformation of Florida* (Chicago: University of Chicago Press, 2008), 246–55.

12. Marguerite Holloway, "Nurturing Nature," in *Environmental Restoration: Ethics, Theory, and Practice*, ed. William Throop (Amherst, NY: Humanity Books, 2000), 27.

13. McCally, "Everglades and the Florida Dream," 154–55.

14. Bruce Babbitt, *Cities in the Wilderness: A New Vision of Land Use in America* (Washington, DC: Island Press, 2005), 41.

15. Grunwald, *The Swamp*, 321.

16. Ibid.

17. Ibid., 341–43; William R. Lowry, *Repairing Paradise: The Restoration of Nature in America's National Parks* (Washington, DC: Brookings Institution Press, 2009), 13–39.

18. Lowry, *Repairing Paradise*, 144–46; Stephen Polasky, "Rivers of Plans for the River of Grass: The Political Economy of Everglades Restoration," in *Large-Scale Ecosystem Restoration*, ed. Doyle and Drew, 51.

19. Lowry, *Repairing Paradise*, 147.

20. National Research Council, Committee on Independent Scientific Review of Everglades Restoration Progress, *Progress toward Restoring the Everglades: The Fourth Biennial Review, 2012* (Washington, DC: National Academies Press, 2012), http://dels.nas.edu/Report/Progress-Toward-Restoring-Everglades/13422; Dexter Filkins, "Swamped," *New Yorker*, January 4, 2016, 35–37.

21. Davis, *Everglades Providence*, 597.

22. Damien Cave, "Renewed Support for an Everglades Land Deal, but Cost Is Still in Question," *New York Times*, March 10, 2010; Damien Cave, "For the Everglades, a Dream Loses Much of Its Grandeur," *New York Times*, August 13, 2010; Lizette Alvarez, "Florida Legislature Has Its Own Ideas for Voter-Approved Conservation Fund," *New York Times*, April 24, 2015.

23. UNESCO, "World Heritage Committee Inscribes Everglades National Park on List of World Heritage in Danger," July 30, 2010, http://whc.unesco.org/en/news/638/.

24. Diane Ackerman, "Will Snakes Inherit the Earth?" *New York Times*, October 28, 2012; Frederick Reimers, "Python Patrol," *Nature Conservancy Magazine*, February–March 2014, 54.

25. Kevin Grange, "Sea Change," *National Parks* 86 (Fall 2012): 25.

26. Kathy Antoniotti, "Florida Resurrection," *Akron Beacon Journal*, March 27, 2011.

27. Christopher P. Cirmo, "Water Resources: The Unique Adirondack Aquascape," in *The Great Experiment in Conservation: Voices from the Adirondack Park*, ed. William F. Porter, Jon D. Erickson, and Ross S. Whaley (Syracuse: Syracuse University Press, 2009), 36–37.

28. Graham L. Cox, "The Adirondack Environmental Nongovernmental Organizations," in *Great Experiment*, ed. Porter, Erickson, and Whaley, 424; Paul Ertelt, "The Battle of Panther Mountain," *Adirondac* 76 (June 2012): 22–23.

29. Philip E. Terrie, *Contested Terrain: A New History of Nature and People in the Adirondacks* (Syracuse: Syracuse University Press and Adirondack Museum, 1997), 160.

30. Ibid., 168–73; Jon D. Erickson, "Introduction: The Park in Perspective," in *Great Experiment*, ed. Porter, Erickson, and Whaley, 200.

31. David Helvarg, *The War against the Greens: The "Wise-Use" Movement, the New Right, and Anti-Environmental Violence* (San Francisco: Sierra Club Books, 1994), 209–17.

32. Erickson, "Introduction," 202.

33. Terrie, *Contested Terrain*, 174–75.

34. Ibid., 175–76.

35. Jon D. Erickson et al., "Public Opinion and Public Representation," in *Great Experiment*, ed. Porter, Erickson and Whaley, 399–401.

36. Cox, "Adirondack Environmental Nongovernmental Organizations," 438.

37. David Straddling, *The Nature of New York: An Environmental History of the Empire State* (Ithaca: Cornell University Press, 2010), 229.

38. Philip E. Terrie, "Stunning Changes," *Adirondac* 73 (May–June 2009): 24.

39. Cox, "Adirondack Environmental Nongovernmental Organizations," 445.

40. Philip E. Terrie, "Compromise, Continuity, and Crisis in the Adirondack Park," in *Great Experiment*, ed. Porter, Erickson, and Whaley, 360.

41. Charles D. Canham, "Upland Forests of the Adirondacks," in *Great Experiment*, ed. Porter, Erickson, and Whaley, 66.

42. Roland W. Kays and Robert A. Daniels, "Fish and Wildlife Communities of the Adirondacks," in *Great Experiment*, ed. Porter, Erickson, and Whaley, 73.

43. William F. Porter, "Wildlife Exploitation in the Adirondacks," in *Great Experiment*, ed. Porter, Erickson, and Whaley, 93.

44. Reed F. Noss and Allen Y. Cooperrider, *Saving Nature's Legacy: Protecting and Restoring Biodiversity* (Washington, DC: Island Press, 1994), 29.

45. Michael E. Soulé, "The Social Siege of Nature," in *Reinventing Nature? Responses to Postmodern Deconstruction*, ed. Michael E. Soulé and Gary Lease (Washington, DC: Island Press, 1995), 160.

46. Kevin Proescholdt, "Guardians, not Gardeners," *Wilderness Watcher* 24 (Spring 2013): 1.

47. John C. Miles, *Wilderness in National Parks: Playground or Preserve* (Seattle: University of Washington Press, 2009), 262–67.

48. David Callihan, *National Wildlife Refuge System* (New York: Nova Science Publishers, 2009), 22.

49. Todd Wilkinson, "Wildlife Needs Wilderness," *Wilderness*, 2003–4, 43–45.

50. Robert B. Keiter, *Keeping Faith with Nature: Ecosystems, Democracy, and America's Public Lands* (New Haven: Yale University Press, 2002), 174–80.

51. Quoted in John Hart, "Two Cheers for Wilderness," *High Country News* 36 (July 21, 2014): 24. Also see Michael P. Nelson and J. Baird Callicott, *The Wilderness Debate Rages On: Continuing the Great New Wilderness Debate* (Athens: University of George Press, 2008).

52. Chad P. Dawson and John C. Hendee, *Wilderness Management: Stewardship and Protections of Resources and Values*, 4th ed. (Golden, CO: Fulcrum Publishing, 2009), 135–39.

53. Keiter, *Keeping Faith with Nature*, 181–82; Jeffrey O. Durrant, *Struggle over Utah's San Rafael Swell: Wilderness, National Conservation Areas, and National Monuments* (Tucson: University of Arizona Press, 2007), 47–53.

54. Dawson and Hendee, *Wilderness Management*, 166.

55. J. C. Hendee, "Emerging Wilderness Understandings," *International Journal of Wilderness* 16 (August 2010): 26.

56. Dawson and Hendee, *Wilderness Management*, 43–45.

57. James Morton Turner, *The Promise of Wilderness: American Environmental Politics since 1964* (Seattle: University of Washington Press, 2012), 91–92.

58. Frank Norris, *Alaska Subsistence: A National Park Service Management History* (Anchorage: National Park Service, 2002).

59. William Worf, "Forest Service Wilderness Legacy," in *Wilderness: Reclaiming the Legacy* (Missoula, MT: Wilderness Watch, 2011), 53.

60. Dawson and Hendee, *Wilderness Management*, 223–34.

61. Ibid., 234–37; R. Edward Grumbine, *Ghost Bears: Exploring the Biodiversity Crisis* (Washington, DC: Island Press, 1992), 203.

62. Dawson and Hendee, *Wilderness Management*, 195–96; Hal K. Rothman, *Blazing Heritage: A History of Wildland Fire in the National Parks* (New York: Oxford University Press, 2007), 197–202; Stephen J. Pyne, *Between Two Fires: A Fire History of Contemporary America* (Tucson: University of Arizona Press, 2015), 345.

63. Stephen F. Arno and Carl E. Fiedler, "Ponderosa Pine and Interior Forests," in *Restoring the Pacific Northwest: The Art and Science of Ecological Restoration in Cascadia,* ed. Dean Apostol and Marcia Sinclair (Washington, DC: Island Press, 2006), 201.

64. Pyne, *Between Two Fires*, 444.

65. Worf, "Forest Service Wilderness Legacy," 53; Kevin Proescholdt, "Wilderness Milestones of 2014: 50th Anniversary of Wilderness Act, 25th Anniversary of Wilderness Watch," *Wilderness Watcher* 25 (Summer/Fall 2014): 4.

8

A Perilous Course

By the first decade of the twenty-first century American conservation reflected the experiences of the previous quarter century together with a growing perception of the natural world as dangerously overcrowded, abused, and nearing catastrophic collapse. In this setting two remedial steps seemed essential. The first was to preserve what remained of that world and restore as much of it as possible. National parks, wilderness areas, and wildlife refuges were an indispensable foundation. But there were many other possibilities as well. In 2009 the WILD Foundation adopted the slogan "Nature Needs Half" to provide a positive long-term objective for activists as well as to suggest the cumulative potential of traditional parks and refuges together with roadless areas, protected wetlands, state and local parks, "working wilderness" areas, other restricted private lands, and a multitude of publicly and privately funded restoration projects. The second step, closely related, was to accelerate the trend toward more ecologically sensitive management. That meant a greater emphasis on connecting core areas, reintroducing natural fire regimes and predators, limiting the spread of nonnative species, remov-

DOI: 10.7330/9781607325703.c008

ing obstructions in waterways, "continuing species-specific intervention" to aid endangered wildlife, including freshwater and marine species, and ecosystem management—in short, reversing many well-established practices, including activities that had formerly fallen under the rubric of "conservation."[1] The magnitude of the crisis led many activists to downplay the danger that new miscalculations might magnify rather than alleviate the legacy of earlier blunders.

If environmentalists had a more coherent and compelling agenda than in the past, were they likely to achieve their goals more quickly? History provided little comfort. Campaigns for national parks, relatively noncontroversial, classic "win-win" projects, had typically taken a decade or more to reach fruition. Twenty years had elapsed between the first serious proposal to reintroduce wolves in Yellowstone and their actual release. The damage caused by cattle grazing had been widely publicized, but the status quo largely prevailed on the western range. Far from responding to the pleas of the conservation community, a substantial minority in the Congress was devoted to overturning the achievements of earlier years.

There were, of course, other avenues, as the burgeoning ranks of the land conservancies and the many initiatives of state and local governments suggested. The question was not whether anything could be done, but the timing, and whether the results would moderate the rate of biodiversity loss and alleviate problems such as the warming of the climate.

THE CONSERVATION LOBBY

Judging from opinion polls, the changes in public policy necessary to implement the conservationists' agenda should have been easy and automatic. For a half century polls showed strong support for various environmental measures, from clean water to parks and wildlife. A 2000 Gallup poll, for example, found 83 percent of respondents in favor of "the broadest goals of the environmental movement."[2] It was customary to note that such general endorsements were not the equivalent of support for specific legislative or regulatory measures and that when questions became more specific, support dwindled. Thus, interest in the environment, it appeared, was broad but shallow. Yet it was also customary to ask what respondents would give up in exchange for a cleaner or healthier environment, suggesting a trade-off involving jobs, economic growth, or higher taxes. In fact most pollution controls and virtually all conservation measures were consistent with economic growth and job creation. The costs, if any, were temporary; the economic and environmental benefits were permanent.

Between 2001 and 2004 public interest in environmental issues "tumbled" as a result of terrorist threats, war, and the systematic opposition of the Bush administration to environmental protection.[3] But this pattern changed again as disenchantment with the Bush policies grew; by 2009, when the Obama administration introduced more aggressive antipollution measures and Congress embraced parks and wilderness legislation, public support was again very high.

What, then, was the problem? The economic interest groups that had spearheaded the Wise Use campaign in the 1990s were willing to spend liberally to defend or enlarge their claims on public resources, and they were often joined by other groups that opposed government spending in general. In many western states traditional activities, such as forestry and ranching, represented a smaller and smaller proportion of the state's economy, but the individuals and businesses devoted to them were still sufficiently influential to threaten meaningful reforms. Environmentalists usually won when the issue was clear and understandable, such as opening the Arctic Wildlife Refuge to oil drilling, but lawyers and lobbyists had the upper hand in disputes over agency rules, legal interpretations, or other esoteric matters. The success or failure of environmental measures thus depended on the number of activists and their ability to organize and operate like traditional special interest groups.

Conservationists had been active in Washington for much of the twentieth century and, by the time of the ANILCA campaign, had become an influential force in national politics. They had typically organized in response to particular challenges, focusing on public lands, forests, wildlife, recreation, or other environmental resources or problems. Several of the national organizations developed broader approaches, but organizational proliferation continued and the movement as a whole remained highly decentralized. This was also true for the land trust movement, which mimicked the larger pattern. In the 1980s Earth First! and other grassroots groups had grown in part by complaining that the Sierra Club, Wilderness Society, Audubon, National Wildlife Federation, and others had become too comfortable in their Washington offices and that their "victories" were often compromises that gave away as much as they gained. Similar criticism became common during the Clinton years, when the administration, avowedly pro-environment, produced only minor gains before 1996 and then virtually nothing until 2000. Influential critiques by Robert Gottlieb (1993) and Mark Dowie (1995) emphasized the disparity between the movement's supposed influence and its impact.

Membership in national environmental organizations peaked in the late 1980s, in response to the policies of Reagan and Bush, and then declined after Clinton's election as activists assumed the change of administrations would remove the most obvious threats. Their complacency was short-lived, and memberships rose again in the second half of the decade. (Whether this pattern was also characteristic of state and local organizations is uncertain; in many cases a narrow, occasionally parochial focus insulated them from national and international trends.) Christopher Bosso reported total US memberships (minus Greenpeace, which fluctuated wildly, distorting the underlying trend) of 6.4 million in 1991–92, 6.7 million in 1996–97, and 7.8 million in 2002–3.[4] How many individuals were involved is unclear, since multiple memberships were common. Still, the growth of the national organizations was sufficiently brisk to cast doubt on the argument that the movement was out of touch and unresponsive.

The financial figures are even more impressive. Bosso reports total revenues for the most prominent groups at $641 million in 1991, $903 million in 1996, and $2.1 billion in 2007. The most successful fundraisers were the biodiversity and wildlife organizations, notably the Nature Conservancy, World Wildlife Fund, and Ducks Unlimited. Much of the money was spent on paid staff, which grew in aggregate from 4,120 in 1990 to 7,630 in 2000.[5] Some organizations depended largely on dues; others derived significant revenues from endowment funds or foundation grants. Most environmental organizations relied on foundations at some point in their history, and that was particularly true of the new groups that emerged at the end of the century. The Pew Charitable Trusts was the single most generous contributor. Smaller, more iconoclastic foundations headed by "ecobarons," notably Ted Turner and Douglas Tompkins, were also influential.[6] They enabled a number of specialized groups, often founded by dissidents from the national organizations, to emerge and in some cases join the ranks of the national organizations.

The Center for Biological Diversity (CBD), one of the most successful of the new organizations, epitomized the larger process. Its focus on endangered species and litigation proved to have wide appeal. The founders, Kieran Suckling and Peter Gabrin, were Earth First! veterans, as were many of the early staff members. They viewed litigation as a powerful and entirely legal substitute for monkey-wrenching. Suckling and his colleagues believed that political pressures would always work against endangered species; only countervailing pressures would force the government to act. Beginning in the early 1990s, the CBD won a number of legal victories in Arizona and New Mexico, its home territory. Its lawsuits on behalf of the Mexican spotted owl halted logging in national forests in the Southwest, spurred additional suits, and won the continuing enmity of the Forest Service. "The use of science in a very aggressive fashion, no matter what the political risk," wrote Robin Silver, another early leader, "is what made us different."[7]

By the late 1990s this approach had proven highly successful, both as a way to protect endangered species and to build an organization. CBD grew rapidly, to 14,000 members by 2004, opened offices outside the Southwest, and attracted the support of mainline foundations. It was responsible for about 70 percent of the additions to the endangered species list after 1992, a total of 335 by 2004.[8] It opposed the Clinton administration's habitat conservation plans, insisted on critical habitat designations, won restrictions on BLM lands in southern California; and secured limits on some ocean fishing. The CBD was the best example of a rebellious outsider group that became, somewhat uncomfortably, part of the mainstream.

With the advent of the second Bush administration the divisions within the environmental movement largely disappeared. Essentially no one had access to the administration or the Republican-controlled Congress, and a unified front was essential to oppose anti-environmental initiatives. Gridlock again became the goal rather than the complaint of environmental lobbyists.

BUSH AND OBAMA

Given the intensity of the conflicts over public lands forestry and the Clinton monuments as well as the emerging battle over climate change, it is remarkable how little attention was devoted to environmental issues in the 2000 election. Vice President Albert Gore, long associated with environmental causes, was strangely reticent; George W. Bush, who neither knew nor cared much about the environment, was happy to devote his attention to other matters, though he did call for increased spending for national parks. Gore's hesitancy cost him dearly. His refusal to oppose a proposed new airport near Miami, despite the opposition of Clinton, Babbitt, and other administration officials, outraged Florida environmentalists, some of whom defected to third-party candidate Ralph Nader. If one half of one percent of Nader's Florida supporters had voted instead for Gore, the vice president would have scored a narrow but unassailable victory in Florida and in the election.[9]

Bush quickly showed himself to be a "defender of the lords of yesterday."[10] His appointees to key posts in the Interior and Agriculture Departments were all associated with the mining, forest products, and agribusiness industries. Most notably, his new secretary of the Interior, Gale Norton, had been a lobbyist for the mining industry and most recently had worked for the Mountain States Legal Foundation, the anti-environmental legal defense group earlier headed by James Watt. The new undersecretary of agriculture and boss of the Forest Service, Mark Rey, was a longtime timber industry lobbyist, best known as the principal author of the 1995 salvage rider.[11] As veterans of earlier conservation battles, they understood the implications of a divided and intensely partisan Congress. Rather than working to repeal laws, they emphasized "nonlegislative paths." They would emphasize "less visible, less legitimate tracks."[12]

As a result, environmental policy became an endless cat-and-mouse game whereby Bush appointees, usually with as little publicity as possible, tried to change the rules to favor their political clients, while environmental groups used the courts, the media, and their allies in Congress to counter them. When Obama succeeded Bush in 2009, the sides reversed. The result was constant conflict, a permanent sense of crisis, and, for the most part, a standoff. Both sides tried to take advantage of momentary opportunities while awaiting changes in the political climate that would permit a more decisive breakthrough. Thus, several years of severe wildfires in the West led to the passage of Bush's "Healthy Forests" legislation, which encouraged timber cutting in national forests, and Democratic triumphs in the congressional elections of 2006 and 2008 led to the passage of an omnibus lands bill in 2009. In the meantime the behind-the-scenes struggle focused increasingly on the weakest of the federal land management agencies, the BLM.

The bureau was an easy and accessible target. BLM bureaucrats were still largely attuned to the interests of commodity producers, whether ranchers, miners, or oil and gas companies. Secretary Babbitt had established the National Landscape Conservation System within the BLM to manage its conservation lands (approximately 10 percent of the total by 2000) and to create a career ladder that would attract professional employees. His second goal was still largely unrealized when he left office. As one observer noted, "managers and staff saw ecosystem management as either the latest name for traditional multiple-use management or as a lofty and overly intellectual concept." In the meantime, "whiplash" changes in policy led to "confusion over the agency's primary mission."[13] This was hardly surprising, given the agency's history, but it meant that there was little or no internal resistance to the commodity orientation of the Bush appointees.

As if to emphasize this point, Bush and Secretary Norton made it clear that they had little use for the BLM's National Landscape Conservation System. Bush did not add new monuments and only grudgingly signed legislation that designated a total of 2.5 million acres of wilderness, three-quarters of it Nevada desert that remained open to grazing.[14] Meanwhile, in a convoluted agreement with the governor of Utah, Norton tried to limit the number of BLM wilderness areas. The agency's original Utah wilderness survey had been scandalously incomplete and had prompted Secretary Babbitt to order a revision. That effort added 3 million acres (which would have to be managed as wilderness until Congress acted) to the 2.5 million acres already set aside. Local officials sued in 1998 and lost. However, since the decision to add the 3 million acres was an administrative action by the Interior secretary, it could also be reversed by administrative action. In her 2003 agreement Norton cancelled Babbitt's additions and pledged not to conduct additional BLM wilderness reviews in Utah or elsewhere. A sympathetic local federal judge approved the deal without giving opponents a chance to challenge it. In effect, Utah would get no more wilderness unless and until the state's congressional representatives took the initiative.[15] In the meantime the BLM would do as little as possible to preserve the state's wilderness-quality lands.

This arrangement was supposed to show that the federal government was receptive to state interests. Yet the administration's sensitivity to local concerns did not extend to state officials who favored more BLM wilderness areas. The one-sided nature of the process helped galvanize opposition.

The Utah deal also proved to be less significant than it appeared at first. In 2005 the Utah judge who had originally approved the deal ruled in a related suit that it was only temporary; subsequent secretaries of the Interior would have the same powers to authorize BLM wilderness reviews that Babbitt and Norton had had. That meant that the only immediate issue was the fate of the 3 million acres that Babbitt had made wilderness study areas. BLM regional managers, who traditionally worked closely with local commodity producers, drew up resource management plans for the 3 million acres that permitted virtually unrestricted oil and gas leasing and off-road vehicle use, activities that would likely make them ineligible for wilderness consideration in the future.[16]

In May 2001 President Bush had issued an executive order requiring BLM managers to make oil and gas extraction their top priority, regardless of the agency's supposed commitment to multiple use. A "task force" was to monitor field managers.[17] Supposedly "BLM staff . . . were evaluated for raises and promotions based on how rapidly they okayed permits."[18] Between 2001 and 2007 they approved 33,000 oil and gas lease applications in the Rocky Mountain states. The Colorado total rose from 1,500 permits in 2000 to 6,500 in 2007. By 2008 there were 60,000 wells on public lands in addition to lease agreements that could eventually triple the total.[19] Long criticized for its preoccupation with grazing, the BLM now had a new emphasis. A Wilderness Society official voiced the distress of many westerners when she complained that "The BLM is pouring money into oil and gas drilling . . . leaving almost no funds for the protection of the Conservation System."[20] After Bush left office, Ken Salazar, the new Interior secretary, cancelled 77 Utah leases, including some on lands adjacent to Canyonlands and Arches National Parks that had been approved just before Bush left office. (A judge, acting on a lawsuit by environmentalists, had stopped drilling in the leased areas before Salazar acted.) But it was virtually impossible to stop the rush. Oil and gas companies had enough leases to continue drilling in the northern Rockies for decades. In subsequent years, threats of lawsuits by environmental groups and more stringent state regulation, particularly in Colorado, addressed some of the most significant dangers associated with the oil and gas boom, but they only blunted the drilling frenzy.[21]

Next to the Rocky Mountain states the Bush administration's principal target was northern Alaska. Unable to persuade Congress to open the Arctic Wildlife Refuge, it turned to the National Petroleum Reserve–Alaska, the

22 million-acre area just west of the Prudhoe Bay oil field that had been set aside in the 1920s for the US Navy. The question was not whether there ought to be some development in the reserve, but whether any part of it should be off-limits. Environmentalists pointed out that it was home to the largest North American caribou herd and millions of migrating waterfowl. The land around Teshekpuk Lake was particularly valuable and sensitive. It had long been protected from leasing, but a BLM land management plan for the northeastern section of the reserve, published in early 2005, proposed to open the entire section. Vigorous objections by Alaskans, including Native groups, and by the national environmental organizations forced the BLM to delay the lease sale.[22]

Of even greater concern were plans by the Bush administration to offer off-shore leases in the Arctic Ocean and the Chukchi Sea on Alaska's west coast. These areas were known for severe storms, and the industry's ability to clean up oil spills in such an environment was highly suspect. Yet in early 2008 the Fish and Wildlife Service delayed action on a petition to list the polar bear as threatened under the Endangered Species Act in order to allow a Chukchi Sea lease auction to proceed.[23] Despite protests and promises of legal challenges, the sale attracted record bids, setting the stage for what would later become a graphic illustration of the hazards of drilling in that turbulent region. In 2012 a Shell Oil Company drilling rig was wrecked in a storm while being towed to one of the newly leased areas. Shell tried again a year later, only to reverse itself and shut down its Arctic operation at a cost of more than $7 billion. Low oil prices, damaging storms, poor initial drilling results, and an avalanche of public criticism made this a prudent if painful course.[24]

Another Bush goal was to undermine the roadless rule, which had just gone into effect in 2000. After considering several strategies, the president's lawyers decided to make only perfunctory efforts to defend it in court and, if it somehow survived, to attack it directly. In 2002 the Senate Government Affairs Committee reported that the Bush officials "sought to employ whatever tools were available to sabotage the rule."[25] This approach set off a decade-long series of suits and countersuits that seemingly ended in 2011 with the courts upholding the original rule and its application to the Tongass National Forest, which had generated a second, parallel series of lawsuits. (The Tongass decision was overturned on appeal and then reaffirmed on an appeal of that decision.) Having made little progress in the courts, Undersecretary Rey and his staff devised an "amended" rule that allowed governors to exclude national forests in their states. The amended rule went into effect in 2005. It brought immediate protests from a number of governors as well as environmental groups. Consequently, Colorado and Idaho were the only states to introduce modifications. A new round of lawsuits revealed that the revised rule had been poorly prepared and was vulnerable on several grounds, including a failure to consider endangered species. Tom Turner of Earthjustice concluded that Rey and his colleagues "could easily have torpedoed the Roadless Rule if they'd been a little more careful."[26] Environmental groups boasted at the end of the decade that no roadless areas had been opened, despite the uneven application of the rule.

Bush's "Healthy Forests" legislation was probably the best example of the cynicism that underlay the forestry campaign. The pretext for the legislation was the forest fires that devastated many western forests and caused extensive property losses, especially in 2000 and 2002. Drought, together with years of fire suppression, poor forestry practices, and urban sprawl were all factors in the devastation. By that time all of the federal agencies allowed fires in remote areas to burn themselves out and used prescribed burns to reduce fire dangers. But given their aim to minimize property damage, the effects of these seemingly important policy changes were surprisingly slight. In practice the agencies continued to suppress most fires—98 percent by one count. Yet property losses mounted relentlessly.[27] The solution proposed by the timber industry was to remove dense undergrowth and small trees, which contributed to the severity of the fires. Experts agreed that thinning could be helpful but had to done with care to avoid destroying wildlife habitat and damaging the forest floor.[28] And like "salvage" logging, thinning was a potential smoke screen for increased conventional logging. Environmental groups opposed it for that reason, but western politicians found it irresistible.

Blaming environmentalists for the agencies' inability to deal with the fire threat, and by implication the fire damage, Bush called for aggressive thinning, with incentives for timber companies that participated and, most importantly, restrictions on environmental appeals. The legislation was subject to prolonged negotiation and revision, with Democrats insisting that most of the money be spent near developed areas. The final legislation, passed in 2003, was a compromise; environmental lobbyists remained opposed to the end but conceded that the outcome could have been far worse.[29] The law was at best a small victory for the timber industry. Over the next decade, the Forest Service treated over 26 million acres and insisted that the hundreds of millions it spend on thinning, brush removal, and prescribed burns made a difference. But fire losses continued to increase.[30]

Forest "health" was also the official rationale for two Bush attacks on endangered species protections: an attempt to roll back the Sierra Nevada agreements of the 1990s in favor of expanded logging and an effort to scrap the "Survey and Manage" feature of the Northwest Forest Plan. Both resulted in years of litigation and eventual decisions reaffirming the original restrictions.

The irony of the Bush approach became more evident with each new forestry initiative. From the beginning the national forests were supposed to protect watersheds. Over the years they had become increasingly important for preserving endangered species and biodiversity, promoting outdoor recreation, and, in recent years, buffering the effects of climate change. None of these functions was compatible with large-scale commercial logging, clearcutting in particular. Yet the Bush appointees were single-mindedly devoted to commercial logging. They curtailed the decommissioning of unneeded forest roads, reduced restorative activities, and even cut back on reforestation (the planting of commercially valuable species). In 2000 the Forest Service had identified ecological sustainability as the "guiding star" of national forest management in its basic planning document; a 2004 revision reduced the "guiding star" to coequal status with economic and social objectives.[31] A proposal to reduce the scope of the Northwest Forest Plan was not finally scrapped until 2012.[32]

The National Park Service faced similar challenges. In the 1990s NPS officials had finally had the freedom to think more expansively about their responsibilities and in 1998 had gotten congressional approval (though not the requisite funding) for an extensive research program, emphasizing species inventories and ecological monitoring. The Bush appointees, who, according to one critic, "espoused values sharply at odds with long term ecological preservation," were not interested. Their goal was to accommodate commercial interests, especially mechanized recreation. Their efforts on behalf of snowmobile users in Yellowstone Park led to growing controversy and legal challenges.[33] Their boldest initiative was an effort to relax long-standing restrictions on commercial activities in parks through a revision of NPS management policies. It was, in the words of park historian Richard West Sellers, "the most manipulative, pervasive, and politically potent" attack on NPS standards with the goal of "almost unregulated backcountry use."[34] Park professionals were appalled, and environmental groups mounted a sustained counterattack. By 2006 the tide had turned, and the subsequent resignations of Secretary Norton and NPS director Fran Mainella ended the campaign.

The efforts of Bush appointees to subvert the endangered species program were no less egregious. Not only did they oppose virtually every addition to the list (epitomized by the decade-long struggle on behalf of the severely threatened wolverine) but intimidated the beleaguered Fish and Wildlife Service staff and manipulated data. The deputy assistant secretary who had responsibility for the program repeatedly sought to distort or suppress information that favored new listings.[35] She too resigned when her activities became widely known.

The excesses of the Bush administration became an easy target for Obama's appointees. The president's chief of staff supposedly told Interior secretary Salazar to "clean up that mess."[36] The new administration accepted the scientists' warnings about climate change and species extinctions and did not interfere with the work of government scientists. It embraced the roadless rule, the Wilderness Preservation System, and the Landscape Conservation System; scrapped a Bush plan to increase logging in the Pacific Northwest; and slowed the leasing of public lands to energy companies. Obama appointed a new, more aggressive administrator to head the National Park Service and increased the budgets of the conservation agencies and appropriations for the Land and Water Conservation Fund. The new president welcomed the Omnibus Land Management Act of 2009, which added 2.1 million acres of wilderness in nine states, bringing the nation's total to 109 million acres, and made the Landscape Conservation System a permanent feature of the BLM. In 2009 Earthjustice, successor to the Sierra Club Legal Defense Fund, published a scorecard comparing Bush and Obama on nine energy and conservation issues. Bush received a failing grade on all nine; Obama was awarded an A or B+ on seven and failing grades on two—tentative support for an oil pipeline from western Canada's tar sands and an initial refusal to propose removal of dams on the Snake River to facilitate salmon recovery.[37] With these exceptions Obama was as hostile to Bush's policies as Bush had been to Clinton's. The pattern of dramatic policy changes dating from the 1980s continued.

Over the following two years the environmentalists' enthusiasm for the Obama administration gradually waned, in some cases changing to disillusionment. One problem was institutional lethargy. Environmentalists were highly critical of the Forest Service's efforts to revise the Forest Management Act in order to simplify the preparation of forest plans, and of the Fish and Wildlife Service's failure to complete its wildlife refuge management plans.[38] They were outraged by FWS proposals to remove the gray wolf and the grizzly bear from the endangered species list and by the agencies' willingness to violate the spirit and often the letter of the Wilderness Act when it served their immediate purposes.[39]

More serious problems resulted from the administration's desire to increase domestic energy supplies. Secretary Salazar had the unenviable task of promoting domestic petroleum production at the same time that he worked to protect the most ecologically and culturally valuable public lands. The BLM independently canceled a number of leases, and lawsuits by Earthjustice and other environmental groups forced it to cancel lease sales in southern New Mexico's Otero Mesa, the Chukchi Sea, and Bristol Bay, in western Alaska, the most productive fishing area on the Pacific Coast. In November 2011 the administration announced a five-year plan for offshore drilling. It called for new leases in the eastern Gulf of Mexico and, ultimately, the Arctic, but closed the Atlantic Coast. Drilling off Alaska's North Slope would be delayed until the end of the five-year period because of the fragility of the area and the absence of facilities for cleaning up an oil spill. Environmental groups criticized the plan and hoped for the best.[40]

In the meantime the Deepwater Horizon explosion and fire on April 20, 2010, resulting in an eighty-seven-day uncontrolled gusher, a 15,000-square-mile oil slick, and 1,300 miles of fouled coastline became an embarrassing reminder of the inevitable dangers of underwater oil exploration Subsequent investigations concluded that the disaster resulted from slipshod management and blunders by local managers. The Minerals Management Service (MMS), an Interior Department agency that regulated offshore drilling, also bore some responsibility; its subservience to the industry had compromised the possibility of meaningful oversight. Salazar subsequently halted leasing in the Gulf of Mexico and reorganized the MMS, though critics doubted that these actions would have any permanent effect. Kieran Suckling of the Center for Biological Diversity described the Salazar reforms as "baby steps."[41] Salazar's successor, Sally Jewell, introduced other safety-related regulations and doubled the number of inspectors in the Gulf of Mexico, but there was no certainty that these steps would address the kinds of managerial lapses that had led to the 2010 disaster.[42]

Shortly before Deepwater Horizon, prominent Utah writer and poet Terry Tempest Williams interviewed Salazar and reported that "his intention to create a broad, inclusive constituency for conservation is sincere." Still, she found little to like about his policies, especially his approach to Utah's long-troubled BLM lands. He had not repudiated Secretary Norton's backroom wilderness deal or the state BLM's one-sided resource management plans and had pledged not to recommend more monuments in the state without approval of the state's elected leaders. He explicitly rejected the red rock wilderness bill, an effort by the Utah Wilderness Coalition to protect BLM desert lands adjacent to the five southern Utah national parks, Grand Staircase Escalante National Monument, and Glen Canyon National Recreation Area. "I prefer the county by county approach" Salazar had told Utah officials, conceding, in effect, that in the polarized Utah environment little or nothing would be done. Williams concluded that "if this is the kind of public lands policy that is being established by our own 'progressive' administration, friendly to environmental concerns, we are in trouble."[43]

This warning seemed to be borne out in the following months. In November 2010 the Interior Department announced a "Wild Lands" policy that seemed to restore the BLM's authority to identify wilderness study areas. But these Wild Lands were not necessarily wilderness study areas; their exact status would depend on circumstances. "We are not quite where we were before," acknowledged a Wilderness Society official.[44] The "victory," if that's what it was, also proved to be short-lived. In the spring of 2011 the Obama administration agreed to eliminate funding for Wild Lands as part of its budget negotiations with congressional Republicans. The effect was to stifle efforts to protect more BLM land for an indefinite period. The budget agreement also removed the gray wolf from the endangered species list in several western states, canceling a successful lawsuit by environmentalists. Environmentalists complained that the administration "releases generalized reports, then retreats from its own policies."[45]

At the end of his first term Obama's record on conservation issues was obviously incomplete and, perhaps more surprisingly, uncertain. It appeared that his goal was to "balance business and environmental interests, seemingly project by project."[46] The administration had reversed much of what Bush had done but had taken ambivalent stands on public lands, BLM wilderness studies, and endangered species and had generally supported oil and gas drilling on public land. Most of the progress on traditional conservation issues resulted from legal action by environmental groups, not administration initiatives. In a widely reported speech, former Interior secretary Bruce Babbitt summarized the environmentalists' indictment. He noted that Presidents George H.W. Bush and Clinton had protected one acre of public land for every acre they opened to hydrocarbon development. George W. Bush had done far less, protecting one acre for every 7.5 acres opened for the oil and gas leasing. Obama's ratio was one to three, an improvement over the second Bush but a surprisingly unimpressive total for a president who counted environmentalists among his supporters. Babbitt called for an additional 4 million protected acres in order to match Clinton's (and his) record.[47]

In the months following his reelection, Obama seemingly took such criticism to heart. The appointment of Jewell and John Podesta, Clinton's chief of staff, as an advisor on environmental issues; more than twenty new national monuments that protected 550,000 acres in New Mexico, 700,000 in Nevada, 2.1 million in California, and 800,000 square miles of ocean in the central Pacific, quadrupling the size of two existing monuments; an ambitious effort to safeguard northern Alaska; as well as far-reaching measures to combat climate change suggested a reprise of the Clinton pattern. The Obama administration's management plan for the National Petroleum Reserve–Alaska banned leasing on half of the land, including the most sensitive areas.[48] And in early 2015 the president, acting on a recommendation of the Fish and Wildlife Service, proposed to designate the remaining 12 million unprotected acres of the Arctic Wildlife Refuge as wilderness. His proposal included the coastal region long coveted by the oil industry and, if approved by Congress, would effectively conclude the thirty-five-year controversy over that area. In any event, it put the government on record in opposition to drilling in the refuge.[49] Thus, if the record of 2009 to 2014 suggested more "green drift," the gradual, uncertain, messy but slightly positive process of advancing environmental protection, the final accounting was likely to be far more positive.

LAND CONSERVATION POST-2000

Although only sporadically reflected in presidential directives and legislation, land conservation continued to accelerate during these years with relatively little controversy or media attention. Private-sector leadership was the critical element as coalitions of environmental groups mobilized public support, especially in the Northeast and Pacific Coast states. There were also important initiatives in the midwestern states and accelerating efforts to protect farms and ranches in the West. Florida continued to be an area of mixed and contradictory impulses. Many of these efforts combined preservation efforts with seemingly compatible economic activities, including recreation and sustainable forestry.

The most important agent in this activity was the Nature Conservancy (TNC), which continued to grow and undertake ever larger land deals. John Sawhill, the president in the 1990s, brought a ruthless entrepreneurial intensity to the organization, greatly expanding its reach. Sawhill placed greater emphasis on easements, sales to government conservation agencies, "landscape-scale conservation," and ever more ambitious undertakings symbolized by the purchase and resale of New Mexico's Gray Ranch. But Sawhill died unexpectedly in 2000 and was succeeded by Steven McCormick, a TNC veteran who had headed the California chapter.[50] McCormick soon had to confront the downside of rapid growth. In 2007 an investigative reporter for the *Washington Post* discovered a surprising number of skeletons in the organization's closet, including cozy real estate deals with TNC trustees. A congressional investigation added embarrassing details. McCormick and his staff struggled to respond to the charges, correct what had gone wrong, and convince the public that the problems were isolated.[51] Given the adverse publicity, their efforts proved to be surprisingly successful in sustaining the pace of deal making and fund-raising.

In 2008 McCormick was succeeded by Mark Tercek, an investment banker who symbolized the organization's links to the world of finance and corporate management. Reflecting his background, Tercek placed great emphasis on projects aimed at demonstrating the value of "natural capital." His chief scientist, Peter Kareiva, went further and argued that human agency had upended and superseded natural processes altogether. He joined others (including so-called ecopragmatists, who sought engineering solutions to problems such as climate change) in proclaiming the arrival of the Anthropocene, an age in which the human presence had become so pervasive that it no longer made sense to talk about wild areas, wilderness, or "self-willed" natural systems. They urged environmentalists to focus on ecosystem services for humans, only incidentally promoting biodiversity and other largely scientific objectives.[52] An emphasis on ecosystem services was not new and certainly not new for the Nature Conservancy, which had always emphasized the self-interest of individuals and corporations. But did the seeming ubiquity of human influence warrant a "new conservation," focused narrowly on human needs? There were rebuttals from the defenders of the wilderness system and many others. The environmental historian Donald Worster probably spoke for most of them when he charged that the critics had gone too far; they were "blind and indifferent toward the wildness that still exists" and "toward the resilience of organisms to recover and survive."[53] Another irritant was their cavalier dismissal of past achievements, together with what writer-activist Tom Butler characterized as their "celebratory, techno-triumphalist voices."[54] There were also concerns that a more human-centered conservation would doom efforts to protect endangered species and preserve habitat and would serve as a smoke screen for a return to the "resourcism" of the mid-twentieth century, when many of the most challenging problems of subsequent years had emerged.[55]

At a "come to Jesus" meeting in late 2013, Tercek, Kareiva, Michael Soulé, Reed Noss, and other leading biologists explored their differences. Conciliatory and apologetic, Tercek proposed a truce whereby each side would avoid antagonistic language and emphasize common goals.[56] The meeting ended with an agreement to work together whenever possible. Superficially, at least, this ended the dispute. Kareiva and Soulé both signed a 2014 public manifesto recognizing the value of varying perspectives and strategies.[57] Reminiscent of earlier conflicts such as the SLOSS controversy, this debate seemingly had little to do with the real world of conservation. In fact, it coincided with a series of large-scale land transactions that had broad, positive implications for plants and wildlife as well as people.

The Northeast provided the model. New England had a large and active environmental community and a growing outdoor recreation industry. Despite a largely urban setting and high land values, there were numerous opportunities for conservation projects. In southern Connecticut, for example, TNC focused on the Tidelands region bordering the Connecticut River. It identified seventeen core sites within the region and campaigned to preserve those areas. That required land purchases, numerous conservation easements, and considerable restoration work.[58]

Northern New England was different. The threat there grew out of the extensive land holdings of paper companies, which were being pressured to convert their illiquid assets into cash.[59] The likely buyers were real estate companies with plans for resorts and vacation homes, fragmenting the forests and radically changing local society. The future of New England seemed to be on the line. What was to be done? The obvious challenge was to stop the sale of large blocks of land to buyers who would subdivide it. Vermont, New Hampshire, and Maine did not have the resources of New York, meaning that a solution comparable to Governor Pataki's Adirondack Park strategy was not possible. Maine also had a long history of antipathy to the national park system, growing out of an extended controversy over the management of the state's magnificent Baxter State Park.[60]

The Nature Conservancy became involved, almost inadvertently in 1998, when International Paper announced its intention to sell 185,000 acres of its Maine holdings. TNC only wanted the land adjacent to the relatively pristine St. John River, but when other bidders dropped out and the entire tract was offered for $35 million, a bargain price, the temptation proved irresistible. TNC's Maine director had to raise $10 million in six weeks in order to secure a $25 million loan from the national organization. When that effort succeeded, he launched a "For Maine Forever" campaign that raised $57 million over the next four years. That enabled TNC to complete the deal for the International Paper property, plus 40,000 acres of vulnerable lakefront land and conservation easements on 200,000 acres near Baxter.[61]

In the meantime TNC was working with the Appalachian Mountain Club (AMC) to preserve lands adjacent to the famous Hundred-Mile Wilderness, south of Baxter. In 2003 AMC purchased a 37,000-acre tract and launched a "Maine Woods Initiative" to buy more land. The timing proved propitious. Over the next decade AMC and TNC joined forces to thwart a plan by Plum Creek Timber Company to develop hundreds of thousands of acres around Moosehead Lake. In 2012 Plum Creek finally agreed to a permanent easement on 90 percent of its holdings (362,000 acres) and gave TNC and AMC the right to purchase other lands; in return it would develop 17,000 acres. In the meantime AMC and TNC made other large purchases. After a decade of activity, AMC, TNC, other conservation groups, the National Park Service (which acquired lands adjacent to the Appalachian Trail), and the state had protected nearly 800,000 acres.[62]

To the casual observer, the result of a decade of often intense, stressful, and "unparalleled" conservation activity was largely the preservation of the status quo. There would be less clear-cutting, more recreational opportunities, more local business activity, and more secure jobs for forest workers, but the real news was what did not change. Large forested areas and relatively little fragmentation would remain a distinctive feature of northern New England for the foreseeable future. That, in turn, had larger implications. Looking back, an influential report characterized the region as a "second-chance landscape" that was emerging as a "'continental-scale habitat corridor.'"[63]

There were also large additions of protected land in the Adirondacks, with the state of New York and the Nature Conservancy continuing to play leading roles. TNC purchased nearly 200,000 acres, and the state acquired easements on an additional 350,000 acres owned by paper companies. Although other large tracts in the Adirondacks will eventually come on the market, the informal alliance of the state and the Nature Conservancy, together with local environmental organizations, has proven to be highly successful in confronting the most immediate threats to the park. The TNC purchase of Finch Pruyn Company lands in 2006, for example, protected "16,000 acres of wetlands, more than 300 lakes and ponds, over 90 mountain peaks, and 425 miles of rivers and streams."[64]

The combination of private leadership and government assistance was also effective in other regions. TNC helped to coordinate more than a dozen successful state conservation referenda in 2008 and 2010, despite the severe recession, and more still in 2012 and 2014. In Minnesota, probably the most ambitious undertaking, a referendum resulted in the immediate protection of 187,000 acres of forest land and 280 miles of lakeshore.[65] TNC also orchestrated a large conservation land purchase by the state of Tennessee and worked with citizens groups in southern Colorado's San Luis Valley to oppose plans to divert water supplies. Strategic land purchases by TNC helped pave the way for the establishment of Great Sand Dunes National Park, the Baca National Wildlife Refuge, and the protection, through easements, of more than 200,000 acres of privately owned land.[66]

Another landmark deal began with protests against Plum Creek's plans to sell off lands in Montana's remote Swan Valley, adjacent to the Bob Marshall

Wilderness. Working with the Trust for Public Land, local groups arranged to purchase a small area in 1997. With land prices rising, Plumb Creek announced additional large-scale sales in 2000 and 2001, prompting new efforts to ensure that the forests did not become vacation home developments. In 2007 the Trust for Public Land and the Nature Conservancy persuaded Senator Max Baucus (D-MT) to sponsor a new conservation fund in the 2007 farm bill. The state supplied additional money. Altogether, 310,000 acres and more than half a billion dollars changed hands, with two-thirds of the land going to the Forest Service and the state. Other lands will be resold with conservation easements. Logging is to continue on the public lands for at least a decade.[67] In 2015 the Nature Conservancy added another 165,000 acres of former Plum Creek lands in northern Montana and Washington. The Montana purchase adjoined the earlier "Crown of the Continent" acquisition.[68]

In Florida several federal initiatives continued the long-running campaign to preserve the Everglades. Most notably for the park per se, the Park Service began to elevate parts of the Tamiami Trail, which had restricted water flow and wildlife movement through the park. In 2010 the Park Service increased its commitment to more than six miles of elevated highway. At the same time the US Department of Agriculture purchased easements on 26,000 acres south of Lake Okeechobee in order to recreate wetlands. Further north, the Fish and Wildlife Service announced a plan to protect the headwaters of the Everglades with a wildlife refuge and conservation area. The agency proposed to purchase 50,000 acres outright and buy easements on an additional 100,000 acres.[69] Like many earlier efforts, this one depended on negotiations with contentious Florida interest groups and congressional appropriations.

In addition to plans that depended on government assistance, several large private initiatives emphasized the popularity of land conservation in the new century. In 2000 the World Wildlife Fund launched a campaign to preserve 3 million acres of prairie grassland north of the Charles M. Russell Wildlife Refuge in Montana.[70] Another project, similar in scale, grew out of concern that the vast Tejon Ranch in southern California would be sold and subdivided. At the juncture of three major ecosystems and home to a wide variety of plants and animals, the ranch seemed destined for development as the Los Angeles suburbs extended to the north and east. Threats of lawsuits by environmental groups opposed to the sale and dismemberment of the ranch led to a 2008 agreement between the owners and the Sierra Club, Audubon, Natural Resources Defense Council, and other environmental organizations, creating the Tejon Ranch Conservancy. The agreement included open-space easements on 178,000 acres and gave the new Conservancy the right to buy easements on another 62,000 acres. In exchange, the environmental groups agreed not to oppose plans for a luxury resort on the western boundary and as many as 23,000 homes on the southern border. The Sierra Club representative called the agreement the "ecological equivalent of the Louisiana Purchase."[71]

Between 2008 and 2012 the Tejon Conservancy purchased the additional easements and the Nature Conservancy bought development rights to three ranches at the northern end of the property, totaling 32,000 acres. Those purchases created a link between the Angeles National Forest, north of Los Angeles, and Sequoia National Forest. The Tejon Conservancy subsequently opened much of the land to biological research.[72]

Such large-scale conservation deals are the most obvious expressions of a much larger grassroots campaign to preserve rural and suburban landscapes, reflected in the dramatic expansion of the local and regional land trust movements after 2000. Building on an ever-growing infrastructure of 1,700 organizations, the land trusts claimed 5 million members, 100,000 volunteers, and a growing cadre of professionals by the end of the decade. During that period local land trust endowments tripled, and funds set aside for monitoring and stewardship more than doubled. In several areas the conservancies pooled their resources and worked together as "regional conservation partnerships," taking on larger projects. By the end of the decade they owned or held easements on more than 9 million acres, triple the total of 2000.[73]

One notable example of this phenomenon was the rapid growth of the Western Reserve Land Conservancy (WRLC) in northeastern Ohio. The result of a 2006 merger of eight small and largely ineffective local groups, WRLC soon developed a substantial following; assembled a large professional staff; developed a regional strategy emphasizing large blocs of undeveloped land, river valleys, and wildlife corridors; and began negotiating complex deals involving public agencies as well as individual landowners. At the time of the merger the eight land conservancies had preserved about 8,000 acres. By 2014 the total had risen to nearly 39,000 and was growing by more than 2,000 acres per year. At that rate it would soon exceed the acreage of the region's public parks. Yet the impact of this activity was essentially invisible to the public.[74]

Even more dramatic changes occurred in the Rocky Mountain states, where conservation easements played a major role in the struggles of farmers and ranchers to remain economically viable and preserve traditional lifestyles. Agricultural land trusts, modeled after the Malpai Borderlands Group and other pioneers, enlisted many of the region's largest landowners; in Colorado, Wyoming, and Montana they were particularly influential. If the present trend continues, "much of [these states'] open land could remain undeveloped."[75] The results stood in a stark contrast to the interminable conflicts of the Washington politicians. Yet doubts remained. Can the easements be monitored and enforced? Will they withstand aggressive legal challenges? Will land trusts be abused by well-heeled contributors or manipulated by real estate speculators? Richard Brewer summarized these concerns in his 2003 history of the movement. Referring to TNC, he asked whether it "can contribute more to saving the Earth by the pluralistic approach . . . or by continuing to do what it is very good at: buying and accepting donations of land and turning it into preserves. In the long term, will doing all these other things . . . preserve biodiversity?"[76]

The Land Trust Alliance(LTA), the coordinating body of state and local groups, has answered one of these questions. In reaction to several aggressive legal challenges, one of which continued for a decade and cost a Connecticut land trust more than $400,000 in legal fees, LTA organized an insurance company, Terrafirma, to help local organizations "keep the promise of permanence." The Connecticut case was atypical, but a survey suggested that violations are increasingly common and that the cost of defending an easement is, on average, nearly $40,000. By 2013 Terrafirma had more than 400 members.[77] LTA has also formed a network of attorneys who provide pro bono services to local groups on the assumption that legal challenges will play an increasingly prominent role in the private land conservation movement.[78]

WETLANDS, RIVERS, AND OCEANS

For many years scientists and environmental activists had assumed that restrictions on pollutants and obstructions and campaigns to clean up rivers and lakes would protect fish and aquatic populations. They had waged notable and often successful battles against proposed dams, particularly on the Colorado River and its tributaries, won "wild and scenic" designations for an impressive number of rivers, and forced the government to embrace elaborate and costly procedures to sustain the few remaining salmon on the Columbia-Snake and other western river systems. Yet compared with the campaigns for parks, forests, and other protected areas, wetlands, rivers, and lakes had received little attention. A 1990 TNC report revealed "perhaps for the first time" the dire condition of many freshwater species.[79] In the following years the emphasis on biodiversity encouraged a more holistic view of the threats to plants and animals; at the same time a growing body of scientific evidence suggested that efforts to clean up waterways had done little to restore their biological health. The Nature Conservancy, World Wildlife Fund, Ocean Conservancy (1972), and American Rivers (1973) had all sponsored aquatic and marine programs since the 1970s, but they became more aggressive in the 1990s and after and were joined by many others. There was no shortage of challenging projects.

In most areas government regulations had merely slowed the loss of wetlands. The Corps of Engineers had had the authority to regulate their use since the 1970s, but its regulations often clashed with those of other agencies, producing a bureaucratic morass. When the Corps, EPA, Fish and Wildlife Service, and Agriculture Department finally attempted to implement a set of common rules, drafted in 1987, they were undercut by the new Bush administration, which was supposedly committed to "no net loss" of wetlands. Another major setback occurred in 2001, when the Supreme Court severely restricted the agencies' authority. The second Bush administration tried to eviscerate what remained, and a 2006 Supreme Court decision failed to resolve the ensuing conflicts. The legal muddle, coupled with ineffectual mitigation efforts, and politically charged confrontations between developers and environmental groups made "no net loss" an empty slogan. In the meantime the Nature Conservancy, Ducks Unlimited, and other wildlife organizations, together at times with the Fish and Wildlife Service, the Agriculture Department, and state wildlife agencies, provided the only meaningful antidote: the purchase of critical wetlands. The Fish and Wildlife Service's 2009 acquisition of Mollicy Farms in north-central Louisiana, now part of the Upper Ouachita National Wildlife Refuge, and subsequent restoration of the area's wetlands was an impressive example of what could be done.[80] However, there was never enough money to offset continuing losses in virtually every state.

The small defeats and victories of these years may have been locally important, but they were collectively overshadowed by the fates of two immense wetland areas, the Everglades and its central Florida hinterland and the southwestern Gulf of Mexico coast, mostly in Louisiana. The effort to preserve the Florida wetlands had absorbed vast quantities of money, time, and labor and remained a work in progress. At least there was a continuing effort, backed by most of the state's organized interest groups; Louisiana was different. The problem there was much greater and the level of public concern substantially lower. More than a million acres of Louisiana marshland disappeared between the 1930s and 1990, equivalent to 34 square miles per year. That was 80 percent of all coastal wetland losses.[81] The decline may have accelerated in the following decades. By 2010, at least 2,300 square miles of wetlands were under water.

Two related activities accounted for most of the losses: the construction of vast levee systems along the lower Mississippi and its tributaries, ostensibly to prevent flooding, and oil drilling in the coastal plain. The levees deprived the adjacent wetlands of water and sediment and led to the emergence of a huge and growing "dead zone" in the Gulf, as fertilizer-laden waters stimulated algae growth. The wells and nearby canals hastened runoff into the Gulf and led to widespread land subsidence. In the 1980s and 1990s the Corps of Engineers and the state government undertook a number of ineffectual remedial efforts. Only Hurricane Katrina in 2005 and the Deepwater Horizon oil spill of 2010 exposed the full extent of the damage. The Deepwater Horizon disaster "served as a wake-up call," according to a Fish and Wildlife official in Louisiana. The media coverage emphasized "the ecological and economic importance of this region in a way that has never happened before."[82]

Nevertheless, the odds against meaningful wetlands restoration were substantial. After a brief hiatus the Interior Department resumed leasing in the Gulf, and state and local officials continued to promote real estate developments in the coastal area with their accustomed zeal. Their proposed fifty-year restoration plan, projected to cost $50 billion or more, will rely initially on fines imposed on BP and its partners. That record amount includes $8 billion earmarked for rebuilding reefs, planting marsh grass, removing dams and levees on the Atchafalaya River, and buying strategically important properties, such as the Powderhorn Ranch, near Corpus Christi, Texas.[83] Even if these projects are carried out successfully, they will not necessarily improve the management of the river or alter the all-too-common assumption, expressed in numerous discussions following Katrina, that more traditional flood control structures are needed. This problem was not confined to Louisiana, though the influence of traditional remedies was particularly strong there because of the immediacy of the challenges facing public officials.

For many years scientists had recognized the need to modify much of the river infrastructure that had evolved over the previous century. Apart from the dangers associated with the possible failure of the levees and other structures, they had deprived many areas of the sediment and nutrients essential for wetlands preservation. The solution, then, was to undo much of what had been done in misguided attempts to control the river system. But there was a large gap between this realization and meaningful action. Multiple political jurisdictions, competition between economic interest groups, and an Army Corps that had enthusiastically promoted the original initiatives and was not eager to admit its mistakes were among the notable obstacles.

These hurdles also slowed progress on other parts of the river. By 2002 the Corps had embraced ecosystem sustainability as a goal for the upper Mississippi. This "groundbreaking effort," which required planners to consider fish and wildlife as well as navigation, raised other issues, since locks and dams, erected to facilitate navigation, contributed to sedimentation, the "primary cause of habitat degradation."[84] Shippers and local government officials opposed the removal of these structures and, indeed, lobbied for additions. The Corps proposed to hold the line on river "improvements" and to introduce a variety of restorative measures. The result was a seemingly unending series of discussions but little action, apart from some additions to wildlife refuges along the river.[85]

Further south (between Cairo, Illinois, and St. Louis) there was greater progress. William R. Lowry reported in 2003 that "restoration of the middle Mississippi has been substantial and fairly rapid compared to most other large-scale programs."[86] A quarter of the structures built in that part of the river had been modified, with impressive improvements in water quality and fish and wildlife habitat. "Adaptive management," which emphasized responses to changing conditions, became more common. Yet, as Lowry also noted, the effect "on the overall health of the Mississippi remains limited."[87] This judgment also applied to the Missouri and its tributaries, the North and South Platte Rivers.[88] The federal and state governments attempted to buy out floodplain residents, though budget reductions during the Bush years set back even these modest initiatives. It is not surprising, then, that the Gulf Coast disasters and other problems had only a modest impact on the management of the waterway.

In most western river systems, large dams were the central issue. Of the more than 75,000 dams in the United States, the largest and most controversial are on the Colorado and Columbia-Snake river systems, but every major western river except the Yellowstone has at least one and usually more. Products of the federal public works programs of the 1930s to the 1960s, they provide hydropower, water for irrigated agriculture, and opportunities for recreation. As western economies have grown, the rivers and their engineering structures have also become critical factors in the competition for water. Environmentalists complain that they convert rivers into huge "plumbing" systems that are inhospitable to fish and other aquatic organisms. In recent decades they have invoked the Endangered Species Act on behalf of salmon and other fish to force changes. There is an active movement, headed by American Rivers, to eliminate as many dams as possible. In the first decade of the new century alone, more than 400 mostly obsolete and deteriorating dams were removed.[89]

The most significant victory to date in the river restoration campaign has been the removal of two large hydroelectric dams on the Elwha River in Washington's Olympic National Park. Congress approved the plan in 1992, but demolition was stalled by hostile politicians for nearly two decades, an indication of the roadblocks and delays that await any effort to eliminate existing dams.[90] The work finally began in 2011. Removal of the Elwha dams permitted salmon to recolonize the river naturally, and the release of sediment helped to restore downstream beaches. The cost of demolition, new power-generating sources, and other related changes will likely total $350 million.[91] By 2012 salmon "were spotted in a previously inaccessible stretch of the river."[92]

Spurred in part by this highly publicized example, dam removal efforts have gained momentum in recent years. Many small dams on eastern rivers will disappear, largely without controversy. Larger dams on the Penobscot River in Maine and on the Klamath River in Oregon will be removed in the near future. The cost of demolition is the biggest obstacle. In other areas dam removal has become a major political issue, typically pitting farm organizations and other commercial interests against environmentalists, scientists, recreation groups, and Native American tribes. The dams on the Snake River, which block salmon migration and have little commercial value, are a prominent target of antidam activists. The great Glen Canyon Dam is also on many wish lists but is vigorously defended by boaters, concessionaires, and nearby communities that rely on the impounded water. Since 1999 Congress has banned the use of federal funds to study the feasibility of removal.[93]

Apart from the often heated controversies over dam removals, the focus of most debates over river management in the West is water utilization (as opposed to flood control, a relatively minor issue). Multiple competing jurisdictions, parochial interest groups, hostile professional organizations, a plethora of government agencies, and the total dependence of many areas on surface water make all policy decisions difficult, and decisions that benefit the environment at the expense of commercial interests are especially unwelcome. Holly Doremus and A. Dan Tarlock have described the formidable obstacles to ecosystem restoration in the Klamath River Basin, symptomatic of the larger problem.[94] Battles over water distribution have inspired more calls for repeal of the Endangered Species Act than any other category of dispute.

The campaign to restore natural features of western river systems continues despite these controversies. Salmon restoration efforts have resulted in the creation of numerous agencies, boards, and committees that command substantial federal and state resources.[95] One obstacle to success is the sheer number of groups that are involved. Equally significant is the something-for-everyone perspective that has been a prominent feature of these and many other efforts at environmental restoration. As a consequence, the initiatives that do win support are often so compromised that they have little value. An endangered species plan for the lower Colorado, adopted in 2004, is illustrative.[96] Commenting on the Colorado system, Robert Adler addresses the larger picture. "Stepping back from the details of the specific restoration efforts," he writes, "one thing is abundantly clear. For the most part, they are not working. Populations of endangered species continue to decline . . . efforts to restore beaches and sandbars appear futile because most of the necessary raw material remains trapped behind the dam. . . . Restoration of the lower river . . . is left to chance."[97] In 2013 American Rivers named the much-studied Colorado as the most endangered American river due to "outdated water management," "over allocation," and "persistent drought."[98]

Similar difficulties have haunted lake restoration projects. The heralded improvement of Great Lakes water quality and aquatic life, one of the signal achievements of the antipollution campaigns of the 1970s, stalled in the 1990s. Lax regulation, complacency, and budgetary shortcomings played major roles. Of forty-three rivers and harbors with serious pollution problems, only one had been cleaned up by 2010.[99] Nonpoint pollution, due largely to agricultural runoff, together with the continuing appearance of invasive species, numbering at least 180, mostly introduced by oceangoing ships, compromised much of the remedial effort. By the early twenty-first century, trillions of quagga and zebra mussels deprived native fish of their food supply and attached themselves to the shells of mussels and crustaceans.[100] Many native species have simply disappeared.[101] The likely arrival of giant Asian carp could multiply the damage. In 2010 Congress authorized a Great Lakes Restoration Initiative, which funded 2,500 projects in the following years.[102] Yet the list of problems continues to grow, overwhelming the cleanup effort.

Chesapeake Bay and other estuaries have shared the fate of the Great Lakes. Prodding by the EPA in the 1980s led Virginia and Maryland officials to undertake a variety of cooperative initiatives aimed at improving water quality, preserving shorelines from development, and reviving the fish and seafood industries. But "idealistic statements" and "lofty ambitions" were hard to translate into meaningful changes.[103] The historian of the Virginia environmental movement concluded that there was "never enough financial support from the states and the federal government to implement the programs fully."[104] By 2005, 41 percent of the bay was a "dead zone."[105]

The most grievous and compelling example of these problems, however, is the continuing decline of ocean fish stocks, despite (some critics would argue because of) a huge national and international bureaucracy devoted to fishing. Even conservation biologists were slow to grasp the devastation occurring in the oceans. Fish consumption has risen rapidly over the last half century, fishing fleets have expanded, and most fishery species are overfished or depleted; the losses typically range from 75 to 95 percent.[106] Though fish farms now account for nearly half of total consumption, wild fish stocks continue to decline. Overfishing combined with habitat destruction, water pollution, and ocean acidification (mostly a byproduct of higher levels of carbon dioxide in the atmosphere) make the outlook for many species increasingly grim. "What we have done in the last few decades is to mine fish," reports marine biologist Callum Roberts.[107] More and more areas, deprived of wild fish, are taken over by phytoplankton and jellyfish.[108]

The explanation for these developments starts with the growth of large-scale industrial fishing after World War II and the veneer of scientific research and international regulation that obscured the reality of drastic overfishing.[109] The Magnuson-Stevens Act of 1975, which reserved a 200-mile zone off US coasts for US fleets, and the Sustainable Fisheries Act of 1996, which amended Magnuson-Stevens supposedly to prevent overfishing, were intended to address these problems. In reality government simply turned over fishery policy to eight regional councils dominated by the fishing industry and state fishery managers.[110] The elimination of foreigners led to an increase in local boats and crews. "The decision-making process" concludes biologist Alison Reiser, "clearly favors short-term commercial interests over long-term sustainability."[111] Charged with balancing commercial and ecological concerns, regulators typically refused to do anything apart from wringing their hands over the terrible dilemmas they faced. In Roberts's words, they were "always one step behind and perennially ineffective."[112] The North Atlantic, Gulf of Mexico, and Pacific Coast, indeed, every major fishing area except Alaska, which adopted stringent state regulations in the 1970s, have experienced dramatic declines.[113]

The international regulatory bodies that make fishery policy for the high seas, the areas beyond the 200-mile zone, are even more ineffectual, as recent controversies over the fate of the endangered bluefin tuna have emphasized. The tuna regulatory body, the International Commission for the Conservation of Atlantic Tunas (ICCAT), is, in the words of marine biologist Carl Safina, the "International Conspiracy to Catch All the Tunas."[114] Despite a rapidly diminishing population of bluefins, the profits are so great that conservation efforts to date have been wholly ineffective.

What should be done? History and biology provide unambiguous answers. Two notable examples from the twentieth century are instructive: Pacific halibut and Bristol Bay sockeye salmon were threatened by overfishing but have recovered and are now relatively abundant. In both cases the key was restricting the number of fish that could be caught. There have been years when fishing for these species was banned, regardless of the impact.[115] This approach has not worked in every case; drastic restrictions in cod fishing have not had a similar effect, probably because of rising ocean temperatures.[116]

But it shows that recovery is possible and relatively inexpensive by terrestrial standards. The other essential is to restrict deep sea bottom trawling, which has disastrous effects on fish populations and fish habitats.[117]

A popular way of reducing the impact of fishing without confronting the industry directly is the designation of marine protected areas (MPAs). Several states and Congress have created MPAs to prevent certain kinds of fishing (such as trawling), to reduce fishing for certain species (such as sea urchins), or to halt gas and oil exploration. Many MPAs are too small to provide more than minimal protection, as a recent comprehensive survey has pointedly emphasized.[118] Some are larger and have multiple goals, such as the Florida Keys and Channel Islands National Marine Sanctuaries. The most recent ones are very large: the Northwestern Hawaiian Islands Coral Reef Ecosystem Reserve (2001), later absorbed into the Papahanaumokuakea Marine National Monument (2006) and three additional marine monuments established by President Bush (2009) and expanded by President Obama, encompass vast areas of the Pacific and include restrictions on fishing. The most important state effort, California's marine protection program, introduced in stages between 2007 and 2011, has banned fishing from 10 to 20 percent of coastal waters, depending on the area.[119] In 2013 scientists from the United States and other nations launched an ambitious international campaign, Global Ocean Legacy, funded by the Pew Charitable Trusts, to create huge "marine parks" in order to "restore and rebuild our global seascape."[120] Together with protection for endangered species, restrictions on fishing and other extractive industries are essential if fish and ocean fishing are to survive. As in other cases, the laws and institutions of the twentieth century have become inadequate or, worse, obstacles to conservation in the twenty-first century.

Action by the United States alone is not likely to be sufficient, however, because of jurisdictional limits and the migratory behavior of many marine species. Viewing the larger setting, Paul Greenberg, who has written widely on fish and fishing, urges a "profound redirection" in fishing; creation of "significant . . . no-catch areas"; international protection of "unmanageable species" such as bluefin tuna; and "protection of the bottom of the food chain," the small fish that are increasingly caught for animal feed (including farmed fish).[121] No small order, Greenberg's agenda promises to tax the political skills and economic resources of conservationists in many countries.

How should the conservation initiatives of the early twenty-first century be measured? There were few major breakthroughs and more continuity than change. The greatest progress was in land conservation, where the growing number of parks and protected areas contributed to a sense that piecemeal advances might eventually make the slogan "Half for Nature" more than an idle dream. Restoration was less successful, in large part because of the enormous cost of undoing the damage of earlier generations. Yet there were positive developments, such as the rapid recovery of some endangered species (gray wolves, grizzlies), and innovative activities, such as captive breeding and assisted migration, though they inevitably require "increasingly intensive human meddling."[122] In contrast, there was comparatively little positive news about wetlands, rivers, lakes, and oceans. The restoration of the Everglades proceeded at a snail's pace; the Gulf Coast was a continuing disaster. Efforts to remove river obstructions typically encountered entrenched opposition. Lakes and bays suffered new setbacks, and the decline in ocean fish stocks became so severe that it finally began to deflect attention away from the vicissitudes of the fishing industry. Most alarming was the political polarization that made conservation a partisan cause. The problem, as in so many areas, was leadership, or the lack thereof, and an unwillingness to adopt a longer-term perspective.

NOTES

1. J. Michael Scott et al., "Conservation-Reliant Species and the Future of Conservation," *Conservation Letters* 3, no. 2 (2010): 91. The biologist Edward O. Wilson has publicized the "half-earth" idea in speeches and essays. See Wilson, *Half-Earth: Our Planet's Fight for Life* (New York: Liveright, 2016).

2. Deborah Lynn Guber, *The Grassroots of a Green Revolution: Polling America on the Environment* (Cambridge, MA: MIT Press, 2003), 31.

3. Christopher J. Bosso and Deborah Lynn Guber, "Maintaining Presence: Environmental Advocacy and the Permanent Campaign," in *Environmental Policy: New Directions for the Twenty-First Century*, 6th ed., ed. Norman J. Vig and Michel E. Kraft (Washington, DC: Congressional Quarterly Press, 2007), 82.

4. Christopher J. Bosso, *Environment, Inc.: From Grassroots to Beltway* (Lawrence: University Press of Kansas, 2005), 54–55.

5. Ibid., 92, 97–98.

6. Edward Humes, *Eco-Barons: The Dreamers, Schemers, and Millionaires Who Are Saving Our Planet* (New York: Ecco, 2009).

7. Douglas Bevington, *The Rebirth of Environmentalism: Grassroots Activism from the Spotted Owl to the Polar Bear* (Washington, DC: Island Press, 2009), 178; Claudine Lomonacco, "Lost in the Woods," *High Country News* 46 (September 1, 2014): 12–20.

8. Bevington, *Rebirth of Environmentalism*, 162.

9. Bruce Babbitt, *Cities in the Wilderness: A New Vision of Land Use in America* (Washington, DC: Island Press, 2005), 42–43; Guber, *Grassroots of a Green Revolution*, 121; Bosso and Guber, "Maintaining Presence," 91.

10. Christopher McGrory Kyza and David Sousa, *American Environmental Policy, 1990–2006: Beyond Gridlock* (Cambridge, MA: MIT Press, 2008), 294. "Lords of yesterday," a reference to nineteenth-century "laws, policies, and ideas" that defined the western economy, is from Charles F. Wilkinson, *Crossing the Next Meridian: Land, Water, and the Future of the West* (Washington, DC: Island Press, 1992), 17.

11. Jacqueline Vaughn and Hanna J. Cortner, *George W. Bush's Healthy Forests: Reframing the Environmental Debate* (Boulder: University Press of Colorado, 2005), 22–23.

12. Klyza and Sousa, *American Environmental Policy*, 97, 206; Samuel P. Hays, *War in the Woods: The Rise of Ecological Forestry in America* (Pittsburgh: University of Pittsburgh Press, 2007), 159–60; Samuel P. Hays, *The American People and the National Forests: The First Century of the U.S. Forest Service* (Pittsburgh: University of Pittsburgh Press, 2009), 133–35.

13. James R. Skillen, *The Nation's Largest Landlord: The Bureau of Land Management in the American West* (Lawrence: University Press of Kansas, 2009), 188.

14. "Wilderness Data Search," 2001–8, http://www.wilderness.net/NWPS/adv Search.

15. "U.S. Plans to Limit Protected Wilderness to 23 Million Acres," *New York Times*, April 13, 2003; Klyza and Sousa, *American Environmental Policy*, 184–87.

16. Southern Utah Wilderness Alliance, *Redrock Wilderness* 28 (Autumn–Winter 2011): 5.

17. Matthew A. Cahn, Sheldon Kamieniecki, and Denise McCain-Tharnstrom, "Bureaucracy, Politics, and Environmental Policy in the American West," in *Environmental Politics and Policy in the West*, ed. Zachary A. Smith and John C. Freemuth (Boulder: University Press of Colorado, 2007), 40.

18. Daniel Glick, "Putting the Public Back in Public Lands," *National Wildlife* 46 (October–November 2008): 26.

19. Ibid., 28–29.

20. "Western Landscapes Shortchanged Due to Emphasis on Drilling," *America's Wilderness* 9 (Spring 2007): 7.

21. Sarah Gilman, "Sacrifice Zone," *High Country News* 47 (January 19, 2015): 49–51.

22. *Sierra Borealis*, March 2013, 4.

23. "Harmful Drilling Planned in the Chukchi Sea," *Alaska Report* 34 (March 2008): 1.

24. Clifford Krauss and Stanley Reed, "Shell Pulls Plug on Exploration in Alaska Arctic," *New York Times*, September 29, 2015.

25. Tom Turner, *Roadless Rules: The Struggle for the Last Wild Forests* (Washington, DC: Island Press, 2009), 57–58.

26. Ibid., 142.

27. Mark Hudson, *Fire Management in the American West: Forest Politics and the Rise of Megafires* (Boulder: University Press of Colorado, 2011), 30, 136–38.

28. Peter Friederici, *Nature's Restoration: People and Places on the Front Lines of Conservation* (Washington, DC: Island Press, 2006), 34.

29. Vaughn and Cortner, *Bush's Healthy Forests*, 174.

30. Jack Healy, "Cost of Battling Wildfires Cuts into Prevention Efforts," *New York Times*, June 28, 2013.

31. John J. Berger, *Forests Forever: Their Ecology, Restoration, and Protection* (Chicago: Center for American Places, 2008), 60; Howard G. Wilshire, Jane E. Nielson, and Richard W. Hazlett, *The American West at Risk: Science, Myths, and Politics of Land Abuse and Recovery* (New York: Oxford University Press, 2008), 29–31.

32. Earthjustice, news release, November 21, 2012.

33. Ruth S. Musgrave, "Legal Trends in Fish and Wildlife Policy," in *Wildlife and Society: The Science of Human Dimensions*, ed. Michael J. Manfredo et al. (Washington, DC: Island Press, 2009), 152.

34. Richard West Sellers, *Preserving Nature in the National Parks: A History* (New Haven: Yale University Press, 2009), 303–4.

35. Joe Roman, *Listed: Dispatches from America's Endangered Species Act* (Cambridge, MA: Harvard University Press, 2011), 186–87; John McManus, "Winning One for the Wolverine," *Earthjustice Quarterly Magazine*, Spring 2013, 20–21.

36. Bruce Barcott, "It's a Wilderness Out There," *Outside*, December 2013, 91.

37. Earthjustice, *In Brief* 110 (Winter 2009–10), 6, 7.

38. "Threats to Endangered Species Act," *Forest News*, Spring 2011, 4; Todd Wilkinson, "Wilderness Needs Wildlife," *Wilderness*, 2008–9, 44.

39. Earthjustice, *In Brief* 110 (2009–10): 6, 17; "On the Watch," *Wilderness Watcher* 21, no. 2 (September 2010): 3–8.

40. John M. Broder, "U.S. to Open New Areas to Offshore Drilling," *New York Times*, November 9, 2011.

41. Antonio Juhusz, *Black Tide: The Devastating Impact of the Gulf Oil Spill* (Hoboken, NJ: John Wiley & Sons, 2010), 2–14.

42. Coral Davenport, "New Sea Drilling Planned, 5 Years after Spill," *New York Times*, April 11, 2015.

43. Terry Tempest Williams, "The Man with the White Hat," *Redrock Wilderness* 30 (Spring 2013): 6.

44. Leslie Kaufman, "Agency Regains Authority for Wilderness Protection," *New York Times*, November 24, 2010.

45. "Change under the Obama Administration? Not So Fast . . . ," *Redrock Wilderness* 28 (Summer 2011): 6.

46. John M. Broder and Clifford Krauss, "Offshore Oil Drilling's New and Frozen Frontier," *New York Times*, May 24, 2012.

47. John M. Broder, "Babbitt Exhorts Obama to Protect Public Lands," *New York Times* Green blog, February 5, 2013.

48. Jenna Hertz and Pam Mitler, "NAEC Members Speak: Washington Listens," *Northern Line* 34 (Winter 2012): 7.

49. "Celebrate! New Arctic Wilderness Recommendation," *Sierra Borealis*, March 2015, 5.

50. Bill Birchard, *Nature's Keepers: The Remarkable Story of How the Nature Conservancy Became the Largest Environment Organization in the World* (San Francisco: Jossey-Bass, 2005), 130–51.

51. Ibid., 205–33; Abe Steep, "The Natural," *Outside*, August 2010, 84–85.

52. Peter Kareiva and Michelle Marvier, "Conservation for the People," *Scientific American* 297, no. 4 (October 2007): 50–57; Peter Kareiva et al., "Domesticated Nature: Shaping Landscapes and Ecosystems for Human Welfare," *Science* 316, no. 5833 (June 29, 2007): 1866–69.

53. Donald Worster, "The Higher Altruism," in *After Preservation: Saving American Nature in the Age of Humans*, ed. Ben A. Minteer and Stephen J. Pyne (Chicago: University of Chicago Press, 2015), 65.

54. Tom Butler, "Lives Not Our Own," in *Keeping the Wild: Against the Domestication of the Earth*, ed. George Wuerthner, Eileen Crist, and Tom Butler (Washington, DC: Island Press, 2014), x.

55. Dave Foreman, "Around the Campfire," *Rewilding Institute*, no. 45 (March 26, 2013): 4–5.

56. D. T. Max, "Green Is Good," *New Yorker*, May 12, 2014, 54–63. Also Mark R. Tercek and Jonathan S. Adams, *Nature's Fortune: How Business and Society Thrive by Investing in Nature* (New York: Basic Books, 2013); Edward O. Wilson, *A Window on Eternity: A Biologist's Walk through Gorongosa National Park* (New York: Simon and

Schuster, 2014), 136–38, 140–41; Curt Meine, "What's So New about the 'New Conservation'?" in *Keeping the Wild*, ed. Wuerthner, Crist, and Butler, 45–54.

57. Amy Mathews Amos, "Keeping the Faith(s)," *High Country News* 47 (January 19, 2015): 10–11.

58. Nels E. Barrett and Juliana P. Barrett, "Reserve Design and the New Conservation Theory," in *The Ecological Basis of Conservation: Heterogeneity, Ecosystems, and Biodiversity* , S.T.A. Pickett et al. (New York: Chapman and Hall, 1997), 246–48.

59. Andrew M. Barton, *The Changing Nature of the Maine Woods* (Durham: University of New Hampshire Press, 2012), 124–27.

60. Ibid., 128; John W. Neff, *Katahdin: An Historic Journey* (Boston: Appalachian Mountain Club Books, 2006), 282–85.

61. Birchard, *Nature's Keepers*, 116–28.

62. Marc Chalisfour, "A Vision in Green," *AMC Outdoors* 75 (November–December 2009): 33; Kristin Weir, "True North," *Nature Conservancy Magazine*, no. 4 (2012): 57, 60; Carey Kish, "Exploring the 100-Mile Wilderness," *AMC Outdoors* 79 (July–August 2013): 38.

63. Tony Hiss, "The Wildest Idea on Earth," *Smithsonian* 45 (September 2014): 73; Barton, *Changing Nature of the Maine Woods*, 130.

64. "Conservation and Advocacy Report," *Adirondac* 76 (September–October 2012): 10.

65. Erik Ness, "Vote Yes for Conservation," *Nature Conservancy Magazine* 59 (Autumn 2009): 35–37; "Minnesota," *Nature Conservancy Magazine* 60 (Winter 2010): 20.

66. Kirk Johnson, "Deal Is Struck in Montana to Preserve Forest Areas," *New York Times*, July 1, 2008; Tom Dunkel, "Wild Idea," *Nature Conservancy Magazine* 58 (Autumn 2008): 54–55; "Cumberland Plateau Protected," *Nature Conservancy Magazine* 58 (Spring 2008): 20.

67. Melanie Parker, "Swan Story," in *Stitching the West Back Together: Conservation of Working Landscapes*, ed. Susan Charnley, Thomas E. Sheridan, and Gary P. Nabhan (Chicago: University of Chicago Press, 2014), 124–33.

68. Ginger Strand, "A Win for the West," *Nature Conservancy Magazine*, April–May 2015, 52–55.

69. "Everglades Restoration Back on Track," *In Brief*, Winter 2010/2011, 14–15.

70. American Prairie Reserve, "Building the Reserve," https://www.american prairie.org/building-the-reserve, and "Our Story," https://www.americanprairie .org/our-story.

71. Edward Humes, "Where the Wild Things Are, Still," *Sierra*, January–February 2010, 41–43.

72. Jane Braxton Little, "The Missing Link," *Nature Conservancy Magazine* 61, no. 4 (2012): 49–52; Hiss, "Wildest Idea," 73.

73. Land Trust Alliance, 2010 National Land Trust Census Report, November 16, 2011, http://s3.amazonaws.com/landtrustalliance.org/page/files/2010LandTrust Census.pdf; "Easements 101," *Nature Conservancy Magazine*, October–November 2014, 42–45.

74. Western Reserve Land Conservancy, *Connections*, 2013, 20; Western Reserve Land Conservancy, *Branching Out: Donor Report*, July 1, 2013–June 30, 2014, http://www.wrlandconservancy.org/pdf/wrlc-donor-re13-14web.pdf.

75. Jon Christensen, Jenny Rempel, and Judee Burr, "Private Land Conservation in the Western United States," in *Stitching the West Back Together*, ed. Charnley, Sheridan, and Nabhan, 243.

76. Richard Brewer, *Conservancy: The Land Trust Movement in America* (Hanover, NH: University Press of New England, 2003), 214.

77. Western Reserve Land Conservancy, *Connections*, 2013, 20.

78. Felicity Barringer, "Insurance Firm Is Set Up for Land Trusts, Which See Legal Costs Soar," *New York Times*, May 20, 2012; Felicity Barringer, "The Yin and Yang of Conserving Land," *New York Times* Green blog, May 22, 2012.

79. David S. Wilcove, *The Condor's Shadow: The Loss and Recovery of Wildlife in America* (New York: W. H. Freeman and Co., 1999), 106.

80. Jeffrey K. Stine, *America's Forested Wetlands: From Wasteland to Valued Resource* (Durham: Forest History Society, 2008), 44, 62; Dan Ferber, "Into the Breach," *Nature Conservancy Magazine* 60 (Spring 2010): 31–32; Mark R. Terck and Jonathan S. Adams "Nature's Fortune," *Nature Conservancy Magazine* 62 (May–June 2013): 56–58.

81. Ann Vileisis, *Discovering the Unknown Landscape: A History of America's Wetlands* (Washington, DC: Island Press, 1997), 336; David M. Curley, *Losing Ground: Identity and Land Loss in Coastal Louisiana* (Jackson: University Press of Mississippi, 2010), 5.

82. Laura Tangley, "Gulf Coast Revival?" *National Wildlife* 49 (April–May 2011): 29.

83. "Fines Fund Conservation," *Nature Conservancy Magazine*, April–May 2015, 37.

84. Cynthia A. Drew, "The Upper Mississippi River and the Army Corps of Engineers' New Role: Will Congress Fund Ecosystem Restoration?" in *Large-Scale Ecosystem Restoration: Five Case Studies from the United States*, ed. Mary Doyle and Cynthia A. Drew (Washington, DC: Island Press, 2008), 229, 237.

85. Ibid., 153–54.

86. William R. Lowry, *Dam Politics: Restoring America's Rivers* (Washington, DC: Georgetown University Press, 2003), 126.

87. Ibid., 128.

88. David M. Freeman, *Implementing the Endangered Species Act on the Platte Basin Water Commons* (Boulder: University Press of Colorado, 2010).

89. Steven Hawley, *Recovering a Lost River: Removing Dams, Rewilding Salmon, Revitalizing Communities* (Boston: Beacon Press, 2011), 6.

90. Jeff Crane, *Finding the River: An Environmental History of the Elwha* (Corvallis: Oregon State University Press, 2011), 133–67.

91. William Yardley, "Removing Barriers to Salmon Migration," *New York Times*, July 30, 2011.

92. *Earthjustice Annual Report 2012; Preserving Our Natural Heritage*, 6.

93. Lowry, *Dam Politics*, 66, 102, 167–68.

94. Holly Doremus and A. Dan Tarlock, *Water War in the Klamath Basin: Macho Law, Combat Biology, and Dirty Politics* (Washington, DC: Island Press, 2008), 183–84; David Nawi and Alf W. Brandt, "The California-Bay Delta: The Challenges of Collaboration," in *Large-Scale Ecosystem Restoration*, ed. Doyle and Drew, 118–20.

95. Dean Apostol and Marcia Sinclair, "Conclusions: The Status and Future of Restoration in the Pacific Northwest," in *Restoring the Pacific Northwest*, ed. Apistol and Sinclair, 431; Ben Goldfarb, "The Great Salmon Compromise," *High Country News* 46 (December 8, 2014): 10–18.

96. William R. Lowry, *Repairing Paradise: The Restoration of Nature in America's National Parks* (Washington, DC: Brookings Institution Press, 2009), 195–96.

97. Robert W. Adler, *Restoring Colorado River Ecosystems: A Troubled Sense of Immensity* (Washington, DC: Island Press, 2007), 240–41.

98. American Rivers, "American Rivers Announces America's Most Endangered Rivers," press release, April 17, 2013.

99. William McGucken, *Lake Erie Rehabilitated: Controlling Cultural Eutrophication, 1960's–1990's* (Akron: University of Akron Press, 2000); Dave Dempsey, *On the Brink: The Great Lakes in the 21st Century* (East Lansing: Michigan State University Press, 2004), 195–225; Michael Wines, "EPA Unveils Second Phase of Plan to Reverse Great Lakes Damage," *New York Times*, September 25, 2014.

100. Wayne Grady, *The Great Lakes: The Natural History of a Changing Region* (Vancouver: Greystone Books, 2007), 195–98.

101. National Wildlife Federation, "Emerging Nutrient Crisis Causing Massive New Breakdown in the Great Lakes," October 4, 2011, https://www.nwf.org/News-and-Magazines/Media-Center/News-by-Topic/Wildlife/2011/10-04-11-Nutrient-Crisis-Causing-Breakdowns-in-the-Great-Lakes.aspx; "Ecosystem Breakdowns in Great Lakes," *National Wildlife* 50 (February–March 2012): 48.

102. Great Lakes Restoration Initiative, *Great Lakes Restoration Initiative Action Plan II*, September 2014, https://www.glri.us/actionplan/pdfs/glri-action-plan-2.pdf.

103. Stephen Polasky, "Murky Waters and Murky Policies: Costs and Benefits of Restoring Chesapeake Bay," in *Large-Scale Ecosystem Restoration*, ed. Doyle and Drew, 216.

104. Margaret T. Peters, *Conserving the Commonwealth: The Early Years of the Environmental Movement in Virginia* (Charlottesville: University of Virginia Press, 2008), 94.

105. Polasky, "Murky Waters," 222.

106. Elliott A. Norse and Larry B. Crowder, "Preface," in *Marine Conservation Biology: The Science of Maintaining the Sea's Biodiversity* , ed. Norse and Crowder (Washington, DC: Island Press, 2005), xviii. Also Etienne Benson, *Wired Wilderness: Technologies of Tracking and the Making of Modern Wildlife* (Baltimore: Johns Hopkins University Press, 2010), 144–64.

107. Callum Roberts, *The Ocean of Life: The Fate of Man and the Sea* (New York: Viking, 2012), 50; Robert Engelman et al., "Introduction: Climate, People, Fisheries, and Aquatic Ecosystems," in *Aquatic Ecosystems* , ed. Nicholas V.C. Polunin (Cambridge: Cambridge University Press, 2008), 12; Anthony D. Barnosky, *Heatstroke: Nature in an Age of Global Warming* (Washington, DC: Island Press, 2009), 50.

108. Roberts, *Ocean of Life*, 233. Also Lisa-ann Gershwin, *Stung! On Jellyfish Blooms and the Future of the Ocean* (Chicago: University of Chicago Press, 2013).

109. Barnosky, *Heatstroke,* 51–52; Larry B. Crowder, "Back to the Future in Marine Conservation," in *Marine Conservation Biology*, ed. Norse and Crowder, 25; Jeremy B.C. Jackson, Karen E. Alexander, and Enric Sala, eds., *Shifting Baselines: The Past and the Future of Ocean Fisheries* (Washington, DC: Island Press, 2011).

110. Carmel Finley, *All the Fish in the Sea: Maximum Sustainable Yield and the Failure of Fisheries Management* (Chicago: University of Chicago Press, 2011), 2–9.

111. Alison Rieser, Charlotte Gray Hudson, and Stephen E. Roady, "The Role of Legal Regimes in Marine Conservation," in *Marine Conservation Biology*, ed. Norse and Crowder, 367.

112. Callum Roberts, "Keep the Fishing Ban in New England," *New York Times*, January 31 2013.

113. Mansel G. Blackford, *Making Seafood Sustainable: American Experiences in Global Perspective* (Philadelphia: University of Pennsylvania Press, 2012), 81–87.

114. Carl Safina, *Song for the Blue Ocean: Encounters along the World's Coasts and beneath the Seas* (New York: Henry Holt, 1998), 13.

115. Ray Hilborn, "Are Sustainable Fisheries Achievable?" in *Marine Conservation Biology*, ed. Norse and Crowder, 253.

116. Callum Roberts, *The Unnatural History of the Sea* (Washington, DC: Island Press, 2007), 323; Michael Wines and Jess Bidgood, "Waters Warm, and Cod Catch Ebbs in Maine," *New York Times*, December 15, 2014.

117. W. Rashid Sumaila and Daniel Pauly, "The 'March of Folly' in Global Fisheries," in *Shifting Baselines*, ed. Jackson, Alexander, and Sala, 24; Tony Koslow, *The Silent Deep: The Discovery, Ecology, and Conservation of the Deep Sea* (Chicago: University of Chicago Press, 2007), 234.

118. Benjamin S. Halpern, "Conservation: Making Marine Protected Areas Work," *Nature* 506, no. 7487 (February 13, 2014): 167–68; Graham J. Edgar et al., "Global Conservation and Outcomes Depend on Marine Protected Areas with Five Key Features," *Nature* 506, no. 7487 (February 13, 2014): 216–20.

119. Erik Olsen, "No-Fishing Rule Roils Southern California," *New York Times* Green blog, January 12, 2012.

120. "A Rising Tide: A Statement of Support by Scientists for the Designation of the First Generation of Great Marine Parks Around the Globe," Open Channels Forum, October 22, 2013, https://www.openchannels.org/news/news/rising-tide-statement-support-scientists-designation-first-generation-great-marine-parks.

121. Paul Greenberg, *Four Fish: The Future of the Last Wild Food* (New York: Penguin Press, 2010), 247–48.

122. Goldfarb, "Great Salmon Compromise," 18.

9

American Conservation

A Progress Report

In 2011 the director of the National Park Service, Jon Jarvis, asked his advisory board's Science Committee to reexamine the agency's approach to resource management in light of changing conditions and new scientific perspectives. He called explicitly for updating the 1963 Leopold report. The resulting document, "Revisiting Leopold," is an useful starting point for assessing the state of American conservation a half century after Leopold and thirty-plus years after Reagan, the emergence of conservation biology and related disciplines, and the proliferation of environmental organizations and activities, private conservation initiatives in particular.

There are obvious and predictable contrasts with Leopold. Gone are references to the national parks as "vignettes" of "primitive America" and the implied association of "naturalness" with the distant past. Indeed, the scientists now emphasized the challenges of continuous, disruptive change, both natural and human-caused: "Biodiversity loss, climate change, habitat fragmentation, land use change, groundwater removal, invasive species, [and] overdevelopment" together with "air, noise, and light pollution" confront

DOI: 10.7330/9781607325703.c009

and will continue to confront park managers. But the tools for responding to these escalating threats have also multiplied. They include the scientists' prescriptions for fire management, invasive species controls, and the reintroduction of predators. In addition, the report noted, "ecosystem management has matured into a science-based activity." In applying these tools, park officials must remember that "biodiversity, evolutionary potential, and system resilience matter as much as observable features of iconic species and grand landscapes." They must strive to improve "the representation of unique ecosystem types," prioritize "the protection of habitats that may serve as climate refugia," maintain "critical migration and dispersal corridors," and strengthen "the resilience of park ecosystems." At the same time, "management strategies must be expanded to encompass geographic scope beyond park boundaries to larger landscapes and to consider longer time horizons." Employing a "holistic vision" and the "best available sound science," managers should make the park system the "core" of a larger network of protected areas. Such an arrangement, involving parks and other landscapes, will "increase their individual and collective resilience over time."[1]

As the report suggests, a more detailed, extensive, and science-based understanding of what contemporary conservation involves—and broad public acceptance of that expanded perspective—is among the notable changes of recent decades. The continuing success of land conservation is another achievement, reflecting the combination of public and private initiatives that has emerged in the wake of the federal government's often disappointing performance on conservation issues. Efforts to preserve plants and animals, enormously complicated under the best of conditions, have been more challenging and remain high on the priority lists of conservationists. Finally, all of these activities have become more complex and trying because of the rapidly changing, warming climate and its implications for the natural world.

A summary of these changes, using the cores, corridors, and carnivores formula, provides a rough balance sheet of the results of thirty-plus years of activism and conflict.

CORES

By any quantitative measure, there has been rapid progress in creating "protected areas," which the International Union for the Conservation of Nature

(IUCN) defines broadly to include parks, wildlife preserves, and multiple-use areas. In the early 1960s there were fewer than 10,000 parks and preserves worldwide; now there are more than 100,000, accounting for 12.5 percent of the Earth's terrestrial surface.[2] In contrast, less than 2 percent of the world's oceans are protected, and Australia's Great Barrier Reef and the US Pacific monuments account for the largest fraction of that meager total.[3] In 2009 North America had more than 13,000 protected areas, totaling 17.3 percent of its land and 1.2 percent of adjacent marine areas, not counting the Pacific monuments. The United States had 7,800 sites, 21 percent of its area, or half of the protected land in North America. Canada had 5,400 protected areas, nearly 9 percent of its land, and Mexico had 193, about 1 percent of its land.[4] These statistics come with several caveats. Only about half the "protected" land in North America is off-limits to extractive industries, and that includes Greenland, largely a "biosphere reserve." Without Greenland, the total would be only 15 percent of the terrestrial surface. On the other hand, these numbers omit local and state parks and lands protected by private groups.[5]

Thomas Vale, a geographer at the University of Wisconsin, has provided more precise statistics for the United States. He calculates that the Park Service, Forest Service, Fish and Wildlife Service, and BLM manage about 249 million acres in the most secure categories, such as parks, wildlife refuges, and wilderness; the states have more than 28 million acres and local governments about 3 million acres in similar categories.[6] His tally does not include the roadless areas of national forests (58 million acres) or holdings of other federal agencies, such as the Defense Department, some of which qualify as de facto wildlife refuges; and he includes only private lands owned by conservation groups, 2 million acres. The 2009 Omnibus Lands Act increased many of these categories and added 2 million acres to the Wilderness Preservation System. Perhaps half of the privately owned land under conservation easement would also qualify, adding about 5 million acres. The revised totals, for the most secure areas alone, are equal to 13 percent of the United States (15 percent with the roadless areas) and 40 percent of federal land holdings. The federal total is strongly influenced by the vast Alaskan parks and refuges.

What about the future? The nations that signed the Convention on Biological Diversity have pledged to protect 17 percent of their land and inland waters and 10 percent of their coastal and marine areas by 2020. (The original 2012 target for marine areas was also 10 percent. That target was obviously too ambitious, and thus the goal remains at 10 percent.) There is also encouraging evidence of qualitative changes, the spread of official wilderness systems in particular. The IUCN first added a wilderness category to its list of protected areas in 1994 and, in response to growing interest, refined that definition in 2009 to put "the emphasis firmly and equivocally on conservation."[7]

The United States continues to play a leading role in this activity. The national park and national forest systems have successfully preserved the most aesthetically impressive areas of the United States, no small achievement. The positive effect of national parks on tourism and local economic activity, documented in numerous studies, virtually guarantees more efforts to upgrade national monuments (such as Great Sand Dunes National Park in 2004 and Pinnacles National Park in 2012) and to establish new parks in the Pacific Northwest, Appalachia, and northern New England. As environmentalists have taken a closer look at BLM lands, they have discovered, often to their surprise, that these "left-over" lands are, in many cases, merely overlooked and include important aesthetic and geological features. So there is potential for expansion there, too.

The largest additions to the total of protected lands since 1980 have resulted from the rapid growth of the land trust movement. It is hard to interpret the significance of these substantial additions, since conservation easements are tailored to specific properties and can permit oil and gas drilling and other activities inconsistent with the idea of "rewilding." Yet in most cases easements are effective barriers to sprawl and fragmentation; the lands they protect are one example of the buffers that can supplement core areas and facilitate connectivity. They are also indicative of a growing recognition that explicit protective measures are essential to preserve natural settings. No longer is it possible to assume that a remote location or difficult terrain are sufficient to preclude development.

In terms of preserving representative landscapes, the record is less satisfactory, largely because of the opportunistic process by which parks and wilderness areas have been created and a preference for mountains over valleys, prairies, and wetlands. Areas traditionally hostile to federal authority, the Gulf Coast and Plains states in particular, are dramatically underrepresented.[8] The Canadian approach, which has explicitly targeted representative areas, stands in marked contrast. The goal there is to preserve at least 12

percent of each ecoregion, a target that has been met in at least five prov-
inces. Ontario and Quebec have also pledged to ban extractive activities from
at least half of their remote northern lands.[9]

Preserving biodiversity is an even greater challenge, and one that received
little or no attention when most parks and other protected areas were established but that is now inextricably associated with the complexities of ecological restoration. In addition to the location issue, there is the legacy of
managerial practices (predator controls, dams, fire suppression, etc.), which
have accelerated the loss of biodiversity, and vague or ambivalent goals ("naturalness").[10] All of these problems are being addressed to some degree. The
critical issues are timing and the effectiveness of specific remedial measures.

There is general agreement among scientists and public lands administrators that habitat loss and invasive species are the most significant contemporary threats to biodiversity. Habitat loss, primarily though fragmentation, is
an ongoing challenge that largely explains why many protected areas are less
valuable than their acreage totals imply. The invasive species threat has grown
rapidly with the expansion of interregional and international commerce and
travel. The dimensions of the problem are vast and confounding, ranging
from a profusion of nonnative fish; the spread of cheatgrass and other nonnative grasses, which now cover large areas of the intermountain West; the
profusion of phragmites and other plants that are choking wetlands; a host
of feral animals; and many others.[11] Hawaii, with more endemic species than
any other state, faces the greatest challenges. Native birds have largely disappeared from lowland areas due to habitat destruction, the ravages of domestic animals, and disease. A variety of remedial measures, including the fencing of parks and preserves, eradication of feral animals, captive breeding of
birds, and establishment of cooperative Watershed Partnerships that provide
for the uniform management of mountainous areas, have shown promise
but have not yet not reversed the decline.[12]

Probably the most serious threats are found on privately owned lands and in
rivers, lakes, and oceans. Cheatgrass, introduced as cattle feed, has increased
the frequency of wildfires in many areas from once or twice a century to two
or three times per decade.[13] Waterways continue to be victims of abuse and
neglect. The prospect of Asian carp joining the host of invasive species that
currently threaten the Great Lakes has called attention to the enormity of
the problem and the failures of public regulation and management.

In such situations a "do nothing" or "do little" policy often invites more serious problems. Yet intervention poses additional challenges. The range of efforts to preserve or sustain wildlife populations, including captive breeding, assisted migration, reintroduction, and ecological replacement, are a measure of the seriousness of the situation and the scale of scientific ingenuity.[14] Michael Soulé and John Terborgh argue that "no large-scale restoration plan is complete without consideration of the array of current invaders and their individual and cumulative impacts on native species."[15] Distinctions, in short, are essential. The Nature Conservancy has developed a detailed program based on efforts to "prioritize threats and strategies" for dealing with them. It reflects an assumption that some threats are more harmful than others and that even the worst of them do not warrant attention if there is no practical way to eliminate them. TNC scientists focus on species that have "large, harmful impacts." Once the eradication process begins, monitoring and adjustments are essential.

Several examples are instructive. On Santa Cruz Island, off the southern California coast, TNC's removal of feral sheep restored native vegetation, but also provided additional food for feral pigs. The pigs in turn attracted golden eagles, which attacked not only the pigs but a species of fox endemic to the coastal islands. By 2004, when the foxes were added to the endangered species list, the only survivors were removed to a TNC captive breeding program. Eliminating the pigs and relocating the eagles produced what TNC calls 'one of the fastest and most effective . . . recovery programs in U.S. history." In less than a decade the fox population on the island grew to 1,300.[16] In central Florida the target was a fast-growing fern that threatened many endemic plants. Beginning in 2004, TNC and various partners removed ferns from over 1 million acres. With the benefit of that experience, a larger region will be targeted for the second phase of the campaign.[17] In these situations, "priority setting should consider effects on native biodiversity, current and potential distribution and abundance, difficulty of control and the biodiversity value of the areas."[18]

In other words, a cautionary approach is not only prudent but essential. Recognizing that most "native" plants and animals were invaders at one time, it is obvious that hasty or arbitrary distinctions can create more problems than they solve, just as the introduction of new predator species to control earlier introductions has often backfired. Moreover, it is often impractical or even impossible to eliminate invasives, and the expense of eradication campaigns diverts resources from more promising activities.[19]

Even more challenging are campaigns to give freer reign to "abiotic forces," notably water and fire. There is a long list of dam removals and other efforts to improve river flow, but each project has typically faced formidable obstacles and long delays. Opposition from commercial interests is a serious hurdle. And even when there is agreement, the expenses can be daunting. In one notable case, it cost ten times as much to reconfigure the Kissimmee River in central Florida as it had to canalize it a quarter of a century earlier.[20] Efforts to recreate more natural fire regimes are equally daunting, especially in the West, due to the continuing spread of roads and homes into remote, forested areas and the persistence of drought conditions. In 2012 record heat and drought led the Forest Service, in what fire historian Stephen Pyne characterizes as "a bizarre piece of political theatre," to revert to the practice of total suppression in the desperate hope that it would prevent larger and more harmful conflagrations. The costs of this policy were so great that the agency again reversed itself. Its latest strategy, proclaimed in 2014, once again included the goal of "living with fire."[21] In the meantime large fires have become more common and have led to an "uncontrolled rise in suppression expenditures," in no small part because of a burgeoning "fire-industrial complex," a "stream of consultants, contractors, and vendors" that has become a highly profitable "torrent."[22] In terms of its budget, the Forest Service is on the verge of becoming a huge rural fire department.

The other requirements of an effective ecosystem restoration process are a system of linkages between cores and a full complement of "keystone" species, including large carnivores. These have proven to be the most challenging features of the effort to recreate a more natural and sustainable environment.

CORRIDORS AND CARNIVORES

The "good news," Soulé argued in a 2010 essay, "is that there exists one simple, documented, and inexpensive" way to restore terrestrial and aquatic ecosystems. The antidote to "habitat fragmentation, climate disruption, and ecological cascades" is "connectivity." It is, he added, "simple, cost-effective, and even culturally popular. . . . 'Nature's aspirin' is the freedom to disperse, particularly for strongly interacting species such as wolves . . . whose repatriation can restore critical interactions and processes."[23] Though core areas are essential, they are not, and probably can never be, numerous enough or large enough to sustain or revive native flora and fauna. Buffer areas, with a greater human presence and links to other cores, are therefore vital, especially for large "keystone" carnivores. But is connectivity in fact simple, inexpensive, and popular? Twenty years have passed since Soulé and his colleagues first publicized the issue. What has been accomplished?

The most obvious achievement is intellectual. An impressive combination of scholarly and popular writings have persuasively argued the case. Most magazines and newsletters of national environmental organizations regularly feature articles on connectivity. These articles, plus the growing number of endangered species and the warming climate, have convinced most environmentalists and federal land managers that the "freedom to disperse" is often the key to survival for threatened or endangered species.[24]

What exactly is required on the ground is less obvious. Connectivity is an elastic term covering a variety of situations.[25] The ambitious interregional "rewilding" plans of the 1990s represented one end in a spectrum of possibilities. Their progress has largely depended on the remoteness of the areas they encompassed. The best known proposal, Yellowstone to Yukon, or Y2Y, has benefited from the support of dozens of local and regional groups and the willingness of Canadian provincial governments to establish new preserves in remote regions of the corridor. A related effort, the "Crown of the Continent" partnership, began as an attempt by officials of Glacier National Park and the adjoining Canadian park, Waterton Lakes, to work on common management issues. Their actions inspired other cross-border collaborations that have generated wide interest and in recent years have overshadowed Y2Y. Although the emphasis has been on consultation and education rather than restrictive measures, the "Crown of the Continent" campaign, like Y2Y and other ambitious proposals, has aroused opposition in some quarters, a reflection of the diverse challenges—oil and gas drilling, mining, logging, and off-road vehicle use—that face national park and national forest managers and their allies.[26] In the meantime, an agreement among Canadian paper companies, environmental organizations, and provincial governments to preserve large areas of boreal forest has provided the foundation for a similar connectivity proposal for northern Canada.[27]

Another intriguing project, known as the El Carmen–Big Bend Conservation Corridor Initiative, is the most recent chapter in a long and frustrating campaign to establish an international park on the US-Mexico border. The initiative embraces more than 3 million acres and includes Big Bend National Park, an adjoining state park, a large BLM wildlife area, four Mexican protected areas, and a private wilderness of 24,000 acres. This collection of parks and wildlife preserves, occupying an important ecological "hotspot" with many endemic species, is an ideal setting for migrating bighorn sheep, bears, mountain lions, and other wildlife. Despite its potential, the initiative faces significant obstacles and an uncertain outcome. The current campaign for "border security" and restricted movements between Mexico and the United States may well mean that this effort, like its antecedents, will produce only disappointment for its proponents and a less happy fate for the bears, mountain lions, and other potential beneficiaries.[28]

There have also been notable failures. The proposed Paseo Pantera corridor, extending more than 500 miles through Central America from Mexico to Panama, is a notable example. Undertaken with great fanfare in the mid-1990s, the project quickly bogged down as conflicts between international funding organizations, local governments, and residents of the proposed areas overshadowed their common goals. By 2000 the plans were in disarray, and by 2006 "hundreds of millions of dollars had been spent but only a single protected area had been created."[29] Nor was Central America the only region where local opposition became a formidable, often insuperable obstacle As the controversies over the spotted owl, the expansion of the Adirondack forest preserve, and others have demonstrated, it is difficult to rally local support where the impetus comes from outside and the long-term benefits are overshadowed by immediate costs. Except as visionary projects, the grand plans of the early 1990s have made only limited progress. The fates of the more than one hundred other corridor projects reported in 2001 are also uncertain.[30]

Fortunately, there are other possibilities. Comparatively small changes in boundaries or managerial policies of many parks and refuges have created linkages, or at least the potential for linkages noted in a previous chapter. At a more modest level, the results are even more encouraging. It has been relatively easy to mobilize support for projects that enable bears, large ungulates, and birds to move more freely, notably via highway overpasses and underpasses. Banff National Park, a leader in this activity, now has two bridges and twenty-two wildlife underpasses, mostly to benefit grizzlies and wolves. (Altogether, there are sixty "mitigation" structures in and around the park.) It has also helped to publicize the idea of wildlife "bridges" as a simple and cheap way to achieve connectivity.[31] In recent years highway departments and national parks in the United States have added similar structures. There are now forty-one wildlife crossings along a fifty-six-mile section of a highway that bisects the Flathead Indian Reservation south of Glacier National Park; six underpasses and two overpasses south of Grand Teton National Park accommodate the seasonal migrations of pronghorn, mule deer, and elk. Everglades Park has thirty-six crossings in a forty-mile section of its major east-west highway, and others have been built near Mt. Rainier National Park.[32] In recent years the National Wildlife Federation has promoted a "vast habitat corridor" in northern New England to reduce highway wildlife casualties.[33]

There were also imaginative variations on this theme. Scientists working with the BLM have established parts of a "National Migration Corridor" for pronghorn and mule deer in Wyoming and a carnivore "highway" along the Idaho-Montana border.[34] Ranchers and environmentalists in southern Arizona and New Mexico have purchased land in northern Sonora, Mexico, to preserve the habitat of the jaguar and have hired Mexican ranchers to photograph the elusive animals. Their goal is to make preservation financially attractive.[35]

The emphasis on carnivores and predation has raised other issues. In recent years scientists have devoted increasing emphasis to the importance of food webs and trophic cascades, the hierarchical relationships between different groups of animals. The profusion of white-tailed deer and other ungulates is one highly visible result of the absence of predators such as wolves, bears, and mountain lions. Using the Endangered Species Act, environmentalists have forced the federal government to reintroduce carnivores in a number of areas. The good news is that gray wolves, lynxes, black-footed ferrets, sea otters, and jaguars have done well, though opposition continues. A combination of exaggerated concerns over livestock losses, resentment of government regulation, and an atavistic hostility toward animals that resist human controls has slowed the restoration process. The equally daunting job of addressing ocean ecosystems, which suffer from many of the same problems, is just getting under way.

The model for carnivore recovery is the grizzly bear program. Since the controversies of the 1970s and early 1980s, grizzlies in the lower forty-eight states have grown in numbers and expanded their range and, perhaps for the first time in a century, are more numerous outside than inside Yellowstone and Glacier National Parks. In Glacier and surrounding areas there were as many as 930 in 2010.[36] Their range has expanded from about 5 million acres in the 1970s to 21 million today. Proclaiming success, the Fish and Wildlife Service sought to remove the grizzly from the endangered species list in 2007, but environmental groups, citing the perilous state of the whitebark pine and the supply of pine nuts, one of the bears' principal autumn food sources, and, by implication, the impact of a warming climate, persuaded the courts to overturn that decision.[37] Because of diminished food supplies, federal biologists fear that grizzlies in the Yellowstone ecosystem may have already exceeded that area's carrying capacity.[38]

Apart from the growth of the bear population, the other notable feature of this process has been the absence of vocal opposition. Unlike most endangered species, bears occasionally harm people, usually as a result of chance encounters. (In Yellowstone bison cause four times as many injuries.)[39] To minimize bear encounters, the Fish and Wildlife Service in Montana has introduced a number of preventive measures, such as removing dead livestock, bear-proofing beehives, and sealing garbage cans. Sixty to seventy of the Montana bears have been collared, enabling scientists to study their movements. Anticipating potential conflicts is a key to their survival. "Mortality control is our No. 1 tool to bringing the bear back," explains a Fish and Wildlife scientist.[40]

Gray wolves have also made a successful comeback and, like the grizzlies, have spread far beyond Yellowstone and central Idaho. By 2008 there were at least 1,645 wolves living in 217 packs, most of them outside Yellowstone. The largest concentration was in the national forests that run northeast from Boise to Glacier National Park.[41] Preliminary indications are that they are having precisely the effect that biologists hoped they would have. In Yellowstone the elk have become more fearful and mobile, and wildlife that feed on carrion have benefited. Researchers point to sixteen species that have been positively affected.[42] (However, in the upper Midwest, a gradual increase in the wolf population over the last thirty years has had a less dramatic effect on other animal and plant species.)[43] The controversies that raged between rival groups of researchers from the 1950s to the 1990s have become more muted or disappeared altogether.

On the other hand, the conflicts with outsiders, ranchers in particular, have grown more heated. Since 1995 environmental groups have addressed live-stock losses in various ways. Defenders of Wildlife has paid ranchers more than a half million dollars in compensation and in 1998 introduced addi-tional measures, including fencing, range riders, and alarms, to protect cattle and sheep from wolves.[44] The National Wildlife Federation bought grazing leases on 600,000 acres of national forest land in the Greater Yellowstone Ecosystem to create habitat for wildlife, including wolves.[45] Local groups, such as Keystone Conservation, have promoted various nonlethal tactics for protecting livestock.[46] But the rapid growth of the wolf population has kept the issue alive, exposing seemingly intractable differences in perspective. A recent exhaustive study of the Greater Yellowstone region has concluded that opposition to wolves reflects cultural, not economic, anxieties.[47]

Citing the success of the gray wolf program, the Fish and Wildlife Service sought to remove the wolf from the endangered species list in 2007, return-ing management to state wildlife authorities. Environmentalists sued suc-cessfully to prevent the delisting. The same thing happened in 2009. In 2011 western senators successfully attached a rider to a budget bill delisting wolves in Idaho and Montana, the first time Congress had intervened to remove an animal from the endangered species list without a recommendation from a management agency.[48] The Fish and Wildlife Service also delisted the gray wolf in the upper Midwest with less controversy.

The result was reminiscent of Alaska, where wolves have long been blamed for fluctuations in the numbers of caribou and moose, and the state has aggressively promoted wolf hunting. In Idaho the state sold 26,000 wolf hunting licenses in September 2011 for an "allowable harvest" of 220 wolves, one-quarter of the total. Three hundred and seventy-five wolves were killed in the following months, nearly one-third of the total population. At that rate the number of wolves in the state might drop to 150 within a year or two.[49] Environmentalists had warned that the hunter-dominated state wildlife agencies were incapable of responsible management. Nevertheless, the Fish and Wildlife Service has also delisted wolves in Wyoming, which has even fewer restrictions.[50] (This decision was at least temporarily reversed by the courts.) In 2011 and 2012 more than 1,600 wolves died at the hands of hunters, trappers, and government agents, including eight with tracking collars killed outside Yellowstone; another 598 were killed in 2013.[51] State wildlife officials in Idaho, Montana, and Wyoming as well as Alaska plan more aggressive eradication campaigns in the near future.[52] The state of Washington, committed to non-lethal methods of protecting livestock, is the outlier, but it has fewer than 70 wolves at present and only a peripheral role in the reintroduction process.[53]

These setbacks parallel similar problems in the Southwest, where the Mexican gray wolf, a subspecies, had been reintroduced in 1998. In this case, the Fish and Wildlife Service seemingly did as little as possible to ensure the success of the plan. It restricted the wolves to two national forests, refused to designate critical habitat, did not require local ranchers to remove dead cattle or sheep, and killed wolves that left public lands. By 2007, when the target population was one hundred, there were only fifty-two wolves in the area; by 2014, eighty-three.[54] As many scientists had predicted, the surviving wolves quickly moved into more settled areas where they confronted automobiles and angry livestock owners. At least forty-six have been killed illegally, others by federal agents. WildEarth Guardians, a Santa Fe–based environmental organization, is trying to buy grazing leases to reduce conflicts with ranchers. In the immediate future a Fish and Wildlife Service–sponsored cooperative council of ranchers, environmentalists, and other interested parties may have a greater effect. It compensates livestock owners for losses due to predation and is gradually extending the areas where wolves are free to roam.[55]

In contrast to the wolf campaign, the effort to save the greater sage grouse, which has lost much of its traditional Great Plains habitat, has relied on the strategy pioneered by former Interior secretary Bruce Babbitt in the 1990s. Beginning in 2010, the Fish and Wildlife Service enlisted anxious state wildlife officials and private landowners in a massive effort to avoid an endangered species listing, which would likely have meant restrictions on various economic activities. The BLM and Forest Service have introduced protective measures on a total of 66 million acres, the states have limited surface disturbances in habitat areas, and the Fish and Wildlife Service has negotiated conservation easements on hundreds of thousands of acres of arid ranchland. Together they have mapped nesting sites and migration routes, created buffer zones where male birds gather, organized to fight grasssland fires, and restricted oil and gas drilling. One goal is to broaden the single-species emphasis of the

Endangered Species Act to include at least 350 other animals that also depend on sagebrush habitat and are also at risk. A second, equally important goal is to head off confrontations reminiscent of the spotted owl battles and the more recent conflicts over the gray wolf. Jim Lyons, the Interior Department's representative in the campaign, described its objective as "something that works for the bird and provides flexibility for sustainable devlopment."[56]

In the short term, at least, the cooperative approach has succeeded in persuading the Fish and Wildlife Service not to list the sage grouse. Echoing Babbitt, Interior secretary Sally Jewell described the campaign as "historic." Public policy expert James Freemuth agreed. "This is a pivotal Western moment," he argues.[57]

There will soon be opportunities to test these conclusions, given the mounting evidence of multiplying extinctions. Biologist Joe Roman suspects that "someday almost every organism will be on the list."[58] In more and more cases, protecting habitat alone, either through stringent application of the law or cooperative measures, will not suffice. Only direct intervention, in the form of captive propagation or other forms of assistance, often involving elaborate efforts to move or "translocate" animals, are likely to save endangered animals or plants.[59] Captive breeding has already saved the California condor, black-footed ferret, and others. Roman estimates that about 5,000 vertebrates, including most amphibians, need such attention, but zoos, which have become leaders in this conservation niche, can accommodate only about 500.[60] Increasingly, zookeepers are forced to pick and choose among many candidates, knowing that they probably provide the last exit on the road to oblivion.[61] A parallel effort to save the many thousands of threatened North American native plants has led to ex situ collecting (seed banks, gene banks, etc.) and the formation of a North American Collections Assessment to keep score. Thus far, a little more than one-third of threatened species have been "conserved" in this way.[62]

THE CHALLENGES OF A WARMING CLIMATE

Since at least the 1990s the specter of climate change has influenced all discussions of conservation issues, sometimes subtly, at other times overtly. The general assumption has been that a warming climate will require painful, unpleasant, and expensive adjustments; nor can the possibility of catastrophic changes be dismissed.[63] That the process is occurring much sooner than orig-inally predicted has added a sense of urgency and foreboding. The drought of 2000–2004 in the western United States was the worst in that region in 800 years, drastically reducing photosynthesis, agricultural production, and river flow, and, together with disease and pests, led to record losses in forest cover. The following decade brought little relief. Barring drastic changes in human behavior, this experience is almost certain to continue. Indeed, drought con-ditions are likely to become the "new normal" as desertification accelerates.[64] Global warming is also likely to increase the frequency of floods, severe storms, and heat waves, magnifying the challenges associated with human population growth, industrialization, and urban sprawl. In the meantime, other developments, notably recessions in the United States and Europe and rapid industrial growth in Asia and, to a lesser degree, Latin America, have undermined efforts to address the problem.

To grasp the immediate significance of a warming climate, it makes sense to start with Yellowstone Park, the most studied natural area in North America. Since 2009 the Park Service has made climate change one of its major concerns and the subject of much of its planning. In 2010 it completed a Climate Change Response Strategy, detailing possible responses to a range of scenarios, and together with other agencies has assigned a group of sci-entists, headquartered in Bozeman, Montana, to monitor changes through-out the West. Much of that work has featured Yellowstone. It has shown, for example, a large increase in the number of heat-loving invasive plants; a marked decline in the park's kettle ponds and in the population of trumpeter swans that depends on them; and a drying of creeks and rivers that drain into Yellowstone Lake, to the detriment of native fish.[65] In 1992–93 scientists found amphibians in forty-three of the forty-six ponds; in 2006–8, in only twenty-one of the forty-six, and in those cases fewer amphibian species.[66] The park's forested areas are also experiencing dramatic changes, mostly due to insect damage. The mountain pine beetle, formerly kept in check by the region's severe winters, has now spread widely; half of the area's forests have been damaged, 10 percent severely. Scientists predict more large fires and marked changes in forest composition. The whitebark pine is likely to disap-pear, while the larch will probably spread to higher elevations.

Park managers are also becoming more active in combating climate change. They are trying to create corridors for flora and fauna, planting disease-resistant seedlings, and using insecticides on individual trees. In some cases they may move wildlife to new, more suitable areas. Their underlying theme is managing for resiliency rather than historical fidelity.[67]

Other parks face equally formidable challenges. A 2014 study found that 81 percent of national park units had experienced "extreme recent warm conditions."[68] Glacier will soon be glacierless; Joshua Tree is likely to be devoid of Joshua trees; Redwood may lose most or all of its redwoods. Canada's Prince Albert National Park, established to preserve parts of the boreal forest, may have to find a new raison d'être. Adirondack ecologist Jerry Jenkins estimates that three-quarters of the grasses, two-thirds of the trees, birds, and ferns, and half the shrubs in the Adirondack forest will disappear as temperatures rise.[69] "We may be the last generation to see the big bogs and the boreal creatures," he laments.[70]

Outside the parks, forests have attracted the greatest attention. Warmer temperatures prolong the growing season, but they also increase the likelihood of insect infestation, droughts, and fires. In extreme cases forests could cease to be carbon sinks and accelerate the warming trend.[71]

To avoid such disasters, it will be necessary to set aside more forest land, introduce remedial measures similar to those employed in the national parks, and in national forests embrace what "new forestry" advocate Jerry Franklin calls "variable retention harvesting." That means lengthening cutting intervals to allow the trees to become bigger and preserving more of them.[72]

The warming climate is certain to exacerbate the problems of habitat fragmentation, pollution, and unsustainable harvests that plague wildlife on every continent. A study of more than 1,700 terrestrial species found that they were moving an average of 3.8 miles per decade toward the poles, greatly complicating the challenge of connecting core areas. This response will ultimately fail, for temperatures in the polar regions are rising much faster than in temperate zones. The IUCN estimates that 13 percent of bird species, 25 percent of mammals, 41 percent of amphibians, and 29 percent of reptiles are threatened.[73] The most comprehensive study to date predicts that 15 to 37 percent of species will be extinct or nearing extinction by the middle of the current century.[74] The oceans probably pose the most immediate challenges, as increasing acidification threatens coral and other animals that form shells or external skeletons and ultimately will spell disaster for many forms of marine life. Often characterized as global warming's "equally evil twin," acidification results from seawater absorbing carbon dioxide from the atmosphere, greatly exaggerating the effects of the warmer water.[75]

The antidote, as the naturalist Robert Pearson explains, is familiar: reduce "nonclimactic threats," preserve lands "that exhibit as much environmental variation as possible," and "create landscapes that allow species to move freely and naturally between protected areas." The only real issue is the willingness of people to act decisively. Pearson, for one, is optimistic. "More than any other environmental issue . . . climate change is demonstrating to people the connections between the natural environment, the economy, public health, and agriculture. . . . [It] offers huge opportunities for putting an economic value on ecosystem services and financing biodiversity conservation."[76]

Is his optimism warranted? Since the 1980s there have been significant additions to the stock of core areas and buffers—in the form of ecosystem management, the roadless rule, conservation easements, and other arrangements that allow economic activities without shortchanging preservation. Connectivity has become a major concern of public lands officials, fire is an accepted if underused managerial tool, some dams and other river obstructions have been removed, and invasive species are recognized as major threats to biodiversity. Carnivore reintroductions remain controversial and will probably continue only with the aggressive support of environmental groups.

There are also major failures or omissions. The bare-bones endangered species program is still severely limited, despite the increasing severity of the extinction crisis. Lakes and oceans remain a monumental challenge. The modest response to global warming is certain to compromise a variety of positive developments. And that is a clue to the challenges that the conservation community and society in general are likely to face in the coming years: an accumulation of ills related to human population growth, industrial and agricultural development, and urban sprawl, all of which threaten to overwhelm even the most positive, far-sighted organizational and technological advances.

∾

The effort to understand and shape the natural order has thus become the central concern of American conservation and of the diverse groups that have been responsible for most of the innovations in theory and practice described in this account. At the time of the original Leopold report, nature was something "out there," seemingly static, evident in undeveloped areas such as national parks, something that could be taken for granted, thankfully, in a rapidly changing world. But those reassuring assumptions soon gave way to the diametrically opposed view, that nature was in constant flux, not to be taken for granted, and in fact under assault by the same forces that were disrupting human society. From that jarring realization emerged a new approach to conservation, one that continued to emphasize preservation but added a long list of supplemental and remedial measures that were necessary, indeed essential, if nature was to be "self willed" and if the natural order was not to be catastrophically impoverished. It is hardly surprising that that the new perspectives were controversial, at least in the political arena. The parks and wilderness legislation of the 1960s and 1970s was opposed by groups that had a stake in the status quo. As the conservation agenda has expanded, the list of opponents has also grown, but so too has the number of individuals and organizations that support that agenda.

By the second decade of the twenty-first century the results of the new approach are still uncertain, and an interim balance sheet of gains and losses can provide only fleeting impressions. But if the results are tentative, the way that activists—ranging from scientists to lobbyists for national organizations to members of local groups—view their tasks and responsibilities has rapidly evolved. If the events of the years since 1980 are any indication, the new focus on biodiversity and climate change is likely to be the foundation for a more assertive advocacy and a more effective defense of embattled nature.

Notes

1. National Park System Advisory Board, Science Committee, *Revisiting Leopold: Resource Stewardship in the National Parks*, August 25, 2012, https://www.nps.gov/calltoaction/PDF/LeopoldReport_2012.pdf. Also see William C. Tweed, *Uncertain Path: A Search for the Future of National Parks* (Berkeley: University of California Press, 2010), 185–208; Robert B. Keiter, *To Conserve Unimpaired: The Evolution of the National Park Idea* (Washington, DC: Island Press, 2013), 261–70.

2. Stuart Chape et al., "History, Definitions, Values, and Global Perspective," in *The World's Protected Areas: Status, Values, and Prospects in the 21st Century*, ed. Stuart Chape, Mark Spaulding, and Martin Jenkins (Berkeley: University of California Press, 2008), 2; H. Ken Cordell and J. M. Bowker, "The Global Economic Contribution of Protected Lands and Wilderness through Tourism," in *Wilderness, Wildlands,*

and People: A Partnership for the Planet, ed. Vance G. Martin and Cyril F. Kormos (Golden, CO: Fulcrum Publishing, 2008), 70.

3. Martin Jenkins et al., "Protected Areas and Biodiversity," in *World's Protected Areas*, ed. Chape, Spaulding, and Jenkins, 75. Jenkins's data is now obsolete. I have tried to adjust for recent additions.

4. A. Turner, "North America," in *World's Protected Areas*, ed. Chape, Spaulding, and Jenkins, 180–83.

5. Ibid., 185.

6. Thomas R. Vale, *The American Wilderness: Reflections on Nature Protection in the United States* (Charlottesville: University of Virginia Press, 2005), 72–73.

7. Magnus Sylven, "Nature Needs Half: A New Spatial Perspective for a Healthy Planet," *International Journal of Wilderness* 17 (December 2011): 10–11; Cyril F. Kormos, "We Need to Scale Up Marine Wilderness Protection: A Global Perspective," *International Journal of Wilderness* 17 (December 2011): 13–14; Nigel Dudley et al., "Defining Wilderness in IUCN," *International Journal of Wilderness* 18 (April 2012): 9–11; Lawrence Hamilton, "Wilderness on the World Stage," *International Journal of Wilderness* 18 (April 2012): 41–42.

8. Cordel and Bowker, "Global Economic Contribution," 18.

9. Harvey Locke, "Canada Increases Wilderness Protection and Policy Goals," *International Journal of Wilderness* 15 (April 2009): 5, 8; Claire Elizabeth Campbell, "Governing a Kingdom: Parks Canada, 1911–2011," in *A Century of Parks Canada, 1911–2011*, ed. Campbell (Calgary: University of Calgary Press, 2011), 11.

10. David N. Cole, "Beyond Naturalness: Adapting Wilderness Stewardship to an Era of Rapid Global Change," *International Journal of Wilderness* 18 (August 2012): 10–12.

11. John M. Randall, "Objectives, Priorities, and Triage: Lessons Learned from Invasive Species Management," in *Beyond Naturalness: Rethinking Park and Wilderness Stewardship in an Era of Rapid Change*, ed. David N. Cole and Laurie Yung (Washington, DC: Island Press, 2010), 105.

12. Thane K. Pratt et al., *Conservation Biology of Hawaiian Forest Birds: Implications for Island Avifauna* (New Haven: Yale University Press, 2009), 129–50.

13. Randall, "Objectives, Priorities, and Triage," 64.

14. See, for example, Roger DeSilvestro," Pushing Boundaries," *National Wildlife* 53 (October–November 2015): 33–35.

15. Michael E. Soulé and John Terborgh, eds., *Continental Conservation: Scientific Foundations of Regional Reserve Networks* (Washington, DC: Island Press, 1999), 73, 118–19.

16. "The Latest," *High Country News* 45 (June 10, 2013): 6. Also Randall, "Objectives, Priorities, and Triage, 166–73.

17. Randall, "Objectives, Priorities, and Triage," 166–73.

18. Ibid., 175.

19. See for example, Emma Marris, *Rambunctious Garden: Saving Nature in a Post-Wild World* (New York: Bloomsbury, 2011), 102–9.

20. Soulé and Terborgh, *Continental Conservation*, 89.

21. Stephen J. Pyne, *Between Two Fires: A Fire History of Contemporary America* (Tucson: University of Arizona Press, 2015), 460–61.

22. Mark Hudson, *Fire Management in the American West: Forest Politics and the Rise of Megafire* (Boulder: University Press of Colorado, 2011), 36; Pyne, *Between Two Fires*, 436.

23. Michael E. Soulé, "Conservation Relevance of Ecological Cascades," in *Trophic Cascades: Predators, Prey, and the Changing Dynamics of Nature*, ed. John Terborgh and James A. Estes (Washington, DC: Island Press, 2010), 350–51.

24. Dean Apostol and Marcia Sinclair, "Conclusions: The Status and Future of Restoration in the Pacific Northwest," in *Restoring the Pacific Northwest: The Art and Science of Ecological Restoration in Cascadia*, ed. Apostol and Sinclair (Washington, DC: Island Press, 2006), 429.

25. Daniel Simberloff et al., "Movement Corridors: Conservation Bargains or Poor Investments?" *Conservation Biology* 6 (1992): 494.

26. Charles C. Chester, *Conservation across Borders: Biodiversity in an Interdependent World* (Washington, DC: Island Press, 2006), 164–76; Keiter, *To Conserve Unimpaired*, 217–19.

27. Matt Jenkins, "Boreal Breakthrough," *Nature Conservancy Magazine* 60 (Autumn 2010): 15.

28. Patricio Robles Gil, "The El Carmen Wilderness," in *Wilderness, Wildlands, and People*, ed. Martin and Kormos, 22–25; Eryn Gable, "75 Years On, Efforts to Create U.S.-Mexico Park Hampered by Security Concerns," *New York Times* Energy and Environment blog, June 24, 2010. Also Emily Wakild, "Border Chasm: International Boundary Parks and Mexican Conservation, 1935–1945," *Environmental History* 14 (July 2009): 459–64.

29. Caroline Fraser, *Rewilding the World: Dispatches from the Conservation Revolution* (New York: Metropolitan Books, 2009), 69.

30. Jodi A. Hilty, William Z. Lidicker Jr., and Adina M. Merenlender, *Corridor Ecology: The Science and Practice of Linking Landscapes for Biodiversity Conservation* (Washington, DC: Island Press, 2006), 235; Cristina Eisenberg, *The Carnivore Way: Coexisting with and Conserving North America's Predators* (Washington, DC: Island Press, 2014), 28.

31. Fraser, *Rewilding the World*, 35; Eisenberg, *Carnivore Way*, 27–28.

32. Michael Jamison, "Over Under," *National Parks* 87 (Winter 2013): 41, 53; "The Latest," *High Country News* 45 (November 25, 2013): 6; Ben Goldfarb, "The Roads Scholar," *High Country News* 46 (August 4, 2014): 6.

33. "Building a Wildlife Corridor in the Northeast," *National Wildlife* 49 (December–January 2011): 23.

34. Fraser, *Rewilding the World*, 38–40.

35. Ibid., 56–59.

36. Jim Robbins, "Grizzlies Return, with Strings Attached," *New York Times*, August 16, 2011.

37. Brian Kevin, "Everybody Hates Chuck Schwartz," *Sierra* 96 (January–February 2011): 28–29; Leslie Kaufman, "Appeals Court Keeps Yellowstone Grizzlies on Threatened List," *New York Times* Green blog, November 23, 2011.

38. "Taking Stock of Grizzlies," *High Country News* 45 (August 19, 2013): 7.

39. Kerry Gunther (National Park Service wildlife biologist), "Grizzlies!" (lecture), January 20, 2012, Cuyahoga Valley National Park.

40. Robbins, "Grizzlies Return."

41. Douglas H. Chadwick, *Yellowstone to Yukon* (Washington, DC: National Geographic, 2000), 44.

42. Fraser, *Rewilding the World*, 48. Also see Arthur Middleton, "Is the Wolf a Real American Hero," *New York Times*, March 10, 2014.

43. Justina C. Ray et. al., "Large Carnivorous Animals and Biodiversity: Does Saving One Conserve the Other?" in *Large Carnivores and the Conservation of Biodiversity*, ed. Justina C. Ray et al. (Washington, DC: Island Press, 2005), 417.

44. Fraser, *Rewilding the World*, 6, 51.

45. John Carey, "Reducing Conflict on Public Lands," *National Wildlife* 49 (February–March 2011): 12.

46. Leslie Kaufman, "After Years of Conflict, a New Dynamic in Wolf Country," *New York Times*, November 5, 2011.

47. Justin Farrell, *The Battle for Yellowstone: Morality and the Sacred Roots of Environmental Conflict* (Princeton: Princeton University Press, 2015), 89–90.

48. John M. Broder, "Caribou and Oil Companies to Share Alaska Petroleum Reserve," *New York Times*, December 20, 2012; "Making History in the Western Arctic: 11 Million Acres Protected," *Sierra Borealis*, March 2013, 1–2.

49. Jeff Smith, "Wilderness Watch Battles to Protect Wolves and Wilderness in Idaho," *Wilderness Watcher* 21 (April 2010): 1.

50. *Earthjustice Quarterly Magazine* (Fall 2012): 24.

51. Emily Anthes, "Tracking the Pack," *New York Times*, February 4, 2013; Felicity Barringer, "Federal Protection for Gray Wolves May Be Lifted, Agency Says," *New York Times*, June 8, 2013; Elliott D. Woods, "Wolflandia," *Outside*, February 2015, 72.

52. George Wuerthner, "State Agency Game Farming Is Not Compatible with Wilderness or Ecosystem Integrity," *Wilderness Watcher* 24 (Spring 2013): 6.

53. Eric Wagner, "Washington's Wolf Experiment," *High Country News* 47 (October 8, 2015): 7.

54. Fraser, *Rewilding the World*, 54.

55. See "Wolves in the West," *New Mexico Wild* 9 (Fall 2012); April Reese, "The Gila Solution," *High Country News* 46 (February 17, 2014): 14–16.

56. Sarah Gilman, "The Sage Grouse Two-Step," *High Country News* 47 (June 22, 2015): 6; Clifford Krauss, "U.S. Rules Grouse Is Not Endangered in Environment-Business Accord," *New York Times*, September 23, 2015.

57. Jodi Peterson, "Little Big Bird," *High Country News* 47 (August 17, 2015): 13.

58. Joe Roman, *Listed: Dispatches from America's Endangered Species Act* (Cambridge, MA: Harvard University Press, 2011), 191.

59. Jon Mooallen, *Wild Ones: A Sometimes Dismaying, Weirdly Reassuring Story about Looking at People Looking at Animals in America* (New York: Penguin Books, 2013).

60. Ibid., 115. Also Roger DeSilvestro, "Saving the Red Wolf," *National Wildlife* 52 (August–September 2014): 38–42.

61. Thomas J. Foose, "Riders of the Last Ark: The Role of Captive Breeding in Conservation Strategies," in *The Last Extinction*, 2nd ed., ed. Les Kaufman and Kenneth Mallory (Cambridge, MA: MIT Press, 1993), 157–73.

62. Kara Rogers, *The Quiet Extinction: Stories of North America's Rare and Threatened Plants* (Tucson: University of Arizona Press, 2015), 207–8.

63. William Nordhaus, *The Climate Casino: Risk, Uncertainty, and Economics for a Warming World* (New Haven: Yale University Press, 2013), 169–81.

64. Christopher R. Schwalm, Christopher A. Williams, and Kevin Schaefer, "Hundred-Year Forecast: Drought," *New York Times*, August 12, 2012.

65. Julie Cort, "Natural Laboratory," *National Wildlife* 49 (April–May 2011): 40.

66. Anthony D. Barnosky, *Heatstroke: Nature in an Age of Global Warming* (Washington, DC: Island Press, 2009), 103.

67. Emma Marris, "Conservation Biology: The End of the Wild," *Nature* 469, no. 7329 (2011): 150–52.

68. Elspeth Dehnert, "National Parks Feel the Heat of Climate Change," *Climate Wire*, July 3, 2014; William B. Monahan and Nicholas A. Fisichelli, "Climate Exposure of U.S. National Parks in a New Era of Change," *PloS One* 9, no. 7 (July 2, 2014): e101302; Richard Pearson, *Driven to Extinction: The Impact of Climate Change on Biodiversity* (New York: Sterling, 2011), 210; Cort, "Natural Laboratory," 38.

69. Jerry Jenkins, *Climate Change in the Adirondacks: The Path of Sustainability* (Ithaca: Cornell University Press, 2010), 30.

70. Lisa W. Foderaro, "Savoring Bogs and Moose, Fearing They'll Vanish as the Adirondacks Warm," *New York Times*, December 2, 2011.

71. John Carey, "Hot Commodities," *National Wildlife* 49 (October–November 2011): 27; Cally Carswell, "The Tree Coroners," *High Country News* 45 (December 9, 2013): 16–17.

72. Carey, "Hot Commodities," 29; also Nathan Rice, "A New Forest Paradigm," *High Country News* 45 (April 29, 2013): 15.

73. Richard Pearson, "are We in the Midst of a Sixth Mass Extinction?" *New York Times*, June 3, 2012.

74. Carl Zimmer, "Multitude of Species Face Threat of Warming," *New York Times*, April 5, 2011.

75. Elizabeth Kolbert, *The Sixth Extinction: An Unnatural History* (New York: Henry Holt, 2014), 118–24.

76. Pearson, *Driven to Extinction*, 214, 222.

Note on Sources

This book is in large measure a reflection of the remarkable increase in scholarly and popular writing on conservation-related topics that has occurred over the last two decades. Not only has the volume has increased but the focus has shifted, and new and more critical perspectives on land, water, and wildlife conservation have emerged.

From the 1970s through the early 1990s a steady stream of books and articles on the federal agencies, national parks, and environmental organizations largely defined the field. Many of these studies attacked the assumptions and policies of the post–World War II years, when conservation was increasingly identified with "multiple use" and the economic exploitation of public resources. During the Reagan years, when political leaders again emphasized commodity production and other exploitative activities, the emphasis shifted to the legislative and policy innovations of the 1960s and 1970s, now under attack. The focus, however, remained on public policy and the role of economic activity in national parks, forests, refuges, and other public lands.

DOI: 10.7330/9781607325703.c010

The mid-1990s brought more extensive changes. The emphasis shifted to animals, plants, rivers, oceans, wildland fires, climate, and other features of the natural environment. The implicit or explicit theme of much of this writing was the limitations of conservation policies and, by implication, the studies that had described and analyzed them. Most such works, it seems, had overstated the achievements of earlier periods, overlooked harmful activities such as clear-cutting, fire suppression, and predator controls and paid too little attention to the value of biodiversity, the loss of habitat, and the problems of invasive species. The Reagan administration, and several successors, may have been bad for the environment, but even the Clinton and perhaps Obama administrations had not been consistently supportive. In short, a truly effective defense of nature required a far more proactive approach than anything that government had done in the last century.

The most important factor in this change of focus was the influence of scientific research and the emergence of conservation biology and related "mission oriented" disciplines. The publication of Reed F. Noss and Allen Y. Cooperrider's *Saving Nature's Legacy* (1994) was a milestone in this transition, and it and other works that focused on the persistent shortcomings of government policy had a broad and immediate effect. Of the many important works on conservation issues that have appeared since 2000, the vast majority reflect this perspective, whether they focus on government agencies, legislation, wildlife, land conservation, or rivers and oceans. More than an academic fad, the new emphasis represents a broader, more critical conception of conservation and its role in modern environmentalism.

Bibliography

Adler, Robert W. *Restoring Colorado River Ecosystems: A Troubled Sense of Immensity.* Washington, DC: Island Press, 2007.

Allin, Craig W. "Wilderness Preservation as a Bureaucratic Tool." In *Federal Lands Policy*, ed. Philip O. Foss, 32–37. New York: Greenwood Press, 1987.

American Prairie Reserve. "Building the Reserve." https://www.americanprairie.org/building-the-reserve.

American Prairie Reserve. "Our Story." https://www.americanprairie.org/our-story.

Amos, Amy Mathews. "Keeping the Faith(s)." *High Country News* 47 (January 19, 2015): 10–11.

Apostol, Dean, and Marcia Sinclair. "Conclusions: The Status and Future of Restoration in the Pacific Northwest." In *Restoring the Pacific Northwest: The Art and Science of Ecological Restoration in Cascadia*, ed. Dean Apostal and Marcia Sinclair, 427–39. Washington, DC: Island Press, 2006.

Arno, Stephen F., and Carl E. Fiedler. "Ponderosa Pine and Interior Forests." In *Restoring the Pacific Northwest: The Art and Science of Ecological Restoration in Cascadia*, ed. Dean Apostal and Marcia Sinclair, 194–215. Washington, DC: Island Press, 2006.

DOI: 10.7330/9781607325703.c011

Babbitt, Bruce. *Cities in the Wilderness: A New Vision of Land Use in America*. Washington, DC: Island Press, 2005.

Barcott, Bruce. "It's a Wilderness Out There." *Outside*, December 2013, 91.

Bari, Judy. *Timber Wars*. Monroe, ME: Common Courage Press, 1994.

Barnosky, Anthony D. *Heatstroke: Nature in an Age of Global Warming*. Washington, DC: Island Press, 2009.

Barnosky, Anthony D., Nicholas Matzke, Susumu Tomiya, Guinevere O.U. Wogan, Brian Swartz, Tiago B. Quental, Charles Marshall, Jenny L. McGuire, Emily L. Lindsey, Kaitlin C. Maguire, et al.." "Has the Earth's Sixth Mass Extinction Already Arrived?" *Nature* 471, no. 7336 (March 3, 2011): 51–57. http://dx.doi.org/10.1038/nature09678.

Barrett, Nels E., and Juliana P. Barrett. "Reserve Design and the New Conservation Theory." In *The Ecological Basis of Conservation: Heterogeneity, Ecosystems, and Biodiversity*, ed. S.T.A. Pickett, R. S. Osfeld, M. Shachak, and G. E. Likens, 236–51. New York: Chapman and Hall, 1997. http://dx.doi.org/10.1007/978-1-4615-6003-6_24.

Barrow, Mark V. *Nature's Ghosts: Confronting Extinction from the Age of Jefferson to the Age of Ecology*. Chicago: University of Chicago Press, 2009. http://dx.doi.org/10.7208/chicago/9780226038155.001.0001.

Barton, Andrew M. *The Changing Nature of the Maine Woods*. Durham: University of New Hampshire Press, 2012.

Bean, Michael J., and Melanie J. Rowland. *The Evolution of National Wildlife Law*. 3rd ed. Westport: Praeger, 1997.

Benson, Etienne. *Wired Wilderness: Technologies of Tracking and the Making of Modern Wildlife*. Baltimore: Johns Hopkins University Press, 2010.

Berger, John J. *Forests Forever: Their Ecology, Restoration, and Protection*. Chicago: Center for American Places, 2008.

Bevington, Douglas. *The Rebirth of Environmentalism: Grassroots Activism from the Spotted Owl to the Polar Bear*. Washington, DC: Island Press, 2009.

Birchard, Bill. *Nature's Keepers: The Remarkable Story of How the Nature Conservancy Became the Largest Environmental Organization in the World*. San Francisco: Jossey-Bass, 2005.

Blackford, Mansel G. *Making Seafood Sustainable: American Experiences in Global Perspective*. Philadelphia: University of Pennsylvania Press, 2012. http://dx.doi.org/10.9783/9780812206272.

Bookchin, Murray, Dave Foreman, and Steve Chase. *Defending the Earth: A Dialogue between Murray Bookchin and Dave Foreman*. Boston: South End Press, 1991.

Bosso, Christopher J. *Environment, Inc.: From Grassroots to Beltway*. Lawrence: University Press of Kansas, 2005.

Bosso, Christopher J., and Deborah Lynn Gruber. "Maintaining Presence: Environmental Advocacy and the Permanent Campaign." In *Environmental Policy: New Directions for the Twenty-First Century*, 6th ed., ed. Norman J. Vig and Michael E. Kraft, 78–99. Washington, DC: Congressional Quarterly Press, 2007.

Brewer, Richard. *Conservancy: The Land Trust Movement in America.* Hanover, NH: University Press of New England, 2003.

Brinkley, Douglas. *Rightful Heritage: Franklin D. Roosevelt and the Land of America.* New York: Harper Collins, 2016.

Brinkley, Douglas. *Wilderness Warrior: Theodore Roosevelt and the Crusade for America.* New York: Harper Collins, 2009.

Brown, Jessica, Nora Mitchell, and Michael Beresford. "Protected Landscapes: A Conservation Approach That Links Nature, Culture, and Community." In *The Protected Landscape Approach: Linking Nature, Culture, and Community*, ed. Brown, Mitchell, and Beresford, 6–23. Gland, Switzerland: IUCN–The World Conservation Union, 2005. http://dx.doi.org/10.2305/IUCN.CH.2005.2.en.

Bryner, Gary C. *U.S. Land and Natural Resources Policy: A Public Issues Handbook.* Westport: Greenwood Press, 1998.

Carr, Ethan. *Mission 66: Modernism and the National Park Dilemma.* Amherst: University of Massachusetts Press, 2007.

Cawley, R. McGregor. *Federal Land, Western Anger: The Sagebrush Rebellion and Environmental Politics.* Lawrence: University Press of Kansas, 1993.

"Celebrate! New Arctic Wilderness Recommendation." *Sierra Borealis*, March 2015, 5.

Cevasco, George A., and Richard P. Harmond. *Modern American Environmentalists: A Biographical Encyclopedia.* Baltimore: Johns Hopkins University Press, 2009.

Chadwick, Douglas. "Wolf Wars." *National Geographic* 217 (March 2010): 44, 34–55.

Chadwick, Douglas. *Yellowstone to Yukon.* Washington, DC: National Geographic, 2000.

Chalisfour, Marc. "A Vision in Green." *AMC Outdoors* 75 (November–December 2009): 33–37.

"Change under the Obama Administration? Not So Fast . . . ." *Redrock Wilderness* 28 (Summer 2011): 6.

Chape, Stuart, M. Spaulding, M. Taylor, D. A. Putney, N. Ishwaran, J. Thorsell, D. Blasco, J. R. Vernhes, P. Bridgewater, J. Harrison, and E. McManus. "History, Definitions, Values, and Global Perspective." In *The World's Protected Areas: Status, Values, and Prospects in the 21st Century*, ed. Stuart Chape, Mark Spaulding, and Martin Jenkins, 1–34. Berkeley: University of California Press, 2008.

Charnley, Susan, Candice Pillingham, Claudia Stuart, Cassandra Moseley, and Ellen Donaghue. "Northwest Forest Plan—The First Ten Years (1994–2004): Socioeconomic Monitoring of the Klamath National Forest and Their Local Communities." USDA General Technical Report, PNW-GTR-764, August 2008. http://www.fs.fed.us/pnw/pubs/pnw_gtr764.pdf.

Charnley, Susan, Thomas E. Sheridan, and Gary P. Nabhan, eds. *Stitching the West Back Together: Conservation of Working Landscapes.* Chicago: University of Chicago Press, 2014. http://dx.doi.org/10.7208/chicago/9780226165851.001.0001.

Chase, Alston. *Playing God in Yellowstone: The Destruction of America's First National Park.* New York: Harcourt Brace Jovanovich, 1987.

Chester, Charles C. *Conservation across Borders: Biodiversity in an Interdependent World.* Washington, DC: Island Press, 2006.

Christensen, Jon, Jenny Rempel, and Judee Burr. "Private Land Conservation in the Western United States." In *Stitching the West Back Together: Conservation of Working Landscapes*, ed. Susan Charnley, Thomas E. Sheridan, and Gary P. Nabhan, 241–45. Chicago: University of Chicago Press, 2014. http://dx.doi.org/10.7208/chicago/9780226165851.003.0020.

Cirmo, Christopher P. "Water Resources: The Unique Adirondack Aquascape." In *The Great Experiment in Conservation: Voices from the Adirondack Park*, ed. William F. Porter, Jon D. Erickson, and Ross S. Whaley, 33–44. Syracuse: Syracuse University Press, 2009.

Clark, Susan G. *Ensuring Greater Yellowstone's Future: Choices for Leaders and Citizens.* New Haven: Yale University Press, 2008. http://dx.doi.org/10.12987/yale/9780300124224.001.0001.

Clarke, Jeanne Neinaber, and Daniel McCool. *Staking Out the Terrain: Power Differentials among Natural Resource Management Agencies.* Albany: SUNY Press, 1985.

Clary, David A. *Timber and the Forest Service.* Lawrence: University Press of Kansas, 1986.

Cohen, Michael P. *The History of the Sierra Club, 1892–1970.* San Francisco: Sierra Club Books, 1988.

Cole, David N. "Beyond Naturalness: Adapting Wilderness Stewardship to an Era of Rapid Global Change." *International Journal of Wilderness* 18 (August 2012): 9–14.

Cole, David N., Eric S. Higgs, and Peter S. White. "History Fidelity, Maintaining Legacy and Connection to Heritage." In *Beyond Naturalness: Rethinking Park and Wilderness Stewardship in an Era of Rapid Change*, ed. David N. Cole and Laurie Yung, 125–41. Washington, DC: Island Press, 2010.

Coleman, Kate. *The Secret Wars of Judi Bari: A Car Bomb, the Fight for the Redwoods, and the End of Earth First!* San Francisco: Encounter Books, 2005.

"Conservation and Advocacy Report." *Adirondac* 76 (September–October 2012): 10–11.

Cordell, H. Ken. "The Diversity of Wilderness: Ecosystems Represented in the U.S. National Wilderness Preservation System." *International Journal of Wilderness* 18 (August 2012): 15–20, 25.

Cordell, H. Ken, and J. M. Bowker. "The Global Economic Contribution of Protected Land and Wilderness through Tourism." In *Wilderness, Wildlands, and People: A Partnership for the Planet*, ed. Vance G. Martin and Cyril F. Kormos, 69–73. Golden: Fulcrum Publishing, 2008.

Cort, Julie. "Natural Laboratory." *National Wildlife* 49 (April–May 2011): 37–42.

Cox, Graham L. "The Adirondack Environmental Nongovernmental Organizations." In *The Great Experiment in Conservation: Voices from the Adirondack Park*, ed. William F. Porter, John D. Erickson, and Ross S. Whaley, 431–50. Syracuse: Syracuse University Press, 2009.

Cox, Thomas R. *The Park Builders: A History of State Parks in the Pacific Northwest.* Seattle: University of Washington Press, 1988.

Craighead, John J., Jay S. Sumer, and John A. Mitchell. *The Grizzly Bears of Yellowstone: Their Ecology in the Yellowstone Ecosystem, 1959–1992.* Washington, DC: Island Press, 1995.

Crane, Jeff. *Finding the River: An Environmental History of the Elwha.* Corvallis: Oregon State University Press, 2011.

Crowder, Larry B. "Back to the Future in Marine Conservation." In *Marine Conservation Biology: The Science of Maintaining the Sea's Biodiversity*, ed. Elliott A. Norse and Larry B. Crowder, 19–30. Washington, DC: Island Press, 2005.

Culhane, Paul J. *Public Lands Politics: Interest Group Influence on the Forest Service and the Bureau of Land Management.* Baltimore: Resources for the Future, 1981.

"Cumberland Plateau Protected." *Nature Conservancy Magazine* 58 (Spring 2008): 20.

Curley, David M. *Losing Ground: Identity and Land Loss in Coastal Louisiana.* Jackson: University Press of Mississippi, 2010.

Cutler, M. Rupert. "The Evolution of a Wilderness Conservationist." *International Journal of Wilderness* 17 (December 2011): 17–23, 28.

Dagget, Dan. *Beyond the Rangeland Conflict: Toward a West That Works.* Flagstaff: Good Stewards Project, 1998.

Darling, F. Fraser, and Noel D. Eichhorn. *Man and Nature in the National Parks.* 2nd ed. Washington, DC: The Conservation Foundation, 1969.

Davis, Charles, and Sandra Davis. "The Politics of Hard-Rock Mining in the American West." In *Environmental Politics and Policy in the West*, ed. Zachary A. Smith and John C. Freemuth, 133–54. Boulder: University Press of Colorado, 2007.

Davis, David Howard. "Energy on Federal Lands." In *Western Public Lands and Environmental Politics*, ed. Charles Davis, 141–68. Boulder: Westview Press, 2001.

Davis, Gary E., and William L. Halvorson. "Long-Term Research in National Parks: From Beliefs to Knowledge." In *Science and Ecosystem Management in the National Parks*, ed. William Halvorson and Gary E. Davis, 3–10. Tucson: University of Arizona Press, 1996.

Davis, Jack E. *An Everglades Providence: Marjory Stoneman Douglas and the American Environmental Century.* Athens: University of Georgia Press, 2009.

Dawson, Chad P., and John C. Hendee. *Wilderness Management: Stewardship and Protection of Resources and Values.* 4th ed. Golden, CO: Fulcrum Publishing, 2009.

Dawson, Chad P., Blake Propst, and John C. Hendee. "Special Provisions of Wilderness Legislation in the United States, 1964 to 2009." *International Journal of Wilderness* 16 (2010): 32–34.

DeBuys, William. *A Great Aridness: Climate Change and the Future of the American Southwest.* New York: Oxford University Press, 2011.

Dehnert, Elspeth. "National Parks Feel the Heat of Climate Change." *Climate Wire*, July 3, 2014.

DellaSala, Dominick A., Faisal Moola, Paul Alaback, Paul C. Pagnet, John W. Schoen, and Reed F. Noss. "Temperate and Boreal Rainforests of the Pacific Coast of North America." In *Temperate and Boreal Rainforests of the World: Ecology and Conservation*, ed. Dominick A. DellaSala, 42–81. Washington, DC: Island Press, 2011.

DellaSala, Dominick A., and Jack E. Williams. "Special Section: The Northwest Forest Plan: A Global Model of Forest Management in Contentious Times." *Conservation Biology* 20, no. 2 (2006): 274–76. http://dx.doi.org/10.1111/j.1523-1739.2006.00381.x.

Dempsey, Dave. *On the Brink: The Great Lakes in the 21st Century*. East Lansing: Michigan State University Press, 2004.

DeSilvestro, Roger. "Pushing Boundaries." *National Wildlife* 53 (October–November 2015): 33–35.

DeSilvestro, Roger. "Saving the Red Wolf." *National Wildlife* 52 (August–September 2014): 38–42.

Dilsaver, Lary M. *America's National Park System: The Critical Documents*. Lanham, MD: Rowman & Littlefield, 1994.

Donahue, Debra L. *The Western Range Revisited: Removing Livestock from Public Lands to Conserve Native Biodiversity*. Norman: University of Oklahoma Press, 1999.

Doremus, Holly. "Private Property Interests, Wildlife Restoration, and Competing Visions of a Western Eden." In *Reclaiming the Native Home of Hope: Community, Ecology, and the American West*, ed. Robert B. Keiter, 79–88. Salt Lake City: University of Utah Press, 1998.

Doremus, Holly, and A. Dan Tarlock. *Water War in the Klamath Basin: Macho Law, Combat Biology, and Dirty Politics*. Washington, DC: Island Press, 2008.

Dowie, Mark. *Losing Ground: American Environmentalism at the Close of the Twentieth Century*. Cambridge, MA: MIT Press, 1995.

Drew, Cynthia A. "The Upper Mississippi River and the Army Corps of Engineers' New Role: Will Congress Fund Ecosystem Restoration?" In *Large-Scale Ecosystem Restoration: Five Case Studies from the United States*, ed. Mary Doyle and Cynthia A. Drew, 229–68. Washington, DC: Island Press, 2008.

Duane, Timothy P. *Shaping the Sierra: Nature, Culture, and Conflict in the Changing West*. Berkeley: University of California Press, 1999.

Dudley, Nigel, Cyril Kormos, Harvey Locke, and Vance G. Martin. "Defining Wilderness in IUCN." *International Journal of Wilderness* 18 (April 2012): 9–11.

Duinker, Peter, Gary Bull, and Bruce A. Shindler. "Sustainable Forestry in Canada and the United States: Developments and Prospects." In *Two Paths toward Sustainable Forests: Public Values in Canada and the United States*, ed. Bruce A. Shindler, Thomas M. Beckley, and Mary Carmel Finley, 35–59. Corvallis: Oregon State University Press, 2003.

Dunkel, Tom. "Wild Idea." *Nature Conservancy Magazine* 58 (Autumn 2008): 49–55.

Dunlap, Riley E. "Trends in Public Opinion toward Environmental Issues." In *American Environmentalism: The U.S. Environmental Movement, 1970–1990*, ed. Riley E. Dunlap and Angela G. Mertig, 91–113. Washington, DC: Taylor and Francis, 1992.

Dunlap, Thomas R. *Saving America's Wildlife*. Princeton: Princeton University Press, 1988.

Durbin, Kathie. *Tongass: Pulp Politics and the Fight for the Alaska Rain Forest*. 2nd ed. Corvallis: Oregon State University Press, 2005.

Durbin, Kathie. *Tree Huggers: Victory, Defeat, and Renewal in the Northwest Ancient Forest Campaign*. Seattle: The Mountaineers, 1996.

Durrant, Jeffrey O. *Struggle over Utah's San Rafael Swell: Wilderness, National Conservation Areas, and National Monuments*. Tucson: University of Arizona Press, 2007.

Durrant, Robert F. *The Administrative Presidency Revisited: Public Lands, the BLM, and the Reagan Revolution*. Albany: SUNY Press, 1992.

"Easements 101." *Nature Conservancy Magazine*, October–November 2014, 42–45.

Earthjustice. *Annual Report, 2012: Preserving Our National Heritage*. San Francisco: Earthjustice.

Earthjustice Quarterly Magazine (Fall 2012): 24.

"Ecosystem Breakdowns in Great Lakes." *National Wildlife* 50 (February–March 2012): 48.

Edgar, Graham J., Rick D. Stuart-Smith, Trevor J. Willis, Stuart Kininmonth, Susan C. Baker, Stuart Banks, Neville S. Barrett, Mikel A. Becerro, Anthony T. F. Bernard, Just Berkhout, et al. "Global Conservation and Outcomes Depend on Marine Protected Areas with Five Key Features." *Nature* 506, no. 7487 (February 13, 2014): 216–20. http://dx.doi.org/10.1038/nature13022.

Ehrenfeld, David. "Life in the Next Millennium: Who Will Be Left in Earth's Community?" In *The Last Extinction*, 2nd ed., ed. Les Kaufman and Kenneth Mallory, 195–214. Cambridge, MA: MIT Press, 1993.

Eisenberg, Christina. *The Carnivore Way: Coexisting with and Conserving North America's Predators*. Washington, DC: Island Press, 2014. http://dx.doi.org/10.5822/978-1-61091-208-2.

Eisenberg, Christina. *The Wolf's Tooth: Keystone Predators, Trophic Cascades, and Biodiversity*. Washington, DC: Island Press, 2010.

Engelman, Robert, Daniel Pauly, Dirk Zeller, Ronald G. Prinn, John K. Pinnegar, and Nicholas V.C. Polunin. "Introduction: Climate, People, Fisheries and Aquatic Ecosystems." In *Aquatic Ecosystems: Trends and Global Prospects*, ed. Nicholas V.C. Polunin, 1–18. Cambridge: Cambridge University Press, 2008. http://dx.doi.org/10.1017/CBO9780511751790.002.

Erickson, Jon D. "Introduction: The Park in Perspective." In *The Great Experiment in Conservation: Voices from the Adirondack Park*, ed. William F. Porter, Jon D. Erickson, and Ross S. Whaley, 193–205. Syracuse: Syracuse University Press, 2009.

Erickson, Jon D., Graham L. Cox, Anne M. Woods, and William F. Porter. "Public Opinion and Public Representation." In *The Great Experiment in Conservation:*

Voices from the Adirondack Park, ed. William F. Porter, Jon D. Erickson, and Ross S. Whaley, 393–403. Syracuse: Syracuse University Press.

Ertelt, Paul. "The Battle of Panther Mountain." *Adirondac* 76 (June 2012): 22–23.

"Everglades Restoration Back on Track." *In Brief*, Winter 2010/2011, 14–15.

Everhart, William C. *The National Park Service*. Boulder: Westview Press, 1983.

Fairfax, Sally K., Lauren Gwin, Mary Ann King, Leigh Raymond, and Laura A. Watt. *Buying Nature: The Limits of Land Acquisition as a Conservation Strategy, 1780–2004*. Cambridge, MA: MIT Press, 2005.

Farnham, Timothy J. *Saving Nature's Legacy: Origins of the Idea of Biological Diversity*. New Haven: Yale University Press, 2007.

Farrell, Justin. *The Battle for Yellowstone: Morality and the Sacred Roots of Environmental Conflict*. Princeton: Princeton University Press, 2015. http://dx.doi.org/10.1515/9781400866496.

Ferber, Dan. "Into the Breach." *Nature Conservancy Magazine* 60 (Spring 2010): 31–39.

Fielder, Peggy L., Peter S. White, and Robert A. Leidy. "The Paradigm Shift in Ecology and Its Implications for Conservation." In *The Ecological Basis of Conservation*, ed. S.T.A. Pickett, 83–92. New York: Chapman and Hall, 1997.

Filkins, Dexter. "Swamped." *New Yorker*, January 4, 2016, 32–37.

"Fines Fund Conservation." *Nature Conservancy Magazine*, April–May 2015, 37.

Finley, Carmel. *All the Fish in the Sea: Maximum Sustainable Yield and the Failure of Fisheries Management*. Chicago: University of Chicago Press, 2011. http://dx.doi.org/10.7208/chicago/9780226249681.001.0001.

Fischer, Hank. *Wolf Wars: The Remarkable Inside Story of the Restoration of Wolves to Yellowstone*. Helena, MT: Falcon Press, 1995.

Fischman, Robert L. *National Wildlife Refuges: Coordinating a Conservation System through Law*. Washington, DC: Island Press, 2003.

Foose, Thomas J. "Riders of the Last Ark: The Role of Captive Breeding in Conservation Strategies." In *The Last Extinction*, 2nd ed., ed. Les Kaufman and Kenneth Mallory, 149–78. Cambridge, MA: MIT Press, 1993.

Foreman, Dave. "Around the Campfire." *Rewilding Institute*, no. 45 (March 26, 2013): 4–5.

Foreman, Dave. *Confessions of an Eco-Warrior*. New York: Harmony Books, 1991.

Foreman, Dave. *Rewilding North America: A Vision for Conservation in the 21st Century*. Washington, DC: Island Press, 2004.

Foreman, Dave. "Take Back the Conservation Movement." *International Journal of Wilderness* 12 (April 2006): 4–8, 31.

Foreman, Dave, John Davis, David Johns, Reed Noss, and Michael Soulé. "The Wildlands Project Mission Statement." *Wild Earth*, Special Issue, 1992.

Foreman, Dave, and Howie Wolke. *The Big Outside: A Descriptive Inventory of the Big Wilderness Areas of the United States*. Rev. ed. New York: Harmony Books, 1992.

Foresta, Ronald A. *America's National Parks and Their Keepers*. Washington, DC: Resources for the Future, 1984.

Fox, Stephen. *The American Conservation Movement: John Muir and His Legacy.* Madison: University of Wisconsin Press, 1985.

Frank, Jerry J. *Making Rocky Mountain National Park: The Environmental History of an American Treasure.* Lawrence: University Press of Kansas, 2013.

Franke, Mary Ann. *To Save the Wild Bison: Life on the Edge in Yellowstone.* Norman: University of Oklahoma Press, 2005.

Fraser, Caroline. *Rewilding the World: Dispatches from the Conservation Revolution.* New York: Metropolitan Books, 2009.

Freeman, David M. *Implementing the Endangered Species Act on the Platte Basin Water Commons.* Boulder: University Press of Colorado, 2010.

Freeman, Richard. "The EcoFactory: The United States Forest Service and the Political Construction of Ecosystem Management." *Environmental History* 7, no. 4 (October 2002): 632–58. http://dx.doi.org/10.2307/3986060.

Friederici, Peter. "Catching Fire." *Nature Conservancy Magazine*, July–August 2013, 30–41.

Friederici, Peter. *Nature's Restoration: People and Places on the Front Lines of Conservation.* Washington, DC: Island Press, 2006.

Frome, Michael. *Rebel on the Road and Why I Was Never Neutral.* Kirksville, MO: Truman State University Press, 2007.

Frome, Michael. *Regreening the National Parks.* Tucson: University of Arizona Press, 1992.

Furnish, Jim. *Toward a Natural Forest: The Forest Service in Transition.* Corvallis: Oregon State University Press, 2015.

Gershwin, Lisa-Ann. *Stung! On Jellyfish Blooms and the Future of the Ocean.* Chicago: University of Chicago Press, 2013. http://dx.doi.org/10.7208/chicago/9780226020242.001.0001.

Gilman, Sarah. "Sacrifice Zone." *High Country News* 47 (January 19, 2015): 49–51.

Gilman, Sarah. "The Sage Grouse Two-Step." *High Country News* 47 (June 22, 2015): 6.

Glick, Daniel. "Putting the Public Back in Public Lands." *National Wildlife* 46 (October–November 2008): 24–30.

Goldfarb, Ben. "The Great Salmon Compromise." *High Country News* 46 (December 8, 2014): 10–18.

Goldfarb, Ben. "Murrelet Malaise." *High Country News* 47 (December 7, 2015): 6.

Goldfarb, Ben. "The Roads Scholar." *High Country News* 46 (August 4, 2014): 6.

Grady, Wayne. *The Great Lakes: The Natural History of a Changing Region.* Vancouver: Greystone Books, 2007.

Grange, Kevin. "Sea Change." *National Parks* 86 (Fall 2012): 25.

Greenberg, Paul. *Four Fish: The Future of the Last Wild Food.* New York: Penguin Press, 2010.

Grumbine, R. Edward. *Ghost Bears: Exploring the Biodiversity Crisis.* Washington, DC: Island Press, 1992.

Grunwald, Michael. *The Swamp: The Everglades, Florida, and the Politics of Paradise.* New York: Simon and Schuster, 2006.

Guber, Deborah Lynn. *The Grassroots of a Green Revolution: Polling America on the Environment.* Cambridge, MA: MIT Press, 2003.

Gunderson, Lance H., and Craig R. Allen. "Introduction." In *Foundations of Ecological Resilience,* ed. Lance H. Gunderson, Craig R. Allen, and C. S. Holling, xiii–xix. Washington, DC: Island Press, 2010. http://dx.doi.org/10.1163/ej.9789004184688.i-536.12.

Halpern, Benjamin S. "Conservation: Making Marine Protected Areas Work." *Nature* 506, no. 7487 (February 13, 2014): 167–68. http://dx.doi.org/10.1038/nature13053.

Hamilton, Lawrence. "Wilderness on the World Stage." *International Journal of Wilderness* 18 (April 2012): 41–42.

"Harmful Drilling Planned in the Chukchi Sea." *Alaska Report* 34 (March 2008): 1.

Harrison, Ian J., Melina Flaverty, and Eleanor J. Sterling. "What Is Biodiversity?" In *Life on Earth: An Encyclopedia of Biodiversity, Ecology, and Evolution,* vol. 1, ed. Niles Eldridge, 1–30. Santa Barbara: ABC Clio, 2002.

Hart, John. "Two Cheers for Wilderness." *High Country News* 36 (July 21, 2004): 24.

Hartzog, George B., Jr. *Battling for the National Parks.* Mt. Kisco, NY: Moyer Bell Limited, 1988.

Harvey, Gordon E. "'We Must Free Ourselves . . . From the Tattered Fetters of the Booster Mentality': Big Cypress Swamp and the Politics of Environmental Protection in 1970s Florida." In *Paradise Lost? The Environmental History of Florida,* ed. Jack E. Davis and Raymond Arsenault, 350–74. Gainesville: University Press of Florida, 2005.

Harvey, Mark W.T. *A Symbol of Wilderness: Echo Park and the American Conservation Movement.* Albuquerque: University of New Mexico Press, 1994.

Harvey, Mark W. T. *Wilderness Forever: Howard Zahnizer and the Path to the Wilderness Act.* Seattle: University of Washington Press, 2005.

Hawley, Steven. *Recovering a Lost River: Removing Dams, Rewilding Salmon, Revitalizing Communities.* Boston: Beacon Press, 2011.

Haycox, Stephen. *Frigid Embrace: Politics, Economics, and Environment in Alaska.* Corvallis: Oregon State University Press, 2002.

Hays, Samuel P. *The American People and the National Forests: The First Century of the U.S. Forest Service.* Pittsburgh: University of Pittsburgh Press, 2009.

Hays, Samuel P. *Conservation and the Gospel of Efficiency: The Progressive Conservation Movement, 1890–1920.* Cambridge, MA: Harvard University Press, 1959.

Hays, Samuel P. *War in the Woods: The Rise of Ecological Forestry in America.* Pittsburgh: University of Pittsburgh Press, 2007.

"Healing America's Great Waters." *National Wildlife* 54 (February–March 2016): 12.

Helvarg, David. *The War against the Greens: The "Wise-Use" Movement, the New Right, and Anti-Environmental Violence.* San Francisco: Sierra Club Books, 1994.

Hendee, J. C. "Emerging Wilderness Understandings." *International Journal of Wilderness* 16 (August 2010): 25–26.

Hertz, Jenna, and Pam Mitler. "NAEC Members Speak: Washington Listens." *Northern Line* 34 (Winter 2012): 7.

Hess, Karl, Jr. *Rocky Times in Rocky Mountain National Park: An Unnatural History.* Boulder: University Press of Colorado, 1993.

Hilborn, Ray. "Are Sustainable Fisheries Achievable?" In *Marine Conservation Biology: The Science of Maintaining the Sea's Biodiversity*, ed. Elliott A. Norse and Larry B. Crowder, 247–60. Washington, DC: Island Press, 2005.

Hilty, Jodi A., William Z. Lidicker Jr., and Adina M. Merenlender. *Corridor Ecology: The Science and Practice of Linking Landscapes for Biodiversity Conservation.* Washington, DC: Island Press, 2006.

Hirt, Paul W. *A Conspiracy of Optimism: Management of the National Forests since World War II.* Lincoln: University of Nebraska Press, 1994.

Hiss, Tony. "The Wildest Idea on Earth." *Smithsonian* 45 (September 2014): 76–77.

Hoberg, George. "The Emerging Triumph of Ecosystem Management: The Transformation of Federal Forest Policy." In *Western Public Lands and Environmental Politics*, ed. Charles Davis, 55–86. Boulder: Westview Press, 2001.

Hollander, Gail M. *Raising Cane in the Glades: The Global Sugar Trade and the Transformation of Florida.* Chicago: University of Chicago Press, 2008. http://dx.doi.org/10.7208/chicago/9780226349480.001.0001.

Holloway, Marguerite. "Nurturing Nature." In *Environmental Restoration: Ethics, Theory, and Practice*, ed. William Throop, 27–38. Amherst, NY: Humanity Books, 2000.

Hudson, Mark. *Fire Management in the American West: Forest Policies and the Rise of Mega Fires.* Boulder: University Press of Colorado, 2011.

Humes, Edward. *Eco-Barons: The Dreamers, Schemers, and Millionaires Who Are Saving Our Planet.* New York: Ecco, 2009.

Humes, Edward. "Where the Wild Things Are, Still." *Sierra*, January–February 2010, 38–43, 111.

Hunt, Joe. *Mission without a Map: The Politics and Policies of Restoration Following the Exxon Valdez Oil Spill: 1989–2002.* Rev. ed.. Anchorage: Exxon Valdez Oil Spill Trustees Council, 2009.

Jackson, Jeremy B., Karen E. Alexander, and Enric Sala, eds. *Shifting Baselines: The Past and the Future of Ocean Fisheries.* Washington, DC: Island Press, 2011. http://dx.doi.org/10.5822/978-1-61091-029-3.

Jackson, Jeremy B.C. "Ecological Extinction and Evolution in the Brave New Ocean." *Proceedings of the National Academy of Sciences of the United States of America* 105, suppl. 1 (2008): 11458–65. http://dx.doi.org/10.1073/pnas.0802812105.

Jacobs, John. *A Rage for Justice: The Passion and Politics of Philip Burton.* Berkeley: University of California Press, 1995.

Jamison, Michael. "Over Under." *National Parks* 87 (Winter 2013): 46–54.

Jenkins, Jerry. *Climate Change in the Adirondacks: The Path of Sustainability*. Ithaca: Cornell University Press, 2010.

Jenkins, Martin, A. Rodrigues, J. Morrison, I. Lysenko, M. Spaulding, V. Kapos, W. Darwall, C. Revenga, E. Hamilton-Smith, L. Hamilton, and T. F. Allnut. "Protected Areas and Biodiversity." In *The World's Protected Areas: Status, Values, and Prospects in the 21st Century*, ed. Stuart Chape, Mark Spaulding, and Martin Jenkins, 36–75. Berkeley: University of California Press, 2008.

Jenkins, Matt. "Boreal Breakthrough." *Nature Conservancy Magazine* 60 (August 2010): 15.

Juhusz, Antonio. *Black Tide: The Devastating Impact of the Gulf Oil Spill*. Hoboken, NJ: John Wiley & Sons, 2010.

Kareiva, Peter, and Michelle Marvier. "Conservation for the People." *Scientific American* 297, no. 4 (October 2007): 50–57. http://dx.doi.org/10.1038/scientificamerican1007-50.

Kareiva, Peter, and Michelle Marvier. *Conservation Science: Balancing the Needs of People and Nature*. Greenwood Village, CO: Roberts and Company, 2011.

Kareiva, Peter, Sean Watts, Robert McDonald, and Tim Boucher. "Domesticated Nature: Shaping Landscapes and Ecosystems for Human Welfare." *Science* 316, no. 5833 (June 29, 2007): 1866–69. http://dx.doi.org/10.1126/science.1140170.

Kaufman, Les, and Kenneth Mallory, eds. *The Last Extinction*. 2nd ed. Cambridge, MA: MIT Press, 1993.

Kaye, Roger. *Last Great Wilderness: The Campaign to Establish the Arctic National Wildlife Refuge*. Fairbanks: University of Alaska Press, 2006.

Kays, Roland W., and Robert A. Daniels. "Fish and Wildlife Communities of the Adirondacks." In *The Great Experiment in Conservation: Voices from the Adirondack Park*, ed. William F. Porter, Jon D. Erickson, and Ross S. Whaley, 71–86. Syracuse: Syracuse University Press, 2009.

Keiter, Robert B. *Keeping Faith with Nature: Ecosystems, Democracy, and American Public Lands*. New Haven: Yale University Press, 2003. http://dx.doi.org/10.12987/yale/9780300092738.001.0001.

Keiter, Robert B. *To Conserve Unimpaired: The Evolution of the National Park Idea*. Washington, DC: Island Press, 2013. http://dx.doi.org/10.5822/978-1-61091-216-7.

Keiter, Robert B., and Mark S. Boyce, eds. *The Greater Yellowstone Ecosystem: Refining America's Wilderness Heritage*. New Haven: Yale University Press, 1991.

Keiter, Robert B., and Mark S. Boyce. "Greater Yellowstone's Future: Ecosystem Management in a Wilderness Environment." In *The Greater Yellowstone Ecosystem: Refining America's Wilderness Heritage*, ed. Robert B. Keiter and Mark S. Boyce, 379–415. New Haven: Yale University Press, 1991.

Kevin, Brian. "Everybody Hates Chuck Schwartz." *Sierra* 96 (January–February 2011): 26–31, 102.

Kingsland, Sharon E. *The Evolution of American Ecology, 1890–2000*. Baltimore: Johns Hopkins University Press, 2005.

Kish, Carey. "Exploring the 100-Mile Wilderness." *AMC Outdoors* 79 (July–August 2013): 36–39.

Klyza, Christopher McGrory. *Who Controls Public Lands? Mining, Forestry, and Grazing Policies, 1970–1990*. Chapel Hill: University of North Carolina Press, 1996.

Klyza, Christopher McGrory, and David Sousa. *American Environmental Policy, 1990–2006: Beyond Gridlock*. Cambridge, MA: MIT Press, 2008.

Knight, Dennis H. "The Yellowstone Fire Controversy." In *The Greater Yellowstone Ecosystem: Refining America's Wilderness Heritage*, ed. Robert B. Keiter and Mark S. Boyce, 87–104. New Haven: Yale University Press, 1991.

Kolbert, Elizabeth. *The Sixth Extinction: An Unnatural History*. New York: Henry Holt, 2014.

Kormos, Cyril F. "We Need to Scale Up Marine Wilderness Protection: A Global Perspective." *International Journal of Wilderness* 17 (December 2011): 13–14.

Koslow, Tony. *The Silent Deep: The Discovery, Ecology, and Conservation of the Deep Sea*. Chicago: University of Chicago Press, 2007.

Kraft, Michael E., and Norman J. Vig. "Environmental Policy from the 1970s to the Twenty-First Century." In *Environmental Policy: New Directions for the Twenty-First Century*, 6th ed., ed. Norman J. Vig and Michael E. Kraft, Washington, DC: 1–33. CQ Press, 2007.

Kricher, John. *The Balance of Nature: Ecology's Enduring Myth*. Princeton: Princeton University Press, 2009. http://dx.doi.org/10.1515/9781400830268.

Krutch, Joseph Wood. *The Voice of the Desert: A Naturalist's Interpretation*. New York: William Morrow, 1955. http://dx.doi.org/10.5962/bhl.title.50829.

Land Trust Alliance. *2010 National Land Trust Census Report*. November 16, 2011. http://s3.amazonaws.com/landtrustalliance.org/page/files/2010LandTrust Census.pdf

Langston, Nancy. *Forest Dreams, Forest Nightmares: The Paradox of Old Growth in the Inland West*. Seattle: University of Washington Press, 1996.

Langston, Nancy. *Where Land and Water Meet: A Western Landscape Transformed*. Seattle: University of Washington Press, 2003.

"The Latest." *High Country News* 48 (January 28, 2016): 9.

Layzer, Judith. *Natural Experiments: Ecosystem-Based Management and the Environment*. Cambridge, MA: MIT Press, 2008. http://dx.doi.org/10.7551/mitpress/9780262 122986.001.0001.

Lee, Martha F. *Earth First!: Environmental Apocalypse*. Syracuse: Syracuse University Press, 1995.

"A Legacy of Disappointment." *Redrock Wilderness* 28 (Autumn–Winter 2011): 5–6.

Libby, Ronald T. *Eco-Wars: Political Campaigns and Social Movements*. New York: Columbia University Press, 1998.

Little, Jane Braxton. "The Missing Link." *Nature Conservancy Magazine* 61, no. 4 (2012): 46–53.

Locke, Harvey. "Canada Increases Wilderness Protection and Policy Goals." *International Journal of Wilderness* 15 (April 2009): 5, 8.

Lomonacco, Claudine. "Lost in the Woods." *High Country News* 46 (September 1, 2014): 12–20.

Loomis, Molly. "Bison and Boundaries." *Sierra*, November–December 2013, 28–31, 70.

Lopez, Barry. "Uncivilized." *Outside*, September 2014, 72.

Lowry, William R. *The Capacity for Wonder: Preserving National Parks*. Washington, DC: Brookings Institution, 1994.

Lowry, William R. *Dam Politics: Restoring America's Rivers*. Washington, DC: Georgetown University Press, 2003.

Lowry, William R. "National Parks Policy." In *Western Public Lands and Environmental Politics*, ed. Charles Davis, 169–96. Boulder: Westview Press, 2001.

Lowry, William R. *Repairing Paradise: The Restoration of Nature in America's National Parks*. Washington, DC: Brookings Institution Press, 2007.

McCally, David. "The Everglades and the Florida Dream." In *Paradise Lost? The Environmental History of Florida*, ed. Jack E. Davis and Raymond Arsenault, 141–59. Gainesville: University Press of Florida, 2005.

McCloskey, Michael. *In the Thick of It: My Life in the Sierra Club*. Washington, DC: Island Press, 2005.

McCloskey, Michael. "Twenty Years of Change in the Environmental Movement: An Insider's View." In *American Environmentalism: The U.S. Environmental Movement, 1970–1990*, ed. Riley E. Dunlap and Angela G. Mertig, 78–87. Washington, DC: Taylor and Francis, 1992.

MacDonald, Samuel A. *The Agony of an American Wilderness: Loggers, Environmentalists, and the Struggle for Control of a Forgotten Forest*. Lanham, MD: Rowman & Littlefield, 2005.

McGucken, William. *Lake Erie Rehabilitated: Controlling Cultural Eutrophication, 1960's–1990's*. Akron: University of Akron Press, 2000.

MacKenzie, G. Calvin, and Robert Weisbrot. *The Liberal Hour: Washington and the Politics of Change in the 1960's*. New York: Penguin Press, 2008.

McManus, John. "Winning One for the Wolverine." *Earthjustice Quarterly Magazine*, Spring 2013, 20–21.

McMillion, Scott. "Ghost Cats." *Nature Conservancy Magazine*, Winter 2009, 33–35.

McMillion, Scott. "New Life in the Badlands." *Nature Conservancy Magazine*, October–November 2015, 32–43.

McMillion, Scott. "Ranching Rebooted." *Nature Conservancy Magazine*, November–December 2013, 35–36, 42.

McNamee, Thomas. *The Return of the Wolf to Yellowstone*. New York: Henry Holt & Co, 1997.

Mace, Georgina M., Jonathan E.M. Baillie, Steven R. Beissinger, and Kent H. Redford. "Assessment and Management of Species at Risk." In *Conservation*

Biology: Research Priorities for the Next Decade, ed. Michael E. Soulé and Gordon H. Orians, 11–30. Washington, DC: Island Press, 2001.

"Making History in the Western Arctic: 11 Million Acres Protected," Sierra Borealis, March 2013, 1–2, 4.

Mangun, William R. "Wildlife Resource Policy Issues in the West." In Environmental Politics and Policy in the West, ed. Zachary A. Smith and John C. Freemuth, 109–32. Boulder: University Press of Colorado, 2007.

Mann, Charles C., and Mark L. Plummer. Noah's Choice: The Future of Endangered Species. New York: Alfred A. Knopf, 1995.

Marris, Emma. "Conservation Biology: The End of the Wild." Nature 469, no. 7329 (2011): 150–52. http://dx.doi.org/10.1038/469150a.

Marris, Emma. Rambunctious Garden: Saving Nature in a Post-Wild World. New York: Bloomsbury, 2011.

Marsh, Kevin R. Drawing Lines in the Forest: Creating Wilderness Areas in the Pacific Northwest. Seattle: University of Washington Press, 2007.

Marsh, Kevin R. "'Save French Pete': Evolution of Wilderness Protests in Oregon." In Natural Protest: Essays on the History of Environmentalism, ed. Michael Egan and Jeff Crane, 223–44. New York: Routledge, 2008.

Marston, Ed. "The Quincy Library Group: A Divisive Attempt at Peace." In Across the Great Divide: Explorations in Collaborative Conservation and the American West, ed. Philip Brick, Donald Snow, and Sarah Van de Wetering, 79–90. Washington, DC: Island Press, 2001.

Max, D. T. "Green Is Good." New Yorker, May 12, 2014, 54–63.

Meine, Curt D. "The Oldest Task in Human History." In A New Century for Natural Resources Management, ed. Richard L. Knight and Sarah F. Bates, 7–36. Washington, DC: Island Press, 1995.

Meine, Curt D. "What's So New about the 'New Conservation'?" In Keeping the Wild: Against the Domestication of the Earth, ed. George Wuerthner, Eileen Crist, and Tom Butler, 45–54. Washington, DC: Island Press, 2014. http://dx.doi.org/10.5822/978-1-61091-559-5_5.

Mengak, Kathy. Reshaping Out National Parks and Their Guardians: The Legacy of George B. Hartzog, Jr. Albuquerque: University of New Mexico Press, 2012.

Merchant, Carolyn. Radical Ecology: The Search for a Liveable World. 2nd ed. New York: Routledge, 2005.

Miles, John C. Guardians of the Parks: A History of the National Parks and Conservation Association. Washington, DC: Taylor and Francis, 1995.

Miles, John C. Wilderness in National Parks: Playground or Preserve. Seattle: University of Washington Press, 2009.

Miller, Char. Gifford Pinchot and the Making of Modern Environmentalism. Washington, DC: Island Press, 2000.

"Minnesota." Nature Conservancy Magazine 60 (Winter 2010): 20.

Mitchell, Donald Craig. *Take My Land, Take My Life: The Story of Congress's Historic Settlement of Alaska Native Land Claims, 1960–1971*. Fairbanks: University of Alaska Press, 2001.

Molina, Randy, Bruce G. Marcot, and Robin Lesher. "Protecting Rare, Old-Growth, Forest Associated Species under the Survey and Manage Program Guidelines of the Northwest Forest Plan." *Conservation Biology* 20, no. 2 (2006): 306–18. http://dx.doi.org/10.1111/j.1523-1739.2006.00386.x.

Monahan, William B., and Nicholas A. Fisichelli. "Climate Exposure of U.S. National Parks in a New Era of Change." *PLoS One* 9, no. 7 (July 2, 2014): e101302. http://dx.doi.org/10.1371/journal.pone.0101302.

"A Monumental Tug of War." *High Country News* 47 (February 16, 2015): 16.

Mooallen, Jon. *Wild Ones: A Sometimes Dismaying, Weirdly Reassuring Story about Looking at People Looking at Animals in America*. New York: Penguin Books, 2013.

Moseley, Cassandra, and Emily June David. *Stewardship Contracting for Landscape-Scale Projects*. Ecosystem Workforce Program Working Paper, no. 25. Eugene: University of Oregon, Institute for Sustainable Environment, Summer 2010.

Muir, John. *Nature Writings*. New York: Library of America, 1997.

Musgrave, Ruth S. "Legal Trends in Fish and Wildlife Policy." In *Wildlife and Society: The Science of Human Dimensions*, ed. Michael J. Manfredo, Jerry J. Vaske, Perry J. Brown, Daniel J. Decker, and Esther A. Duke, 145–60. Washington, DC: Island Press, 2009.

Nash, Roderick Frazier. *The Rights of Nature: A History of Environmental Ethics*. Madison: University of Wisconsin Press, 1989.

National Park Service. *National Parks: Our Treasured Landscapes*. June 2009. https://wilderness.org/resource/national-parks-our-treasured-landscapes.

National Park System Advisory Board, Science Committee. *Revisiting Leopold: Resource Stewardship in the National Parks*. August 25, 2012. https://www.nps.gov/calltoaction/PDF/LeopoldReport_2012.pdf.

National Research Council, Committee on Independent Scientific Review of Everglades Restoration Progress. *Progress toward Restoring the Everglades: The Fourth Biennial Review, 2012*. Washington, DC: National Academies Press, 2012. http://dels.nas.edu/Report/Progress-Toward-Restoring-Everglades/13422

National Wildlife Federation. "Emerging Nutrient Crisis Causing Massive New Breakdown in the Great Lakes." October 4, 2011. https://www.nwf.org/News-and-Magazines/Media-Center/News-by-Topic/Wildlife/2011/10-04-11-Nutrient-Crisis-Causing-Breakdowns-in-the-Great-Lakes.aspx.

Nawi, David, and Alf W. Brandt. "The California-Bay Delta: The Challenges of Collaboration." In *Large-Scale Ecosystem Restoration: Five Case Studies from the United States*, ed. Mary Doyle and Cynthia A. Drew. Washington, DC: Island Press, 2008.

Neff, John W. *Katahdin: An Historic Journey*. Boston: Appalachian Mountain Club Books, 2006.

Nelson, Daniel. *Northern Landscapes: The Struggle for Wilderness Alaska*. Washington, DC: Resources for the Future, 2004.

Nelson, Daniel. *A Passion for the Land: John F. Seiberling and the Environmental Movement*. Kent, OH: Kent State University Press, 2009.

Nelson, Michael P., and J. Baird Callicott. *The Wilderness Debate Rages On: Continuing the Great New Wilderness Debate*. Athens: University of Georgia Press, 2008.

Ness, Erik. "Vote Yes for Conservation." *Nature Conservancy Magazine* 59 (Autumn 2009): 32–43.

Newmark, William D. "Extinction of Mammal Populations in Western North American National Parks." *Conservation Biology* 9, no. 3 (June 1995): 512–26. http://dx.doi.org/10.1046/j.1523-1739.1995.09030512.x.

Nie, Martin. *The Governance of Western Public Lands: Mapping Its Present and Future*. Lawrence: University Press of Kansas, 2008.

Noon, Barry, and Jennifer A. Blakesley. "Conservation of the Northern Spotted Owl under the Northwest Forest Plan." *Conservation Biology* 20, no. 2 (2006): 288–96. http://dx.doi.org/10.1111/j.1523-1739.2006.00387.x.

Nordhaus, William. *The Climate Casino: Risk, Uncertainty, and Economics for a Warming World*. New Haven: Yale University Press, 2013.

Norris, Frank. *Alaska Subsistence: A National Park Service Management History*. Anchorage: National Park Service, 2002.

Norse, Elliott A., and Larry B. Crowder. "Preface." In *Marine Conservation Biology: The Science of Maintaining the Sea's Biodiversity*, ed. Elliott A. Norse and Larry B. Crowder, xvii–xx. Washington, DC: Island Press, 2005.

Noss, Reed F. "Biodiversity, Ecological Integrity, and Wilderness." *International Journal of Wilderness* 2 (August 1996): 5–8.

Noss, Reed F., and Allen Y. Cooperrider. *Saving Nature's Legacy: Protecting and Restoring Biodiversity*. Washington, DC: Island Press, 1994.

"Obama II: Disappointment Dampens Desire to Hope." *Redrock Wilderness* 30 (Spring 2013): 5–6, 8.

"On the Watch." *Wilderness Watcher* 21, no. 2 (September 2010): 3–8.

Oregon Explorer. "A Monumental Accord: Steens Mountain Cooperative Management Area." http://oregonexplorer.info/content/monumental-accord-steens-mountain-cooperative-management-area?topic=86&ptopic=62.

Parker, Melanie. "Swan Story." In *Stitching the West Back Together: Conservation of Working Landscapes*, ed. Susan Charnley, Thomas E. Sheridan, and Gary P. Nabhan, 123–35. Chicago: University of Chicago Press, 2014. http://dx.doi.org/10.7208/chicago/9780226165851.003.0009.

Pearson, Richard. *Driven to Extinction: The Impact of Climate Change on Biodiversity*. New York: Sterling, 2011.

Peters, Margaret T. *Conserving the Commonwealth: The Early Years of the Environmental Movement in Virginia*. Charlottesville: University of Virginia Press, 2008.

Peterson, Jodi. "Little Big Bird." *High Country News* 47 (August 17, 2015): 13.

Pettibone, David. "Rocky Mountain National Park: Wilderness after 35 Years." *International Journal of Wilderness* 19 (April 2013): 9–13, 25.

Pinchot Institute. *Independent Science Panel Report: Herger-Feinstein Quincy Library Group Forest Recovery Act*. Washington, DC: Pinchot Institute for Conservation, July 31, 2013.

Polasky, Stephen. "Murky Waters and Murky Policies: Costs and Benefits of Restoring Chesapeake Bay." In *Large-Scale Ecosystem Restoration: Five Case Studies from the United States*, ed. Mary Doyle and Cynthia A. Drew, 215–24. Washington, DC: Island Press, 2008.

Polasky, Stephen. "Rivers of Plans for the River of Grass: The Political Economy of Everglades Restoration." In *Large-Scale Ecosystem Restoration: Five Case Studies from the United States*, ed. Mary Doyle and Cynthia A. Drew, 44–54. Washington, DC: Island Press, 2008.

Porter, William F. "Wildlife Exploitation in the Adirondacks." In *The Great Experiment in Conservation: Voices from the Adirondack Park*, ed. William F. Porter, Jon D. Erickson, and Russ S. Whaley, 87–95. Syracuse: Syracuse University Press, 2009.

Power, Thomas Michael. *Lost Landscapes and Failed Economies: The Search for a Value of Place*. Washington, DC: Island Press, 1996.

Prato, Tony, and Dan Fagre. *National Parks and Protected Areas: Approaches for Balancing Social, Economic, and Ecological Values*. Ames, IA: Blackwell Publishing, 2005.

Pratt, Thane K., Carter T. Atkinson, Paul C. Banko, James D. Jacobi, and Bethany L. Woodworth. *Conservation Biology of Hawaiian Forest Birds: Implications for Island Avifauna*. New Haven: Yale University Press, 2009.

Primack, Richard. *Essentials of Conservation Biology*. 5th ed. Sunderland, MA: Sinauer Associates, 2010.

Pritchard, James A. *Preserving Yellowstone's Natural Conditions: Science and the Perception of Nature*. Lincoln: University of Nebraska Press, 1999.

Proescholdt, Kevin. "Guardians, not Gardeners." *Wilderness Watcher* 24 (Spring 2013): 1.

Proescholdt, Kevin. "Wilderness Milestones of 2014: 50th Anniversary of the Wilderness Act, 25th Anniversary of Wilderness Watch." *Wilderness Watcher* 25 (Summer/Fall 2014): 4.

Pyne, Stephen J. *Between Two Fires: A Fire History of Contemporary America*. Tucson: University of Arizona Press, 2015.

Pyne, Stephen J. *Fire in America: A Cultural History of Wildland and Rural Fire*. Seattle: University of Washington Press, 1997.

Quammen, David. *The Song of the Dodo: Island Biogeography in an Age of Extinctions*. New York: Scribner, 1996.

Rakestraw, Lawrence. *A History of the United States Forest Service in Alaska*. Tongass Centennial Special Edition. Washington: US Department of Agriculture, 2002.

Randall, John M. "Objectives, Priorities, and Triage: Lessons Learned from Invasive Species Management." In *Beyond Naturalness: Rethinking Park and Wilderness*

Stewardship in an Era of Rapid Change, ed. David N. Cole and Laurie Yung, 162–78. Washington, DC: Island Press, 2010.

Ray, Justina C., Kent H. Redford, Robert S. Steneck, and Joel Berger, eds. *Large Carnivores and the Conservation of Biodiversity* Washington, DC: Island Press, 2005.

Ray, Justina C., Kent H. Redford, Joel Berger, and Robert Steneck. "Large Carnivorous Animals and Biodiversity: Does Saving One Conserve the Other?" In *Large Carnivores and the Conservation of Biodiversity*, ed. Justina C. Ray, Kent H. Redford, Robert S. Steneck, and Joel Berger, 401–29. Washington, DC: Island Press, 2005.

Reese, April. "The Gila Solution." *High Country News* 46 (February 17, 2014): 12–16.

Reimers, Frederick. "Python Patrol." *Nature Conservancy Magazine*, February–March 2014, 50–59.

Reimers, Frederick. "Shifting Ground: A Stunning Landscape Is Saved after a Decade-Long Fight over Its Water." *Nature Conservancy Magazine*, May–June 2013, 30–43.

Rice, Nathan. "A New Forest Paradigm." *High Country News* 45 (April 29, 2013): 15.

Rieser, Alison, Charlotte Gray Hudson, and Stephan E. Roady. "The Role of Legal Regimes in Marine Conservation." In *Marine Conservation Biology: The Science of Maintaining the Sea's Biodiversity*, ed. Elliott A. Norse and Larry B. Crowder, 362–74. Washington, DC: Island Press, 2005.

Righter, Robert W. *The Battle over Hetch Hetchy: America's Most Controversial Dam and the Birth of Modern Environmentalism.* New York: Oxford University Press, 2005. http://dx.doi.org/10.1093/acprof:oso/9780195149470.001.0001.

"A Rising Tide: A Statement by Scientists for the Designation of the First Generation of Great Marine Parks around the Globe." *Open Channels* online forum, October 22, 2013. https://www.openchannels.org/news/news/rising-tide-statement -support-scientists-designation-first-generation-great-marine-parks.

Robbins, Jim. *Last Refuge: The Environmental Showdown in Yellowstone and the American West.* New York: William Morrow and Co., 1993.

Robbins, Jim. "On the Life List." *Nature Conservancy Magazine*, no. 1 (2012): 38–43.

Roberts, Callum. *The Ocean of Life: The Fate of Man and the Sea.* New York: Viking, 2012.

Roberts, Callum. *The Unnatural History of the Sea.* Washington, DC: Island Press, 2007.

Robinson, Michael J. *Predatory Bureaucracy: The Extermination of Wolves and Transformation of the West.* Boulder: University Press of Colorado, 2005.

Robles Gil, Patricio. "The El Carmen Wilderness." In *Wilderness, Wildlands, and People: A Partnership for the Planet*, ed. Vance G. Martin and Cyril F. Kormos, 22–28. Golden: Fulcrum Publishing, 2008.

Rogers, Kara. *The Quiet Extinction: Stories of North America's Rare and Threatened Plants.* Tucson: University of Arizona Press, 2015.

Roman, Joe. *Listed: Dispatches from America's Endangered Species Act.* Cambridge, MA: Harvard University Press, 2011. http://dx.doi.org/10.4159/harvard.9780674061279.

Rome, Adam. *The Bulldozer in the Countryside: Suburban Sprawl and the Rise of American Environmentalism*. Cambridge: Cambridge University Press, 2001. http://dx.doi.org/10.1017/CBO9780511816703.

Rome, Adam. *The Genius of Earth Day: How a 1970 Teach-In Unexpectedly Made the First Green Generation*. New York: Hill and Wang, 2013.

Rose, Debra A. "Implementing Endangered Species Policy." In *American Fish and Wildlife Policy: The Human Dimension*, ed. William R. Mangun, 94–118. Carbondale: Southern Illinois University Press, 1992.

Roselle, Mike, with Josh Mahan. *Tree Spiker: From Earth First! to Lowbagging: My Struggles in Radical Environmental Action*. New York: St. Martin's Press, 2009.

Roth, Dennis. "The National Forests and the Campaign for Wilderness Legislation." In *American Forests: Nature, Culture, and Politics*, ed. Char Miller, 229–46. Lawrence: University of Kansas Press, 1997.

Roth, Dennis. *The Wilderness Movement and the National Forests*. College Station, TX: Intaglio Press, 1988.

Ross, Ken. *Environmental Conflict in Alaska*. Boulder: University Press of Colorado, 2000.

Rothman, Hal K. *Blazing Heritage: A History of Wildland Fire in the National Parks*. New York: Oxford University Press, 2007. http://dx.doi.org/10.1093/acprof:oso/9780195311167.001.0001.

Rothman, Hal K. *The Greening of a Nation? Environmentalism in the United States since 1945*. Fort Worth: Harcourt Brace College Publishers, 1988.

Rothman, Hal K., and Char Miller. *Death Valley National Park: A History*. Reno: University of Nevada Press, 2013.

Runte, Alfred. *National Parks: The American Experience*. 3rd ed. Lincoln: University of Nebraska Press, 1987.

Safina, Carl. *Song for the Blue Ocean: Encounters along the World's Coasts and beneath the Seas*. New York: Henry Holt, 1998.

Salt, Terrence "Rock," Stuart Langton, and Mary Doyle. "The Challenges of Restoring the Everglades Ecosystem." In *Large-Scale Ecosystem Restoration: Five Case Studies from the United States*, ed. Mary Doyle and Cynthia A. Drew, 5–33. Washington, DC: Island Press, 2008.

Savory, Allan. "Re-Creating the West . . . One Decision at a Time." In *Ranching West of the 100th Meridian: Culture, Ecology, and Economics*, ed. Richard L. Knight, Wendell C. Gilbert, and Ed Marston, 155–72. Washington, DC: Island Press, 2002.

Sayre, Nathan F. *Working Wilderness: The Malpai Borderlands Group and the Future of the Western Range*. Tucson: Rio Nuevo Publishers, 2005.

Scarce, Rik. *Eco-Warriors: Understanding the Radical Environmental Movement*. Walnut Creek, CA: Left Coast Press, 2006.

Schrepfer, Susan R. "Establishing Administrative 'Standing': The Sierra Club and the Forest Service." In *American Forests: Nature, Culture, and Politics*, ed. Char Miller, 125–42. Lawrence: University of Kansas Press, 1997.

Schrepfer, Susan R. *The Fight to Save the Redwoods: A History of Environmental Reform, 1917–78.* Madison: University of Wisconsin Press, 1983.

Schullery, Paul. *Searching for Yellowstone: Ecology and Wonder in the Last Wilderness.* Boston: Houghton Mifflin, 1997.

Schulte, Steven C. *Wayne Aspinall and the Shaping of the American West.* Boulder: University Press of Colorado, 2002.

Scott, Doug. *The Enduring Wilderness.* Golden: Fulcrum Publishing, 2004.

Scott, J. Michael, Dale D. Goble, Aaron M. Haines, John A. Wiens, and Maile C. Neel. "Conservation-Reliant Species and the Future of Conservation." *Conservation Letters* 3, no. 2 (2010): 91–97. http://dx.doi.org/10.1111/j.1755-263X.2010.00096.x.

Sellers, Richard West. *Preserving Nature in the National Parks: A History.* New Haven: Yale University Press, 1997.

Sheridan, Thomas E., Nathan F. Sayre, and David Seibert. "Beyond 'Stakeholders' and the Zero-Sum Game: Toward Community-Based Collaborative Conservation in the American West." In *Stitching the West Back Together: Conservation of Working Landscapes,* ed. Susan Charnley, Thomas E. Sheridan, and Gary P. Nabhan, 53–75. Chicago: University of Chicago Press, 2014.

Shivik, John A. *The Predator Paradox: Ending the War with Wolves, Bears, Cougars, and Coyotes.* Boston: Beacon Press, 2014.

Shogren, Elizabeth. "Legacy Maker." *High Country News* 47 (May 25, 2015): 12–14.

Simberloff, Daniel, James A. Farr, James Cox, and David W. Mehlman. "Movement Corridors: Conservation Bargains or Poor Investments?" *Conservation Biology* 6, no. 4 (1992): 493–504. http://dx.doi.org/10.1046/j.1523-1739.1992.06040493.x.

Skillen, James R. *The Nation's Largest Landlord: The Bureau of Land Management in the American West.* Lawrence: University of Kansas Press, 2009.

Smith, Jeff. "Wilderness Watch Battles to Protect Wolves and Wilderness in Idaho." *Wilderness Watcher* 21 (April 2010): 1–2.

Snow, Donald. *Inside the Environmental Movement: Meeting the Leadership Challenge.* Washington, DC: Island Press, 1992.

Soulé, Michael. "Conservation Relevance of Ecological Cascades." In *Trophic Cascades: Predators, Prey, and the Changing Dynamics of Nature,* ed. John Terborgh and James A. Estes, 337–52. Washington, DC: Island Press, 2010.

Soulé, Michael. "The Social Siege of Nature." In *Reinventing Nature?: Responses to Postmodern Deconstruction,* ed. Michael E. Soulé and Gary Lease, 137–70. Washington, DC: Island Press, 1995.

Soulé, Michael. "'A Vision for the Meantime." *Wild Earth,* Special Issue: The Wildlands Project (1992): 7–8.

Soulé, Michael E., and John Terborgh, eds. *Continental Conservation: Scientific Foundations of Regional Reserve Networks.* Washington, DC: Island Press, 1999.

Soulé, Michael E., and Bruce A. Wilcox. "Conservation Biology: Its Scope and Its Challenge." In *Conservation Biology: An Evolutionary-Ecological Perspective,* ed. Michael E. Soulé and Bruce A. Wilcox, 1–8. Sunderland, MA: Sinauer Associates, 1980.

Southern Utah Wilderness Alliance. *Redrock Wilderness* 28 (Autumn–Winter 2011): 5.

Speth, James Gustave. *Red Sky at Morning: America and the Crisis of the Global Environment*. New Haven: Yale University Press, 2004.

"Spotted Owls in Rapid Decline." *Forest News*, Fall 2015, 7.

Stahl, Andy. "Ownership, Accountability, and Collaboration." In *Across the Great Divide: Explorations in Collaborative Conservation and the American West*, ed. Philip Brick, Donald Snow, and Sarah Van de Wetering, 194–99. Washington, DC: Island Press, 2001.

Stanley, Thomas R., Jr. "Ecosystem Management and the Arrogance of Humanism." *Conservation Biology* 9, no. 2 (April 1995): 255–62. http://dx.doi.org/10.1046/j.1523-1739.1995.9020255.x.

Starrs, Paul F. *Let the Cowboy Ride: Cattle Ranching in the American West*. Baltimore: Johns Hopkins University Press, 1998.

Steep, Abe. "The Natural." *Outside*, August 2010, 84–85.

Steneck, Robert S. "An Ecological Context for the Role of Large Carnivorous Animals in Conserving Biodiversity." In *Large Carnivores and the Conservation of Biodiversity*, ed. Justina C. Ray, Kent H. Redford, Robert S. Steneck, and Joel Berger, 9–32. Washington, DC: Island Press, 2005.

Stine, Jeffrey K. *America's Forested Wetlands: From Wasteland to Valued Resource*. Durham: Forest History Society, 2008.

Straddling, David. *The Nature of New York: An Environmental History of the Empire State*. Ithaca: Cornell University Press, 2010.

Strand, Ginger. "A Win for the West." *Nature Conservancy Magazine*, April–May 2015, 52–55.

Sumaila, W. Rashid, and Daniel Pauly. "The 'March of Folly' in Global Fisheries." In *Shifting Baselines: The Past and Future of Ocean Fisheries*, ed. Jeremy B.C. Jackson, Karen E. Alexander, and Enric Sala, 21–32. Washington, DC: Island Press, 2011. http://dx.doi.org/10.5822/978-1-61091-029-3_2.

Sundstrom, Shiloh, and Johnny Sundstrom. "Stewardship Contracting in the Siuslaw National Forest." In *Stitching the West Back Together: Conservation of Working Landscapes*, ed. Susan Charnley, Thomas E. Sheridan, and Gary P. Nabhan, 159–75. Chicago: University of Chicago Press, 2014. http://dx.doi.org/10.7208/chicago/9780226165851.003.0013.

Sutter, Paul S. *Driven Wild: How the Fight against Automobiles Launched the Modern Wilderness Movement*. Seattle: University of Washington Press, 2002.

Swanson, Frederick H. *The Bitterroot and Mr. Brandborg*. Provo: University of Utah Press, 2011.

Swanson, Frederick H. *Where Roads Will Never Reach: Wilderness and Its Visionaries in the Northern Rockies*. Salt Lake City: University of Utah Press, 2015.

Sylven, Magnus. "Nature Needs Half: A New Spatial Perspective for a Healthy Planet." *International Journal of Wilderness* 17 (December 2011): 10–11.

Szylvian, Kristin M. "Transforming Lake Michigan into the 'World's Greatest Fishing Hole': The Environmental Politics of Michigan's Great Lakes Sport Fishing, 1965–1985." *Environmental History* 9, no. 1 (January 2004): 102–27. http://dx.doi.org/10.2307/3985947.

"Taking Stock of Grizzlies." *High Country News* 45 (August 19, 2013): 7.

Tangley, Laura. "Gulf Coast Revival?" *National Wildlife* 49 (April–May 2011): 24–29.

Terborgh, John. "The Green World Hypothesis Revisited." In *Large Carnivores and the Conservation of Biodiversity*, ed. Justina Ray, Kent H. Redford, Robert S. Steneck, and Joel Berger, 84–99. Washington, DC: Island Press, 2005.

Terck, Mark R., and Jonathan S. Adams. "Nature's Fortune." *Nature Conservancy Magazine* 62 (May–June 2013): 56–58.

Terck, Mark R., and Jonathan S. Adams. *Nature's Fortune: How Business and Society Thrive by Investing in Nature*. New York: Basic Books, 2013.

Terrie, Philip E. "Compromise, Continuity, and Crisis in the Adirondack Park." In *The Great Experiment in Conservation: Voices from the Adirondack Park*, ed. William F. Porter, Jon D. Erickson, and Ross S. Whaley, 354–69. Syracuse: Syracuse University Press, 2009.

Terrie, Philip E. *Contested Terrain: A New History of Nature and People in the Adirondacks*. Syracuse: Syracuse University Press and Adirondack Museum, 1997.

Terrie, Philip E. "Stunning Changes." *Adirondac* 73 (May–June 2009): 24.

Thomas, Jack Ward. *The Journals of a Forest Service Chief*. Seattle: University of Washington Press, 2004.

Thomas, Jack Ward, Jerry F. Franklin, John Gordon, and K. Norman Johnson. "The Northwest Forest Plan: Origins, Components, Implementation Experience, and Suggestions for Change." *Conservation Biology* 20, no. 2 (2006): 277–87. http://dx.doi.org/10.1111/j.1523-1739.2006.00385.x.

Thorne, E. Tom, Mary Meagher, and Robert Hillman. "Brucellosis in Free-Ranging Bison: Three Perspectives." In *The Greater Yellowstone Ecosystem: Refining America's Wilderness Heritage*, ed. Robert B. Keiter and Mark J. Boyce, 275–88. New Haven: Yale University Press, 1991.

"Threats to Endangered Species Act." *Forest News*, Spring 2011, 4.

Trust for Public Land. "Final Chapters of New World Mine Are Complete." June 15, 2010. https://www.tpl.org/media-room/final-chapter-new-world-mine-controversy-complete.

Turner, A. "North America." In *The World's Protected Areas: Status, Values, and Prospects in the 21st Century*, ed. Stuart Chape, Mark Spaulding, and Martin Jenkins, 179–89. Berkeley: University of California Press, 2008.

Turner, James Morton. *The Promise of Wilderness: American Environmental Politics since 1964*. Seattle: University of Washington Press, 2012.

Turner, Tom. *Roadless Rules: The Struggle for the Last Wild Forests*. Washington, DC: Island Press, 2009.

Tweed, William C. *Uncertain Path: A Search for the Future of National Parks*. Berkeley: University of California Press, 2010.

USDA. *Forest Service Roadless Area Conservation: Final Environmental Impact Statement*. Vol. 1. Washington, DC: USDA, 2000.

USDA. *Status Report to Congress, Fiscal Year 2011, Herger-Feinstein Quincy Library Group Forest Recovery Act Pilot Project*. http://www.fs.fed.us/r5/hfqlg/publications/congress_report/2011/FY2011%20HFQLG%20Report%20Final%20for%20Release.pdf.

Vale, Thomas R. *The American Wilderness: Reflections on Nature Protection in the United States*. Charlottesville: University of Virginia Press, 2005.

Varley, John D., and Paul Schullery. "Reality and Opportunity in the Yellowstone Fires of 1988." In *The Greater Yellowstone Ecosystem: Refining America's Wilderness Heritage*, ed. Robert B. Keiter and Mark S. Boyce., 105–22. New Haven: Yale University Press, 1991.

Vaughn, Jacqueline, and Hanna J. Cortner. *George W. Bush's Healthy Forests: Reframing the Environmental Debate*. Boulder: University Press of Colorado, 2005.

Vileisis, Ann. *Discovering the Unknown Landscape: A History of America's Wetlands*. Washington, DC: Island Press, 1997.

Voight, William, Jr. *Public Grazing Lands: Use and Misuse by Industry and Government*. New Brunswick: Rutgers University Press, 1976.

Wagner, Eric. "Washington's Wolf Experiment." *High Country News* 47 (October 8, 2015): 7.

Wagner, Frederick H. *Yellowstone's Destabilized Ecosystem: Elk Effects, Science, and the Policy Conflict*. New York: Oxford University Press, 2006. http://dx.doi.org/10.1093/acprof:oso/9780195148213.001.0001.

Wakild, Emily. "Border Chasm: International Boundary Parks and Mexican Conservation, 1935–1945." *Environmental History* 14, no. 3 (July 2009): 453–75. http://dx.doi.org/10.1093/envhis/14.3.453.

Wall, Derek. *Earth First! and the Anti-Roads Movement: Radical Environmentalism and Comparative Social Movements*. London: Routledge, 1999.

Weber, Edward P. *Bringing Society Back In: Grassroots Ecosystem Management, Accountability, and Sustainable Communities*. Cambridge, MA: MIT Press, 2003.

Weber, Michael L. *From Abundance to Scarcity: A History of the U.S. Marine Fisheries Policy*. Washington, DC: Island Press, 2002.

Weir, Kristin. "True North." *Nature Conservancy Magazine*, no. 4 (2012): 57–60.

"Western Landscapes Shortchanged Due to Emphasis on Drilling." *America's Wilderness* 9 (Spring 2007): 7.

Western Reserve Land Conservancy. *Branching Out: Donor Report*. July 1, 2013–June 30, 2014. http://www.wrlandconservancy.org/pdf/wrlc-donor-re13-14web.pdf.

Western Reserve Land Conservancy. *Connections*, 2013, 20.

Wheat, Frank. *California Desert Miracle: The Fight for Desert Parks and Wilderness*. San Diego: Sunbelt Publications, 1999.

Wheeler, Sara. *The Magnetic North: Notes from the Arctic Circle.* New York: Farrar, Straus and Giroux, 2009.

White, Courtney. *Resolution on the Range: The Rise of a New Ranch in the American West.* Washington, DC: Island Press, 2009.

Widick, Richard. *Trouble in the Forest: California's Redwood Timber Wars.* Minneapolis: University of Minnesota Press, 2009.

Wilcove, David S. *The Condor's Shadow: The Loss and Recovery of Wildlife in America.* New York: W. H. Freeman and Co, 1999.

Wilcove, David S. *No Way Home: The Decline of the World's Great Animal Migrations.* Washington, DC: Island Press, 2008.

Wilkinson, Charles F. *Crossing the Next Meridian: Land, Water, and the Future of the West.* Washington, DC: Island Press, 1992.

Wilkinson, Todd. "Wilderness Needs Wildlife." *Wilderness,* 2008–9, 42–46.

Wilkinson, Todd. "Wildlife Needs Wilderness." *Wilderness,* 2003–4, 43–45.

Williams, James D., and Ronald M. Nowak. "Vanishing Species in Our Own Backyard: Extinct Fish and Wildlife in the United States and Canada." In *The Last Extinction,* 2nd ed., ed. Les Kaufman and Kenneth Mallory, 115–48. Cambridge, MA: MIT Press, 1993.

Williams, Terry Tempest. "The Man with the White Hat." *Redrock Wilderness* 27 (Summer 2010): 6–8.

Wilshire, Howard G., Jane E. Nielson, and Richard W. Hazlett. *The American West at Risk: Science, Myths, and Politics of Land Abuse and Recovery.* New York: Oxford University Press, 2008.

Wilson, Edward O. "Afterword." In *Silent Spring,* by Rachel Carson, 357–63. Boston: Houghton Mifflin, 2002.

Wilson, Edward O. *The Diversity of Life.* Cambridge, MA: Harvard University Press, 1992.

Wilson, Edward O. *Half-Earth: Our Planet's Fight for Life.* New York: Liveright, 2016.

Wilson, Edward O. "Island Biogeography in the 1960s: Theory and Experience." In *The Theory of Island Biogeography Revisited,* ed. Jonathan B. Losos and Robert E. Rickles, 1–12. Princeton: Princeton University Press, 2010.

Wilson, Edward O. *A Window on Eternity: A Biologist's Walk through Gorongosa National Park.* New York: Simon and Schuster, 2014.

"Wolves in the West." *New Mexico Wild* 9 (Fall 2012): 2–25.

Woods, Elliott D. "Wolflandia." *Outside,* February 2015, 70–79.

Woodward, Molly. "Obama's Environmental Record: Comparison with the Bush Years—Part 1." *In Brief* 110 (Winter 2009–10): 10–11.

Worf, William. "Forest Service Wilderness Legacy." In *Wilderness: Reclaiming the Legacy,* 49–56. Missoula: Wilderness Watch, 2011.

Worster, Donald. "The Higher Altruism." In *After Preservation: Saving American Nature in the Age of Humans,* ed. Ben A. Minteer and Stephen J. Pyne, 59–65. Chicago: University of Chicago Press, 2015.

Worster, Donald. *A Passion for Nature: The Life of John Muir*. New York: Oxford University Press, 2008.

Worster, Donald. *The Wealth of Nature: Environmental History and the Ecological Imagination*. New York: Oxford University Press, 1993.

Wuerthner, George. "State Agency Game Farming Is Not Compatible with Wilderness or Ecosystem Integrity." *Wilderness Watcher* 24 (Spring 2013): 6.

Yaffee, Stephen Lewis. *Prohibitive Policy: Implementing the Federal Endangered Species Act*. Cambridge, MA: MIT Press, 1982.

Yaffee, Stephen Lewis. *The Wisdom of the Spotted Owl: Policy Lessons for a New Century*. Washington, DC: Island Press, 1994.

Yellowstone National Park. *Yellowstone's Northern Range: Complexity & Change in a Wildland Ecosystem*. Mammoth Hot Springs: Yellowstone National Park, 1997.

Yochim, Michael J. *Protecting Yellowstone: Science and the Politics of National Park Management*. Albuquerque: University of New Mexico Press, 2013.

Zaffos, Joshua. "Up in the Air." *Nature Conservancy Magazine*, Fall 2012, 12.

Zakin, Susan. *Coyotes and Town Dogs: Earth First! and the Environmental Movement*. New York: Viking, 1993.

Zielinski, Elaine. "The Northwest Forest Plan." http://www.blm.gov/wo/st/en/info/history/sidebars/ecosystems/Northwest_Forest_Plan.html.

Zimmer, Carl. "Ecosystems on the Brink." *Scientific American* 307, no. 4 (October 2012): 60–65. http://dx.doi.org/10.1038/scientificamerican1012-60.

About the Author

DANIEL NELSON received a PhD in American history from the University of Wisconsin–Madison and taught at the University of Akron for three decades, specializing in business and labor history. The author of a half-dozen books and more than fifty essays and articles on industrial history and public policy, he has increasingly devoted his attention to environmental topics. Recent publications include *Northern Landscapes: The Struggle for Wilderness Alaska* (2004) and *A Passion for the Land: John F. Seiberling and the Environmental Movement* (2009).

An enthusiastic hiker and gardener, he is also active in a variety of local and national environmental organizations.

Index

www.ingramcontent.com/pod-product-compliance
Lightning Source LLC
Chambersburg PA
CBHW022138020426
42334CB00015B/951